The History of Western Alliance
after the World War II
1945-2005

Zhou Rongyao - Jiang Nan - Jin Hai

CANUT INTERNATIONAL PUBLISHERS

Istanbul - Berlin - London - Santiago

The publication is authorized by Jiangxi People's Publishing House Limited Liability Company, China.

The publication is funded by China Classics International.

The History of Western Alliance after the World War II (1945-2005)
Edited by Zhou Rongyao, Jiang Nan, Jin Hai
Translated by Dimitri Spirodis
Original Title: 战后西方联盟 / ISBN: 978-7-210-04924-1
Copyright © Jiangxi People's Publishing House, October, 2011.

Canut International Publishers

Canut Intl. Turkey, Teraziler Cad. No.29. Sancaktepe, Istanbul, Turkey

Canut Intl. Germany, Heerstr. 266, D-47053, Duisburg, Germany

Canut Intl. United Kingdom, 12a Guernsay Road, London E11 4BJ, England

Copyright © Canut International Publishers, 2016

ISBN: 978-605-9914-48-2

Printed in UK
Lightning Source Ltd. UK
Chapterhouse, Pitfield Kiln Farm
MK11 3LW
United Kingdom
www.canutbooks.com

Contents

CHAPTER VI

THE END OF COLD WAR AND THE WESTERN ALLIANCE 255

Acknowledgements

The post-War Western Alliance is one component part of the "International Relations Volumes" published by Jiangxi Publishing House under the title of Comprehensive World History which includes 39 volumes. The sixth part of the whole series probes into the analysis of the relations between Western nations in the post-World War II era, from the perspective of history. The reason to begin the International Relations Volumes with the "Western alliance" is because the author suggests that the world, its order and structure in the Post-War period were maintained by various alliance systems. And in the post-War era, the post-War Western alliance is the most central and complete reflection of the relations between Western countries.

According to tradition, the "alliance" means forming a group among countries to achieve certain common goals through covenant, and developing common behaviors, and, as for the term "Western" as abundantly used in this book, refers to the political meaning rather than a geographical one. In accordance with this traditional conception, the post-War Western alliances include North Atlantic Alliance (the US-European alliance), the US-Japan alliance, South Korea-US alliance, ANZUS and the EU. In this book we mainly focus on the three: the North Atlantic Alliance – the US-European alliance, the EU and the US-Japan alliance. Since we discuss the relations between Western countries, the focus is given to major Western powers (the US, Europe, and Japan). Careful readers may notice that the contents of the US-European alliance and the European Union outweighs that of the US-Japan alliance. This is because, with the status of Europe ascending and transforming, the conflict between the US and Europe has gradually transformed from direct, internal disputes of interests to emphasizing disagreements on external issues and external relations, which is quite different from the contradictions between the US and Japan. The reason is that, unlike Europe, Japan depends too much on the US policies and cannot initiate significant steps on the international stage without the US backing. That's why the content of the book related to US-Japan alliance quite lesser.

All the aspects of international relationships are included in the book. The content covered in this book mainly concentrates on the issues of strategy, security, politics and economy which affect the overall relationship status of the Western powers. Based on a thorough analysis and research on the Western alliance, this book attempts to reveal the basic factors influencing the relationship between major developed countries and points out to those "lasting characteristics" "variations" "similarities" and "particularities" with special attention to those factors related with the overall situation. Being influential in the past, we notice that these factors, to a certain extent continue their effects still today and will also be effective in the future, which demonstrate regularity. Besides, this book tries to theoretically analyze and evaluate the function and significance of ideologies, social system, values, and national interests in contemporary Western international relations. Certainly, the analysis in the book includes the influence of historical traditions and cultural backgrounds, as we see in the obvious differences between the US and Japan, and in the similarities and differences of the old and the new continent. Although the book covers the main aspects of the Western alliances, there are also some events or issues partly omitted due to the limitations of writing space. As a convenience to the reader the book is divided into six chapters. Chapters with relatively independent monographic characteristics correlate with each other historically and are narrated on a relatively independent time span accompanied by a relatively independent content. Nevertheless, all the chapters follow the main thread of "post-War Western alliance".

The first chapter covers the period starting from the end of World War II to the armistice in the Korean War. This chapter analyses the gradual formation of bipolar world which was eventually established in this period, and which deeply influenced the relationships between Western powers. As verified more than once by the past history, in the world of human society, where still antagonisms and conflicts exist, once the common enemies disappear, usually the concord between allies fade, discord and even disputes emerge as a common phenomena and such a discord situation is evolving currently. But it has been so complex, long-lasting, and influential that, any chapter of history cannot be compared with the post-World War II era.

The features of relationships among Western powers analyzed in this chapter are as follows: First, with the emergence of the US-Soviet confrontation and the shaping of the Cold War structure, the formation of an alliance has been the mainline of developments in the relationships of Western powers—we should say that the Western alliance has preceded the Soviet-Eastern Socialist Germany alliance. Second, the US has established its leading status during the formation of the Western alliance; third, the allies of the US have begun forming sub-alliances within the alliance to guard their own interests—which has caused the alliance relations become increasingly complex.

Due to its dominant role in the Western alliance, naturally, this chapter focuses on the US party. However, we have not ignored the complex psychology and attitudes of other parties of the alliance, though being helpless or weaker, did not always simply obey and to follow the US dictates. At the first phase of the Western alliance, the relationships between the top leading figures of the US and its allies were not strong but have developed gradually.

The time span of the chapter two is quite long, from the end of World War II, to the German reunification in 1990s. Japan and Federal Republic of Germany are two countries, which have occupied special status in the post-War international relations and in Post-War Western alliance. The main issues discussed in this chapter are: first, how could the Western nations led by the US overcome doubts and disagreements within a short period of time and turn the relationships with Japan and Federal Republic of Germany from a hostile to a cooperative pattern and even achieve an alliance. Were there any other factors behind this phenomenon, besides the need of for a proper adjustment in to Cold War world structure? Second, how could Japan and Federal Republic of Germany hide their capacities and bide their time, and gradually build up their national strength although they were faced with a severely difficult situation, with certain dilemma or even extinction? How did they utilize the "asylum" of alliance to change themselves from vanquished and conquered nations to major economic powers and later to political ones? What were the inevitabilities and contingencies of this specific historical process? Third, the chapter examines the positive and negative influences imposed on the relationships between Western powers by the rising status of Japan and Federal Germany. The third chapter focuses on the relationships and formation of the European integration among Western powers, especially, among European countries since the end of World War II. The European Union, which emerged and formed in the process of European integration, has become one of the most important forces of the international political and economic configurations. Since after the establishment of European Coal and Steel Community in 1951, the formation of the EU has overcome several challenges; established itself and achieved its unity and established a wisdom with abundant experience and lessons which indeed attracts admiration. This chapter reveals two points: in the course of its development, how did the EU realize reconciliation and cooperation between major old rival nations and achieved the regional peace? Next, how could the EU, progressively eliminate the conflicts and disputes of interests between different contesting nations and deepened the degree and scope of integration, which promoted the economic prosperity and social stability of the European region.

The fourth chapter studies the influence of national liberation and independence movements on the relationships among the Western powers. After the World War II, national liberation movements saw an unprecedented development. Many colonized and semi-colonized peoples resumed their sovereignty in succession by diverse means of struggle. This has been one prominent feature of the post-War international political life. It did not only represent the characteristics of the times—the tendency of peaceful development around the whole world, but also imposed great impacts on the Western alliance formed under the bipolar structure. This chapter illustrates three points. The first one is the inherent historical necessity and motive force of national movements aiming national liberation and sovereignty, which both divided and allied major Western powers against the former.. The second one focuses on the essence and means employed in fighting for and maintaining sphere of influences both in colonial and neo-colonial eras. The third part of this chapter examines struggles to maintain national independence and sovereignty as one main feature of post-War international relationships. These efforts have been manifested in the fights of oppressed nations for independence in the old colonies, but in the second phase it assumed a new form as the struggles to break the unequal economic and international relations in the world order. The elaboration in the fifth chapter mainly covers the US-EU relationships within the transatlantic alliance led by the US. The US attitude towards European integration has been generally positive after World War II., whereas the US strategy aimed to limit the European integration within the framework of the transatlantic alliance. The post-War Western or Eastern alliances under the bipolar structure of the international relationships system, throughout an evolution of a decade or so, have gradually lost their original strong ideological colors and national interests came to the fore. Thus national interests of allied partners have become the main factors that constantly nurtured their ideological consensus; either within the Soviet led Eastern alliance or the US Western alliance.

It is under such enduring impact that bilateral relations with distinct features have formed within the Western alliance and the transatlantic alliance and between the EU and the US. This chapter explores the universal and particular aspects of relationships between the allied parties and focuses on dependencies in Japan-US, German-US and the special US-UK relations plus the peculiar feature of independency, which is obvious in France-US relations.

The sixth chapter expounds on the relations of major powers within the Western alliance in the post-Cold War era. The great setback of world socialism, the collapse and disintegration of the Soviet Union, German unification in 1991, and the rise of Asian nations, a series of great changes in the world politics and economy have put an end to the old system of bipolar international structure. Since after this great change, almost every major actor or group of actors have strived hard to determine the rules and the structure of the prospective international relations system before it will eventually shape. Yet they did so led by their own specific interests and aimed to gain optimal status in the new system of international relations being gradually shaped. The collapse of the old bipolar world order have shaken the foundations of Western alliance and made the US become the sole super power. There started a new exploration to find a new foundation on the heritage of previous alliance, and have been making efforts to strike new balance among the partners within the alliance. In this respect, they have sought to strengthen the role of factors, such as the economy, moral values, and forging new security concepts, etc. which all have made the relations among the Western alliances more complicated. In a word, the old alliance has been facing brand new challenges.

Anything in the long process of history, inevitably reaches an end and this will apply for the post-War Western alliance, too. Currently, what we should do is to carry on research and discussion on the basis of summarization, of the historical facts that have accumulated more than a half century, figure out which trends are reversible, and those irreversible, find out those which have declined with the history passing by, and those which will remain active in the future history, in order to negative aspects of the Western alliance.

Creation of this volume has been a cooperative work: The first, third, and fifth chapters of the book was written by Prof. Dr. Jin Hai and Prof. Dr. Jiang Nan respectively, and Prof. Dr. Zhou Rongyao has written the second, the fourth and the sixth chapters and provided conceptual design of the whole book and compiled the drafts written by the other colleagues and first draft of the complete book.

We would like to extent our sincere gratitude to Prof. Dr. Gu Junli who reviewed and made valuable suggestions for the final draft and leaders of Jiangxi Publishing House who have enabled the realization of the book.

Zhou Rongyao
Deputy Director-General,
Institute of World History, Chinese Academy of Social Sciences

Publisher's Note

This book is 27th Volume of Comprehensive World History Series book project by the World History Institute of CASS, which was started in 2000s, which comprises 39 volumes altogether. The book is co-written by renowned scholars Zhou Rongyao, Jiang Nan, Jin Hai, who are researchers of Institute of World History attached to Chinese Academy of Social Sciences. Comprehensive World History Series is a pioneering project, which demonstrates the theoretical achievements of China's world history studies, and will certainly contribute to the international history academy.

The book series is published by Jiangxi Publishing House, in Nanchang. We have started our publishing plan with the volume "The History of Western Alliance After the World War II-1945-2005" and the "International Relations Volumes" include 8 books.

The reason to begin the International Relations Volumes with the "Western alliance" is because the author suggests that the world, its order and structure in the Post-War period (WW II) were maintained by various alliance systems. And during this era, the post-War Western alliance has been the most central and complete reflection of the relations between Western countries.

All the aspects of international relationships are included in the book. The content of the book mainly concentrates on the issues of strategy, security, politics and economy which affect the overall relationship status among the Western powers. Based on a thorough analysis and research on the Western alliance, the book attempts to reveal the basic factors influencing the relationship between major developed countries and points out to those "lasting characteristics" "variations" "similarities" and "particularities" with special attention given to those factors more directly related with the overall situation. We hope this precious book will promote the academic communication in the field of world history.

Dennis Simon
May 2017, Berlin

Chapter I

The US-European Alliance
in Early Post-War Era

World War II brought fundamental changes in the international relations of the Western world. The damage brought by the war seriously weakened the power of the European countries. How to avoid a destructive a new war became their common concern. Soon later with the outbreak of the Cold War and the emergence of the powerful Soviet Union and Eastern Europe allied to it made this issue even more urgent. In order to ensure their own security, the countries of Western Europe, on the one hand, strengthened their cooperation, and opened a new path to European unity. On the other hand, they tried their best to obtain the assistance of the United States to hinder the withdrawal of the United States from Europe. The United States whose comprehensive national power experienced a rapid growth in the World War II, also started to more and more deeply involved in the international affairs as the world's most powerful country, hoping to re-arrange the world according to their interests. The traditional isolationism which had dominated the foreign policy of the United States for 170 years gradually gave way to "internationalism".[1]

During 1940s and 1950s, the policy of the United States towards the European countries saw certain changes as follows: from retreating back and implementing the British-style "splendid isolation" to providing limited economic assistance; from supporting the independent development of Europe to cooperating closely with the European countries, from the

[1] The internationalism mentioned here, which is a terminology in the field of the US international relations studies, is used as a contrast with isolationism. The former approach to foreign relations which involves foreign international affairs was quite active (especially European affairs.

establishment of the collective defense under the framework of NATO (North Atlantic Treaty Organization) to assuming military obligations, all these have led to the formation of the Western alliance headed by the United States, thus completing the historical shift in the US policy towards Europe. In this way, with the policies of Western European countries and the United States affecting and promoting each other, the framework of the post-War Western international relations finally took shape.

1.1. The conceptions of the bilateral relations of the post-War Europe and the US

1.1.1 The European aspirations and the intentions of the United States

At the most exciting moment during the World War II, the post-war US-European relations became the important issue for many European countries. The outbreak of the World War II and the early victories of Germany over Western European countries, have made the latter recognize such a painful fact: It was insufficient to depend solely on themselves to maintain the international order in Europe or even safeguard their own security. The United States, as a vigorously ascending power, was destined to replace Europe and become a key actor on the stage of international relations. The US had gained a decisive status on these major issues of war and peace. So, after the war, how to adapt to this change in US-European relations, to make it produce a favorable result in the maintenance of international peace and security were of great significance for the European countries.

It was Trygve Lie from Norway who brought up the earliest idea of establishing a transatlantic security system. In November 1940, it was not long before he took the position of the deputy foreign minister of the government in exile of Norway; Lie had a conversation with the British Foreign Ministry officials. In the conversation, he suggested the United States and UK establish bases in Norway after the war, the United States, UK and Norway set up outpost in Greenland, Iceland and the Faroe Islands. On December 15, 1940 Trygve Lie declared his idea in his address through the radio to the occupied Norway. He completely broke the tie with the Norway's tradition of the non-aligned in the past, and stresses that in order to safeguard the security of the West they must cooperate with those countries who have the common ideals and motivation, first with UK and the United States. In Trygve Lie's words, the efforts of the states and the wartime alliance which was established and strengthened during the wartime should "constitute the basis of cooperation in the post-war era and be further carried on. Such cooperation includes the political cooperation ensuring the freedom of our nations and avoid the danger of being attacked by the arrogant and tyrannical aggressors and include economic cooperation that will provide social security and prevent our welfare from being destructed"[2].

Trygve Lie's view quickly aroused the interest of the British Foreign Office. In 1941, the British assistant under-Secretary of the Foreign Ministry Sir Sergeant wrote: "One of the major problems of the Post-War era is how to maintain the status of Britain on the European continent. A lot of evidence suggests that the failure of France has made the cooperation with the United States become the crucial premise for achieving this goal. Does Trygve Lie's proposal provide a practical means to achieve such cooperation? According to Mr. Trygve Lie's suggestion, Britain and Norway can both have bases in Norway, so, a similar British-American base can exist in the Irish port even in the British Port."[3]

However, in 1941 when the Nazi Germany was still in the stage of strategic offensive people's attention focused mainly on how to win the war, and only had a vague vision of the relationship between the US and Europe in the post-war. era

Along with the reversal of the war situation and the failure of the axis powers, the contemplations on post-war US-European relations became more and more active and specific. The representative of those advocating strengthening the US-EU cooperation was Britain's Winston Churchill. In his famous "three-circles diplomacy", Anglo-American alliance gained an upper hand. As Churchill said:

Without the alliance of the English speaking countries like brothers, it would be was impossible to effectively prevent the war. This alliance is to establish a special relationship between the two parties: one party is the Commonwealth and the British Empire, the other the USA. Now is not the time for abstract and general evaluations, I wish to make it clearer and specific. The brotherly alliance requires not only the establishment of growing friendship and mutual understanding in our two huge, blood connected social systems, but also calls for both parties' military advisers to continue maintaining close contacts, in order to jointly observe the potential danger,

---

2   Olav Riste, "Norway's 'Atlantic Policy': The Genesis of North Atlantic Defense Cooperation", in Nicholas Sherwen ed. NATO's Anxious Birth: The Prophetic Vision of the 1940s, St.Martin's Press, New York, 1985.

3   Foreign ministry archives, memorandum on April, 8, 1941,(FO 371/29421, N 1307/87/30).

the similarities and differences of weapons, training materials, as well as the exchange of military officers and students of military academies. It should also include joint use of all of the air and naval bases of the two countries in all parts of the world, so that the existing facilities can be used for the purpose of common security as before. It will greatly expand the power of the British Empire and render important financial savings – if the world calms down.[4]

Under Britain's leadership, the other small states also followed suit. Lie once again proposed to the British Foreign Ministry that it was necessary to take permanent measures on the issue of transatlantic defense with regard to the security of Norway and the future peace in Europe. The Dutch Foreign Minister Van Kleffens informed the British government that Belgium, Netherlands and Norway were considering whether to make proposals to the United Kingdom and the United States on the same issues.

The Dutch Foreign Minister also made contact with the US Secretary of State Cordell Hull and his deputy Sumner Welles to discuss the regional arrangement of the US and the Netherland forces in the Pacific Ocean, the Indian Ocean, and the Atlantic, the Mediterranean and the Baltic Sea. The requirement of the European states to strengthen cooperation with the United States got increasingly stronger.

Europe after the Second World War

However, the US policy towards Europe was still swinging in those days. Of course, the focus of the argument wasn't on the question of whether the US should play a leadership role on the international political stage, but on the question of how to exert the leadership in order to serve the US interests. The disputers included two main groups. One of the parties have argued that they should support and maintain balanced power relations among the major European nations, so that US could easily manipulate Europe from the other shore of Atlantic by playing one against the other. Without largely involving into the affairs of the European continent, the US could use the classic British "splendid isolation" policy to achieve this goal. The second party has advocated that the US could never greatly distance itself from European affairs, because the US's relationships with European nations have been strong for a long time in the history, anyway. Therefore, the US should positively interfere with and coach the European affairs, and establish close relationships with the European countries to secure its leading position in the world.

---

4   Winston Churchill, The Complete Speeches of Churchill, Vol. 7, N.Y. Chelsea House Pub.,1974, p.6923-6924.

The debate on the US policy towards Europe, as it is said to be "historic". After World War I, a great debate which erupted was on how to arrange and design the post-War world. At that time, representatives of the two debating parties were the former President Roosevelt and the incumbent President Woodrow Wilson. President Wilson's internationalist ideology was fully showed in his "Fourteen Points" peace program (See Appendix of the book). He hoped to completely abolish the old balance of power in Europe, and to build the peacekeeping hope on the basis of a collective security system including the United States as one of its members. Wilson, on January 22, 1917, published his "peace without victory" speech, where he declared, "There must be, not a balance of power, but a community of power; not organized rivalries, but an organized common peace."[5]

In order to facilitate the US intervention in European affairs, Wilson hoped to weaken the European countries. So his main target of the "Fourteen Points Agenda for Peace" was not the defeated Germany, but the victors led by the United Kingdom. For instance, he attempted to weaken the British tradition of economic-trade warfare capabilities through "freedom of the sea", and was ready to establish a world's most powerful navy to tie the hands of the British.

In contrast, the old Roosevelt-led faction (Theodore Roosevelt) had a geopolitical point of view, and opposed to destroy the traditional balance of power in Europe. "The Day of the Saxon", a book published by Homer Lea in 1912 was the representative of this geopolitical view. He claimed, "It was Britain rather than the United States that ensured the independence of American States. It is the existence of the British Empire, not the Monroe Doctrine, has established a basis for their security." In the old Roosevelt's opinion, the British Navy was the fringe defense force in the Western Hemisphere. As long as the British successfully maintained the balance of power in continental Europe, the United States did not have to interfere in European affairs, and safely maintained its splendid isolation. In the battle of arguments on both sides, the geographical limitations that the United States is far from Eurasia and the limitations of traditional isolationist view eventually headed to the victory of isolationism led by old Roosevelt. As the Congress refused to ratify "the Treaty of Versailles", the US returned to the isolationism which meant indifference to European affairs in the 1920s.

What violated the objective of the isolationism was that Europe failed to prevent the outbreak of World War II. At the end of World War II, arranging the Post-War world issues had brought on to the agenda of the United

---

5   John Lambert Harper, American Visions of Europe:Franklin D. Roosevelt, George F. Kennan and Dean G. Asheson, Cambridge University Press, 1994, p.93.

States. Franklin Roosevelt's answer to this question was a mixture of the two propositions. On the one hand, as a former Assistant Secretary of the Navy in the Wilson government, he inherited Wilson's idea of maintaining world peace through international organizations and collective security, and thought that the United States should join international organizations and obligations. In Roosevelt's understanding, the United Nations and its mechanisms had become the main tool to maintain the international peace. On the other hand, he was still affected by the isolationist forces, unwilling to see long-term US military presence in Europe. He hoped that after the end of the war the US would be able to withdraw from Europe as soon as possible.

In order to achieve these two objectives simultaneously, Roosevelt put his hopes on the cooperation among the great powers. This was prominently demonstrated in his US, Soviet, British and Chinese "Four Policemen" concept. These four countries would seek for the maintenance of international peace: The United Kingdom and the Soviet Union would be responsible for Europe. The United States would be responsible for the Western Hemisphere. China would be in charge of Far East issues by the US's support. Roosevelt insisted that only the "four policemen" should be massively armed to maintain peace on the basis of regional coordination, Aside from the four countries the other countries and regions should be debilitated to the extent that the revisionism against the international order which four countries were at the core could be minimized. Thus, the world leadership of the United States, would be simplified, because ensuring the coordination between the four countries would end the complex contests. In Roosevelt's view, this would truly be a world-wide system, which no longer led by Europe but by the four balanced powers. To some extent the other three major great powers had to depend on United States. The US, as the founder of the "balanced power system" and the unity, under the premise of avoiding to bear heavy duties, would help the US to control Europe and Asia and complete the leadership of the world with help of other three countries. Roosevelt's main idea was to weaken the free power of Europe, making it subordinate under the control of United Kingdom and the Soviet Union, thus facilitate the United States' remote control. So he focused on the reform of non-centralization and re-arranging territories in the European regions. In March 1943, Roosevelt told the British Foreign Secretary Eden, "Serbs and Croats have nothing in common and that is ridiculous to try to force to such antagonistic people to live together under the same government." Belgium had also "artificial binary system," which should suffer the same fate as Yugoslavia. The same argument was also applied for Germany and France, which were two main European problem producers in the eyes of the Roosevelt. Roosevelt believed Alsace-Lorraine should be separated from France and included into a new state entity together with Belgium and Luxembourg. Moreover, he said:"after the German disarmament, there is no reason for France to maintain a strong military force?"[6]

Charles E. Bohlen once commented that the aim of the Soviet Union in the Tehran conference also applied to Roosevelt's views. These goals were:

Germany should be divided up and kept divided. The Eastern European, the South-Eastern and the Central European countries should not be allowed to from any federal states or alliances. France should be deprived of colonies and strategic bases abroad, and France should not be allowed to maintain any large-scale military forces. Poland and Italy should maintain the territorial size which is close to the current situation, but whether they would be allowed keep armed forces was doubtful. Consequently, the Soviet Union would become the sole major political and military power in the European continent. The rest of Europe would be weakened politically and militarily until they become insignificant.[7]

Although Roosevelt had recognized the need for the United States to join international organizations and shoulder the obligations in the collective security system in order to maintain international peace, in contrast as to the European policy, he still had not given up his idea of distancing from Europe. A newspaper quoted: "The President disagrees with those who foresee the US forever embroiled in foreign quarrels and required to keep large military forces abroad." Roosevelt had repeatedly said that the US military forces would soon withdraw from Europe after the war. In the Yalta conference, he explicitly told Churchill not to expect the US military would remain in Europe for more than two years. When discussing allocation of occupation zones of Germany, Roosevelt told British leaders, expressed his desire to occupy the north-west zone, since the port facilities in this zone would be convenient for the future transport of US military facilities and equipment back home. In those days, Roosevelt was quite optimistic about the outcomes of cooperative relationships among the major world powers, especially he was expectant for the prospects of cooperation between the US and the Soviet Union. This approach had made him blind to possible

6   The Department of State, Foreign Relations of the United States, 1943, Vol.3, USGPO, 1957, pp.13,16. The issues about Belgium referred here is the conversation between Roosevelt and the State Council officials, Foreign Relations of the United States, 1943, Vol.1,543. The issues about Alsas and Lolin which has referred is Foreign Relations of the United States, 1943, Vol.3, p.153.
7   Charles E. Bohlen, Witness to History, 1929-1969, Norton, New York, 1973, p.153.

threats the post-war Europe could face, and which required US's vigorous involvement, which made him strongly favor the US's withdrawal from Europe, as soon as possible. The idea of distancing and withdrawing from Europe was by no means confined by Roosevelt and his team; this was also the mainstream view in the American society. The famous international relations columnist Walter Lippmann once wrote in 1943, "Our ambitious goal must be one not requiring the involvement of the United States forever in Europe to maintain its peace... so if we, like Jefferson, who was aware of the interests of the United States, we can see that the traditional policy against involvement in European affairs is consistent with strengthening of the vital interests of the United States, in any case."[8]

Roosevelt's policy of distancing from Europe and entrusting it to Britain and the Soviet Union contrasted the desire of European countries to strengthen ties with the US. On the one hand, rather than the expecting that US domination would decide their destiny, European countries needed and aimed to promote their self-interests by the help of Roosevelt's approach and policy of weakening the power of Europe was critical for their territorial integrity and independence, sovereignty. On the other hand, European countries did not believe that Britain and the Soviet Union could effectively safeguard their interests. They did not trust the Soviet Union, while Britain was in decline, so only the United States could provide the security umbrella and economic assistance which they needed. Therefore, the European countries were also very reluctant and worrisome to see the United States isolating itself from Europe. They tried to allow and persuade the United States continue to play its role in Europe. Representatives of these two opposing ideas and forces were Charles de Gaulle of France and Winston Churchill of the United Kingdom.

Charles de Gaulle even as early as March 1944 had already pointed out sharply that the essence of Roosevelt's European policy was "enabling a weak Europe and a weak France and letting four countries—the United States, the Soviet Union, China, Britain—jointly deciding the world's affairs. In the meantime, Roosevelt's European policy includes deciding on the Europe-related affairs, such as the fate of Germany, the fate of the Vistula River countries and the Danube River Basin countries, the fate of the Balkan countries and Italy, in his view, all these views of Roosevelt were the problems of belonging. Roosevelt cannot sacrifice and pull back from his concepts which aims to achieve satisfactory and favorable agreement on these issues."[9]

---

8   Walter Lippmann, US Foreign Police: Shield of the Republic, Little Brown, Boston,1943, pp.126,163.
9   Charles de Gaulle, Memoires de Guerre, L'unite 1942-1944, Librairie Plon, 1956, p.282-284.

Charles de Gaulle said, "His (Roosevelt's) plans will endanger the Western world. By considering the issue of western Europe as a second-rate business, would he not ruin the goal – the goal of civilization to which he is pursuing? Today, although western Europe has faded and is in a split, it is still indispensable for the West." Charles de Gaulle concluded: "On Foreign affairs, the logical and emotional strength will become completely insignificant in the face of the real, solid power. What is effective is something solid which state possess in its hands and be able to control. In order to restore her position, France can only rely on herself."[10]

After 1942, Roosevelt championed general Henri Giraud, more compliant with US interests than de Gaulle, as the leader of the French Resistance. At the Casablanca Conference (1943), Roosevelt forced Charles de Gaulle to cooperate with Giraud, but Charles de Gaulle was considered as the undisputed leader of the Resistance by the French people and Giraud was progressively deprived of his political and military roles.

In order to restrict the United States from freely manipulating French affairs, Charles de Gaulle took a series of steps to guard the interests of France and its national dignity. He tried to get rid of the adverse effects of the France's defeat in 1940 to restore its great power status. He opposed Roosevelt's attempts to promote Giraud replace his leadership in the "Free French movement" and urged the allies to immediately recognize the French Committee of National Liberation as France's provisional government; he tried to protect French interests in the colonies and tried hard to avoid France being a subordinate world actor in the major powers club of the Britain, US, and SU. France should have its own say and stake in the post-war arrangements, consequently he pursued to have France's own occupation zone in the defeated Germany and so on. De Gaulle's France became the symbol of safeguarding independence and rights, and resistance against US domination over the European countries. Charles de Gaulle asserted that France's "will for independence" offered "an example and comfort ... [for] all kind of nations."[11]

Churchill posed a challenge to Roosevelt's European policy by proposing another approach. If, we can say that Charles de Gaulle has realized the importance of maintaining independent status of the European countries in the post-war recovery era, we might say that Churchill has realized that the US support for the recovery and revival of the European countries was equally indispensable. If we can say that Roosevelt was indulged in the

---

10   Zhou Yaorong, Critical Biography of Charles de Gaulle, Oriental Press ,1994, p.166.
11   Ibid.

merits of the wartime alliance with the Soviet Union, then Churchill might be evaluated as viewing the communist Soviet Union as an arch rival in the post-war era. As early as in the days when the Soviet Union was founded, Churchill had strongly advocated a joint international armed intervention to destroy the newborn SU: "Bolshevism is not a policy; it is a disease. It is not a creed; it is pestilence...." "let it meet the mischief in its infancy; strangle it in the cradle."

Even in the 1930s, faced with the approaching threat of Nazi Germany, although he began to vigorously argue in favor of Anglo-Soviet alliance, he still did not abandon his past anti-Soviet and anti-Communist stand. In March 23, 1938, Churchill said to the London representative of Soviet Union the following:

20 years ago, I did everything within my power to oppose communism, because at that time I thought communism and its revolutionary ideals to be the greatest danger to the British Empire. On the contrary, Nazism today and hegemony craze established in Berlin forms the biggest danger to the British Empire. So now I do everything within my power to oppose Hitler. If one day the danger of Fascism disappears, and the danger from the communism erupts again, I would like to say – being quite frankly – I will once again start fighting to oppose you.[12]

For Churchill, the cooperation with Soviet Union was only a temporary measure to deal with urgent threats. With the reversing of the war situation and victory approaching during the Second World War, Churchill had felt a growing concern about the Soviet threat. As early as October 21, 1942, he pointed out in his telegram to Foreign Secretary Eden: "If Russian barbarism overlaid the culture and independence of ancient states of Europe it would be measureless disaster."

We can say Churchill, if not being entirely negative, at least had serious doubts about Roosevelt's vision of the post-war configuration as "the four major powers co-governing" the world and its affairs. It seemed to Churchill that Roosevelt's approach embodied a huge danger which depended on the practice of being commissioned by Britain and the Soviet Union when dealing with European affairs and which desired to ensure getting out from Europe, since Roosevelt's main goals throughout all the peace conferences was to ensure that the US was not going to be a permanent presence in Europe. Once the US troops withdrew from Europe, Britain which heading towards a decline, simply could not resist the pressures coming from

12   Robin Edmonds, The Big Three: Churchill, Roosevelt, Stalin in Peace and War, W.H. Norton & Co., New York, 1991, p.87.

the Soviet Union, the result would be the Soviet Union's sole control over the whole Europe. Moreover, without the US's help, it was difficult for the European countries that had been cannibalized by the war to complete the revival and recovery task alone by themselves. No matter whether from the security concerns or from the economic point of view, there was a need to persuade the United States firmly connect and engage with the Europe.

Thus, Churchill became the most powerful advocate of US-European co-operation. He repeatedly emphasized "the Anglo-American relationship as a special relationship"; rejected the withdrawal of the US troops from Europe before solving the problem of dividing the occupied territories; and vigorously advocated the wartime Anglo-American military cooperation. In order to reverse Roosevelt's approach of "establishing a post-war configuration which would lead US distancing from Europe and at the same time to have a decisive say regarding the fate of Europe". In 1943, Churchill put forward his own idea about the post-war world configuration and international organizations when he met with the US Vice President Wallace in Washington, He suggested that the US and Britain should lead the world and added: There should be a "Supreme World Council," guided by three principal powers— the UK, the US, and the USSR—which he invariably called "Russia." And subordinate to the Supreme World Council there should be three Regional Councils of Europe, the American Hemisphere and the Pacific, i.e. "a three-legged stool structure". He proposed that Russia would participate the Pacific Council. American Hemisphere Council would naturally include Canada and Canada would represent the British Commonwealth. The US would be represented in the three Regional Councils. European Council might consist of twelve states or confederations.

Members of the "Supreme World Council," would "join the relevant Regional Council directly", while the US should "in addition to be a representative of the Pacific Council it should also become the representative of the European and Pacific Councils." His comments put Roosevelt in a dilemma.

If the United States participated in the European Council, it meant that the United States would be deeply involved in European affairs and would not distance itself from Europe. If the United States did not participate in the European Council, it would mean that it would lose the golden opportunity to have a say regarding the European affairs. The result would be the emergence of a united powerful Europe which US would not be able to control. Such a united Europe would make the United States unable to design and lead the international order and diminish its say on the World affairs. We can say that Churchill's "three-legged stool structure" had posed a difficult choice for the United States between actively involving in European affairs and losing control over the European affairs.

1.1.2 The trend of thoughts that motivated the United States to keep distance from Europe

Churchill and Charles de Gaulle were the advocators of two major approaches for the post-war European policy towards the United States, these two approaches combined can be formulated as follows: we should not only firmly connect and engage the United States to Europe, so as to enable Europe benefit from US's maximum support and protection, but we should also try to maintain the independence and the freedom of the European nations in order to prevent it from becoming "a pawn" in the global strategy of the US. These two approaches related to European policy towards the US were interrelated and mutually conditioned, and constituted an organic whole which has been pursued throughout the entire post-war era. Thus European countries have played a huge role in the establishment and development of the post-War framework of US-European relations on the basis of these two approaches.

In the brief epoch after the war, the US government did not seem to be affected by the approaches, demands and acts of the European countries at all. Even in April 1945, after Roosevelt's death and Truman's assumption of power, Roosevelt's original idea of a weakened Europe and keeping the US at a certain distance from Europe had not changed. Just after the war in Europe had ended, the US State Department had notified the European countries that "the US aid in the framework of Lend-Lease agreement, which had not yet been dispatched or which was on the way to Europe" was halted," and the notification was based on the order signed in May 8, 1945 by Truman. This notification had caused strong protests in Britain and the Soviet Union.

Clayton and Collado "were horrified to hear of the action taken over the weekend in Washington to cut off Lend-Lease." Truman had indeed terminated Lend-Lease abruptly on August 21, 1945. Clayton immediately phoned Secretary of State Jimmy Byrnes in Washington, DC. Although he was famous for his even temper and uncommon self-control, Clayton was furious with Byrnes. The British were also shocked and angry. Hugh Dalton soon arrived with Lord Brand from the British Treasury. Dalton exclaimed: "What's the use of sitting here talking to you about what will happen when suddenly we learn from Washington what you're really doing!" Fortunately,

Clayton and Brand knew each other from when Brand served as British Treasury Representative in Washington. "The British were terribly upset, and this showed how close [Clayton] was to Brand, for together they bound up the hurts.

Although Truman commented that the State Department officials misunderstood him and ordered to re-start the aid deliveries, this event had provoked a stir among the European countries.

In September 1945, after the Japanese government surrendered, the Truman administration notified the United Kingdom to terminate various Anglo-American Joint Commissions which were set up during the war for coordinating transportation, food, raw materials, and naval issues between the two countries. By the suspension of the joint meeting of Anglo-American Joint Chiefs of Staff with the pretext of "necessity to review the articles of the treaty in the new circumstances" United States' attitude to distance and withdraw from Europe as soon as possible had become more apparent.

While the United States gradually alienated from Europe, it also adopted a series of policies undermining the power of European countries. In this regard, a veteran of the British colonial powers bore the brunt. Britain's "Imperial Preferential system" became the main target of the US critiques. On November 6th, 1945, the US Secretary of State Byrnes in his speech expounded on the intentions of the US foreign economic policy, he criticized the British "imperial ex-gratia system" under the banner of free trade said:

In such a situation (huge losses caused by the war), what can a country do? It can seek loans for its needs for Foreign exchange, which enables it to adapt to free trade principles which served as the basis of any permanent prosperity.

Or it can tighten its belt. It can reduce the living standards of the people, using a variety of methods to store the foreign currency that is difficult to get, and to shift its foreign trade to those countries where it is easier to get money by government decree.

The latter approach would increase trade discrimination and trade division now existed in xenophobic groups. If we cannot help eliminate the state of forcing other countries, usually in violation of the will of their own, to create the xenophobic group, we cannot reject these xenophobic groups.

We must not only be against these xenophobic trade groups, but also we have to cooperate with other countries to eliminate the situation of fostering trade discrimination in the world trade.

...... We cannot play the role of Santa Claus in this world, but we can offer loans to those reputable governments, if the government can change its trade policy which will enable us to increase trade with them.

...... Trade between countries is one of the greatest powers leading to fuller use of these production capacities with a huge expansion. But if those countries cannot learn to trade like neighbors and friends, they will lose the opportunity to improve the living standards of their people. If we want to have peace in the world, we cannot let the heavy restrictions strangle world trade.[13]

Byrnes indicated in his speech that the US would exert pressure through economic aid, required the recipient to clearly manifest their policy of opening their markets to US products, Britain should accept this rule in the preferential loans given to her by the US. War had almost brought Britain's finance to the point of collapse. In August 1945, when "Lend-Lease" treaty came to an end, the British had been facing a serious crisis of pound. British Prime Minister Attlee said in the Parliament that the deficit of Britain had reached 1.2 billion pounds, as an economist Kenneth called "financial Dunkirk". "The Economist" magazine, estimated that just in order to meet the needs of the next two years; the British government would need to borrow 2 Billion US Dollars. If it wanted to restore the long-term ability to pay, then the total amount of its loans will reach 6 billion US Dollars.. So Britain sent a delegation to negotiate the preferential loans with the United States, with the originally proposed figure of 1.5 billion pounds. During the negotiations, the public opinion in the United States simply astonished the British people. A Gallup poll showed that 60% of the US people opposed to provide any loans to the United Kingdom, only 27% of them were in favor of the loan agreement. The American people did not seem to fully understand that Britain had to pay such a high price because of war. One important condition for the loan agreement proposed by the US government was also very demanding, which has requested that the pound to be fully convertible within 15 months. Churchill called the loan agreement as "it so perilous that in practice would become self defeating."

Although the British had no choice but to accept the plan but it could be imagined how dissatisfied British people were. Sunday Times reflected the mood of the British people like this, "There is a feeling in this country that it seems we, as the winner, are required to pay compensation instead." "The Anglo-American special relationship" advocated by Churchill seemed to have received a serious blow.

---

13   Arthur M. Schlesinger, The Dynamics of World Power: A Documentary History of United States Foreign Policy, 1945-1973, Vol. 1, Western Europe, Chelsea House Publishers, New York, 1973, pp.32-34.

In addition to the harsh attitude exhibited in the aspect of economic assistance, the US unwilling to take on more political and military obligations in Europe also made Britain politicians frustrated. In December 1946, Attlee wrote a long personal letter with his private typewriter to Foreign Minister Bevin who was talking on the peace treaty with the Secretary of United States in Washington. From his long personal letter, we can see his distrust in the United States was deepening, "In the US, there is a tendency to see us as an outpost, whom it doesn't need to protect. I'm very worried about the sign that shows US is establishing a safety zone around on its own and left us and Europe in the deserted land. I think we should seek to understand what the Americans are going to do, then we must be very careful not to involve in it."[14]

In the brief epoch when the World War II had just ended, the prospect of US-European relations seemed pessimistic.

1.2 The Political and Economic Basis for the US-European Alliance

When the European countries were frustrated by the growing isolationist tendencies in the US Foreign policy, they seemed to ignore another traditional principle of the US Foreign policy towards Europe which was almost equal to the isolationism. The US should absolutely not allow a big country rule Europe and stay neutral. This principle was announced by Jefferson in 1812. At that time, the United States and Britain were at war. In this case, Jefferson still thought the US should not let the enemy of the Britain (Napoleon) rule Europe. He wrote, "Letting Europe go under the rule of a monarch does not comply with our interests. If Napoleon marches to Moscow again, I would hope that he will meet a kind of disaster that had prevented him conquering St. Petersburg in his former attempt. Although its consequence might be the further extension of our ongoing war, I would rather accept the consequences than see the power of the whole Europe falling in the hands of one person."[15]

The development of the international situation after World War II caused the revisiting of this principle which increasingly became more important, which gradually overwhelmed the isolationist tradition, and eventually led to a change in the relationship between Europe and the US.

---

14   Don Cook, Forging the Alliance: NATO, 1945-1950, Arbor House/William Morrow, New York, 1989, p.67-68.
15   Arthur M. Schlesinger, The Dynamics of World Power: A Documentary History of United States Foreign Policy, 1945-1973, Vol. 1, Western Europe, Chelsea House Publishers, New York, 1973, p.32.

1.2.1 The Truman Doctrine

With the end of World War II, conflicts and differences between wartime allies began to emerge. The conflicts among the western allies and the Soviet Union was intensifying about how to arrange the post-War world. After the war, the Soviet Union helped Eastern European countries to establish socialist regimes with a series of hasty interventions which caused a strong reaction and doubts in the US government. The US believed the socialist regimes in the Eastern Europe did not represent the free choice of their people, but imposed on them by the pro-Soviet puppet governments established after the liberation by the Red Army. The Soviet Union's measures of expanding its sphere of influence in Eastern Europe became increasingly aggressive in the eyes of The US government. They began to suspect that whether the purpose of the Soviet Union was trying to take advantage of the post-war chaos to establish hegemony in Europe. Starting from the end of the war in Europe, the United States policy towards the Soviet Union had gradually hardened. In April 1945, when Molotov met with Truman in Washington on his way to attend the inaugural meeting of the United Nations in San Francisco, Truman conducted a comprehensive attack with fierce rhetoric against the Soviet Union actions after the war. Molotov protested that no one had ever spoken to him in this tone. Truman replied, "Fulfill your agreement, and you will never hear this tone." Truman said to the Secretary of State Byrnes that he was tired of repeatedly making compromise with the Soviet Union. In a series of controversial issues after the war, his attitude towards the Soviet Union gradually changed. For example Truman insisted unshared US occupation of Japan and accused the Soviet Union's actions that fostered pro-Soviet regimes in Eastern European countries as the violation of Yalta treaty; he strongly urged the Soviet Union to withdraw its troops from Iran according to the original agreement reached between Britain and the Soviet Union. Thus relations between the Soviet Union and the US quickly got tense.

In this atmosphere, Roosevelt's policy of maintaining international order by cooperation between big countries received increasing concerns. Was the Soviet Union a reliable Post-War cooperation partner, or a potential international order breaker? State Department began to feel the need to re-evaluate the policy of the Soviet Union. Thus, early in 1946, State Department officials asked the US Embassy in the Soviet Union to provide a memorandum about their views on the Soviet Union policies as soon as possible for reference. In February 22, 1946, an 8000-word telegram wrote by George Kennan, the US ambassador in the Soviet Union and the telegram was one of the classic documents containing the policy,

Kennan's Long Telegram

In this telegram Kennan analyzed the root of history and reality about the policy of Soviet, and came to this conclusion, "To sum up, we are facing a political force. The Soviet Union is fanatically convinced that there is no permanent compromising between itself and the United States. It believes that if the Soviet regime will be consolidated, then it is necessary and desirable to mess up the internal harmony of our society, destroy our traditional way of life and damage the authority of the country in the international arena." This ran counter to Roosevelt's idea of maintaining the international order by inter-country cooperation. But Kennan did not therefore consider the war between the Soviet Union and the US was inevitable. He believed that the Soviet Union "is different from Hitler's Germany...... when it encounters strong resistance at any place, it can easily retreat". From this point of view, in terms of how the US should deal with the Soviet Union's policy, Kennan made the following recommendations:

A large part of the problem depends on the health and vitality of our own society. The world communist movement is like vicious parasites relying on sick muscle tissue to feed them. This is the counterpart of the domestic policy and the Foreign policy. Every bold and effective measure that we take to solve internal problems of our own society, and strengthen our people's confidence, discipline, morale and esprit de corps is a diplomatic victory over Moscow. Its value is equal to a thousand diplomatic notes and joint communiqués. If we cannot abandon fatalism and indifferent attitude in the face of defects in our society, Moscow will benefit from it, there would not be any benefit for Moscow from its Foreign policy.

We have to plan for other countries and propose a more positive and more constructive way than we have risen in the past that we wish to see. It is not enough to just urge other countries to develop similar political process of our country. Many Foreign people, the peoples of Europe, at least, have felt tired and afraid of the past experiences. They have less interest for abstract freedom than for safety. They are looking for guidance, rather than responsibility. We should provide better guidance to them than the Russians. If we do not give guidance, the Russians will definitely give.[16]

This was the basic logic of Kennan's containment policy. In his view, the Soviet social structure and its ideology had great weaknesses. It was impossible to maintain those weaknesses in a peaceful competition with the West. It can only maintain the social cohesion to ensure the survival by provoking

---

16   Wang Chunliang, Selected Documents and Modern World History 1900-1988, Oriental Press,1990, pp.464,466-467.

tensions and continuing to expand. Therefore, if the West pursued a firm policy of containment, there would be no opportunity left for the Soviet to expand, the internal contradictions of Soviet society would eventually lead to the total destruction of the communist system. Given the poverty and unrest was a hotbed of communism, Western Europe's current economic situation would provide the best opportunity for the expansion of the communist forces. At this time, the pressing question in front of the US was how to help European countries to restore economic and social stability and streng then their resistance against the domestic communist subversion. On May 23, 1947 a report submitted by Kennan to Acheson stated that more clearly. He said the State Department's Policy Planning Board did not believe that "the activities of the Communist Party was the root of the difficulties in the Western Europe", and what caused chaos in Europe is the devastating impact of the war on Europe's social structure, economic structure and political structure, and the depletion of materials and equipment and spiritual strength. Therefore, the "US aid work in Europe should not fight against the existing communist, but should restore the health of the European economy and social vitality". It was the economic imbalance trend in Europe that caused the prevalence of all totalitarian movements. When the economy of the Western European countries had been recovered, society had been stabilized, and the danger of the subversion of Communism will be eliminated then the US recovery plan was going to overcome this trend.[17]

So their political, economic, and military alliance would constitute the best barrier to contain Soviet expansion. US policy towards Europe was going to change.

In Europe the first beneficiary of this shift in the US policy was France. In the spring of 1946, the French delegation led by the former French Prime Minister Léon Blum and Jean Monnet arrived in Washington to discuss the issue of loans with the US government. Different from the United Kingdom, lending requirements of France received the full support of the US ambassador in France. In a letter sent from Paris to the State Department in February, the US ambassador stated:

Currently ... I wish to emphasize my view that our national interests require us to provide a lot of dollar loans to France. Although from a banker's perspective, the risks faced by the French may not be the biggest, but certainly, the political situation in recent weeks has seriously deteriorated. Ordinary people are still cold, hungry, and unable to buy the goods they need, and feel no progress in resolving the problem, and therefore have deep frustration. Today, extremists have been out of control. Our interests demand that the

---

17   Forrest C. Pogue, Marshall Biography, World Knowledge Publishing House, 1991, p.213.

public morale cannot be reduced to the level where extremists seem to be the only opportunity to improve leadership and material conditions. France now need our help in urgent. If coal cannot be shipped from the Ruhr, the United States will be the only country who has extra for export. When the wheat production reduces in France, it will turn to the United States for help. It is also important that the industrial machinery and equipment for its industrial modernization also only come from the United States.... Refusing assistance or (decrease) assistance ... will deprived those who wish France remains as an independent and democratic country of the last pillar and hope.[18]

The result of this proposal of US ambassador is that, during the critical period of the French presidential election, the United States lent 650 million US dollars to France (which happened a few months after that it had obtained a 550 million US dollar loan from the Export-Import Bank). France agreed except for allowing free access of US goods into its markets, "Disclaimed obligation."

When the United States began to realize the importance of aiding the revival of Europe to its global interests, the United Kingdom provided an important stage for the shift in the US policy. On February 21, 1947, the British ambassador in Washington met with the US Secretary of State noted that after March 31, 1947, the UK would not be able to continue to assume the economic and military responsibilities incurred in maintaining the independence and the security of Greek. In addition, the UK would also stop the assistance to Turkey. Since France's experience showed that emphasizing the Soviet threat was the best way to achieve US aid, the Britain naturally would not miss this opportunity. British Ambassador stressed in a note, "Due to the military and strategic reasons, Greece and Turkey should not be allowed to fall under the Soviet control." Accordingly, he urged the United States to undertake the burden of aiding Greece and Turkey financially.

The meetings with British politicians and experts provided Truman a great opportunity to re-examine the US policy on Europe.

Due to new developments in the international situation, Roosevelt's original policy goal of United States alienation from Europe and controlling European affairs from afar through cooperation among major powers had become increasingly improper, but so far, the US government only made some amendments in certain specific policy implementation, instead of thoroughly re-adjusting its European policy. Truman recognized the need for the US government to change course, and developed a new policy towards Europe. The United Kingdom's requirement of taking on to assisting

---

18   The Department of State, FRUS, 1946, Vol.5, Washington: US GPO, 1967, p.413.

Greece and Turkey provided an opportunity for Truman to enable him to explain the changes in the international situation and the importance of assisting Europe to America's interests. Motivated by the European countries, the Truman Doctrine was introduced.

In order to get congressional support, Truman organized a briefing in the White House for a number of important members of Congress. State Department officials explained the necessity of the aid which will be given to Greece and Turkey. So accordance to this detection first, Secretary of State Marshall introduced the case. But Marshall's speech was too bounded by the situation in Greece and Turkey and the Undersecretary of State Dean Acheson did not feel his speech highlight key points, then he requested to take the floor. He directly said in his first sentence that, "Gentlemen, in 2000's since the Punic Wars, human society is under the bipolar pattern for the first time." Acheson's speech focused on the worldwide conflict between two superpowers and the threat to the strategic interests of the United States caused by the Soviet Union. When he finished, Senator Vandenberg said to Truman, "Mr. President, if you say the same thing in the Congress, then I think the Congress will approve your request."

At the same time, a large-scale propaganda war had started. On March 3, 1947, British Embassy in Washington described the situation about mobilizing public opinion to the Ministry of Foreign Affairs in the United States in the weekly political summary, "It is almost impossible to find a serious newspaper or magazine with no articles on describing in detail the current international situation and discussing the measures that this country should take. The conclusion of most of these articles is that the United States cannot avoid the responsibility brought by the status as the world's number one power out of its own interests."[19] This propaganda quickly achieved the effect which provided a beneficial environment to introduce the Truman Doctrine. On March 17, 1947, the British ambassador in Washington summed up the views of Americans towards the Truman Doctrine, "People often compare the Truman Doctrine with the Monroe Doctrine. People naturally think that the United States has every reason, including moral reasons, to change the basic guiding principle of its Foreign policy from separating the US sphere of influence to protect the rest of the world from the erosion of the Soviet forces.... As for the Truman Doctrine, Americans took anti-Soviet public policy as the deformation of the thought of Americans who consider themselves as Crusaders to maintain the world democracy."[20]

---

19   Weekly Political Summary from Washington to Foreign Office, 3 March, 1947, FO 371/61054.
20   Ibid.

In this environment, Truman read at the joint meeting of Congress in March 12, 1947, claiming that:

In order to ensure that countries can develop in peace without outside pressure, the United States played a leading role in the establishment of the United Nations. The United Nations is designed for making the lasting freedom and independence of all member states possible. But unless we are willing to help free people to ensure that their freedom and national integrity are not threatened by the invading attempt which imposing a totalitarian regime on them, our goal cannot be achieved. This is just too frankly admit, the totalitarian regime imposed on free people of all countries through direct or indirect aggression weakens the foundations of international peace and thus endangers US security.

...... At this stage of development in the world history, nearly every nation must make a choice between different ways of life, and this choice is usually not free.

A way of life is based upon the will of the majority of people, and it is showed by the mechanism for freedom, representative government, free elections, guaranteed freedom of individual, freedom of speech and religion and freedom from political persecution.

Another way of life is built on basis of the will of the minority imposed on the most people. It relies on terror and repression, the control of newspapers and radio stations, pre-arranged election result and the suppression of individual freedom.

I believe that the US policy must help those free people who resist armed minorities or outside pressures with attempt to conquer them.

I believe that we must assist free people with their own way to determine their own destiny.

I believe we should first provide essential financial and economic assistance to establish political process with political stability and orders.[21]

This was the so-called "Truman Doctrine." It was announced from the perspective of the struggle between freedoms and totalitarians and because of that US security obligation was all over the world, and acknowledged the need for the United States to assume the obligations of aiding Europe, which overthrew the Roosevelt policy on peacekeeping by cooperation among the major powers and getting out of the Europe. "Truman Doctrine" provided political basis for the US large-scale assistance to the Europe and this was

---

21   http://avalon.law.yale.edu/

the next political basis for the US-European alliance. And the bill approved by the US Congress to aid Greece and Turkey demonstrated the change in the US policy towards Europe. The first important sign of this change was the European Recovery Program, known as the "Marshall Plan."

1.2.2 The Marshall Plan

For a long time, the scholars who study the history of international relations of post-War and the Cold War eras or the US diplomatic history generally agree with the importance of the Marshall Plan in promoting the revival of the European economy. But after entering the 1980s, the revisionist school led by Alan S. Milward, Melvyn. P. Leffler, Charles S. Maier and Immanuel Wexler proposed a different interpretation, attempting to overthrow the traditional view on the Marshall Plan. The economic historian of London School of Economics, Milward said, "The so-called Western European economic crisis in the summer of 1947 did not actually exist. It is just the shortage of Foreign exchange caused by the large-scale investment and production prosperity in Europe." He believed that the Marshall Plan was a carefully designed scam to push forward US hegemony in Europe. As for the economic boom during the implementation of the Marshall Plan in Europe, the Amend School thought it was not completely owed to the US aid. Milward believed the role of the Marshall Plan was only to compensate the deficit to the dollar zone in the international trade which has brought by the US aid for the participating countries. Charles Maier also held the same view. He believed in the first two years of the Marshall Plan, 80% to 90% of the capital of the major European countries' economy was provided by local resources. The contribution of the United States was only marginal, and the amount was small, and since 1949 it began to decrease.[22]

To examine the history more calmly and objectively 40 years can be a sufficient time period but also it is a long enough time to ignore or do not understand the seriousness and urgency of the problems as well as the social and psychological impact at that time. After World War II which lasted for 6 years, Europe's economy had been hit by a devastating blow, and people's life almost approached to the brink of collapse. In September 1945, the French government announced food rations as follows: 1 pound of fat per month, 1 pound of sugar, 5 ounces of cheese, 4 pounds of potatoes; 8

---

22 Alan Milward, The Reconstruction of Western Europe, 1945-1951, London, 1984; Melvyn Leffler, "The United States and the Strategic Dimension of the Marshall Plan", in Diplomatic History, 12, Summer 1998, p.277-306; Immanuel Wexler, The Marshall Plan Revisited: The European Recovery Program in Economic Perspective, Westport, Connecticut, 1983; Charles P. Kindleberger, The Marshall Plan Days, Boston, 1987.

ounces of meat per week, 1 quart of wine, 4 ounces of coffee synthesis; milk supply only to children; 100 pounds of coal for the whole winter.[23] A poll held in France in January 1946 showed that 49 percent of the people regarded their basic needs as the most important issue they cared about, 26% of the people primarily concerned with health, 15% of the people concerned about the money first. These were directly or indirectly related to the economic issues, while there was almost no one who mentioned the so-called Communist threat. This proportion had not changed until 1949. This was not the worst case. During 1946 and 1947, the cold winter which had never been seen in a hundred years led to further deterioration of the economic situation in Europe. Half the industry completely paralyzed in Britain. Production levels in the Western Zones of Germany decreased to 29% in 1936, and continued to decline. The cold winter led to the poorest harvest during a century in 1947 in Europe. So the countries continued to cut food supplies. In Germany, Austria and Italy, the per capita calorie intake had been reduced to the point which cannot sustain life for long. The traffic got paralyzed and they were unable to transport food and fuel, and the demand of wage rise by the workers made the situation in European countries more severe. During 1947 and 1948, The US reporters in Paris Theodore White described the situation in Europe at the time, "It (Europe) is like a whale stranded and hardly reach the beach, if it cannot be saved, it will die, rot and pollute everything around it".[24] At that time, the severity of the situation in Europe was beyond doubt for ordinary people.

In 1947, the Kennan version of the policy of containment was popular in the US politics. As mentioned before, this version of the containment policy considered the Soviet threat was not lying in its military force but in the political subversion and infiltration through the local Communist force. The worsening economic situation in Europe was the hotbed for the local Communist forces to develop and grow. US weapon to deal with this threat should be economic and political aid rather than military obligations. From this viewpoint, the earliest advocates of the policy of containment in the US government had recognized the necessity and the emergency of a comprehensive aid policy in Europe. After three days from the State Department Policy Planning Board was established, at its second meeting, there was a discussion on the relation between the revival of the European economy and the US security. Its report claimed that the participants agreed that "There is a close link between the economic difficulties abroad and the

---

23 New York Times, 30 Sep, 1945.
24 Wilson D. Miscamble, George F. Kennan and the Making of the US Foreign Policy, Princeton University Press, Princeton, New Jersey, 1992, p.43.

ability and willingness of the United States to quickly and effectively deal with it.... The greatest and most important issue is in Western Europe; ... the problem is political and economic, rather than military (except to maintain the ability of the United States); now the way to solve the political problems is to use economic methods"[25]. The undersecretary of state for economic affairs, Will Clayton went further in this aspect. On May 27, 1947, he submitted a memorandum to the Secretary of State, Marshall, and once again he stressed that "if there will be no further promotion and substantial assistance from the United States, the split of the economy, society and politics will cover the whole Europe." Clayton believed that it would cost US the 6 billion to 7 billion dollars a year to aid Europe within three years, and particularly pointed out that in spite of the US aid should be based on a European project, "this scene must be directed by the United States"[26].

The Soviet attitude made the US worried too. On April 15, 1947, the Secretary of State Marshall met with Stalin in Moscow after attending the meeting of the four countries' Foreign ministers. In the talk, Marshall complained to Stalin about the Soviet Union that seems doesn't want to reach an agreement with its wartime allies on post-war arrangements. He also told Stalin that the US decided to provide all assistance within its capacity to those countries facing economic collapse, and hoped to improve democracy in recipient countries through aid. Stalin replied him with a cold tone. He told Marshall "not to make too pessimistic interpretation of the issue that the allies failed to reach agreement. Because, "when people become exhausted", they will be aware of the need of compromising. This is a rule." So the Moscow Foreign Ministers' Meeting "was just the first skirmish." Stalin hoped Marshall could have some patience. "Even though we still cannot reach an agreement the next time, then there is a third time." In Marshall's view, this unmistakably showed that the Soviet wanted to make profit from the current deteriorated economic situation in Europe. He hoped the growing economic pressure would eventually make the West "become exhausted," and therefore, accept the Soviet Union's requirements. Marshall also began to feel the urgency of the aiding Europe action. In the phone with Truman after he returned home, Marshall said, "We cannot ignore the time factor. The revival in Europe is slower than imagined. The separating forces have existed. If the doctor thinks carefully, the patient's condition can rapidly get worse. So I think we cannot compromise after we get exhausted. New problems arise every day. Whatever the action, so long

25   Minutes of Meeting, May 8, 1947, Department of State Records, PPS Records, P.Box 32, National Archives, Washington D.C.
26   Wilson D. Miscamble, George F. Kennan and the Making of the US Foreign Policy, Princeton University Press, Princeton, New Jersey, 1992, pp.51-52.

as it is able to cope with these increasingly urgent problems, then it must be taken without hesitation."

On June 5, 1947, on the ceremony where Harvard University awarded him an honorary doctorate, Marshall made a 15-minute speech. Usually, this type of speech is only ceremonial, without any substance. But in the speech, Marshall illustrated the necessity, purpose and manner of the US aiding plan to Europe, which marked the start of a comprehensive action to aid European recovery. Marshall said, "Currently, Europe had become a ruin with no foreign aid. Europe was going to "face very serious economic, social and political deterioration", so "the United States should do everything to help the world economy restore to the normal state." The purpose of US aid in Europe was "to restore the effective economic system in the world to provide the political and social conditions for the free system". He claimed that the United States was unable to provide assistance to European countries separately. European countries needed to cooperate to ensure that US aid was "a way to cure disaster rather than a temporary measure coping with emergencies." Marshall insisted that the initiative of European recovery must be taken by the Europeans. The role of the United States "should include providing friendly help in the process of drafting the European programs and support this program as soon as it becomes practicable".[27]

In order to ensure that European countries were able to make favorable responses, State Department officials kept close contact with the European diplomats and journalists so that European governments can be aware of the trends of US policy at any time. As early as May 22, when Undersecretary of State Acheson had lunch with the British Chief Justice John Balfour and the editor of London's "News Chronicle" Gerald Barry, he revealed to them that the US was thinking the problem of aiding Western Europe "from the perspective of the whole European continent rather than individual country". Belfort immediately reported Acheson's conversation to the Department of State. In a private conversation, Kennan also expressed informally to Balfour that US policy was changing. On June 2, 1947 just three days before Marshall's speech, Acheson met with the BBC's Leon Leonard Millard, Malcolm Macquarie Ridge from "Daily Telegraph" and Rene McColl from "Daily Mirror". Acheson asked them to pay attention to Marshall's speech and highlighted the difficulties of aiding Europe in the Parliament. He said that "Europeans must cooperate and take some dramatic action to change the impression of Congress". After the Marshall speech on June 5, 1947 the three British journalists made their moves immediately.

---

27 Wilson D Meath Campbell, George F. Kennan and the Making of US Foreign Policy, pp.53-54.

Macquarie Ridge sent Marshall's speech to the "Daily Telegraph" with a note for the editor, and asked him to send a copy to the Ministry of Foreign Affairs. Millard told the BBC's news editor that Marshall made an important proposal to the Europe, asking them to broadcast this message in the extended evening news as soon as possible. BBC agreed to his request, British Foreign Secretary Bevin was one of the audiences of Millard that day.[28]

European countries reacted immediately just like the US government had expected. British Foreign Secretary Bevin said Marshall's speech was "the world's greatest speech," French President Vincent Auriol also announced that France would "not hesitate" to participate in Europe's economic plan. On June 17, 1947 Britain and France met in Paris to discuss about inviting the Soviet Union to participate in the Marshall Plan. Although Marshall announced in his speech that the US aid policy was "not against any country or doctrine, but against hunger, desperation, poverty and chaos", but in fact the United States did not want the Soviet Union to join. On June 24, Kennan and Bohlen phoned the British Embassy, and conveyed the prerequisite of the Soviet Union to participate to the British Ambassador Vladimir Chapel and Belfort judge. Kennan showed the Soviet Union and Eastern European countries that they could only participate in the Marshall Plan under the condition of joining the economic cooperation in Europe which was advocated by Marshall's speech, especially that "the Soviet should permit its satellite countries to fully establish economic ties with neighboring countries in Western Europe". Kennan said that if the Soviets rejected this condition, Europe should understand "by then the United States would carry out this plan with Western Europe alone." Sure enough, in Britain, France and the Soviet Union Foreign ministers' meeting held on June 27, Molotov firmly opposed to the European countries to develop a unified economic revival plan, claiming that this was interfering with the internal affairs of states. As a result, on July 2, Molotov left the meeting. Bevin and French Foreign Minister Georges Bidault immediately issued invitations to 22 European countries, wanting them "to send representatives to Paris to attend the meeting and to formulate a unified recovery plan". Under the pressure of the Soviet Union, Eastern European countries had to reject the invitation, but there were still invited representatives of 16 countries came to the meeting. The exit of the Soviet Union and Eastern European countries allowed the United States to reaffirm Europe's goal of stabilizing the political and economic order. The European Recovery Program and political containment strategy eventually linked together.

---

28   Don Cook, Forging the Alliance: NATO, 1945-1950, pp.86-87.

On July 12, the European economic conference was held in Paris and 16 of the Western European countries have attended the conference, where a decision was made on some organizational issues.. The European Economic Cooperation Commission was set up with the United Kingdom as the president, four committees were also established for the problems of food and agriculture, coal and steel, energy and transportation, and elected the Executive Committee comprising of the United Kingdom, France, Norway, the Netherlands and Italy. But after making these organizational arrangements some problems had occurred. European countries were looking at the issues from their own perspective and trying to pursue their economic goals. Britain was reluctant to change its trade arrangements; France refused to consider the issue of Germany's economic recovery, and insisted to include Monnet plans of French industrial modernization to the European Recovery Plan. Officials of the US Embassy in Paris asked the US government to exert influence to speed up the developing process of the European Recovery Program, but the State Department's officials in Washington insisted that the initiative must be taken by the European countries. As a result, the plan firstly proposed by the Paris Conference which required the United States to provide 28.2 billion US dollars in four years, was equal to the sum of all European countries' economic plans. The Undersecretary of State for Economic Affairs Clayton immediately told the President of the European Economic Cooperation Committee meeting frankly, "This is impossible." Further discussion made about not fall but rising this figure. When Kennan was sent to Paris to coordinate the requirements of European countries, the amount of assistance that the Europeans required was 29.2 billion US dollars in four years. While recognizing the efforts of European countries alone cannot make a feasible recovery plan in the near future, Kennan proposed a compromising proposal: the US government would consider Europe's demands, but the executive branch will eventually proposed their plans to Congress. In Kennan's words, "This means that we will listen to the words of all the Europeans, but we do not ask what they need. We just tell them what they will get." United States finally put the responsibility of developing the European Recovery Program on their shoulders. US involvement in Europe had deepened one more step.

On December 19, 1947, President Truman submitted the statement on "The United States supports the European Recovery Program" to Congress, requiring a funding of $17 billion from 1948 to 1952 and to establish the Economic Cooperation Department handling Foreign aid led by the President. After a three-month-long debate, the US Congress finally passed the "Foreign Assistance Act of 1948", providing 5.3 billion US Dollars in funding within 15 months, of which $ 4 billion was used to aid Western Europe, 1.3 billion US Dollars for the Western Zones of Germany, China, Greece, Turkey, the International Refugee Organization and the United Nations International Children's Emergency Fund and the amount of the fund for future would be approved year by year. US Economic Cooperation Department was founded as the implementing agency of the Marshall Plan, and Harriman was the special representative of the department in Europe. The Marshall Plan was formally implemented.

In the Marshall Plan, there are two points worth noting;

First, the Marshall Plan was the first large-scale aid operation in the US after the announcement of Truman Doctrine, it greatly deepened the US involvement in European affairs and it marked the beginning of the abandoning the isolationist tradition for the United States. However, the transfer from the isolationist policy to the internationalism policy did not happen at once. Getting away from Europe was still the goal of many Americans. Even those earliest advocates of the containment policy did not give up of the US dream of controlling the European affairs from afar without too much obligation. The representative of this aspect was George Kennan. In a letter on October 13, 1947, Kennan explained the European policy that he imagined. He said, "I did not hesitate to put forward the containment policy ...... the primary reason is to encourage and develop other forces against Communism." Kennan believed that in the early post-war world, "the power of Germany, Italy and Japan were destroyed; British and Chinese forces were severely weakened. In these circumstances the actual problem is that Russia surrounded by a power vacuum now. " Only direct action of the United States could fill this vacuum. But Kennan did not wish to do it. He said, "The most important point that our policy is based on ensuring to develop other power in Eurasia as soon as possible to share some burden of 'bipolar world' on our shoulders." And this was "the charm of the Marshall Plan", because "it obviously had this effect."[29]

For Kennan, US involvement in European affairs brought by the Marshall Plan was only temporary, it was specifically for the hard time ahead. It was the emergent measure to help European countries to stabilize, and its purpose still was to establish a power balance in Europe that could ensure safe escaping of the United States.

Such thoughts of getting away from Europe also had a huge impact on the Marshall Plan. On May 27, 1947, the State Department's Policy

---

29   Minutes of Meeting, May 8, 1947, Department of State Records, PPS Records, P.Box 32, National Archives, Washington D.C.

Planning Board had proposed a memo "on US aid policy in Western Europe ". It recommended:

a. It is necessary to clearly separate the European economic revival plan from the United States support to this revival. If the US government unilaterally develops a plan which is designed to stir up the burden of the Western European economy, and takes the initiative to announce officially, this is not suitable and will not have much effect.

Economic revival is the Europeans' business, so it should be formally proposed by the Europeans. The plan should be made in Europe, and they should shoulder the primary responsibility. America's role is to give friendly assistance at the time of drafting the European Recovery Program. Later, the US should give financial and other support to this project as the Europeans requested.

......

c. European recovery plan should try to maintain the general standard of living on the basis of financial self-reliance for Western Europe. The program must be committed to carry out all the work. It should also be added with a reasonable assurance that, if you need our support, this program should be the last plan in the near future we want to support.

......

e. This does not mean that the United States can standby, or ignore all the consideration and formulation of the European Recovery Program. ...... But in order to understand correctly, in order to have an exact concept, in order to protect the self-esteem of the Europeans, we must insist that the initiative and the main responsibility must be taken by Europe. In fact, those who are unwilling to help themselves, even though the American people have the best wishes, they cannot be helpful. If the European government is going to show the initiative as we required, and not ready to publicly take responsibility, then this would mean that the European political institutions have something wrong as we know it. For us, it will be too late to reverse the process of the event.[30]

It was under the influence of this view that Marshall listed the full cooperation of European countries as the prerequisite for US aid in his speech, and he repeatedly claimed that "the initiatives must be taken by the European countries." This attitude prevented the US officials to play an active role in European economic conference, showing the unwillingness of the United

30 Wang Chunliang, Selected Documents and Modern World History 1900-1988, Oriental Press,1990, pp.473-474.

States to have long and deep involvement in European affairs. In order to strengthen Europe's position in front of the Soviet Union, the United States used the help of the Marshall Plan as a lever to actively promote the European alliance, and called for the establishment of a customs union in Western Europe. Kennan even suggested that he supported Europe to become the "third force" between the US and the Soviet Union. In some US strategists' view, the European alliance which have urged by the Marshall Plan would make Europe stronger enough to withstand the Soviet threat. At the same time, it would facilitate the US remotely in control of the Western Hemisphere with the penetration of the US economic power, so that the United States would be able get out of Europe safely. On the one hand, it could be seen that the residual effects of isolationism still existed. On the other hand, the Marshall Plan provided the economic base for European integration as well as for the US and European alliance relations.

Secondly, although the European countries responded actively to the Marshall Plan, their reactions also exhibited duality.

On the one hand, European countries were pleased at the fact that the United States finally was willing to assume the responsibility of aiding Europe, but they were also worried about the swing and uncertainty shown on US policy. They feared that the US aid to Europe was only temporary. Once the economic and social development in Europe returned on the normal track, it would leave Europe. The Marshall Plan brought only economic aid, but it said nothing about the political and military security in Europe, which added to the concerns of the European countries. They wanted the United States to assume greater responsibility for security in Europe. This attitude was shown the most obviously by France. With the World War II the security problem that the French were most concerned about, become an issues. The changes of international situation in the early post-war period made the French people consider how to solve the traditional problem of containing the Germany revival while they were facing the new threat caused by the Soviet forces. Under heavy security pressure, the French government began to accuse America of its half-hearted attitude when aiding Europe and said that "the Marshall Plan was not sufficient in coping with the situation in Europe". They pointed out that without strengthening the military forces in Europe, " the wealthy Europe will be more attractive target to the Soviet Union." The French government suggested changing the focus of the Marshall Plan: To put the military defense before economic recovery, to compensate the Soviet military advantage of 16 to 1 in the eyes of Frenchman. For the French, "the Truman Doctrine started a dangerous era. It would continue until the military forces supported by the US which was enough to shake Russians appeared in Europe. The US government must recognize that there would not be any different results of the incendiary rhetoric itself. A guarantee without force would only lead to trouble." France hoped that the United States could assume the political and military obligation to ensure the security in Europe and reach a military agreement with the 16 Western European countries who participated in the Marshall Plan, and to make the US military stay in Europe. France also proposed a package plan to defend along the Rhine, and even more to the east, along the Elbe river.[31]

On the other hand, European countries maintained their independence while accepting aid from the US. They were unwilling to become the handmaid of the United States forces, but become the equal partner in the global strategy of the United States. Britain was the representative of this attitude. Different from other European countries, Britain hadn't been conquered by Nazi Germany's blitzkrieg. On the contrary, it made a decisive contribution to the victory of the World War II together with the Soviet Union, becoming one of the three great countries during the war. So, in the early post-war period, the Britain continued to regard itself as a great power in the world and a leader in Europe. Even in decline, the Britain did not want to give up its leadership on the world stage. To this end, the United Kingdom repeatedly stressed "the Anglo-American special relationship", unwilling to let US think that they were the same as the other European countries, and tried to highlight its status as a great power. But on June 24, 1947, the meeting was participated by the Undersecretary of State, Clayton Douglas, the US ambassador of Britain and the British Cabinet officials, on clarifying the role that the US wished the Britain to play in the Marshall Plan, they refused Bevan's requirements about establishing the specifically important status of Britain, on the grounds that this would lead to a special financial relationship between the Britain and the US. Clayton Douglas conveyed the views of the United States as: Britain must be treated as "a part of Europe", because the special assistance to British violates the principle of dealing with the European issues separately."

This hinted descending of the Britain's position made her become aware of the need to safeguard their independence in the face of the United States. The British Government thought that in order to make this happen, first they must get rid of the dependence on the US aid as soon as possible, and to establish a self-sufficient economy. In October 1947, Finance Minister Cripps told the Cabinet did not hold too much hope for the US aid since the Marshall Plan was the only help they could get from the US. Besides, this aid would not last

---

31   Irwin M. Woll, The United States and the Making of post-War France, 1945-1954, Cambridge University Press, 1991, pp.133-134.

long, and the numbers were not much. The British Cabinet held almost unanimous opinion that they could not lay their hope completely on the US. Sir Edward Bridges said, "If we use up our reserves and hope the US aid to help, then we will have to accept any conditions chosen by the United States – by that time we will be faced with a disaster. If aid does not come, our reserves and capacity of bargaining in the world will disappear."[32]

In order to build the necessary reserves, Cripps proposed again to reduce the spending. He tried to save dollars which worth 73 million pounds from the cost of buying food, which led to the result that the per capita calorie intake will reduce to 2800 calories or less in the first half of 1948. Food minister protested that because this figure was even lower than the worst period during wartime before the start of the "Lend-Lease Act". But the cabinet still approved the proposal to decrease the amount of sugar from 10 ounces to 8 ounces, to reduce egg supply to 66 per year, the amount of meat was one shilling a week, the amount of bacon was 1 ounce per week, so that to achieve the target proposed by the Chancellor of the Exchequer. Sheffield Lord Roger Margins described the British Cabinet's view like this, "Once we have taken all necessary measures to ensure that we can survive regardless of whether the US aid can arrive, we will improve our position to a great extent."[33]

The British policy of sticking to their unique position was mainly presented in its attitude towards the European integration that United States strongly advocated. Britain was not opposed to the European integration but hoped to lead establishing European integration which was independent, and able to strengthen the cooperation between the United States and Europe, instead of a European integration that allowed the United States to escape and remotely control Europe. Britain posited itself as a bond connecting the United States and Europe in the international arena. This attitude was first manifested in Churchill's "Three Rings" diplomacy. The so-called "three-ring" meant the union of the English speaking countries; the European alliance; the Commonwealth or the British Empire. Britain, as the only country who played an important role in the "three-ring" and at the same time would become a link among the countries in the world. Therefore, the British could never completely involve in any one ring and loss the free activities in the other two rings, while ensuring close contact between "three-ring". This attitude constituted the basic position of the United Kingdom towards the European Union, which meant Britain firmly

---

32 CAB 130/27, Gen. 197/1.
33 Elisabeth Barker, The British between the Superpowers, 1945-1950, University of Toronto Press, Toronto and Buffalo, 1983, p.97.

rejects to play a role of an ordinary member in a united Europe and strongly emphasize that the European Union including the United States and Canada should be placed in the wider framework of the Atlantic. On May 9, 1949, the sub-official committee under the leadership of Ministry of Foreign Affairs Permanent Secretary Officer William Strong submitted a memorandum to articulate the basic policy of the United Kingdom for the European alliance. The memorandum stated: Only the "Western unity" including the United States can contain the Soviet Union and be in line with "the interests of the Commonwealth and the European union". But the joint was not equal to alliance. "It is wise not to sacrifice our relationship with the United States and the Commonwealth while trying to unduly rely on the European economic association, because if we go too far on this road, we will find that Europe goes beyond the limit of its capacity, and our own economic sector is unable to perform its functions." Britain's policy should keep loyalty to Commonwealth countries, play a leading role on the European continent and act as a balance wheel of "the Western system" to expand activities. Minister Committee hoped that as the time passed, the "dependency factor" in US-European relation would give way to "interdependence", while Britain would show up as an equal partner of the US in the economy and the security system serving the interests of both countries.[34] This attitude made the UK reluctant to be thoroughly involved in European integration affairs. But without the leadership of the United Kingdom, the small European countries were also skeptical of European integration issues and kept waiting, which hampered the European integration policy advocated by the United States. After the Schuman Plan announced in 1950 and the European Coal and Steel Community established in 1951, the European integration entered a new stage of development in a completely different way from the leadership of France and Germany, which was beyond the expectation of the US government officials.

In short, the presence of the Truman Doctrine and the Marshall Plan greatly changed the US policy. They became the turning point of the US-European relations in the early post-war period, and provided the political and economic foundation for the US-European alliance and European alliance. However, it was only the beginning of change. The US-European relations were not finalized. The United States policy of getting out of Europe did not completely disappear, European countries also needed to make greater efforts to ensure that the United States assumed more obligations in Europe, especially in the security field. The contact and cooperation between Europe and America needed yet to be further strengthened.

---

34   PUSC 22, PREM8/1204.

1.3 The Foundation of North Atlantic Treaty Organization (NATO)

During 1947 and 1948, further changes in the international situation had undergone. At the same time when the United States launched the Truman Doctrine and the Marshall Plan, and got more and more deeply involved in European affairs, the Soviet Union had also taken a series of measures to consolidate its sphere of influence in Eastern Europe. At the behest of the Soviet Union, the Communist or the representatives from the Workers Party of the Soviet Union, Romania, Yugoslavia, Poland, Hungary, Czechoslovakia, Bulgaria, France and Italy held its inaugural meeting of the 9th European Communist Party and Workers Party's Intelligence in Poland between 22-27th of September 1947, by the invitation of the first secretary of the Polish Workers' Party Gomulka. The declaration of the meeting made clear that the world had split into two major camps, imperialist and anti-imperialist, and asked the Communists to develop a common program of action and strategies to oppose imperialist aggression and expansion. In Western countries' opinion, this seemed a resurrection of the "world revolution" theory of the Third International. For the Marshall Plan, the Soviet Union also proposed a "Molotov Plan" in 1947. The economic networks between countries of Eastern Europe were formed by making a series of bilateral economic agreements with Soviet and Eastern European countries. The Soviet Union and the Eastern Europe did most of the trade within their region. This further defined the division of Europe from the perspective of economy. The council for mutual economic association was built on this basis in 1949. The "two world market" called by Stalin gradually formed. In addition, Eastern European countries established and strengthened the regime leading by the Communist. In 1947, the Romanian king abdicated. The People's Republic of Romania leading by the Communist Party was announced to establish. February incident happened in Czechoslovakia in February 1948 and President Benes accepted the new list of the government proposed by the Communist Party of Czechoslovakia. On June 24, 1948, the Soviet Union used road maintenance as an excuse to cut the water and land transportation between the west occupation in Germany and Berlin, thus the first Berlin crisis erupted. This series of actions of the Soviet Union made "the Soviet invasion threat" in the eyes of the West more serious and concrete. In order to deal with the "Soviet threat", they began to strengthen cooperation in security, which resulted in further changes in the US-European relations.

1.3.1 Europe before the alliance

It should be noted that security cooperation between the US and Europe was not taken into consideration at first in 1947. Shortly after World War II, this cooperation had proceeded. When the Soviet Union refused to withdraw from Iran as the agreement of Tehran require them to withdraw and held bilateral talks on the problem of Black Sea Straits with Turkey in 1946, Truman ordered the Deputy Secretary of State Dean Acheson to call the State Department–Department of the Army and Navy Coordinating Committee to discuss the reaction of the United States. At the meeting on August 15, participants agreed that the actions towards the Soviet Union should "fight at all costs". They recommended sending Air Force reinforcements to the north of Italy, and sent warships to help the Missouri battleship which was cruising in the Eastern Mediterranean after a visit to Istanbul to show the US military power and determination. On the 6th of September, Secretary of State Byrnes gave a speech with a hint that the US was going to be involved in European security issues in Stuttgart. He claimed, "The security forces may have to stay in Germany for a long period. I do not want any misunderstanding. We will not shirk our responsibilities. We will not back down. We are going to stay here, and share reasonable responsibility in the security forces."[35] His speech completely changed what Roosevelt had declared to Churchill and Stalin at the Yalta Conference, that the US troops might only station in Europe for "a few years". For Western European countries and the Soviet Union, this was a signal that the United States would firmly stick to its position.

However, since the US military was in the large-scale demobilization period at that time, it did not have enough strength to support its hard attitude. On August 22, 1946, Secretary of the Navy Forrestal's diary described the scene of the rapid decline of the US military:

Our rapid demobilization sharply reduced the fleet size, our fleet efficiency reached bottom in July. Although there has been a slight recovery since then, it is still low to a dangerous degree. Our fleet in active service has a large amount of ships, but they are unable to sail due to the lack of sufficient personnel. When we wanted to make a command ship Katuoketing move, the commander had to deploy staff from other warships in the port of Norfolk. Even so, the warship still had a few minor incidents.

---

35   Don Cook, Forging the Alliance: NATO,1945-1950, p.43.

In order to perform the task in Europe, the estimated Army force at hand is about 460 fighters, 90 bombers, and 175 trained frontline pilots.[36]

I talked with Acheson and told him I was very worried about our strength. In my opinion, our responsibility is to leave the impression to others that we are able to support these (to the Russians) declaration.[37]

In order to compensate for the lack of power, the United States had to seek cooperation with European countries, firstly with Britain. On August 30, 1946 the representatives of the Royal Navy in the military services of British Embassy were invited to the Joint Chiefs of Staff in the Pentagon to generally discuss that "if an emergency situation occurs how the US and the UK use to deal with such a situation." Thus, they took the first step to re-establish the Anglo-American military liaison and planning agency. Then, in mid-September, the British Empire chief of staff, Field Marshal Viscount Montgomery arrived in Washington to have a "friendly visit." On September 16, Eisenhower invited Montgomery and the US Chiefs of Staff to conduct a parade on the Potomac River. Under this cover, the two sides held secret talks and agreed to hold secret talks between the US and British chief of staff at the earliest possible time in order to coordinate their strategic plan. At the same time, Byrnes in Europe took an action. He proposed to the Foreign Minister Bevin for his requirement of allowing the United States to establish bases in the Pacific and other regions of the British territory. He suggested that the United States and Commonwealth countries could adopt a "common use policy", sharing each other's ports and air bases. This proposal was quite similar to the exclamation of Norway Foreign Minister, Trygve Lie during the war. Britain's chief of staff who expressed his support suggested that it would be better not to write such important proposal but to restore the convention in wartime that the ports of two sides can be automatically used for other warships of the other side, and to begin naval visits as soon as possible. Under the impetus of this agreement, the United States took further actions. On October 1, 1946, Secretary of the Navy Forrestal announced the establishment of a new headquarters as a permanent base for the US Navy in the Mediterranean, and a new task force would be stationed there with Franklin D. Roosevelt at the centre. Later, this task force was renamed as the US Mediterranean Sixth Fleet. To the end of 1946, three cruisers and eight destroyers joined the Roosevelt, and the fleet was officially formed. Thus, with the resumption of the US-British

---

36   The US Air Force was not independent at that time, but exerted its function as a part of the Navy Air Force which is the so-called Army Air Force and Naval Air Force—Author noted.

37   Don Cook, Forging the Alliance: NATO,1945-1950, p.41.

military cooperation, military construction began. Meanwhile, the military cooperation between European countries was gradually established. In March 1947, Britain and France signed a "Treaty of Alliance and Mutual Assistance between Britain and France" in Dunkirk, declaring the two countries decided to "help each other if German invades again". Although the objective of this treaty was against Germany, it laid the foundation for further cooperation in the field of security among European countries in the future.

However, during 1946-1947, the biggest threat in the eyes of the US and European countries was not the Soviet Union's military power but the social chaos brought by the economic collapse in Europe. At that time, the United States was still in nuclear monopoly. Although Western countries were in disadvantage in conventional forces compared to the Soviet bloc, they still counted on the nuclear weapons of the United States to provide adequate protection, so that the Soviet Union did not dare to win the European hegemony by military means. Therefore, the United States and European countries put their focus on the restoration of normal economic and social order. As Kennan said in his "8000 word telegram", as long as the economic and political life in Western countries turned on the track, political subversion and infiltration of the Soviet Union could not succeed. The result would be two groups of East and West facing the long-term confrontation. Due to the weaknesses of the Soviet social system, it could not afford such long-term confrontation. The final result would be the failure of the Soviet party. According to this logic, the United States didn't need to assume excessive military obligations in Europe. Under the influence of the isolationist tradition, the US public opinion had not transformed to accept the military alliance of the United States and Europe in peacetime. "Let the children come home" was still the overwhelming voice. So, at this time, the obligations undertaken by the United States on European security remained vague and limited.

Even European countries did not seriously consider about their military security issues. The collapse of the economic situation had made them battered. They cannot afford the massive arms. Until early 1948, the majority of British politicians still kept indifferent attitude to the suggestion of establishing a Western group which can be political or economic or military group with the target to resist the Soviet threat. Churchill clearly expressed the attitude of Britain towards the establishment of a Western security group in a letter to Eden in November 1944:

Before a really powerful French army appears – it may take 5 years or 10 years – there is nothing left except for desperate weakness in these countries. Belgians are extremely weak and their act before the war was wavering. Dutch are completely selfish, and they will fight only when they are attacked, but it will only persist for several hours. Denmark is helpless, and there is no protection. In fact, this is also true for Norway. Before France re-establishes an army in Europe, the UK can only rely on any help that can be provided by these countries to take on the task of defending them. In my opinion it is unwise or even imprudent...... Foreigners will immediately ask, "How big an army will you provide?" I cannot imagine whether we can maintain the expeditionary force with 50-60 divisions if we continue to collect taxes at the current tax rate – I'm sure the rate would undermine the economic recovery, and if we want to play a game of war on the continent, these forces are minimal.[38]

Even Montgomery which stressed the need for a "continental army" did not show any respect to the strength of the Western European countries. France was wandering between Germany and the Soviet Union and cannot determine who was more of a threat. Without the leadership of the United Kingdom and France, the other small countries in Western Europe were a mess. Compared with the security threats, they cared more about their own economic revival and social problems.

In correspondence, European countries constantly cut military spending in order to reduce their military burdens. Since at present there was no imminent threat of the military attack from the Soviet Union, there was no reason to maintain a strong military. In early 1948, the accepted view in Britain was that the Soviet Union would not to take the risk of war in the next few years. In January, 1948, Bevan told the Cabinet that the primary goal of Russia was to catch up with the West in terms of material prosperity. At the mean time, they "would grab a lot of vital interests for their own in the chaos of the post-War world". He did not believe that "the Soviet government consciously wanted to risk war for that purpose, especially when the Anglo-Saxon states monopolized the atomic secrets; they thought they might be able to get what they want through the 'Cold War' struggle".[39] This view had a direct impact on defense spending. Chancellor of the Exchequer told the Defense Committee, "We must consider our defense from this point of view...... it is not only preventing the possibility of a more distant armed aggression, but also preventing the possibility of a much more urgent economic and financial collapse." Under the pressure of the Chancellor of the

38   PRE 4/308, M.1144/4.
39   CAB 129/23, CP(48)6.

Exchequer, the defense minister A.V. Alexander had to announce that in a decade from the beginning of 1947, the annual defense budget could not be more than 600 million pounds. British Chiefs of Staff must develop their plans based on such a principle. It was worth mentioning that the more European countries cut military spending, the more they were dependent on the US aid in defense issues, their wish that the US assume more responsibilities in the field of security in Europe. In January 1947, the British Chiefs of Staff issued a statement that the United States might become an ally in future wars, although the time to participate the war could not be predicted. Therefore, it was absolutely necessary for the United Kingdom to shorten the time persisting alone to a minimum.

1.3.2 The "Brussels Treaty"–a prelude to the alliance

Begin from the end of 1947 and the beginning of 1948, as the Soviet Union's control over the Eastern European countries was strengthened and the conflict between the east and the west got intensified, European countries began to change their opinion towards the Soviet threat. Though at that time, most of the people believed that the Soviet Union was unlikely to launch a full-scale military attack to the West in the foreseeable future. But with the support of a large military force, the political pressure of the Soviet Union made European politicians increasingly feel worried. In the same memo of Bevan on January 4, 1948 which claimed that the Soviet Union could not take the risk of war, he also highlighted the threat caused by political pressure of the Soviet and the measures to be taken by Western countries. He said, "We must recognize the Soviet Government built a strong political and economic group on the way from the Baltic Sea to the Oder River, behind the Trieste to the back line of the Black Sea. In the near future, we cannot reconstruct and maintain a normal relationship with European countries behind this line. In this situation what Russia policy caused, half-hearted measures are of no use. If we want to maintain peace and our own security, we can only mobilize our moral and material forces. On the one hand we have to build our own confidence and ability, on the other hand, to force the Soviet Union to respect us and be careful. Otherwise we can only accept the continuous infiltration of the Russia in silence, and watch helplessly that the Western camp crash one after another."[40]

In the meeting of Chief of Staff on March 17, Admiral Sir John Cunningham proposed to set up a "Stop Line". Over this line, the Soviet Union's "infiltration and communism transmission" must be curbed. This

---

40   The north corner refers to the north end of border line between Norway and Swedish on Scandinavia -Author noted.

line he drew started from the North, passing the east of Scandinavia, France and the Low Countries, northern Italy, Greece, Turkey, Iran to Afghanistan.[41]

Attlee asked, if communist influence pushed westward over this "stop line", did chief of staff consider this constituted the reason of a declaration of war. The answer to this question was that if France and the Low Countries were under the Soviet Union's control, "It will almost lead us to a war."

Therefore, from the end of 1947, the British began to make exploratory effort to strengthen security cooperation with the Western countries. Foreign ministers meeting of the US, Britain, France and the Soviet Union held in London between 25th of November–the 6th of December 1947. Bevan took the opportunity to have private talk with French Foreign Minister Bidault and the US Secretary of State Marshall separately to discuss the issues of strengthening security cooperation among Western countries. He told Bidault that Europe now had split along with the line from Greece to the Baltic, from Oder River to the Trieste. We must concentrate all the strength to save Western civilization. He said Europe must restore its military power, especially France. Bidault agreed to let the French army chief of staff came to London to coordinate their military efforts. Bevan then proposed a "Western democracy" program for Marshall. This system would be composed of the United States, Britain, France, the Netherlands, Belgium, Luxembourg, Italy and the United Kingdom Dominion, hoping to strengthen the connection between the United States and the European countries. For Bevan's suggestion, Marshall's first reaction was positive, but he expressed the hope to see a more detailed plan. Thus, on January 13, 1948, Bevan issued a memorandum to the US State Department, explaining his "Western Alliance" program in detail. He proposed to invite the Netherlands, Belgium and Luxembourg to join a defense system like the "Dunkirk Treaty". Then this system would be gradually expanded to Greece, Portugal and the Scandinavian countries. Once Germany and Italy established democracy, they would be absorbed in.[42]

In such system, the US role was to provide financial assistance for Europe through the Marshall Plan. At the same time, Britain, France, Belgium, Netherlands, Luxembourg had negotiations on strengthening security cooperation between each other.

Bevin's proposal immediately led to a controversy in Washington. Just within one year, the United States had to rethink its European policy for the second time. What was the nature of the Soviet threat in the end? Was

---

41   Ibid.
42   The Department of State, FFRUS, 1948, Vol.3, Washington, US GPO, 1973, p.4-5.

it necessary for America to assume more obligations in Europe, or even involved in a military alliance? One side led by John D. Hick Mickelson, the chef of the European Affairs in the State Department had a fierce debate with another side led by George Kennan. Hick Mickelson agreed with the goal of Bevin from the outset. He had told his deputy Theodore Achilles, "I do not care about the idea that the involvement of an alliance is worse than the original sin since George Washington. We must hold negotiations with the European Union on the issue of establishing a military alliance in an era of peace, and we must do so as soon as possible." Just after 6 days receiving the memorandum of Bevan, he presented his views to Marshall. He believed Bevan's goal was "very good", but he opposed Bevan to achieve it by expanding "Dunkirk Treaty". Hick Wilson advocated that "Western Union" should follow the model of "Rio de Janeiro Treaty" between the United States and Latin American countries to establish a regional collective security arrangements. Because he believed that compared to those military strict obligations and the imaginary enemy "Dunkirk Treaty", a loose regional arrangement was easier for US to accept. The possibility of the US participation was greater. Hick Mandelson said quite openly that if such a treaty was to be in force, we must have the participation of the United States. In the ongoing negotiations among five countries of Western Europe, the issue was that what form the "Western Union" should take. Britain and France advocated the Netherlands, Belgium and Luxembourg to join "Dunkirk Treaty", while the Netherlands, Belgium and Luxembourg advocated establishing a loose regional collective security system based on the spirit of section 51 in the UN Charter. Apparently, the consideration of Europe and the US had involved the problem of the relationship between the United States and regional collective security system. In this aspect, the idea of Hick Mickelson went a step further than Bevan's.

On the second day after Hick Mickelson presented his ideas, Kennan also told Marshall his proposal. Kennan insisted his views put forward in the "8000 word telegram", that the Soviet threat was not military but political. Now the main threat to Western European countries was "the Communist Party political partner" in the country rather than direct military invasion of the Soviet Union. Thus, in Kennan's opinion, the military alliance established between the US and Europe was unnecessary. He claimed, "Military alliance is a wrong starting point, the current focus should be on the political, economic and spiritual alliance". He insisted that Europeans should take the initiative on their own security issues, and cannot allow the issue of security relations of the United States and Europe "catch hold of their minds". Kennan was reluctant to see the United States too deeply involved in European affairs, which ultimately harm the chance to get out of Europe. In the face of this basic disagreement of State Council, Marshall was almost unable to give a definite answer to Bevan. He expressed that in his reply on January 20, 1948, "Your initiative was highly praised in the United States. I hope you know I am very interested in this proposal and it touches me deeply. I would like to see the United States do everything it can to guide the program to success. If you think I can help, please feel free to consult with me".

When the fierce debate on strengthening security cooperation with Europe in the US government was continuing, the Soviet Union's action had prompted Western European countries to accelerate the pace of their action. In February 1948, Czechoslovakia incident occurred in February. President Benes accepted the list of government proposed by the Czech Communist Party. Soon, people found Foreign Minister Jan Masaryk's body downstairs in the Ministry of Foreign Affairs who was the only non-Communist member in the new government. Although it was not clear whether it was suicide or homicide, it provoked a huge panic and anger at the time. In Western countries' eyes, Masaryk's death was a concrete symbol of the demise of the bourgeois-democratic regime in Czechoslovakia, and they connect it with Hitler's attempt to win the hegemony of Europe in Munich. They got more worried about whether it would be a prelude to another world war. What made matters worse was that Finland and the Soviet Union signed a "friendship treaty" like the Soviet Union and Eastern Europe signed in the same week when the Czech Communist seize political power. In this treaty, the Finns allowed the Soviet Union to build a naval base on the territory of Finland, while regarded the Soviet Union as their main trading partners. On March 11, Foreign Minister of Norway Halvard Lange met with the US and British ambassador separately in Oslo, and conveyed them the message Norway had received from three different sources of information. It might become the next country with which the Soviet Union required to sign "friendship treaty". Lange said that the inner circle of Norway's Labor government had begun to think about the Soviet's demand but decided to reject it. He talked more about it to the British ambassador. Lange said that the Soviet Union might ask Norway ceded territory and while the Finns allowed them to build a naval base in the north of Finland the Norway government was determined to reject any such request of the Soviet Union. If this would cause an attack to the territory of Norway by the Soviet Union, Norway would fight. He hoped to consult the British government, "When there is an attack would Norway count on British government?"

Bevin immediately contacted Marshall for this issue to discuss the current situation and the countermeasures to be taken by the West. He claimed, " For the Soviet Union losing Norway could lead to the collapse in the Atlantic Ocean and in the entire Scandinavian system, which will further threaten any plans of the Soviet Union concerning relentlessly push forward to Western Europe. In conclusion, there were two serious threats: the strategic threat of Russia's sphere of influence extending to the Atlantic Ocean as well as the political threat destructing any effort to establish the Western European Alliance". But Bevan did not intend to include Scandinavian countries into the ongoing negotiations among the five countries. Because he believed the five countries of Western Europe could not afford to play a mission to protect the Scandinavian countries. He argued, "Before the Norwegian yield the most effective measures should be the signing a regional Atlantic Mutual Assistance Treaty as soon as possible according to section 51 in the UN Charter. All countries threatened by the Soviet Union advancing in the Atlantic should participate in this treaty, such as the United States, Britain, Canada, Ireland, Iceland, Norway, Denmark, Portugal, France (and Spain, after the establishment of a democratic regime)". The Western security system envisaged by Bevan was divided into three parts: Britain, France and the Low Countries alliance with the support of the United States, Atlantic security plan with more closely watching by the US as well as a Mediterranean system which had a significant impact on the Italian. Bevan said, "We are building the first part, but as for the threat faced by Norway, the Atlantic security system is even more important and urgent. Therefore, I believe that we should discuss the problem of establishing an Atlantic security system without delay. Thus, if the threat faced by Norway continued to develop, we should able to immediately strengthen the confidence and solidarity while the West is against the Soviet Union dominance and forcing the Soviet government to fully respect the West, eliminate incentives of their actions in order to ensure long-term peace. .... If other countries outside the Soviet system can really be organized, we will be able to make the whole world away from the war, and thus save Russia itself".[43]

When encouraging the United States to provide greater support, Western European countries had also accelerated the pace of their negotiations. On March 17, 1948, on the same day when Bevan's telegram reached Washington, representatives of the five countries, England, France, Belgium, Netherlands, and Luxembourg ended their negotiations and signed the "Treaty of Brussels". The final treaty accepted the views of lowlands,

---

43   Don Cook, Forging the Alliance: NATO,1945-1950, p.125.

and took the form of regional collective security system advocated by Hick Wilson. Treaty states, "In accordance with the UN Charter, every country should provide assistance to each other when maintaining international peace and security and resisting any aggression; to take measures are considered necessary in case of the resurrection of German aggression policy". Although on the surface, the treaty was signed to prevent the German resurrection of the policy of aggression, it emphasized the time when "resisting any aggression", involving countries should "provide assistance to each other". It primarily aimed at the so-called "communism westward". The highest governing body of "Brussels Treaty" was the Foreign minister of the Consultative Committee. At the same time, the Western Union Defense Committee joined by the Defense Minister was also established to study the problem of collective defense. In addition, General Staff of the Western Union and the Commander of the Committee of Western Union were set up to be responsible for coordinating military action. Brussels Treaty Organization was officially formed.

1.3.3 The "North Atlantic Treaty" was signed – (The United States and Europe Alliance)

At this time, the United States showed increasing concern on security issues in Europe. Commander of the US occupation forces stationed in Germany, General Lucius Clay strongly urged that the national government should pay attention to the urgency of the situation in Europe. In early March 1948, he called Secretary of Defense Forrestal from Berlin, "For several months, according to the analysis of logic, I feel and think war cannot happen within at least a decade. In the past few weeks, I've felt the attitude of the Soviet Union changed dramatically. I cannot describe this change, but my feeling is that it can happen suddenly. I cannot prove my feeling with any evident. ...... But my feeling is real".[44]

At the State Department, more and more officials inclined to accept Hick Mickelson's view rather than Kennan's. Even the strongest supporters of Kennan, Bohlen also reminded him that despite the judgment, "Russians did not have any intentions to use of military force against us", was certainly correct, but it was too risky to regard it as a widely accepted basis for policy. With Bohlen's words, "Whether Europeans' concern about the Soviet armed attack is an exaggeration but the fear is genuine. Europe's problem is the existence of the Red Army itself, rather than whether Soviet Union will use it or not". Even Truman, the President also began to consider

---

44   Ibid., p.121.

strengthening cooperation of security with Europe. On March 5, 1948, in the briefing Marshall proposed, Truman said, "What will be the next move of the Soviet Union? Who will pull the trigger? Where are we heading?" In the day of signing the "Brussels Treaty", Truman delivered a speech at the joint meeting of Congress, asking Congress to pass the legislation of military service election in peacetime to strengthen the US military, and to enable it to cope with the deepening security crisis. In his speech, Truman publicly declared that the United States would aid European countries and determined to defend their security. He said, "When I am delivering my speech to you, there are five European countries signed an agreement in Brussels which is a 50-year economic cooperation and mutual defense agreement...... This development deserves our full support. I am confident that the United States will support these countries in an appropriate way according to the needs of the situation. I have no doubt that our determination of assisting free European countries to self-defense is stronger than their determination to defend itself".[45]

In the five days before signing the "Treaty of Brussels", Truman approved Marshall to inform the British Ambassador, "We are ready to discuss immediately on the topic of establishing an Atlantic security system. I recommend the British representative to attend next week".

Bevan responded immediately. He warmly welcomed Marshall's proposal. On March 14, the Permanent Secretary of the British Foreign Office, Sir Oliver Sargent told Bevin in Paris that the British Cabinet will consider the proposed "Atlantic Treaty" at the 16th, proposed on behalf of the British representative, Gladwyn Jebb's stance in Washington talk. The final instructions given to Jebb reflected that the British policy in the negotiations was still focused on two principles:

To establish the possible closest security cooperation between the US and Europe and to emphasize in the Anglo-American special relationship in the cooperation. As direction proposed, Jebb should first mention "the Brussels Treaty", and clarify how the United States will support it, or even to join the treaty. Secondly, Jebb should focus on the Atlantic Treaty, avoiding including other areas to enlarge discussions. "In our opinion, one of the reasons of approving Atlantic system that including us and maybe France is that Low Countries may be reluctant to assume additional obligations to invite other countries, for example Norway. In addition, because the proposed Atlantic system was only defensive, perhaps it was best to avoid the economic problems brought by the joint of non-European countries". Thirdly,

---

45　Harry Truman, Truman's memoirs, Vol.2, SDX Joint Publishing Company,1974, p.288.

Jebb should first suggest defining the treaty among the United States, Britain and Canada. The three countries constituted the core of the Atlantic system, while other European countries on the Atlantic coast can join in the future. Jebb can also draw a frame on the geographical scope in the treaty, and it would "extend from 30 degrees north latitude, including all the co-untries on the Atlantic coast, namely Norway, Sweden, Denmark (including Greenland), Germany, Holland, Belgium, France, Spain, Portugal, Iceland and Ireland".[46]

In 1948, from March 22 to April 1, three Countries (America, Britain, Canada) held a secret talk that lasting 9 days in the Pentagon. Both sides quickly agreed on the need to strengthen mutual cooperation on security. As a result, the "Pentagon Papers" was approved, and they decided to "for-mulate a regional collective defense agreement of the North Atlantic area".

However, the "Pentagon Papers" was just a secret understanding reached between the three countries on the future intentions. It was not a formal treaty, which did not have the force of law. Transforming it into concrete policies also needed the support of Congress. In fact, since Truman invited some important Members of Congress to the White House to hear briefings in March 1947 in order to pass the bill of aiding Greece and Turkey, the so-called "bipartisan Foreign policy" was gradually formed in Congress. Its representative was the president of the Senate Foreign Affairs Committee Arthur Vandenberg.

He used to be a famous isolationist. But since the Japanese attacked Pearl Harbor, he had abandoned the isolationist stance, saying that "the world today had been linked so closely, the United States cannot be transcenden-tal". Truman Doctrine and the Marshall Plan can be successfully accepted by Congress. Vandenberg played an important role in it. Now, he also began to focus on the problem of strengthening the US-European security coope-ration. Vandenberg was not ignorant to the situation. In the US delegation attending the Foreign ministers' meeting in London at the end of 1947, the representative of Vandenberg, John Foster Dulles was in the meeting. Dulles knew about Bevan's suggestion to Marshall and conveyed it to Vandenberg. Thus, when the Truman administration solicited the views on the establish-ment of the "Atlantic Alliance" problem to Vandenberg, and wanted to get his support, Vandenberg was not entirely unfamiliar to this problem. He believed that this policy is wise. But for partisan political considerations,

46   Alexander Rendel, "Secret Explorations: The Anglo-American Initiatives", in Nicholas Sherwen, ed., NATO's Anxious Birth: The Prophetic Vision of the 1940s, St. Martin's Press, New York, 1985, pp.15-16.

he was unwilling to let Truman get all the credit in the establishment of alliances, but advocated the Senate taking the initiative, "recommending" the president to negotiate on such a treaty. Truman also recognized that this would greatly increase the likelihood of the treaty adopted in Congress, so he agreed. Thus, Vandenberg proposed a motion to the Senate asking the Senate to "advice" the government to hold a negotiation on establishing alliance that can contain the aggression by its very nature. On June 11, 1948, the Senate overwhelmingly passed the bill, which was called the "Vandenberg Resolution". It stated as follows:

Because just peace and to defend human rights and fundamental freedom need more effective international cooperation among United Nations agencies, so:

Declare, the Senate reaffirmed the policy of the United States achieve international peace and security through the United Nations. It doesn't need armed forces any more except the occasion of safeguarding the common interests. The Senate recommended to the President that the constitutional procedures passed by the current government need to pay attention on fulfilling the following objectives in the structure of the UN Charter:

(1) Consenting voluntarily not to use the veto on all the issues involving the peaceful settlement of international disputes and the situation, and on the issue of accepting new members.

(2) According to the target, principles and provisions of "UN Charter", developing positively the nature of the region and other collective arrangements on the issues of individual and collective self-defense.

(3) Through the method of selection procedures, developing the cooperation among the United States and other regional and collective arrangements that are set up on the basis of effective self-help and mutual aid and affect the security of the United States.

(4) The approval shows if any armed aggression involving its national security occurs, it is determined to perform individual or collective self-defense powers in accordance with the section 51 in the UN Charter, in order to contribute to the maintenance of peace.

(5) Making the maximum effort to reach an agreement on providing the armed forces to the United Nations in accordance with the provisions of the Charter, and to agree on an agreement among the member states of achieving a comprehensive limitation and disarmament issues under adequate and reliable conditions.

(6) If necessary, after making enough efforts to strengthen the United Nations, holding a plenary meeting or General Assembly at the right time according to the section 109 of the constitution to re-examine the UN Charter.[47]

"Vandenberg Resolution" proposed participation of the US in international security cooperation under the banner of strengthening the United Nations institutions. Its adoption eventually paved the way for the US to take bolder measures to undertake security duties in Europe.

At the same time, European countries were taking measures in that respect, pushing the United States to joining the European Security Alliance. After the Pentagon talks, Assistant Secretary of State Lovett met with the British Ambassador Vladimir Britain Chapel who was leaving his post. He told Britain Vladimir Chapel, congressional leaders were mostly agree with the US and European alliance, but at the same time they were realistic. Therefore, European countries needed to make more effort, "to convince them to believe that "the Brussels Treaty." Five countries were actively taking action themselves. He suggested that "the Brussels Treaty" countries should put forward a report on the memo of actual military situation, the size of the armed forces, the supply situation and increasing the potential sources of armaments, their military planning and the required strength of executing these plans. Thus, the Brussels Treaty Organization immediately held a meeting of five defense ministers to consider the Lovett requirements. In April 30, Brussels Treaty Military Committee was established. Its first task was to prepare a memorandum that the US required. Bevan further recommended the United States sending "military observers" to the Brussels Treaty Organization, and to study the issue of military supplies and plans with the military committee. The United States agreed with it. In this way, the first organized military connection between the United States and Europe had been formed a year before signing the North Atlantic Treaty. Meanwhile, the Military Committee also came up with the initial military report generally assessing Europe's military within two weeks. What worth special noting was that it regulated the Western Europe's defense strategy, "In the case of the Russian attack, the five countries are determined to fight in eastern Germany. Their goal is to prevent the Russians occupy the territory of Germany in order to win enough time for the US military to make the decisive intervention because it was within the attack distance of the five countries ...... They realize that their plans are closely connected with the strategic concept in the United States and from the start they are prepared to use the troops to defend Europe".[48]

47   Arthur M. Schlesinger, The Dynamics of World power: A Documentary History of US Foreign Policy, 1945-1973, Vol. 1, p.133.
48   Don Cook, Forging the Alliance: NATO,1945-1950, p.169.

In this strategy, the European countries not only expressed that aid of the United States was crucial for European security, but also showed their determination and will to fight, to prove that they were reliable partners of the United States. This statement had constituted NATO's basic defense strategies until the Drastic Change happened in 1989.

The negotiation on establishing the US-European security cooperation finally began on July 6, 1948 with the efforts made by both the US and European countries,. The participating countries included the United States, Canada and five Brussels Treaty countries. However, during the talk, there were still many differences, one of which was the problem of the basis of the negotiation. The United States, Canada and Britain hoped to negotiate on the basis of the "Pentagon Papers". But other European countries, especially France, which did not participate in secret talks before, hoped to lienvent the wheel and to start from scratch. European countries were extremely unhappy and worried about a secret negotiation that the US, the UK and Canada made behind them, but only used some broad statement of principles to stall them. So rather than dwelled in the framework of the Atlantic security system they asked the US aid to be more specific. This attitude was most evident in France. From the outset of the negotiation of seven countries, France had repeatedly claimed that the most important question was what kind of military assistance the US can provide to the Brussels Treaty Organization. Until the end of August, the French still insisted that the most important thing was not the Atlantic treaty, but two specific and urgent requirements: the US provided military equipment to France; in curbing attacks by the Soviet Union to Western Europe, the obligations of the United States should extend to East. French Ambassador Henri Bonnet had phoned Secretary of State Marshall in mid August, saying that France only accepted an Atlantic Treaty under the following three conditions, "Establishing a unified command to the armed forces of various countries; delivering the US military supplies to France immediately; delivering the US military personnel to France immediately". According to Lovett, "This greatly irritated Marshall ... so much that he even wanted to immediately interrupt the negotiations of the Atlantic Treaty".[49] In the telegram sent to US ambassador in Paris at the end of August, Lovett used one sentence to indicate the feeling of the US at that moment, "The French tormented us to an unbearable level". But under the mediation of Canada and other countries, the French gradually recognized that it was still early

---

49   Escott Reid, "The Art of the Almost Impossible: Unwavering Canadian Support for the Emerging Atlantic Alliance", in: Nicholas Sherwen, ed., NATO's Anxious Birth: The Prophetic Vision of the 1940s, St. Martin's Press, New York, 1985, pp.79-80.

to require the US to assume specific obligation of the Western European defense, and it would reduce the possibility of ratifying the treaty by the United States Congress. After some mediation, France gradually gave up their demands, and agreed to focus on constructing a system of collective security of the Atlantic region.

Another difference lied in terms of the structure of the North Atlantic system. The United States asserted to firstly expand the Brussels Treaty Organization to Norway, Denmark, Ireland, Portugal, as well as Italy, if possible. Then the United States and Canada provided guarantee to these European countries. This was the "two pillars" principle with one pillar of the United States and Canada, and the other pillars were the European countries.

But European countries expressed opposition to this principle. French worried that these countries' participation in Brussels organization will "make the piece of cake smaller". Canada was also unwilling to become the vassal of the United States at the "two pillars" structure. Finally, the United States had to give up their assertion, agreeing that "Norway and other countries can become a member of the North Atlantic Treaty without their approval of the Brussels Treaty".

After two months of negotiations, on September 9, 1948, the meeting finally reached a "Washington File". Its full name was "the memorandum to their governments by the participating countries about the discussion on security issues held on July 6, 1948 until the September the 9th in Washington " It was divided into the preamble; "situations impacting European security", "the area of the security arrangements in the North Atlantic and its relationship with other countries' security", "the nature of the security arrangements that may arise in the North Atlantic" and other parts, which regulated the nature, scope of the North Atlantic Treaty Organization and obligations of involving states and the relationship with other European organizations and so on. Then participants sent invitations to Norway, Sweden, Denmark, Iceland, Ireland, Portugal and Italy, wanting them to participate in the North Atlantic Treaty. Norway and Denmark immediately accepted. Iceland realized that there was a need to strengthen the security cooperation in Atlantic, but due to its policy of neutrality since it became independent and its situation of having no established armed forces, so it raised a question whether this would cause conflicts with the rights and obligations of NATO member countries. After getting a negative answer, it also expressed its willingness to join. Portugal was worried that if Spain was not invited to join NATO, then it would be a small country in Iberian

Peninsula surrounded by Spanish. How could Spain ensure to have links with NATO countries and what will its role be? When the Portuguese heard that the Spanish will be invited to join NATO when it is established the democracy they also dispelled the concerns, and accepted the North Atlantic Treaty. But Sweden rejected with the excuse that joining NATO went against its tradition of keeping neutral. Ireland claimed that the prerequisite for joining NATO was the ending of the division of Ireland, because the dispute it had with Britain on the ownership of Northern Ireland for a long time. The United Kingdom naturally did not meet this requirement, so the problem stopped here. France started to oppose Italy to join, fearing it would take away some of the aid it received from the United States. But then it changed its attitude out of the considerations of their own safety of Mediterranean borders, and expressed support for Italy to join.

Washington Meeting in 1949: NATO declared its establishment

So, on April 4, 1949, Foreign Minister of United States, Canada, Britain, France, Belgium, Luxembourg, the Netherlands, Denmark, Norway, Iceland, Portugal and Italy, in a total of 12 countries, met in Washington, and signed the North Atlantic Treaty. On August 24th, the convention entered into force. North Atlantic Treaty Organization (NATO) was officially established.

North Atlantic Treaty stated, "States Parties, according to the spirit of the UN Charter, determined to use peaceful means without endangering the peace, security and justice to resolve international conflicts they were involved in, and to avoid using force or threat against the target which was inconsistent with the United Nations in international relations." It stated, "in order to more effectively achieve the objectives of this Treaty, the states parties, individually or collectively, uses the measures to self-help or mutual aid which are sustainable and effective. This will maintain and develop their individual and collective ability to resist armed attack when they think the territorial integrity, political independence and national security of any involved party are threatened. The Parties will consult each other". Once the armed attack occurred, "the Parties agree to regard the armed attack to one or several Contracting State in Europe and North America as an attack on all States Parties. ...... According to the individual and collective self-defense authority recognized by the section 51 in the UN Charter, any contracting state may individually or collectively take the necessary action to assist countries affected by the attack, in order to maintain and the restore the security in the North Atlantic region. Such armed attack and the countermeasures taken by the state party should be reported to the UN

Security Council. Once the Security Council has taken measures necessary to maintain and restore peace and security, countermeasures taken by the state party will end".[50]

NATO's highest authority was the Council, which was composed by the Minister of Foreign Affairs, Defense and Finance of the member states. When the meeting adjourned, every country appointed a representative to form the Permanent Council which was responsible for implementing the policies of NATO. The permanent executive body was the Secretariat, which was in charged by the Secretary-General. Thus, an organized system of US-European security cooperation initially came into shape. It marked the formation of the post-war Western alliance under the new international pattern. The United States finally got caught up in European security affairs, and began to play a leadership role in it.

The establishment of the NATO showed a qualitative change in the United States attitude towards the Soviet threat. It gradually turned its attention from the threat of "political infiltration and subversion" to the threat of military force of the Soviet Union. On June 25, 1949, in the message suggesting Congress providing military assistance to Western Europe, Truman pointed out:

The main task of the free countries of Western Europe over the past four years was to restore their economy destroyed in the war. The inherent difficulties in this task were worsened by the Soviet Union's Foreign policy. It did whatever it can to prevent Europe's recovery.... In this environment, the Soviet Union carefully created a climate of fear and danger by violent propaganda, manipulation of the conspiracy of the world communist movement and the largest army to maintain the peacetime in history. Facing with the events in Greece and Berlin, facing with threats and pressures that Iran and Turkey suffered, we see the repression of human freedom under the control of the communist. Western European countries cannot ignore the necessity of protecting themselves by military means.... They realize that there must be a shield to protect their political mechanism from invading and to ensure their own economic and social life can be restored.[51]

Thus, the United States military aid to Europe had brought on the agenda. On September 26, 1949, Congress passed the common Assistance Act. The Act stated, the United States would "provide the necessary military assistance" based on "the principle of self-help and mutual aid" to other

---

50   http://avalon.law.yale.edu/
51   Arthur M. Schlesinger, The Dynamics of World power: A Documentary History of US Foreign Policy, 1945-1973, Vol. 1, p.144-145.

countries. Fiscal aid authorized by Congress to Foreign military in 1949 was 1.314 billion US Dollars, of which1 billion US Dollars for NATO. This was the prelude of the first large-scale US military aid to Europe, as well as the first step of the US involvement in European security affairs.

The establishment of NATO pushed forward the US involvement in European affairs for one more step, and made the scope of obligations to Europe expand from economic to military. But, like the Truman Doctrine and the Marshall Plan, it did not mean the end of the process of fixing the relations between the US and Europe after the World War. Although the United States established NATO, it still had questions about the extent of its involvement in European security issues. Whether the United States should send ground troops to Europe remained a sensitive issue. Many MPs and government officials avoided this problem, because they both believed that the US and European security cooperation was necessary, but did not want to face the possible result of this requirement that the United States might send ground forces. In the debate on the Congress ratification for the North Atlantic Treaty, in order to get more support from Members, Senator Vandenberg who actively claimed, "I think a member can vote on the issue of supporting the treaty, while at the same time vote against the issue of funding to implement it. Because for me, announcing this treaty in public is to remind Mr. Stalin that he is now in the opposite position to Mr. Hitler. Because Mr. Hitler viewed us with a Neutrality Act. Mr. Stalin now sees us with a pact of cooperative action." So this actually means that the North Atlantic Treaty was just valid on paper, people did not have to make substantial efforts to implement it. In the hearing, although Secretary of State Dean Acheson did his best to oppose "winning votes by seriously belittle treaty obligations", when isolationist Republican senator from Iowa Bourke Hickenlooper asked him whether this treaty required the US to "send large numbers of troops there (Western Europe), and how much permanent contribution can be made for developing the resistant ability of those countries", Acheson replied, "Senator, the answer to this question is obvious and absolute 'no'". In the summer of 1949, the Pentagon did not have the attempt and plan of sending troops to Europe. Marshall had a clear suggestion to the Secretary of Defense James Forrestal, "Our policy should be the construction of ground forces in Western Europe ...... At this stage, we cannot use the goal of US which is to promote the construction ground forces in Europe"[52].

---

52   Don Cook, Forging the Alliance: NATO,1945-1950, pp.225-226.

Thus, in 1949, even if NATO had been established, for the European countries, there were still too many uncertainties in the US policy. The US's unwillingness to send ground troops to Europe and the reality that it had not appointed a supreme commander of the army stationed in the European alliance not only made European countries suspect that once the war broke out whether the United States would offer support decisively and timely. This suspicion had greatly offset the positive effect of strengthening the morale of the European countries by North Atlantic Treaty. European countries still had to prepare themselves for the worst scenario: if the United States would not provide substantial assistance, then they would resume to a neutral position. French Le Monde claimed that Europe felt insecure and the West could not stop the Soviet offensive The US isolationism and European neutrality still had certain basis. The US Embassy in France had argued that this view "was poisoning the minds of the French people, but it was more dangerous than the Communist Party". Until 1950, Europe's morale had not much improved. The US ambassador to France, Counselor Bohlen stated, "Europe is one patient that we are healing now, and we can already say that he will not die, but it is showing a tendency to return to the split state in the past". US Embassy in London also thought that "this tendency will lead to the neutral atmosphere in Western Europe". News from Germany was about the same. McCloy said, "Over the past six months, due to the significant increase of Soviet propaganda and the growing sense of fear which has permeated this country in the eyes of the German caused by the lack of Western power, "for German Foreign Minister, "the world situation is gradually worsening".[53]

This negative attitude in Europe, in turn, exacerbated the US suspicions that the European countries did not really want to resist the Soviet threat, but to use the shadow of the Soviet threat to defraud the US aid. Once the war broke out, they would immediately crash. In fact, the suspicions between the two sides were derived from a fundamental problem which was the kind of position Europe had been put in the US global strategy. This was the crux that the United States and Europe had to face in the next few years.

1.4 The Korean War and the Formation of the US-European Alliance

On June 25, 1950, the Korean War broke out. It produced the international situation and the impact was far beyond the importance of this narrow peninsula in Northeast Asia. Although the US politicians and strategists had repeatedly claimed that the Korean peninsula almost had no strategic

---

53   The Department of State, FRUS, 1943, Vol. 3, pp.620, 810.

value to the United States. Although Korea was invaded the US military commander strongly urged the Government to withdraw troops from South Korea as soon as possible. Although Acheson and MacArthur excluded the Korean peninsula from the defense chain of the United States in the Asia-Pacific islands, after the outbreak of war, the US government still made a strong reaction with surprising speed. On June 25 (New York time), the United States used the opportunity of the Soviet's absent to manipulate the UN Security Council to adopt a resolution condemning North Korea. Two days later, Truman commanded the US Navy and Air Force to provide air and sea cover and support to the South Korean army, while sending the US Seventh Fleet to the Taiwan Strait, "in order to prevent attacks between the mainland and Taiwan to ensure the stability of the local situation". On June 30, in the absence of authorization by Congress, Truman ordered Supreme Commander of the Allied Powers in Japan, MacArthur to send ground troops to Korea. Five days later, the twenty-fourth division of the US Army's first regiment combat team entered North Korea. On July 7, under the United States manipulation, the UN Security Council passed a resolution, authorizing the US organization "United National Army" to interfere in the Korean War. MacArthur was appointed as the commander in chief of the "United National Army". In less than half a month, the United States was involved in the war in order to protect a place with no strategic importance.

Truman and MacArthur

The United States took such a bold initiative because they thought that the Korean War overthrew the previous containment policy makers completely — primarily George Kennan. Kennan's considered the nature of the Soviet threat was primarily political rather than military. Even after the establishment of NATO, this view still had a great influence within the US government, mainly showed on the fate of document, NSC-68. In 1949, the success of the Soviet atomic bomb test led to Truman to develop the hydrogen bomb. He ordered Acheson chaired the National Security Council, "re-evaluating our goal in the time of war and peace as well as the effect of the implementation of our strategic plan". The document NSC-68 was then eventually produced. The document stressed the importance of military power, claiming, "The single most important power is the power of the military. If the military force existed and ready to mobilize but not dominant, then the containment policy – as a well-designed and overall receives unanimous consent policy–it is just a deception policy. In the face of a significant increase of the Soviet military forces, our strength is weakening. We cannot fully fulfill the fundamental part of the containment policy". Document NSC-68 proposed to change the focus of the US containment policy, and strengthen military forces in Western countries. In conclusion, "The whole success or failure depends entirely on whether the government, the US people and the people of the world, recognize that the Cold War is actually a real war that decides the survival in the world".[54] However, document NSC-68 was strongly opposed by Kennan and other congressional representatives of containment policy and the Congress. Kennan thought that it put too much emphasis on that military field in containment policy which would lead to the intensification of the US-Soviet conflict and destabilizing the international situation. The Congress believed the claim of strengthening the military power in document NSC-68 would lead to a huge defense budget (document estimated $ 50 billion per year), which would affect the national economy. With the end of the Berlin crisis, people thought there was no need to increase armaments. Therefore, the government would cut the defense budget in the fiscal year of 1951 to $ 13.5 billion (defense budget was $ 81.6 billion in the fiscal year of 1945). The number of the armed forces was also cut to 160 million (1260 million in the fiscal year of 1945). With this trend of cutting military spending, the fate of document NSC-68 can be imagined. Truman quietly shelved the document, and announced at a press conference after a month that the military spending may be less in the fiscal year of 1952.

However, the outbreak of the Korean War changed everything. Overnight, the military threat replaced the political infiltration and became a top priority for governments. In less than six months after the Korean War had broken out, the US Joint Chiefs of Staff required additional funding for three times, and the President approved without hesitation. In the fiscal year of 1951, the funding amount finally passed by Congress reached $ 48.2 billion with a 257% increase compared with the originally proposed figure of 13.5 billion US dollars. Meanwhile, document NSC-68 thought that the US military now was not sufficient to curb the communist aggression had also been a point of attention. It seemed that the situation in Europe was more urgent than that in North Korea, because in North Korea, the US could mobilize all its forces stationed in Japan and the Western Pacific, but in Europe there was no US ground troops in addition to occupying army in Germany. In May 1949, at the end of the airlift in Berlin crisis, the US troops stationed in Europe reached a total of 14 million people, nearly equaled to the power of three combat divisions.

They scattered in southern Germany to perform the functions of the police and occupation, which was totally inconsistent with the actual requirements. British troops were closer to the actual state, but they only had

54   Don Cook, Forging the Alliance: NATO,1945-1950, pp.235-236.

two and a half divisions. France stationed three poorly equipped divisions in Germany. Its reserve forces dispersed on the vast land from Morocco to Indochina. In addition, there were several ill-equipped Dutch and Belgian divisions. It was impossible to expect these weak forces would be effective against 35 Soviet divisions stationed in Eastern Europe and the place near the dividing line between East and West in East Germany. Acheson warned that if the Soviet Union entered the Greek, the US would not be able to make a strong response. Because "we do not have any forces in the region where was 1000 miles away from Greece". In addition, "we cannot take any action in Iran; if we want to take action in Berlin, we will go through a terrible period".[55]

After being aware of this threat, for the US, the first thing to do was to encourage European countries to fight, and to show them that the United States would not back down when the war came. Truman's first reaction to the news of the outbreak of the Korean War was pointing to a globe and said, "This is the Far East, Greece. As long as our actions can be determined enough, there will be no crisis". On July 8, 1950, the US State Council issued a telegram to national missions in Europe, saying, "You should take all measures to show that as a result of the North Korean situation, the leadership of the United States will be bolder and more credible. The basis tone should be the more effort of all countries. You should show that the United States prepares to fully discharge its responsibilities in cooperation with each other".

European countries almost reached the same conclusion. They also began to feel the seriousness of the Soviet military threat and that in this case the US aid to Europe was indispensable. In order to fight for greater obligation that America could fulfill in Europe, European countries suppressed the neutrality in 1949, and tried to show their will to fight. They wanted to prove that European countries would be a reliable partner in the coming battle. On some issues, the position of the European countries was even tougher than the United States. For example, in the problem of sending troops to North Korea, the United States also wanted to be able to get the UN Security Council resolution to prove the legality of their actions. The British thought that the Western countries could put aside the United Nations when necessary (such as the Soviet veto) and acting alone. On July 5, 1950, Prime Minister Attlee revealed this intent in a speech to the House:

---

55   Ronald E. Powaski, The Entangling Alliance: The United States and European Security, 1950-1993, Greenwood Press, Westport, 1994, p.5.

The general principle of international law recognized any attacked country has the right to defend itself, and any other countries have the right to help the country which becomes the target of aggression.

UN Charter does not cancel this right. On the contrary, in section 51 it explicitly claims, "When armed aggression occurs against a Member Stat. Before the Council takes necessary measures to maintain international peace and security, the right of its Member States individually or collective self-defense has not been changed in the existing charter of the United Nations". Indeed, Article 51 only mentions the case of armed aggression against the UN member state. However, South Korea is not a UN member. The objective of the section 51 of the Charter is not to create a new power but to merely indicate that the power can be applied to every country.

All countries participate in the North Atlantic Treaty are clearly aware that the collective self-defense right applies to the attack to those countries who are not UN members, such as Italy and Portugal, according to section 51 of the Charter.... Our general principle is that if the aggression on any part of the world is allowed to get achievement of aggression, it will endanger all countries.[56]

According to the request of the United States, Britain, France, Canada, the Netherlands, Belgium, Luxembourg and other countries sent troops to join the "United National Army" to interfere in the Korean War in order to show the unity of the newly established alliance between the US and Europe and Western countries in the face of the threat of aggression.

The US and Europe showed their strong will to fight and desire to mutual collaboration. At the same time, both of them also took practical means to strengthen defense forces of the Western world. The outbreak of the Korean War made Truman accept the expansion program mentioned in document NSC-68, and he put the completion data ahead from 1954 to June 30, 1952. By then, the army would increase 2 extra divisions on the base of 10 divisions; the number of navy active warship would be total 1,176 from 618 (There would be 16 CVBG in all, comparing with the former 9 CVBG); navy would increase to 3 divisions; affiliated Air fleet would possess 3 divisions; and air force would reach 80 regiments from past 42 ones. And the total amount of air force strategic bomber would be increased to 37 united from 21 united. Meanwhile, the US aid to Europe would shift the focus from economic aid listed in Marshall Plan to military aid. The US government declared that it would reduce the economic aid to Europe and focus

---

56   John W. Spanier, The Truman-MacArthur Controversy and the Korean War, The Norton Library, W.W. Norton &Company Inc. New York, 1965, p.38.

its aid on supporting the defense production, not the civilian production. In 1951, appropriation used in Mutual Defense Assistance Act raised from 1.2 billion to 5.0 billion US dollars, corresponding, appropriation used in Marshall Plan was cut to $ 2.25 billion. The mutual security program official communication proposed by the Truman administration in 1951 called for Congress to authorize funding 8.5 billion US dollars as Foreign aid funds in 1952, including 6.5 billion US dollars for military aid, and 2.25 billion US dollars for economic assistance. Congress finally approved the "Mutual Security Act in 1951", and decreased the total Foreign aid funds to 7.483 billion US dollars, which was operated almost entirely within the scope of economic aid. And economic aid fund was cut down from 2.25 billion to 1.44 billion US dollars. According to this Act, Europe received 1 billion US dollars as economic aid and 4.8 billion US dollars in military aid. What the more far-reaching impact on the US policy was that the act provided for Economic Cooperation Department would be revoked in the end of 1951 instead of 1952, and also established Mutual Security Agency (MSA) in charge of Foreign aid matters. In fact, it declared the victory of the "cannon priority" doctrine and the death of the Marshall Plan. Even Economic Cooperation Department itself endorsed the US aid priorities which led to its close. At the end of the Marshall Plan, its report on the achievements of the program claimed that "There are still many dark points in the economic panorama in Europe. What the darkest point is inflationary pressure caused by the widening dollar gap on rearmament efforts".[57]

As the change of the aiding focus on Europe, the United States began to take the measures that European countries had repeatedly asked for since the establishment of NATO: sending four divisions of ground troops to Europe, and appointing General Eisenhower as the supreme allied commander in Europe, which took the pace to establish a unified Western defense. Although these actions sparked a debate about Foreign policy in the United States, MacArthur and others claimed that Truman sent troops on the ground to Europe but refused their demands to escalate the Korean battlefield was putting the cart before the horse, the senate approved that Truman sent troops to the European action and claimed in the resolution that "ground forces under the leadership of the General Eisenhower should be mainly provided by the European members of the North Atlantic Treaty Organization", and "in addition to the four divisions, it is not allowed to send more troops on the ground further in accordance with article 3 of the North Atlantic Treaty without congressional approval to Western Europe";

---

57   Arthur M. Schlesinger, The Dynamics of World Power: A Documentary History of US Foreign Policy, 1945-1973, Vol. 1, p.106.

the congress finally admitted in the approval that "threats to the United States and our NATO Allies security made it necessary for US to bear fair share in the army, and stationed abroad necessary and appropriate scale of armed forces to defend north Atlantic area, then accepted the fact that the necessary military commitment in Europe.[58]

Until this moment, military alliance really established in the US and Europe. After that, NATO's military strength developed rapidly. By December 1951, its strength was increased to 35, 3000 aircrafts and 700 ships. In early 1952, NATO's headquarters were set up one after another. In the words of Truman, "Western European defense rack" was established before his final departure from the White House."

The US military commitment in Europe was confirmed. But another problem emerged gradually as the Korean War continues, and received more and more attention; what was the status of Europe in the global strategy of the United States? Will the United States sacrifice Europe for the interests of other parts? Will Europe get involved in a new world war due to the problem which has nothing to do with its interests? MacArthur's action in North Korea increased this fear of European countries.

At the beginning of the war, the European countries strongly supported the action of expanding the war in order to attract aid of US. Bevan, British Foreign secretary, came up with the goal of the unification of the Korean peninsula in 1950, at the end of September. The goal was that there was not so-called North Korea or the so-called South Korea, they were the Koreans, and the division was not eternal. At the UN General Assembly debate, Kenneth Young, the British representative, enthusiastically supported the unification of the Korean peninsula. Other European countries were un-willing to lag behind. British representative put forward the bill that propo-sitioned indirect authorization for moving northward, which was strongly supported by France, Norway, the Netherlands and other NATO members. Final assembly with 47 votes for, five votes against, the result of seven abstentions passed across the 38th parallel north into the resolution. During this period, the support of its European allies to MacArthur in the Korean peninsula had almost complete freedom of action.

However, Chinese People's Volunteer Army (CPVA) joined the battle in October 25, 1950, and its victory in the first and the second battle before the end of 1950 have reversed the situation of North Korea, after those Western countries were faced with a new war. In this war, the UK was opposed to have a new enemy with broad territory, large population, and the land of

---

58   Ibid., pp.168-169.

the enemy was located beyond the attack coverage of the "United Nations Command" (if refraining limited war from a full-scale war). The US generals, government officials and the public suddenly lost patience in the face of the sudden failure and started considering whether they should consider more intense war. General MacArthur was the representative of this view. He even took risks on a full-scale war with China in order to win the victory of the Korean War. He put forward a rhapsodic strategic plan which was bombing military bases and the Yalu River Bridge in northeastern China, using Chiang Kai-Shek's troops to land in southeast coast, and throwing 30-50 tactical atomic bombs in North Korea. What's more, he wanted to set a radioactive cobalt belt which was 30 km in breadth along the both sides of the Yalu River to cut off the relationship between China and North Korea. Even Truman also considered the use of nuclear weapons under the shadow of failure at the end of 1950. In a press conference, Truman said the atomic bomb was just an ordinary weapon, and whether to use it was decided by the war district commanders. This word blurted out and immediately sparked uproar in Europe. Attlee, British prime minister, immediately flew to Washington in December, and talked with Truman to ensure that the US government needed full consultation with the European countries before the use of nuclear weapons.

Dulles revised the militaristic democracy line

European countries were even more worrisome that MacArthur openly declared that the US's strategic focus was in Asia and the Pacific. If necessary, the United States could put aside the idea of acting alone in European countries. In March 1951, in a telegram to Rep. Martin, MacArthur declared, "it seems incredibly difficult for some people to recognize that the Communist conspirators have chosen Asia to begin the conquest of the world. We have participated in the disputes about the battlefield. It is difficult for them to realize that we are here using weapons to fight for Europe, while diplomats are still there in a war of words. And if we are defeated by communism in Asia, Europe will follow, the fall is inevitable. If we win here, then it is possible to avoid war in Europe and to maintain European freedom. As you pointed out, we must win. We have no other way but to win".[59]

In Congress hearing held to inspect and judge MacArthur's career, MacArthur expressed his views more clearly. At that time senator from Rhode Island Green asked MacArthur that whether his policy on the Korean War meant that "we should act alone and do not need help from other UN member states", the question caused the following conversation:

---

59   Harry Truman, Truman's memoirs, Vol.2, SDX Joint Publishing Company,1974, pp 531-532.

MacArthur: I cannot tell you any ideas concerning the United Nation, Senator.

Green: What is your hope?

MacArthur: I certainly hope that the United Nations act with wisdom and determination in this process, but if they do not, I still believe that US interests in North Korea is in domination. It requires us to act.

Green: Acting alone?

MacArthur: If necessary, acting alone. If other countries in the world do not have enough insight, and still cannot see where another appeasement will go after the appeasement led to the Second World War in Europe, if they do not see the path we should follow in Asia , then we'd better protect themselves and act alone.[60]

MacArthur was not alone. He received the support of Congress and Republican isolationists. Just when the Truman administration prepared to assume greater European military obligations, these forces caused great trouble to the smooth implementation of the US-European policy. Republican conservatives attacked the government's European policy from three major aspects: Government policy of supporting Europe made the US economy more intense; it would make the United States involve into a "European ground combat"; because the United States had a strong naval and air forces by which it can control Atlantic and Pacific and defend any invasion of the Western Hemisphere. Therefore, Europe was not the vital area to the United States. Republican conservatives' attack caused a big debate on the US Foreign policy. It gave European countries a huge shock. A French reporter summed up the impression of the Europeans on the debate: The US Congress, especially the Senate, seemed to be the world's most unstable and most unpredictable legislature. Europeans started to view the United States as the equivalent to European senator who they distrust rather than the President. He said, "If the basis of trust cannot be quickly established, it will have serious political influence. In this period, the morale and political foundation upon which to build the Atlantic alliance will collapse in distrust".[61]

---

60   Richard H. Rovere & Arthur Schlesinger, General MacArthur and President Truman, the Struggle for Control of The US Foreign Policy, Transaction Publishers, New Brunswick and London, 1992, 222.
61   John Spanier, Truman-MacArthur Dispute and North Korea War, pp.159-160.

In this case, the European countries increasingly worried about the reckless act of the US. In early 1951, when the United States accused China of being the invader and blockaded, embargoed China at the UN General Assembly, the British Chancellor of the Exchequer Hugh Gaitskell expressed his worry in his diary, "international situation becomes darker. The US is talking about a limited war, but we all feel that there is no such limited war. The worst thing is that if the organization blocked China or the US bombed China, Chinese people may retaliate by occupying Hong Kong or move southward through Indochina to Malaysia. The embarrassing plight is that if we can not restrict the US, we would either have to enter China with them which no one hopes, or to abandon them. This will have very serious impact on the US participation in European defense".[62] British cabinet set off a wave of anti-Americanism. Ministers led by Aneurin Bevan and Kenneth Young strongly opposed the resolution of the United States, insisting to vote against it in the UN General Assembly. Gaitskell's abstain was even not agreed. That was mainly because Bevan insisted that they cannot let Anglo-American strategic partnership be exposed to any risk and got the support of Prime Minister Attlee, which finally suppressed opponents' views.

French people considered the relationship between Europe and America much deeper level. Monet wrote in his notes in 1950: People's thoughts are focused on a simple but dangerous point—the Cold War. All recommendations and actions have been interpreted as a contribution to the Cold War by public opinion. This kind of public opinion creates a narrow thinking that only pursues single target rather than explores solutions to the problem.

The situation in Germany is rapidly becoming cancer that in the near future will imperil peace , and it will immediately turn into threat to France, unless it is directed to the direction that not only German hope to see but also promotes cooperation with the people of free nations. We must not attempt to solve the problems in Germany under current situation. We need to make changes happen by changing the basic facts.

If France cannot speak or act now, what will happen? There will be a group around the US with the purpose of inciting Cold War with more craze. European countries will be filled with fear and they starts to seek help. Britain will more closely combine with the US. Germany will develop quickly. We will be not able to prevent it from arming. France will be involved again, which will inevitably lead to its crash.[63]

---

62   Philip M. Williams, The Diary of Hugh Gaitskell, 1945-1956, Jonathan Cape, London, 1983, pp.225-226.

63   Don Cook, Forging the Alliance: NATO,1945-1950, pp.235-236.

While the British stressed the importance of US-European strategic partnership, Frenchmen began to realize that European countries need to maintain their independence, and they cannot become a puppet of the United States in the Cold War. This very idea resulted in the most imaginative and most far-reaching diplomatic policy action of France—the establishment of the European Coal and Steel Community (ECSC).

Although Britain and France had different starting point and conclusions about the US-Europe Alliance, there was still one thing in common— that Europe was the real interests of the Western world, thus the strategies of Western countries should be based on Europe, at the same time interests of other regions should not be gained at the expense of Europe. Even Churchill, a hard-line anti-communist, believed that it was necessary to end the Korean War as soon as possible, so that the United States could concentrate its power on European defense issues. He pointed out, "the Soviet plan is to force the US and the U.N. involved in China as deep as possible, thus prevent reinforcements for Europe and build our defense forces strong enough to effectively curb them. This is the best—almost perfect—strategic and tactical means: To put the opponent's resources bound in part of the battlefield, and then at the right time attack the other part (of the battlefield)... The United Nations must by all means avoid war with China that will bring inextricable problems. Conflict in the Far East—because on the whole, it is just a conflict—can develop into some kind of stable situation the sooner the better... because it is Europe that decides the fate of the world. Here there is a danger of a lack of morale. We have this view is perhaps because we live here, but one cannot say that this bias distorts facts."[64]

In fact, the Truman administration considered intervening into the Korean War when Europe was at the centre of the US global strategy. On January 13, 1951, when the 3rd campaign launched by Chinese People's Volunteers it was also the darkest time in the Korean War for the US. At this very time, Truman sent a letter to MacArthur, pointing out that their operational objectives in the Korean War, 'In order to show that aggression will not be accepted by us and the UN, and if the Soviet Union takes any action, spirit and strength in the free world can be mobilized to face the worldwide threat it brought; fulfill our obligation to South Korea and indicate the immeasurable value of the friendship of the US when facing the outbreak of hostilities; increase not only Asia's determination but also the determination of many countries in Europe and the Middle East that lives under the shadow of the mainland powers, so that they know it is not necessary

---

64   United States Department of State, Historical Office, The US Foreign Policy, 1950-1955, Basic Documents, GPO, Washington D.C., 1957, pp.2621.

to conclude a treaty of surrender with the Communists; encourage those countries that are willing to resist Soviet Union under sudden attack; show the benefits and urgency of the rapid establishment of the Western world defense; the UN make great efforts for collective security and establish the free world alliance at the first time which has inestimable value for the US national security; warn the people behind the Iron Curtain that their master tends to aggression, and such crimes will be resisted by the free world."[65] We can see that when intervened into the Korean War, the Truman administration focused its attention on strengthening coalition of the Western world. Therefore, Truman instructed McArthur 'Our current action policy should be uniting the overwhelming majority of the member nations in the United Nations. These countries are not only part of the UN, but also our reliable allies in urgent need when the Soviet Union launches any attack.' The US Joint Chiefs of Staff (JCS) stressed repeatedly that military and economic assistance to Western Europe should not be influenced by the Korean War, and that the decisive battlefield is still in Europe. A famous remark made by General Omar Bradley goes that the expansion of the war in Korea would be 'the wrong war, at the wrong place, at the wrong time, and with the wrong enemy'. On June 1, 1951, Secretary of State Dean Acheson issued a statement before the Senate Armed Services Committee and the Foreign Relations Committee and established the crucial status of Europe in America's global strategy. He said,

We should also analyze the consequences of take proactive measures to expand the war outside North Korea from the perspective of our allies. The link between us would be seriously weakened, and in some cases even cut off.

It can be understood that they do not want to be involved in a full-scale war in the Far East—a war that could evolve into a worldwide full-scale war. They are more reluctant to join such a war especially under the circumstances that the US has lost patience with the slow progress in efforts to counter aggression (in their view such efforts provide decent and not so disastrous solutions) and thus caused the full-scale war. If we take these measures, our risks and obligations will simultaneously increase, and they will weaken the strength and determination of our alliance so that our strength is compromised.

If we take measures which expose those people with us in the collective security system to unnecessary risk, then we cannot expect our collective security system be perpetuated. It can be imagined that they will be

---

65 Ibid.

reluctant to connect with an ally who guide them crossing a difficulty fracture through a highly risky shortcut.

What links to the threat of the whole world is that our security needs us to strengthen. It is not the bond that weakens our collective security system.

Our power of deterring attack coalition partly depends on our allies' will and mutual trust. If we, for taking the measures suggested above, weaken this effect, especially in the North Atlantic region, we will endanger the safety of this region which is crucial for our own national security.[66]

In this way, the collision and the influence among the US government that advocates European countries finally solve the last but the most fundamental question in the post-war US-European relations: Namely the European status was the US's global strategy. Truman established the "Europe first" strategic principle by firing MacArthur and strengthening of the European aid action. Eisenhower was elected president in 1952 and defeated the isolationist in Republican Party, and finalized this principle. European countries also recognized that they were still dependent on the US aid. They must accept the leadership of the United States to some extent. Britain eventually supported the US in the Korean armistice negotiations, insisted on the principle of the voluntary repatriation of prisoners of war with the United States, and accepted the statement drafted by the US using forces to fight against the action that destructed the armistice announcement. European countries also stepped up efforts to build national defense forces and included the war of defending their colonial (especially the British war in Malaysia and France war in Indochina) to the US global anti-communism track. This showed that European countries accepted following proposition of the US: That in order to get the US protection and assistance, they must play their role in the containment strategy of the United States. Until then, the strategic partnership between the United States and Europe was finally established after the war.

Overall, the evolution of the early post-war relations between the US and Europe was mainly about how the US was involved in European affairs and assume more and more obligations in Europe through the European alliance. This change was a part of the process that the US Foreign policy transformed from isolationism to internationalism with the strengthening of the US power throughout the 20th century. The inherent reason of the failure of Roosevelt policy which is maintaining international order by cooperation between the major powers and ensuring the US exiting from Europe, was

66 Henry Kissinger, trans, Gu Shuxin & Lin Tiangui, Diplomacy, Hainan Publishing House, 1997, p.146.

the connection in the world had been strengthened compared with the peak time of "splendid isolation" in the 19th century. There were other reasons like the intensified conflict between the post-war interests of the West and the East, increased strength of the Soviet and inability to balance the Soviet Union against European countries which they weakened by war. The unstable and changing international arena was more intense than the one in 19th century. A crisis could happen any time. In this case, detached from daily affairs of Europe, it was difficult to deal with the rapid change of the situation and the sudden crisis. If the United States wanted to maintain its interests effectively, it must be deeply involved in European affairs. Kissinger divided the balance of power policy into two categories in his Diplomacy: One was British-style "splendid isolation" policy; the other was Bismarck continent system. He said, "In an interdependent world, it is very difficult for the United States to achieve the British Empire-style 'splendid isolation'. It is impossible to establish an elaborate security system that can take care of every part of the world. The most possible and constructive way to solve the problem is to establish an alliance systems that have many layers, some layers should focus on safety, some on economic relations. United States will fight against the challenges with a common goal, imbued by the US values and to use this common goal to unite different groups".[67]

Perhaps these words will enable us to better understand the process of the changes in the US policy towards Europe in 40s, 50s of the last century and the inevitable trend of US-European alliance.

It is worth noting that, in the process of transformation of the post-War the US-Europe relations, the European countries were not passively accepting this change. They did everything to exert their influence on the United States. Preventing the United States to abandon Europe, and protecting the interests and the independence of Europe in cooperation with the United States were two major objectives of the European countries' policy towards the United States. Therefore, the development of the post-war US-European relations was the process of the European country and the United States collided and affected with each other, which also became a feature of the post-war US-European relations.

---

67   Diplomacy, by Henry Kissinger, trans, by Gu Shuxin & Lin Tiangui, Hainan Publishing House, 1997, p.146.

Chapter II

The Changes of Japan's and the Federal Republic of Germany's International Position

With the end of World War II, the wartime anti-Fascist alliance came to an end. Originally, how to deal with vanquished country should be a key issue between the allies after the war. However, because the arrangement and designing of the Post-War world had become a major conflict between the Western countries and the Soviet Union, how to deal with the problem of Japan and Germany became a major chip in the strategic rivalry between the Soviet Union and the US after World War II. The US forced Western countries to follow its leading role as part of its grand strategy in order to realize its own national interest. Its policy towards Japan and Germany had undergone a complex process of change. For the United States, with the passage of history, Japan and the Federal Republic of Germany turned from rivalry to partnership, from collaboration to alliance. Moreover, in the course of time the two allies also became competitors of USA.

2.1 From Conflict to Cooperation– The US Fostering Japan and FRG

2.1.1 The United States policy towards Japan and Germany

The US policy towards the FRG

As the victory of the World Anti-Fascist War became clearer, the problem of how to deal with the defeated Germany and Japan, besides the problem of how to accelerate the process of peace and end the war as quickly as possible, became important issues of negotiations among the allies. The method of dealing with the defeated Germany was gradually determined at the conference in Tehran (November 28, 1943-1 December), the

Yalta Conference (February 4-1, 1945), and the Potsdam Conference (July 17-August 2, 1945).[1]

At the meeting in Tehran, the US advocated "de-centralization" of Germany. According to Roosevelt, it was necessary to make the Germans forget the word "empire". Roosevelt's idea was to split Post-War Germany into five parts, and let victorious allies be in charge of important German cities and regions. Stalin and Churchill also agreed to split Germany. But the three leaders all compromised to let the European Advisory Committee to decide the way of segmentation. On the eve of the Yalta Conference, as the victory of the war was a foregone conclusion, dealing with the Post-War matters had become a more pressing issue. Before the meeting, Britain and the US leaders had exchanged views on controlling zones in Germany after the World War. The United States had proposed to make post-war Germany the pastoral country's "Morgenthau Plan". At the Yalta Conference, three leaders reaffirmed the division of Germany and reached an agreement on principles. They also decided to set up a committee in charge of dividing Germany. However, in order to avoid any further complications about the surrender of Germany, they decided not to mention the split of Germany in the meeting bulletin, but only to load the protocol. In the bulletin it is announced that France, America, Britain and the Soviet Union would take charge of the divided part of the surrendered Germany. When the Potsdam Conference was held, Roosevelt had died of illness (on April 12), Germany surrendered unconditionally (on May 8), the US atomic bomb test succeeded (on July 16). In the agreement signed in the Potsdam Conference involving Germany, they identified that the four countries could occupied different zones in Germany; the disarmament of all armed forces of Germany and made it completely demilitarized, they should eradicate or control all German military production industry, put down National Socialist Party and all its institutions, and dissolute all Nazi organizations; they should arrest and bring all war criminals to trial; the German central government would not be set up now. German economy should be dispersed, whose level should be remained at the level no higher than the average living standard of European countries. Among those, there was not a word involving partition of Germany.[1]

---

1   FRUS, Diplomatic Papers: The Conferences at Cairo and Teheran 1943, GPO, Washington, D.C, 1961; The Conferences at Malta and Yalta 1945, GPO, Washington, D.C, 1961; The Conferences at Malta and Yalta 1945, GPO, Washington, D.C, 1955; The Conference of Berlin 1945, GPO, Washington, D.C, 1960; Collection of German Problem, People's Publishing House, 1953; Meeting Record Roundup of Teheran, Yalta, Potsdam Conference, Shanghai People's Publishing House, 1974; The Meeting Files of Teheran, Yalta, Potsdam Conference, SDX Joint Publishing Press, 1978, pp.12-20.

After Germany's unconditional surrender, three countries completely abandoned the idea of dismembering Germany. Many domestic scholars identified that as because the US and British conflict with the Soviet Union kept upgrading, and both sides felt that a unified Germany was more favorable to them. Because, if one could control a unified Germany, that meant it could control the post-war Europe.[2]

This prospect was too attractive for ambitious countries.

According to the agreement, the Soviet Union, the US, Britain and France drew the dividing line in the actual territory of Germany at the end of 1937. Thus, the Soviet Union occupied the eastern region, the United States occupied the southwest region, the United Kingdom occupied the northwest region, and France occupied the Western region; although Berlin was under Soviet's control, Berlin also occupied a region according to the same principle. On May 10, 1945, the US government conveyed their basic objectives of the occupation policy of Germany through military, namely the Joint Chiefs of Staff with the Command No.1067 . The general Clay served as the US military governor of the occupied territory said the order "dominated the actions in the early months of occupying Germany". The order stated that Germany was occupied because it was defeated; the consequence of war was caused by Germany, so Germany should take the responsibility themselves. The command also developed strict control measures in occupied regions. For example, all political activities were banned, free migration was not allowed, censorship was implemented, and living standard was limited and so on.[3]

Therefore, even though the US policy towards Germany was closely linked to its policy towards the Soviet Union, the goal of the war was destructing militarism, eradicating Nazism, and making Germany lost its economic strength to invade other countries forever had not been changed.

The US policy towards Japan

During November 22-26, 1943, the three leaders Roosevelt, Churchill, and Chiang Kai-shek respectively from the United States, Britain and China met in Cairo. The theme of the meeting was the China problem, which inevitably involved the policy towards Japan. The conference published the "Cairo Declaration" to announce to the world that the purpose of the

---

2   Zi Zhongjun, The Post-War The US Diplomatic History, Vol. 1, World Affairs Press, 1994, p.42; Liu Jinzhi, History of Cold War, Vol. 1, World Affairs Press, 2003, 68; Wang Shengzu, History of International Relations, Vol. 7, World Affairs Press, 1995, p.65.
3   Beate Von Oppen, Documents on Germany under Occupation, 1945-1954, Oxford University Press, London, 1955, pp 13-27.

war against Japan "was to halt and punish the aggression of Japan", and to deprive all the islands that Japan seized or occupied in the Pacific since 1914. It also specifically pointed out that the northeast of China, Taiwan, and Penghu Islands which were "stolen" by Japan from China should be returned to China. The three countries declared they would keep long-term fight to make Japan finally "surrender unconditionally".[4]

This was the first time that anti-Fascist allies coordinated on the policy towards Japan and declared the policy of how to deal with Japan after the war.

Then, in January 1944, the United States established a committee for post-war plan in the State Department, which was responsible for developing policies towards major vanquished countries after the war. Soon, the committee brought out several documents about policies towards Japan. From these documents the US position towards Japan in Tehran, Yalta, Potsdam meetings was shown that although there were differences and controversies in the United States, the two basic principles of the US in dealing with Japan were clear: In order to destroy Japan's war machine and prevent Japan becoming a threat to countries in the Pacific region, Japan firstly surrender unconditionally. Second, allies must occupy Japan with military force. But they said nothing about whether to retain tenno and tennoism[5] in Japan.

In1945, Fascist Germany's ultimate failure was evident and the struggle of dividing Europe between the Soviet Union and the US exposed in the Tehran and the Yalta Conference was increasingly prominent after the war. In order to prevent the friction in Asia similar to Europe which took place after the war, and to avoid further strengthening impact of the Soviet on the world, Truman began to consciously act alone in the problem of defeating and controlling Japan after the war. On July 26, 1945, China, the United States and Britain published a joint declaration "Potsdam Proclamation" to make Japan unconditionally surrender. On July 28, Japan published a government statement showed its ignorance of the declaration. The United States regarded this as to reject unconditional surrender. On August 6h, the US dropped an atomic bomb on Hiroshima, Japan (dropped another on Nagasaki on August 9). At 17:00 on August 8 (Far Eastern time at 0:00 on the 9th), the Soviet Union declared war against Japan and participated in the Potsdam Proclamation. On August 10, the Japanese government issued notes to China, the United States, Britain, the Soviet Union, accepting the Potsdam Proclamation, but Japan hoped they could leave tennoism alone.

---

4   International Treaties, 1934-1944, World Affairs Press, 1961, p.407.
5   Tenno refers to Japan's traditional Kingdom dynasty.

After obtaining the subtly consent of the United States, Mikado announced a truce and surrendered on August 15.[6]

In this case, about how to deal with the defeated Japan, the US attitude was very clear. Truman said, "I decided not to repeat Germany's mistakes in occupying Japan and I do not intend to split or divide control. I do not want to give the Russians any chance to let them act like they were in Germany and Austria".[7]

The United States strongly rejected the Soviet's requirement of being the supreme commander of the alliance of occupying Japan, and unilaterally appointed MacArthur as the supreme commander. This determined that the defeated Japan would be militarily occupied by the United States alone. Because the Soviets could not comply with the command of the US, China could not sent troops due to domestic reasons; Britain and other countries would not compete with the United States to get fruits of the victory.

Claiming to be "the absolute ruler of eight million Japanese", MacArthur followed the international strategic policy of the United States at this time, he implemented indirect rule through the Japanese government at the premise of reserving Mikado in Japan. Mikado, before the defeat of Japan, had absolute authority which was unshakable in Japanese society and politics. Therefore, the Emperor of Japan had inescapable responsibility for the war of aggression. Within the allies, including the United States, especially in the countries that suffered from Japanese aggression, there was a popular voice of punishing Mikado. But, after all, Mikado's name did not appear in the list of war criminals. Moreover, under the influence of the US occupation, among the hundreds of Class A war suspects were only 25 of them actually prosecuted, of which only seven were sentenced to death. In order to stabilize the Japanese political situation as soon as possible, the United States included Japan into its absolute sphere of influence. How to deal with the crimes of Japan's war of aggression was left unsaid, which constituted one of the reasons that the Japanese ultra-right forces used for defending war crimes until today.

After occupying Japan, the US implemented a series of "post-war reforms" to make the Japanese soon embark on the road of the Western democracy as a country which the United States could take advantage of in

6   In less than 20 days, Japanese wartime government changes its decision from rejecting Potsdam Proclamation and sticking to fight locally to surrendering. This left the world history a problem that has been discussing until today: The role of atom bomb played in ending the war against Japan, was it necessary? See, Nan Fangshuo, Different Opinion on the Atomic Bomb in Hiroshima, Ming Pao News, Hong Kong, 08.08.2005.
7   Harry Truman, Truman's Memoirs, Vol.1, SDX Joint Publishing Press, 1974, p.371.

the US post-war global strategy. The reform was comprehensive, mainly including amending the constitution, agricultural land reform, the dissolution of the zaibatsu, as well as the reform of labor and education. Among them, the revision of the constitution, the making of the new constitution was the most important part in a series of reforms. Published in November 1946, the Constitution of Japan implemented in May 1947 (also known as Peace Constitution or 1946 Constitution) reserved the nominal Mikado, and left the Mikado who used to have supreme authority with only symbolic meaning. It identified that Mikado was a symbol of the country "without any authority of making national policy". The new Constitution also specifically provided that Japan "cannot maintain land, sea or air forces as well as other forces for war. The right of belligerency of the State will not be recognized" (Article 9 in the constitution). This had important historical significance on determining the direction of Japan's Post-War development.

It should be said that although in order to adapt to their new strategic needs, the US government's policy towards Japan was relatively relaxed at this time compared with the wartime policy towards Japan. And America rarely took the allies into account, especially the interests of the neighboring countries of Japan. In overall, Japan was still a hostile defeated country. Preventing it from becoming a new threat was the gist of the US policy towards Japan when the war ended.

2.1.2 The Formation of subordinate affiliation — New statuses of Japan and FRG

In the early days of 1946, the world situation experienced a significant and qualitative change. Since the war had ended, the basis of the US-Soviet wartime alliance ceased to exist, and the conflict of interest between the Soviet Union and the US heated up. Although the bickering of differences about the problem of vanquished states continued, the vision of both sides had reached far beyond Japan and Germany, and stared their international political arrangements focusing at their own sphere of influences. The United States policy towards Japan and Germany had changed due following changes in the US polices: From having close links with the Soviet Union, to fully shifting to the policy of " containment against the communist threat", from the policy of controlling, punishing and promoting Japan's and Germany's demilitarization to the policy of the controlled rearmament of them under the conditions of approaching Cold War causing divided camps in Europe, and other divisions of North and South Vietnam, North and South Korea, and the East and West Germany, the outbreak of the Korean War, and the formation of two military blocs and two camps. It was due to these strategic adjustments by the US that the post-War Japan and Germany, which used to be the rivals of the United States, embarked on a road to rely on the US. Thus post-War Japan and Germany were willingly to become smaller allies in order to exercise state functions and return to the international stage as early as possible.

The US-Japan alliance

The shift in the US policy towards Japan after World War II was an important part of the Asian strategy after the US relocated its global strategy in the new situation, and it was also closely related to the US policy towards China.

During the war, the United States still believed post-War Japan would be disqualified as an Asian power in a fairly long period of time, and Japan's position could only be substituted by China. In order to gain China's support on the policies and position of expansion in Asia after the war, the Roosevelt administration put their hopes on Chiang Kai-shek's regime. After Truman took office, he still claimed that "the US interests in Asia depended on Chiang Kai-shek's regime which strengthened China", "The KMT should take the position of Japan to become a stable force in Asia."[8]

However, as the Chinese people's revolutionary struggles achieved victories, the US was astonished, and had to shift its attention to Japan again. "After 1947, the US found that it was facing a task that was to transform a country into an ally, whose sovereignty was fully grasped in the hands of the United States."[9]

Changes in the US policy towards Japan were mainly reflected in two aspects. First was to revive the Japanese economy. Second was to make peace with Japan as soon as possible.

On October 9, 1948, formed on the basis of two reports of George Kennan, a specialist of the "containment policy", the No.NSC13/2 National Security Council document signed by the Harry S. Truman was regarded as the turning point of the US policy towards Japan in historical records during the occupation period.[10]

---

8   Walter LaFaber, America, Russia, and the Cold War 1945-1980, the Commercial Press, 1986, p.30.
9   George Freidman, Merendith Lebard, trans, He Li, The Coming War between America and Japan, Xinhua Publishing House, 1992, p.102.
10   FRUS, 1948, Vol.1, pp 523-525.

In fact, this was just a formal symbol. The change of the actual policy had begun before this.

In the initial period of occupying Japan, the United States was primarily concerned about Japan's demilitarization and democratization of its political establishment and institutions. With the curtain of the Cold War rising, the US-Soviet relations became tense and on the other hand Japan with the totally collapsed economy, was not just a power that the United States could use for its interests, but might become a heavy burden for the US in terms of its strategy towards the Soviet Union. So, vigorous support of the revival of the Japanese economy was started officially with the aim of "reducing the burden of occupation". The US measures to support Japan's economic revival were:

1. Significant revision to reduce Japan's compensation. The original plan of Japan's compensation designed by the United States was very strict. According to President Truman's special envoy Pawley's plan of Japan's compensation in December 1945, Japan's industry should be remained at the level of the late 1920s; the living standard of people should stay below the standard of the Asian countries it had invaded. According to this principle, Japan's military industry and all the heavy industrial equipment should be handed over to the United States or removal of 50% of steel production in Japan might not be more than 2.5 million tons (later reduced to 1.5 million tons). Since 1947, the compensation plan had been revised for several times. The level of industrial production in Japan was raised to the level in 1936, and was later raised to the level in 1948. The plan significantly reduced the number of demolished factories.[11] In May, 1949, the United States hastily announced the accomplishment of the demolition plan.

2. Losing the sanctions and restrictions on Japanese zaibatsu. Chaebol company form which was a form of monopoly-capitalist group with strong feudal characteristics was unique in Japan. It was the economic foundation behind Japan's foreign expansion. During the early period of the US occupation, the US laid down the basic principles for the dissolution of the zaibatsu, especially for Mitsui, Mitsubishi, Sumitomo, Yasuda zaibatsu; lifted or limited Chaebol families' control of the business and management; promulgated the "the Act of Exclusion of Excessive Concentration of Economic Power" ("Concentrating Exclusion Act") and the "Antimonopoly Act" to

---

11   Some say about 50 thousand machines were dismantled which is only 7% of Pawley's plan. Kobayasi, Japan's post-War Economic History, the Commercial Press, 1985, 24; Some say when the dispensation was declared in 1947, only 17 arsenals and 16 million equipments were dismantled. Yu Qun, Research on the US Policy towards Japan, NFNU Press, 1996, p.86.

prevent the emergence of new monopolies. From May in 1948, the United States made major adjustments to "Concentrating Exclusion Act". The US eased the "Concentrating Exclusion policy", relaxed "Concentrating Exclusion object", and repeatedly modified the "Antimonopoly Act". To early 1950, according to the "Concentrating Exclusion Act", only 18 companies were dismissed. Later, a number of new monopoly groups gradually emerged.

3. The United States strengthened the economic assistance to Japan. In 1947-1949, the United States, as the Japanese government required, provided the assistance of scarce materials for the revival of Japanese economy, such as heavy oil, coke, iron ore, raw rubber and so on. To 1950, levels of the main economic production, such as the production of coal, iron, steel, electricity and other supplies in Japan, had exceeded the levels in 1935. Although the US aid began to decrease at this time, the Japanese economy soon caught "a ride" of the Korean War, and entered the "special needs in Korean boom period" in Japan.

Of course, the shift in the US policy towards Japan was more obvious in the aspect of politics. Especially in making peace with Japan in a hurry, the objects of political purges were mostly removed from the original war crime-related people to the leftists and because that the US proposed to rearm Japan.[12]

Declaring the end of the war and making peace with Japan meant for the countries invaded by Japan re-admitting Japan's an equal and friendly country status. About the main principle on Peace Treaty with Japan was discussed as early as in wartime in several major summits, such as how to deal with the Japan's armed forces, and the withdrawal of the occupation forces in Japan. Soon, the United States included the Japanese Peace issue into its strategic needs against the Soviet Union. Making peace with Japan for the US means to be faced with numerous warring countries, which made the question of the Japanese Peace inevitably become the focus of the early Cold War confrontation. Such differences were also reflected in the US domestic politics.

Before the end of 1946, although the United States had considered the issue of making peace with Japan the conditions were not yet mature because of the transformation in Japan was still in progress. So, making peace with Japan was not brought on the agenda. To the end of 1946, the transformation of Japan basically completed; particularly those involving the disposal of the Japanese army and the promulgation of the new constitution,

---

12   Zi Zhongjun, The Post-War the US Diplomatic History, Vol. 1, World Affairs Press, 1994, pp.154-155.

the composition of Congress. Besides, the pressure of the international situation in the Far East and the democratic movement in Japan, the United States government and the occupation authorities thought they must begin to implement the Peace Treaty with Japan.

The initial plan of the US Peace Treaty with Japan's was drafted by the Secretary of the State Council Office of Northeast Asia Far East Division, George Burton. The main principle of "Burton plan" basically followed the Roosevelt era, with emphasis on punishing Japan and preventing the revival of Japanese militarism from posing new threats.[13]

Obviously, the main structure of "Burton program" became outdated when the post-Cold War began. It was natural that "Burton program" caused the opposition of the US military and occupation authorities from different perspectives. The burden of quelling the controversy fell on the shoulder of George Kennan, who had been very popular in the US State Department. From August 1947, the US State Department Policy Planning Board led by Kennan took two months to present a memorandum of Peace Treaty with Japan, namely the Policy Design Committee document PPS/10. Kennan advocated postponing Peace Treaty, thinking the treaty was unfavorable to both Japan and the US security, and it might create an opportunity for the communist to rule. He suggested carrying out "making peace in actual", which meant more support to the self-reliance policy for Japanese economy and to broaden the administrative authority of the Japanese government, but it would not end the military occupation. On this basis, Kennan drafted the "Proposal on the US policy towards Japan" (document PPS/28) in March 1948. G. Kennan suggested not to make peace negotiations in quite a long time, and made it clear that, "If Russia still threats the world's security, the coalition forces will continue to stay in Japan; or convince Japan to rearm, until it has the ability to withstand public armed aggression".[14]

At the same time, in order to avoid the German-Soviet stalemate in the problem of making peace with Japan that had appeared on Germany issue, the United States established a policy just for Japan. This meant that even though the US was about to make peace, it was among America and only a small number of allies who could make peace with Japan.

From the second half of 1949, the world situation became further clarified. Soviet atomic bomb test was successful, New China was founded, the Sino-Soviet alliance was established, the Asian countries were very active in national democratic movement and the communist movement; in Europe, Germany had been split into two countries, NATO had also been composed, and confrontation

---

13   FRUS, 1947, Vol.6, p.452, 459; FRUS, 1948, Vol.6, pp.656-660.
14   FRUS, 1948, Vol.6, p.713.

between the two camps was laid on the Cold War arena. In Japan, the National Democratic Movement also heated up, emotions of opposing the US military occupation became increasingly intense, while the fact that Japan was isolated from the world and Asian countries had become a constraining factor for the United States to foster economic recovery in Japan. So, in order to make Japan its allies and helpers in the Cold War as soon as possible, the United States accelerated the peace making with Japan alone.

First, the United States negotiated with the Atlantic allies who had the same strategic interest—Britain and France. Since the Korean War broke out, some countries gave up the ideas that the US would be different on the issue of the Japanese Peace. In September 1950 three foreign ministers reached a consensus on the problem of Peace Treaty with Japan without including the Soviet Union; on the eased policy towards Japan and the US military presence in Japan and other issues. Britain also promised to agree with this position in Asia-Pacific region and British Commonwealth countries associated with making peace.

The Treaty of Peace meeting was held on September 4, 1951 in San Francisco with the United States orchestration. A total of 52 participating countries attended the meeting, Yugoslavia, India, Myanmar received an invitation but did not participate; Mongolia, North Korea, Vietnam, and even China, which had the longest time fighting against the war, lost the most, and was the main battlefield of the Sino-Japanese War (including Taiwan authorities), were not invited. After several days of bickering, on September 8, with the exception of the Soviet Union, Poland, Czechoslovakia, the 49 countries (including Japan) signed the peace treaty. San Francisco Peace Treaty rejected the participation of China, and did not mention that Japan should return China coastal island that usurped by Japan. The peace treaty intended to foster economic recovery and re-arming of Japan, allowing long-term US military occupation of Japan and other unequal terms. This was not only contrary to the historical facts, but also violated the principle of wartime agreement among a few big powers.[15]

Therefore, it was illegal and invalid, it was unacceptable for the Chinese people and the people of other countries suffering from the pain of Japan's aggression. It was only a ticket to the drama directed by the United States to build a strategic system against communism in Asia by taking Japan into the alliance as soon as possible. Soon, the US formed a military alliance in the Asia Pacific region through a series of bilateral or multilateral military treaties and agreements.

15   Japan's Political Situation, China Social Sciences Press, 1984, pp 364-379. -Author's note Japanese people opposed US-Japan Security Treaty.

In the process of planning the San Francisco meeting, because a large number of Asia-Pacific countries still doubted about Japan, and were dissatisfied that the US monopolized the authority of disposing Japan, which endangered their interests. The United States had to appease these countries first. Coordinating with the establishment of the North Atlantic Treaty Organization in the west, America took the excuse of ensuring military security to take these countries into its military alliance network in Asia. On August 30, 1951, the United States and the Philippines signed the "US-Philippine Mutual Defense Treaty". On September 1, America signed the "ANZUS" with Australia and New Zealand.

In only a few hours after signing "San Francisco Peace Treaty", "Japan and the United States Security Treaty" was signed between the United States and Japan, which marked the formal establishment of the US-Japan military alliance. Thus, Japan embarked on a path of rearmament, and became the US most important strategic stronghold and military bases in Asia, as well as the United States' most powerful ally in Asia against the Soviet-led socialists, and the servant of the United States in opposing the new China.[16] The US-Japan alliance relationship was further strengthened by "US-Japan Mutual Defense Assistance Agreement" in March 1954, "Southeast Asia Collective Defense Treaty" in September, and "US Taiwan Mutual Defense Treaty" signed by the United States and Taiwan authorities in December.

The Federal Republic of Germany joined the North Atlantic Treaty

The US and Britain had publicly declared they would no longer pursue to dismember Germany after the establishment of the transitional system of separate occupation in Germany by the Soviet Union, the US, Britain and France. Naturally this was declared after the signing of the peace treaty with Germany. Germany on the other hand still wanted to establish unified central government agencies to become a unified European country. However, against the Cold War background, a unified Germany would inevitably have a problem of attribution. Should it stand to the side of the US-led Western camp, or to side of in the Soviet-led Eastern bloc? Because in Europe the strategic position and foreseeable effect of Germany determines the final outcome for both sides of the Cold War. This issue was crucial because it determined that Germany under occupation could not become a unified country. After splitting two Germanys went separate ways.[17]

---

16   FRUS, 1951, Vol.6, pp.1466-1467.

17   The first Prime Minister of the Federal Republic of Germany, Adenauer said, "Our geographical location put us between two big countries which have contrary ideals of life. If we don't want to be pulverized, we have to choose a side". Adenauer's memoirs, Vol.1, Shanghai People's Publishing House, 1976, pp.98-99.

The Federal Republic of Germany, with the support of the United States, became the European bridgehead for the United States against the Soviet Union.After Germany was occupied separately, the four countries had been solving the problem of Germany through foreign ministers' meeting. Entering 1946, with the Cold War's prelude and harsh changes in the international environment, except France and the Soviet Union still maintained vigilance towards Germany revival, the United States and Britain had been locked into strategic adversary to the Soviet. Their policy towards Germany began to change from punishment and restriction to steering and support. Thus, it was difficult to reach a consensus on the issue of Germany in the foreign ministers' meeting.

The United States and Britain argued that they should unify the economy of all the occupied territories in Germany as soon as possible, and establish a unified economic management institution. The Soviet insisted to firstly determine the future political direction of Germany, and then to talk about economic recovery in Germany. Germany also insisted to fulfill the agreement to obtain compensation from the United States occupied district. From June 15, 1946 to July 15, foreign ministers' meeting was held in Paris without any agreement on the Germany issue. During the meeting, the US Secretary of State Byrnes issued a statement, and formally suggested merging the occupied territories. This proposal was later rejected by France. The Soviet Union ignored, while the British gave it a warm response, and claimed if they could not agree, the United Kingdom would act alone in the British occupation zone. On September 5, 1947 United States and Britain reached an agreement on the merging of the US and British occupied zones, and the agreement was officially signed in Washington on December 2, 1947. This was the first step to post-war division of Germany. In March 1947, the Truman Doctrine came out, in June, the Marshall Plan was introduced. In this environment, French policy towards Germany had to gradually move closer to the policy of the United States and Britain. Facing the adverse situation of "three-one", in the Soviet Union's behest, "Congress of the German people" was held in East Berlin on December 6, 1947. They required achieving the reunification of Germany. The Soviet Union took this as pressure and required the US and Britain to listen to "People's opinions", but was rejected. Thus, the four foreign ministers' meeting for solving German issue had come to an end. In February 1948, the US, Britain and France put aside the Soviet Union, and invited Netherlands, Belgium, Luxembourg, the three countries to hold a meeting in London to discuss the merger of three occupied zones in the West, the treaty towards Germany and other issues. The Soviet Union became extremely angry.

On March 20, 1948 the Soviet Union announced its withdrawal from allies-controlled German Commission. The two sides began to design and build a different future in Germany according to their own wishes and needs in their occupied region.

During the period before the formal establishment of the two Germanys, the Soviet Union and the US competed to build the future of Germany. Since September 1947, the Soviet Union set up the Cominform, together with the communist parties of eight European countries. It focused on consolidating its position of strength in Eastern Europe from the political and military aspect. In February 1948, Czechoslovakia bourgeois parties failed to seize the power, and this shocked the West. In April, under the pressure of the Soviet Union, Finland had to sign a friendship treaty with the Soviet Union and ensure not using the policy of neutrality with an alliance with a third country. In February, 1948, the Soviet Union announced a ban on Western representatives participating in the German political rally in the occupied zone of Berlin. From April 1, the Soviet began to check all documents of the Americans passing by the Soviet occupation zone, and to check all items except personal baggage. It also implemented irregular restrictions on ground transportation to Berlin. The United States rejected the requirement of the Soviet that the flight passing three sky paths between the west zone and Berlin should be approved ahead of flying. On June 18, according to the spirit of London meeting, America, Britain and France announced to implement currency reform after three days in the Western occupation zone, and would issue new B mark. The Soviet Union also immediately announced the currency reform, D mark would be issued. The Soviet Union stepped up traffic blockade of Berlin, implemented full control of land and sea traffic between the Western occupied zone and Berlin. The United States was forced to use an air corridor to airlift daily requirement to Western occupied zone in Berlin. The Berlin crisis ended until May 12, 1949. In March 1948, the Second People's Congress was held in the Soviet occupation zone. The elected General Assembly became the governing body of the Soviet occupation zone. It was not only responsible for handling daily affairs, but also had the authority to formulate the draft constitution and conclude treaty. As the three countries urged the West, in September 1948, the German parliamentary committee (Constituent Assembly of the Western Zones) started to work, drafting the Basic Law for separate nations after the emerging of the Western zones. Adenauer was elected the President of the Constituent Assembly.

On April 4, 1949, the North Atlantic Treaty was signed in Washington. Only days later, US, British and French foreign ministers signed nine files including the Occupation Regulations on Germany issues. These documents determined the relationship among the three countries which will occupy the Germany in the future, and set the tone for establishing a new state system of post-war Germany. On May 8, the German Parliament Committee adopted the draft of the Basic Law and was approved by the occupation authorities. On May 23, when four foreign ministers were in the meeting in Paris, the ceremony was about celebrating the signing of the Basic Law and bringing it into effect in the Western zone. On August 14th, the Bundestag election was held in the Western occupied zones. On September 15, Adenauer was appointed as the prime minister. On September 20, the Federal Republic of Germany was founded. And on October 7th, socialist oriented German Democratic Republic was proclaimed in the Soviet occupied zone. (We used to call them as West Germany and East Germany.) Germany was officially split into two countries, although they were not legally considered as fully independent sovereign states.

In the latter half of the 19th century, in half a century, the unified German state composed of the "iron and blood", was repeatedly intimidating and scary in Europe and throughout the world. But it eventually failed to escape the punishment brought by launching the war, and also failed to stop splitting that had lasted more than forty years arranged by two superpowers, The Soviet Union and America. In retrospect, perhaps this was the only most appropriate outcome at the time. Because neither Germany could be unified, nor be occupied endlessly. No one could offer a better solution. This was the result of the situation and the history. However, an interesting fact which should not be ignored at the outset was that at the beginning of the establishment of the two German states, although they both didn't recognize each other as an independent sovereign state, they never gave up wishes and requirements of re-unifying Germany when they were maintaining and fighting for their national sovereignty. Adenauer said in his speech at the opening ceremony of the parliamentary committee, "Given the difficult situation in Germany and the realization of the responsibilities for our people, we gathered to work together to draft a Basic Law. The firm goal of our parliamentary committee is to write such a constitution was making Germany permanently unified and making the eastern part of Germany exist in this new country".[18]

---

18   Adenauer's memoirs, Vol.1, Shanghai People's Publishing House, 1976, p.163.

Such aspirations and demands were realized forty years later through several generations' efforts and historical conditions. This is the fact that we witness today. However, this Germany at this moment is not the same Germany at that moment.

After the Federal Republic of Germany was founded, in order to make it became a full member of the Atlantic Alliance soon; the United States accelerated their full support. The United States believed, to make West Germany become a truly functioning ally, it must first be recognized as an independent state in the international law, and then to speed up the development of its economic revival, and finally, the most important objective was rearming West Germany. Thus, with the auspices of the United States, West Germany was allowed to establish quasi-diplomatic relations with other countries–consular and trade relations, and allowed to participate in the international organizations in European region and to exert the rights and fulfill the obligations. It was allowed to accept the terms of the Marshall Plan, some heavy industry base and equipment that were planned to be removed originally, were also ceased to demolish. From 1950 onwards, as the "Schuman Plan" came into reality, "Pleven Plan" with main content of establishing a "unified European army" was launched. With the pressures and needs of the Korean War, the United States was determined to promote a joint European military to achieve the rearmament of the West Germany.

On September 12 until 19th, 1950, when NATO Council meeting was held in New York, the United States, British and French foreign ministers held a meeting on the German issue. It was announced that the Federal Government of Germany was the sole legitimate government of Germany; the three countries would end the state of war with Germany. In May 1951, the US, Britain and France began negotiations with the West German government on the specific content of "German Treaty". In July, the three countries announced the end of the war against Germany. In November, Britain, France and the United States foreign ministers initialed the German Treaty (its official name is "Convention on the relationship between the three countries and the Federal Republic of Germany", also known as "General Treaty", ", "Bonn Treaty" or "Bonn Pact"), and was formally signed on May 26, 1952. In fact, the treaty was a peace treaty just among the United States, Britain, France and the Federal Republic of Germany. In the next day, the "Pleven Plan" based "European Defense Community Treaty" was signed. The essence of this treaty was to rearm Germany and to take it into the North Atlantic Treaty Organization military bloc. Thus, on August 30, 1954, it finally received a veto from France which was always hesitant about German rearmament. France's veto disembarked the Western bloc.

However, at this time, the British did seize the opportunity to act as a mediator. British Foreign Secretary Eden proposed a new solution that was to simultaneously accept the Federal Republic of Germany to participate in the North Atlantic Treaty and the modified Brussels Treaty (later renamed as Western European Alliance). Because of the persuasions and pressure from the United States and Britain, France had to agree to accept this plan in principle. On September 28, 1954, foreign ministers of the United States, Canada, Germany, Italy and the five countries signed the Brussels Treaty (Britain, France, the Netherlands, Belgium, Luxembourg) had a meeting in London to discuss the problem of re-arming Germany and issued a "final resolution agreement"("London agreement"). On October 23, nine foreign ministers meetings continued to be held in Paris, and they reached an agreement on accepting participation in "the Western European Alliance" of the Federal Republic of Germany and Italy. At the same time, the US, Britain, France and Germany had a consensus on canceling the occupation in Germany. Fourteen NATO foreign ministers, defense ministers' council also agreed to absorb Federal Republic of Germany into the NATO. This was the famous "Paris agreement" in the history of Western alliance. On May 5, 1955, "Paris Agreement" entered into force. From the perspective of international law, the Federal Republic of Germany had formally gained an independent sovereign status.

Corresponding with the Western alliance, the Soviet Union had been taking countermeasures. On November 29, 1954, before the "Paris Agreement", the Soviet Union, Poland, Romania, Hungary, the Czech Republic, Bulgaria , Slovakia, and "German Democratic Republic" held a meeting of peace and security in Moscow, explicitly declared that if any US offensive would occur, the Soviet Union and Eastern countries would be ready to take joint actions. Consequently, on May 14, 1955, Treaty of Friendship and Mutual Assistance was signed by eight countries in Warsaw. "Warsaw Pact" was officially established. Since then, the two major military and political blocs in the East and the West began a tense face to face confrontation for decades in Europe.

2.1.3 The differences among the Western major powers on the issue of defeated countries in the post-War era

Most of the people had fixed opinions towards the relations among the super powers in the West, especially the relations between the US and European countries. For instance, Charles de Gaulle criticized the government of the French Fourth Republic was at the US beck and call, saying that it could not do anything except for executing the US order; another example, many committed the special relations between the US and Britain, of which the main implication was that Britain did whatever the US ordered; besides, Germany was dependent on the US and so on. In fact, this was only one side of the problem. The problem was not that simple. Their differences and conflict existed from the very beginning to the end with fluctuated degree, and were often covered by the conflict between the NATO and the Warsaw Treaty Organization.

At the end of the World War II, the situation that the US solely occupied Japan determined the struggle between the one-sided policy and full-rounded policy towards the issue of making peace with Japan. The argument existed among the US and other countries that had been invaded by Japan, existed in Japan and the US, and existed between the US and its new allies, such as Britain.

In 1948, the US adjusted its policy towards Japan, and established the policy of recovering Japanese economy and rearming Japan. Entering 1949, not long after the establishment of the NATO, Soviet Union had achieved the successful atom bomb test and , the People's Republic of China was founded it. All these made the US have to turn its eyes to Asian issues and speeded up its efforts to make unilateral peace with Japan when it was also focusing the European issues As a matter of fact, the focus of the struggle regarding achieving a peace treaty with Japan was the question of whether China could become one of the signing parties of treaty and China's attitude towards Japan's rearmament. Whether the new China would participate as one party in the peace treaty with Japan became severe conflict between the US and Britain. Early in September, 1949, Britain and the US reached an agreement on the issue of making a joint peace with Japan after several negotiations, and Britain compromised with the US policy. After Britain announced its recognition of the People's Republic of China in the beginning of 1950, it had different opinion with the US on the issue of China's right to sign the peace treaty with Japan. The US argued that the representative of P.R China should represent China in the peace treaty with Japan, while the US insisted Taiwan authorities should represent China. In 1951, in order to make up the differences and to sweep the obstacles in the issues of Japan peace treaty, Dulles, Dulles started intense diplomatic negotiations in the Asia-Pacific region, in which he gave Britain both lure and pressure at the same time. Dulles paid three visits to Japan, and ran across Britain, France, Australia, New Zealand and Philippines.

Around March, 1951, draft treaty with Japan was prepared by the US government and sent to 14 countries. Only after one month, Britain also sent its own the treaty drafts to the Commonwealth countries besides the US, the West Germany and Holland. The draft suggested that China could participate as one party in the peace treaty towards Japan, and that Taiwan should be returned to China.

Under the manipulation of the US, in spite of the domestic voice of dissent, Japan's Yoshida's government showed its intent that they were willing to make peace treaty with the government of Kuomintang (Taiwan) instead of the PRC, or they would rather delay the signing of the treaty. On the other hand Dulles utilized the difficult situation of France in Indochina, with the attempt to sign a separate a treaty with the puppet regime of French Indochina and forced Japan to pay war compensation to Indochina, in order to please the Indochina nations. He probably planned to show this act as a support to France which was faced with increasing pressure coming from Indochina's native forces. From April to June, foreign ministers of the US and Britain held abundant negotiations. At last, Dulles promised to Morrison, the Foreign Secretary of Britain, that he would use its influence on Iran and compromise with Britain on the problem of Iran which demanded sovereignty on its oil wells.[19]

This promise persuaded Britain to agree with US side that the People's Republic of China and Kuomintang would both be excluded from the peace treaty with towards Japan, this agreement determined the future Japan towards China relations and Japan was also given the status a sovereign state.[20]

This meant that the initiative of arranging its relations with China or Taiwan was given to the Japan. Since Japan had agreed and preferred to make peace with Taiwan, this hindered the possibility of China signing a separate treaty with Japan in the future. British leader Morrison was fully aware of this, he felt to express regret publicly. On 12 July, 1951, Britain and The US announced the details of jointly drafted treaty with towards Japan.

---

19   Iran government asked to nationalize oil field, and prepared to take over the control of Anglo-Persian Oil Company which was in charge of Iranian oil field from the hand of Britain. Britain sent navy to demonstrate at the Persian Gulf, but it was powerless to take greater military moves.

20   FRUS, 1951, Vol.6, Part 1, pp.1106-1109.

According to its global strategy the US opposed to P.R China's participation in the peace treaty with Japan. . The US intention was clear enough,
but why the British side, as the most important and the closest ally of the
US during the World War II, and which sometimes had much louder voice
than the US in the US-UK led anti-communist camp had a different opinion
from the US on the issue of P.R. China's participation in the peace treaty?

This policy was determined by the British interests in its relations with
China. After the foundation of new China, Britain was faced with a dilem-
ma regarding its policy towards China. On the one hand, the ruling class of
Britain regarded new China's system as a rival ideologically and politically.
In the beginning of the Cold War the contradiction was very clearly appa-
rent after Churchill's famous speech of Iron Curtain. With the addition of
the US pressure and influence, it was hard for Britain to immediately accept
China's "Three Principles" of establishing relations with other nations.[21]

However, among the capitalist countries, the proportion of British investment in China was the highest. Especially on the issue of Hong Kong
which was a major relation between China and Britain, it tended not to
completely submit to US views. During the late civil war (1946-1949) period in China, Britain was worried that China would liberate Hong Kong by
force after the victory of revolution, so it had developed defense program
to maintain the status of Hong Kong. After the new China was founded,
Chinese government did not attempt to liberate Hong Kong by force, instead just confined itself to announce that it would not accept the past unequal
treaties related to Hong Kong, and reclaimed that Hong Kong was Chinese
territory, which demonstrated that "it aimed to solve Hong Kong issue by
negotiations at an appropriate time in the future". It seems that China didn't
prioritize the settling of the Hong Kong issue. Chinese stance of maintaining the current status and not rushing to solve the Hong Kong issue was
very obvious. China preferred that British government should refrain to stir
any trouble damaging China's interests. In October, 1949, Britain recalled
its "ambassador" from Kuomintang ruled Taiwan, and officially declared
recognition of the legal position of P.R. China in June 1, 1950, though US
was in favor of maintaining its former position.[22]

---

21   "Three principles" means to confirm through negotiations that: cutting the diplomatic
relations with Taiwan authorities; supporting China to recover its legal position in the UN;
respecting China's independent sovereignty. – Author's note.

22   Documents of China's Foreign Relations, Vol.1, World Affairs Press, 1957, p.19.
Author's note: Since Britain kept in touch with Taiwan authorities, and abstained on the
issue of Chinese position in the UN, China and Britain only established charged' affaires to
the level of diplomatic relations since 1954, which was upgraded to the ambassadorial level
until 1972.

This meant that, Britain didn't want to have souring relationship with China after it had annoyed it on the peace treaty issue with Japan After the end of World War II and during the 1950s, the German issue had always been the focus of international relations. It was not the only severe controversial issue between the US-led Western allies and the Soviet-led Eastern alliance, but also a topic of disagreement among the Western allies, especially between the U.S and France.

Since the US, Britain, and the Soviet Union changed their original consensus of dismembering Germany in the Potsdam Conference into regulations on occupying and controlling Germany, and after they took charge of different zones in Germany, France kept a closer watch on Germany about its rising power and still insisted to take dismemberment as its policy towards Germany. On August 7, 1945, French government informed three countries that it accepted the main regulations in Potsdam Agreement, but declared that "it would not accept to re-build a German central government at the beginning".[23] French policy towards Germany showed more obvious differences with British and the US policy.

The inherent objective of the French policy towards Germany was to completely destroy or weaken Germany by all means, so that it would not become a threat to France any more. After the Potsdam Conference, France mentioned the major points of its policy towards Germany. First, since the Potsdam Agreement a piece of land should be separated from the Eastern Germany, so, "there should be a balance between the Eastern and the West Germany", which meant a piece of land should also be separated from the West Germany. Ruhr was the "potential of the war" in Germany, Rhineland was "the access point to invading France", they should be separated or monitored, and Germany should be dismembered. Second, France insistently opposed to establish the German central regime. The French thought, a unified Germany would "become a threat sooner or later", and opposed the decision made by Britain and the US about founding German central government. France wanted to merge with the US-UK occupation zone. Third, a strict compensation plan should be made and executed. France required to take control of the German production of coal and steel and to destroy the military production to restrain the industrial production at a low level. At last, Saar should be put under Germany's administration.

The French strict policy towards Germany firstly came from the historical lessons learnt from the relations between France and Germany. France and Germany had a long history of resentment with continuing wars. No

---

23   Alfred Grosser, La IVe Republique et sa Politique exterieure, Armond Colin, 1961, p.197.

matter which side caused the wars and what was the nature of the wars, if we only see from the consequences, France suffered a lot from German aggression. Especially the France-Prussian War and World Wars caused almost catastrophes for France. After the World War II, though Fascist Germany was defeated, France was afraid that it would rise again. "For France, Germany issue was firstly about security and politics". Therefore, all plans and suggestions that were relevant for recovering sovereignty of Germany and reviving Germany caused a lot of rejection and restlessness in French government and in public. Just as Adenauer said, "The worry about Germany's revival obviously manipulated the political thoughts in France".[24]

However, the historical reason was neither the only factor nor the essential factor for French attitude towards Germany. The essential reason was the political and economical needs of France after the war.

France lost its status as a superpower that it had for centuries in the World War II. In politics, France was rejected from the Tehran Conference, the Yalta Conference, and the Potsdam Conference by the US. No one paid attention on France. French people on the other hand generally thought if France didn't protect its interests on the issue of Germany that had a close relationship with France, and continued to follow others' orders, it would have the danger of being placed in the rank of inferior countries. In economy, industrial production value in France when the war ended was only 40% (In Britain, the percentage was 80%). In 1946, the production price raised 80%. In 1947, GDP could not even reach the standard of 1910. In the early years after the war, the biggest agricultural production country in Western Europe had lower ration of bread than any period when it was occupied by Germany. This political and economical situation was far away from its ambition of restoring the status as a superpower. Therefore, France, as a country that had been plundered and destroyed when being invaded, not only rejected every political and economic condition of Germany's revival, but also wanted to get more compensation to recover and develop itself. Of course, from a historical perspective, besides worrying about Germany's revival, French strict policy towards Germany included some elements of vengeance. Thus, the prior task of post-war France was to take all the means to permanently change the power contrast between France and Germany. In another word, after the war, in terms of its national interests France needed a feeble Germany.

---

24   Adenauer's Memoirs, Vol.1, Shanghai People Press, 1976, p.95.

The French hard-line policy towards Germany, of course, was incompatible with the policy of the United States that takes the Soviet Union as the main opponent, supporting and rearming Germany. It was also not conducive to the establishment of the Western alliance. With the division of Europe, and the Cold War got intensified, the United States didn't wish France and Germany remain in a state of hostility. The United States repeatedly blamed the French for wanting others takes into consideration of its doubt about Germany, regardless of "communist threat". The US asked the British to put pressure on France together to refuse its requirements, except to meet the requirement of France on the Saar question (The purpose was to return to the agreement with the United States and Britain and to establish German central government for the merger). In fact, under the pressure of the US and Britain, French policy towards Germany had gradually softened since after the four foreign ministers meeting in Moscow in 1947. At the end of the London meeting with the six-nation which was in June 1948, France had agreed to establish the German central administrative bodies in the Western occupation zone in Germany, and then developed the interim constitution, and held government elections on this basis. It recognized that Germany would eventually achieve reunification. France also agreed to cooperate with the US and British policy and recognized the Western Zones of Germany as a single economic unit to participate in the Marshall Plan, and established an international regulatory bodies in the Ruhr, but its main function was to allocate coal and steel as needed.

The reason of softening French policy first of all was because the pressure of the dollar. Between 1945-1947, all kinds of assistance or loans from the United States that France had received was approximately $ 5 billion combined, France got nearly $ 2.5 billion aid from April 1948 to September 1951 from the Marshall Plan, accounting for 4% of the income (United Kingdom accounted for 3%, Germany 2.5%). The United States also often clamped France by deferred payment, refusal to supply coal and other means. This helpless economic dependence naturally had to be paid politically. Ramadier, the French Prime Minister, had to admit, "Every loan given will depend on the political reality. Every time we get a loan, our independence would reduce to some extent."[25] At the same time, the domestic political situation in France also changed. Early in 1946, Charles de Gaulle, head of the government of France, who had been advocating a strict policy towards Germany and had always been wary of the United States, advocating conditional acceptance of the US aid, was forced to resign. In May 1947, the French Communist Party was also pushed out of the cabinet. This also reduced the resistance of France to soften its policy towards Germany.

---

25   Davis Horowitz, the US Diplomatic Policy in Cold War, Shanghai People Press, 1974, p.55.

Due to the situation at the time and the pressure from the US, the idea of prevent the pressure through a tough policy and restoring economy by abundant resources was unable to be achieved, Frenchman need to find another way, so they brought out "Schuman Plan", intending to prevent German rearmament by putting German coal and steel under the co-management. French move received a positive response in Germany. Germany's return to the international arena must be understood by France firstly. Adenauer said, "I often think that the adoption of international cooperation of the most important European steel industry may become the bud of the widest implementation of the international cooperation in the field of coal and steel. In so doing, I seem to be more strongly hope that France and Germany can make reconciliation."[26]

However, softening of the French policy, did not mean that it paid less attention on the change of the political and military status of France and Germany. French softened policy towards Germany was based on the premise of French political and military advantage over Germany.. Later, when the Federal German economy was soaring, France became particularly sensitive to changes in Germany's political and military status. Thus, although the United States continued to exert pressure on the rearmament of Germany, France was still reluctant to agree. France had not agreed the Federal Republic of Germany to participate in the NATO, and refused to discuss the approval of "European Defense Community Treaty". Later, just because the domestic political instability and the pressure of ongoing colonial war and ally, the French finally agreed to expand the Brussels Treaty as a stopgap measure, and accepted the Federal Republic of Germany and Italy. Until 1955, Federal Republic of Germany formally joined the NATO. In 1956, France and Germany signed an agreement on the return of the Saar and making Moselle a canal. So far, France and Germany relations in the Post-War period was very difficult.

It could be seen that, before this, the member states of the Western Union had different views on the principal contradiction in the international political arena. They had problems of their own priorities. The United States and Britain, in particular, the United States' first consideration was how to prevent the Soviet Union, and how to further develop and consolidate its position in Europe. France's first consideration was how to prevent the normalization of Germany, in order to ensure its own security and development.

---

26   Alfred Grosser, La IV. Republique et sa Politique exterieure, Armond Colin, 1961, p.210.

2.2 From Cooperation to Competition–
The Economic Growth of Japan and FRG

Under the enthusiastic support of the US, through a series of treaties and agreements, Japan and the Federal Republic of Germany gained the status of a sovereign state in politics, and had been placed militarily under the security umbrella of the Western alliance. They soon got rid of the vanquished status, and immediately began the era of creating economic miracle. In the history of the development of the world economy after World War II, from the mid 1950s to the early 1970s, Japan and the Federal Republic of Germany experienced a period of nearly 20 years of rapid economic development, created an economic miracle. Developing on the weak basis of being destructed and restricted by the war, the two countries became the pillars of the capitalist world's economy and the world economic powers. As the reasons, some said it was because of the United States' help, some others said the reason was that even though they participated in the confrontation, they were not dragged down by the arms race. Some people thought the two countries made a profit from the war. Some people even said that the reason was their nationality. Anyway, many problems were worthy studying. But for the Western allies of Japan and the Federal Republic of Germany, one more important question was how to deal with the competition of these two emerging economic powers.

2.2.1 The historical background of the economic rise of Japan and the Federal Republic of Germany

Ever since the Cold War began, when we discuss any issues of international affairs, I am afraid we cannot think without the background of the Soviet Union against the US. It was especially true to the economic rise of Japan and the Federal Republic of Germany. This was determined by the special international status of Japan and Germany after World War II. Originally, the status of being defeated doomed the future of these two countries: military occupation, political decomposition, financial compensation, although the two countries were called country, they were deformed countries not allowed having the qualification as a complete nation. Before and after the end of the war was sufficient to prove that all these were entirely possible as all the political declarations of allies and the history of World War I showed. However, at the end what people had expected and Japan and Germany were worried about did not occur. With the outbreak of the Cold War, the fight between the Soviet Union and the US got more and more intensified, which changed the fate and future of Japan and Germany.

On the big strategic chessboard of the United States and the Soviet Union, Japan and Germany were no longer the main rivals and enemies. Under the situation that the Soviet Union and the US regarded each other as the main rival and enemy, they had no intention of, or were unable to put the vanquished countries to death. For instance signing the "Treaty of Versailles" after World War I, especially the United States, did not want to put Germany and Japan in the dead end, but to turn them "its friends", so that Japan and Germany could become its outposts against the Soviet Union in the East and the West. Then there was the strategic adjustment to support and re-arm Japan and the Federal Republic of Germany. Moreover, the specific policy adjustments under all these strategies had created the conditions and laid the foundation for the subsequent economic rise of Japan and the Federal Republic of Germany.

When the famous German economist Karl Hardach analyzed from the point of view of German, he said, "If there is no East-West conflict, the occupation policy of the four victors will certainly be much more severe, or at least they will not treated Germany so kindly, the burden on Germany will be heavier, and time will be longer. German is certainly not being seen as the only gainers of the Cold War, but as the main gainers. There is a reason to emphasize that the Cold War created the conditions of decisive significance for the rise of Germany."[27]

The US aid was the key factor behind the economic revival of Japan and Germany

The war did not only bring disaster to the victims of aggression, but also to the invaders themselves. Japan lost 25% of the national wealth in the war, 40% of urban buildings and 50% of industrial and transportation facilities were destroyed. In 1946, Japan's industrial output only reached 26.4% of the 1935 level; the agricultural output was only 60% before the war level, the whole economy collapsed. In Germany, the industrial production in 1946 only reached 22.9% of the figure in 1938, in which coal production as the main driving force of production and life accounted for 60%, the country's national income was less than one-third in 1938. Such adverse economic conditions did not last long in Japan and Germany. After spending the most difficult time in 1946, with the adjustment of the US strategy, the two countries' economic production has been restored to pre-war levels through the efforts of five or six years in the early 1950s, and achieved economic recovery as the foundation for the next economic rise.

---

27   Karl Hardach, German Economic History in 20th Century, the Commercial Press, 1984, p.182.

In the economic recovery of Japan and the Federal Republic of Germany, the US aid had the significant effect. It played the key part. One of the most effective ways was reducing and ending the war reparations program ahead of the schedule, which were indirect assistance with incalculable value given by the United States to Japan and Germany. It retained a large number of industrial infrastructures and saved a lot funds for the economic revival and the rise of the two countries. The second was to provide direct assistance of a large number of much-needed supplies and funds. In the early Post-War period, from the perspective of resuming production, Japan had the scarcest resource and the most short of energy. Japan asked the United States to provide heavy oil first, so that it could recover coal and steel production as soon as possible. With the US support, the coal production of Japan in 1947 reached nearly 30 million tons, the coal supply in the steel, fertilizer, the power sector increased by 57%, 44%, and 121%. Since then, the United States became a major supplier of ore, coke, and rubber of Japan. During the occupation, the United States provided $ 2.1 billion economic assistance to Japan. In Europe, if the US assistance to Britain and France taken as the indirect aid to Germany then Germany was the biggest beneficiaries of the US "Marshall Plan" and on the other hand this could decrease the compensational claims of these countries to Germany. Germany accepted the US aid firstly by "receiving the relief funding for the occupied territories from the US government". From the end of the war to March 1950, the United States provided $ 1.62 billion to Germany including all types of assistance; another channel was opened through the "European Recovery plan "(the "Marshall plan"). From 1948 to 1952, the United States provided nearly $ 1.6 billion. The third was to provide convenience through various international organizations. After the war, the United States fully used the international financial and trade organizations of the Bretton Woods international monetary system, the International Monetary Fund, the General Agreement on Tariffs and Trade, etc. When Japan and the Federal Republic of Germany were once regarded as a sovereign state, they would be immediately accepted as a member of these organizations and would enjoy preferential treatment. For example, they could choose not to fulfill the regulations of liberalizing capital and trade. It was until 1962 that Japan implemented trade liberalization, implemented capital liberalization in 1966. The Federal Republic of Germany accepted all obligations of the revocation of import restrictions in 1957.

The Korean War: A special opportunity for Japan

The Korean War that broke out in 1950 provided a special opportunity for the economic recovery of Japan and the Federal Republic of Germany. Originally, during the occupation period, Japan and the Federal Republic of Germany needed not to spend defense spending substantially, even though they were "re-armed" by the United States. Given all the "restrictions", Japan's and the Federal Republic of Germany's military spending was not so much under the umbrella of the US nuclear weapons and troops. This saved a lot of money for the production and scientific research, and effectively improved their economic potential and competitiveness. The Korean War became a turning point in Japan's Post-War economic revival. Because of the war, military orders and demand of services for the US military had increased. In Japan, this was known as the boom of "Korean special needs". In 1949 Japan's foreign exchange reserve was about $ 200 million and in 1951 and 1952 Japanese annual "special needs income" reached 800 million dollars. Korean War stimulated the Japanese economy, especially the key industries like iron and steel, manufacturing, chemical fiber and other "special needs" industry developed faster. By 1953, the production indicators of major sectors in Japan reached or exceeded pre-war levels.

Although the Korean War was far away from the Federal Republic of Germany, it had a major impact on its economic recovery. In the context of the Korean War, the United States and its allies made further significant changes, adjusting the policy that imposed limit on Germany's industry and industrial technology. For example, it changed certain conventional weapons production that was prohibited to limit the production, abolished the ban on the manufacture of certain merchant, and completely abolished the restrictions on the production of heavy machine tools, aluminum, ammonia and chlorine. The Federal Republic of Germany did not get directly involved in the Korean War, "but the North Korean crisis had a beneficial effect to Germany's foreign trade in general".[28] In the second half of 1951, foreign trade had residual for the first time. In the same year, industrial production for the first time exceeded 1938 level. From 1952, the Federal Republic of Germany entered a "Golden Age" of rapid post-war economic growth.

The Great economic boom in the capitalist world

In Japan and Germany post-War economic growth of high-speed was outstanding, even it can be called miracle in its own unique feature. It should be noted that, the economic miracle of Japan and the Federal Republic

---

28   Karl Hardach, German Economic History in 20th Century, the Commercial Press, 1984, p.181.

of Germany was part of the economic development of capitalist world, or the most prominent part. If there was no post-war economic development of the capitalist world, it was difficult for Japan and Germany to create economic miracles.

From the mid-1950s, the major capitalist countries entered a period of great economic development. During this period, which had lasted for about 20 years, ended until the end of 1973 when the oil crisis triggered the global economic crisis. During this period, the average annual economic growth rate of the major capitalist countries reached 5.3%, the growth rate was more than any other time in history. In the United States, Britain and France, for example, from 1953 to 1973, the average annual GDP growth rates were 3.5%, 3.0% and 5.2%. In the United States, 1960s was known as the "decade of prosperity". In the past 20 years, the growth rate of France kept up with Germany. The cooperation of the European Economic Community effectively contributed to the economic advantages of Federal Republic of Germany. Although the growth rate of British economy in the past 20 years lagged behind, it still kept growing. It was particularly worth noting that the United States completed the technical breakthroughs of the electronics industry with the lead of technological revolution, not only made the old and the new industry leap to a new level, but also made Japan and the Federal Republic of Germany which consistently used "bringism" (invented by Lu Xun, one of the greatest Chinese thinker; The ethics accepts but analyzes, takes but selects, and inherits but improves all ethical resources, whether Confucian, socialist, or Western ethics. Ed.) Japanese synthetic fiber, petrochemical technology came from the United States DuPont and the British Imperial Chemical Industries, the semiconductor industry came from the transistor technology of the Bell Labs, the world famous TV industry benefited from the Radio Corporation of the US technology licenses. The Federal Republic of Germany was the world's second largest technology importer following Japan. In the first half of the 1950s, the German deficit in annual purchasing technology licenses reached 50 billion marks, to as much as 450 million marks in 1961, and maintained that for several years. All these constitute the indispensable environment for Post-War economic rise of Japan and the Federal Republic of Germany, and effectively motivated the high-speed economic development of both countries.

2.2.2 The "golden age" of the Federal Republic of Germany's and Japan's vigorous economic rise

The economic rise of Federal Republic of Germany

When it comes to the economic rise of the post-war Federal Republic of Germany, we cannot avoid talking about Germany's "social market economy" and its main initiator, Ludwig Erhard.

The so-called "social market economy" derived from the Freiburg School of neoliberal economic theory. It was not laissez-faire style market economy, but a conscious control of the market economy from a social policy perspective. The social market economy was to act according to the law of the market economy, but was complemented by the economic system of social security. It basically means combining the free market principles with social justice, so that it would ensure effective competition in the market. It was both denied the statist economy, affirmed the necessity of state intervention and regulation of the economy at the same time. From the Post-War history of Germany's economic development, the social market economy played a positive role in promoting the German economic recovery and development and the maintenance of social stability and progress in Germany. In the process of the implementing the social market economy, Ludwig Erhard certainly contributed a lot. During Erhard's PhD at the University of Frankfurt, he was tutored by the renowned economist, the sociologist Fritz Oppenheimer. After graduation he engaged in economic research, and accepted the German neo-liberal theory. During the war, when Erhard was conducting research work, he was involved in activities against Hitler. Therefore, once the war ended, he was immediately hired by the occupation authorities. Erhard was the Bavarian Minister of Economic Affairs in 1945, and took the position of director of Economic Authority in British and The US occupation zone in 1948. Erhard held the post of economy minister from the foundation of Federal Republic of Germany in 1949 to the previous government of Adenauer in 1963. Following Adenauer, Erhard also served as Prime Minister of the Federal Government from 1963 to 1966. Of course, he was a much less successful prime minister than the economy minister. Erhard advocated harmonizing the relationship between individual freedom, wealth growth and social security depending on state intervention and regulation on the basis of the maintenance of private ownership, and regarded market economy as the core issue. Erhard's economic thought identified that the social market economy became an economic management system of post-war Federal Republic of Germany for a long period, and provided a theoretical foundation and institutional guarantee for the economic rise of Germany.

Strictly speaking, the "golden age" of the Federal Republic of Germany's Post-War economic rise should refer to the 1950s, and specifically refers to the years from 1952 to 1959.[29]

However, although from after 1959 to the early 1970s, economic growth in the Federal Republic of Germany was not like before and still among the best in the capitalist world. Therefore, broadly speaking, it can be called the fifties and sixties as "Golden Age" of economic development. Overall, during this period, Germany's economic growth rate was faster, amplitude of growth in consumer prices was small, inflation was moderate, labor market was active, the unemployment rate remained at a low level, the country's overall economic strength continued rapid growth and came from behind to the top in the capitalist world, and became one of the pillars. If calculated by dollar, Federal Republic of Germany's gross domestic product (GDP) average annual growth rate was 9% from 1952 to 1959, 9.9% from 1960 to 1965, 10.2% from 1952 to 1965, exceeded the United States, Britain, France, but Japan. During this period, the absolute terms of GDP increased by 3.4 times, this was ahead of other capitalist countries except the United States. The average annual gross national product (GNP) growth rate in Federal Republic of Germany was lower than Japan and France and higher than the US and the UK between 1960 -1973.

During 1952 and 1965, following Japan, the Federal Republic of Germany's average annual growth rate of national income reached 10.2 %;d it was far more than the United States, Britain and France. Before 1967, the national income of Federal Germany was just after the United States, and ranked second among capitalist countries.[30]

Let's take a look at the most representative production rate of the industry. From 1952 to 1965, the average annual growth rate was 7.9%, only inferior to Japan, far more than the United States, Britain, and France (4.2%, 3.4%, and 5.9%). During this period, the Federal German industrial production rose 1.68 times, higher than the United States (71%), Britain (55%), and France (1.1 times), behind Japan (4.2 times). In terms of crude steel production, in 1950, Germany produced only 12 million tons of crude steel. It reached 33 million tons in 1960, 44 million tons in 1970. Japan respectively reached 500 million tons, 22 million tons, 93 million tons in the same period; the figures for French were 9 million tons, 17 million tons, and 24 million tons; Britain 16 million tons, 24.7 million tons, 28

---

29   Some researches refer to years between 1953-1959.
30   IMF, International Financial Statistics, 1977; Statistical Abstract of the United States, Jan 1981; OECD, Main Economic Indicators, 1950-1968.

million tons. Then auto production output, the Federal Germany produced 300,000 in 1950, 2.96 million in 1965, 3.83 million in 1970. Japan reached 30,000, 1.88 million, 5.29 million units over the same period; France reached 360,000, 1,620,000, 2,750,000; British reached respectively 780,000, 2,180,000, 2,100,000 units.[31]

During this period, the Federal Republic of Germany's consumer price growth rate was also lower than the figures in other major capitalist countries. Taking the statistics of 1960 for example, the United States reached 1.5%, the UK 1.1%, France 4%, Japan 3.7 %, Germany 1.6%, behind the United States and the United Kingdom. In the 1970s, Federal Republic of Germany replaced the US-British position. In 1975, the United States reached 9.2%, the UK 24.2%, France 11.7%, Japan 11.9%, Germany only 5.9%. The price stability and the low inflation were the important features of German high-speed economic growth in this period. Shortly after the economic recovery of Germany in the early 1950s, foreign trade surplus occurred and kept unchanged in the run, so the Federal German gold reserves always occupied a dominant position in the capitalist countries. Taking the statistics in 1952 for example, the United States accounted for 50.1%, the UK accounted for 4%, France 1.4%, Japan 2.2%, and Germany 1.9%. By 1960, this figure became 32.3% for the US, 6.2% for the UK, 3.8% for France, 3.2% for Japan, 11.7% for Germany, while after 1970s, Federal Republic of Germany replaced the United States as the country with the highest proportion of gold reserves among all the capitalist countries.[32]

Japan's economic rise

The speed of Japan's economic rise was more prominent than Germany's. But the Federal Republic of Germany outstripped the Japan.

In the economic history of Japan, it was generally believed that Japan's economic growth boomed in 1955-1972. The starting point was in 1955, from a political perspective, it was because the "1955 system" which was governed by the Liberal Democratic Party, the combination of Japan's Liberal Party and the Democratic Party; from an economic perspective, it was because the harvest agriculture in 1955, crops' price fell sharply, while product price was stable. This was known as the "Year of the most satisfying for consumers". In this year, in addition to the import and export trade, the main economic indicators exceeded the prewar level. The real gross national income was 136% of pre-war, industrial output value 158%; agricultural output 148%, real per capita gross national income 105%, achieved

31   Figures above are extracted from official documents of respective countries.
32   IMF figures, International Financial Statistics, 1980.

"the number of boom" and the revival goal of "economic independence" without inflation, the year was called as "the best year of the post-war economy". In fact, in Japan's economic history, the most promoting thing of Japan's Post-War economic rise was the "White Paper on the economy" announced by the Japanese government in 1956. The white paper gave a landmark impetus to the Japanese economy:

First, "now is not the post-war", and the second was "the future is based on the modern period as the center of economic growth". It established the foundation of quickly leaving behind "the burden of war" and "Post-War consciousness" for the Japanese in terms of ideology, and the establishment of a national goal to achieve modernization. It was a very important "emancipation of the mind" in Japan's post-war economic history. On this basis, in 1957, the Japanese Cabinet developed a "new long-term economic plan" and "national income doubling plan" in 1960 (1961-1970). Driven by technological innovation, energy revolution, consumer revolution, and other economic strategic measures, after the Japanese economy experienced a variety of so-called "boom" (such as "brilliant boom", "Rock households boom", "Olympic boom", "mythological boom" or even "Vietnam War boom"), Japan maintained the leadership position for a fairly long time in the capitalist world.

From an economic point of view, the average annual growth rate in Japan in 1955-1960 was 8.5%. In 1960-1973, up to 10.5%, far more than the United States' 4.2%, UK's 3.2%, France's 5.75%, Germany's 4.8%. In 1955-1970, Japan's GDP growth rate increased 7.2 times. The figure was over Canada in 1960, exceeded Britain and France in 1967, exceeded Germany in 1968. Among these, the industrial output grew faster. In 1950-1970, the figure increased by 15.7 times, the average annual increased by 14.1%. In the Post-War booming period of Japan's economic growth, the development automobile, shipbuilding, steel, electronics and other sectors of the Japanese industry were of the most representative. In the 1960s, Japan's auto industry developed rapidly. 1961-1970, the average annual growth of Japanese car production was 34.4 percent, faster than all countries, and vehicle production ranked second in the world. After technical innovations in the 1970s, Japanese auto production surpassed the United States and became the world's first. Japan's shipbuilding industry had been the traditional industries. It was limited in the early post-War period, but because of the Korean War needs, the annual output in 1951 was just after the UK as the world's second. In 1956, it became the first again. The number of boats launched in Japan totally accounted for 20.7% of the sum of the world in 1960, 43.9% in 1965, 48.3% in 1970, and maintained at around 50%

thereafter. Japan's steel industry entered the period of great development from reaching pre-war levels of crude steel production in 1953. Around 1960, steel production in Japan was more than France, Britain, Germany, and became the world's third major steel-producing country. Crude steel production in 1973 exceeded 100 million tons, 10 times of 1956. Japan was also the world's largest steel exporter, accounting for 20% to 30% of total world exports. In the post-war economic boom period, the Japanese electronics industry developed rapidly. Electronic Industrial output in 1970 grew by 33.4 times more than in 1956; the average annual growth rate reached 238.6%. In 1959, Japanese transistor radios production ranked first in the world. In 1970, TV production value was 51 times than in 1965, accounting for one fifth of the entire electronics industry. In 1970, computer output increased 123 times than that in 1960 and occupied the world advanced level. Especially that the household appliances of Japan's electronics industry were inexpensive, full-featured, and easy to operate, they had swept the world for many years, monopolizing the world market. In short, with the 1970s, Japan became a developed, affluent country, and the world's second largest economy only next to the US.[33]

2.2.3 Foreign policies of Japan and Federal Republic of Germany

Since the end of the Cold War in the 1990s, to achieve national interests in international relations the economic factor as a diplomatic means was used more frequently and became more and more important, especially that the United States that became the only superpower used the economic sanction frequently as a diplomatic means to achieve its political goals. The reason why people paid attention to this was because a major change in the international political and economic relations. In fact, for the defeated nations in World War II like Japan and the Federal Republic of Germany, in quite a long period after the war, there was nothing new about using economic factors conventionally as the basis and a means for foreign policy as a result of being deprived or restricted of political rights and military forces. But with the political status enhanced and Japan continued to take part in military activities, it had dominant position in diplomatic activities which other countries did not have.

---

33   The reference of the figures above is IMF, International Financial Statistics, 1980; Chinese Academy of Social Science, Concise Japan Encyclopedia, China Social Science Press, 1994.

Japan's economic diplomacy

It is a normal activity to dealing with national affairs between a sovereign state and other countries. If a country loss its sovereignty completely or its sovereignty is under treat, it has no right to diplomacy or complete diplomacy at all. In the early period after World War II, Japan belonged to this case. When Japan militarily occupied by the United States, it is completely obeyed the order of the "allies' commander in chief" in its domestic, political, economic and social life, and lost its national sovereignty, so there was no independent foreign right. To obtain diplomatic rights, Japan should first end the war through peace treaty with foreign states to return to the international community as an independent sovereign state. In September 1951, under the US initiative, Japan was honored a favorable peace treaty. In May 1952, the United States supported Japan to join the International Monetary Fund and the World Bank. In September 1955, Japan formally became a GATT member state. Japan applied to join the United Nations from 1952. In October 1956, Japan resumed diplomatic relations with the Soviet Union and issued a joint declaration to clear the way for Japan to join the United Nations in December. In September 1957, Japan issued a "Diplomatic Blue Book", which was considered as the biggest turning point in Japan's Post-War diplomacy to reassume diplomatic relations with the Soviet Union and to join the United Nations. Japan finally "returned to the international community" and became "an equal member." In fact, at this time, although Japan could be seen as a sovereign state, its sovereignty was still restricted. Therefore, although Japan had diplomatic power, it could not implement full diplomacy.

Despite the fact that Japan had been accepted into the United Nations, the United Nations was a product of the anti-Fascist war, UN Charter was "a regional agreement to prevent a repeat of the enemy's aggressive policy" made by the victors of World War II, which clearly contained "enemy clause" aimed at Japan, Germany and other vanquished countries. Living in such an international environment, and lacking convincing correct view of history, Japan would naturally find it difficult to enter the "high society" of politics and diplomacy. Besides, Japan's military was still in supervision and regulation, and Japanese Constitution Article IX regulated war and military power, Japan's military diplomacy had no way to go, so the economic diplomacy was the only way for them. This choice was completely in line with the actual situation in Japan, because it was consistent with the main strategy of Japan's Post-War development. Post-War Japan implemented a development strategy that to firstly recover economy, and then to establish the status of an economic power based on economic prosperity, in order to seek political power and military power.

In the "Diplomatic Blue Book" published in September 1957, the Japanese government identified three principles of diplomacy on the basis of the Japan-US alliance, namely the United Nations Centre for Foreign Affairs, Coordination with the Western States (liberal state), insisting the position of Asian countries. But the core of the three principles was the implementation of economic diplomacy. During the 1950s to the 1970s, Japan's economic diplomacy's main objective was to obtain, consolidate and expand overseas markets, to build and determine the status of economic power. Japan was a long, narrow island, raw materials and commodity markets were the key to its economic development and survival. Due to limitations of the post-war international status, Japan could not afford the market competition with other Western countries for the moment. It had to first develop and occupy Asian markets on the basis of the Japan-US alliance. Originally, China should be the first choice for Asian markets. This was not only because there was a long tradition of economic exchanges between Japan and China, but also because Chinese supplies, human resources, geopolitical conditions were extremely attractive for Japan. However, due to the post-war Japanese government followed the US and took the hostile policy towards China, Japan-China relations before the 1970s had been in a non-normalization phase. Even so, the "non-governmental diplomacy" between Japan and China had never stopped, and this "private diplomacy" was mainly carried out in economic and trade activities between the two countries. In fact, the diplomacy could also be referred as "non-governmental economic diplomacy", which laid the foundation for the normalization of Japan-China diplomatic relations in the future. Japan blocked the economic diplomatic channel with China in Asia, so the Southeast Asian countries became the preferred target for Japan's economic diplomacy. In retrospect, the Southeast Asian countries played a tremendous role in Japan's Post-War economic rise. Japan firstly used war reparations and economic aid as a gimmick, and returned to the Southeast Asia. Under the influence of the United States, the Southeast Asian countries had accepted the small amount of compensation and financial assistance of Japan, and the Philippines ratified "the San Francisco Peace Treaty" in 1956. In 1958, Indonesia signed a separate peace treaty with Japan.[34]

Japan reopened the resource and commodity markets in Southeast Asia, and gained access to the safety guarantee of sea lanes that was important.

---

34   Philippine got 550 million dollars, as compensation to be released in 20 years and a long-term loan of 250 million US dollars; Indonesia got 223 million US dollars and a private loan and investments of 400 million US dollars. Other states which received Japanese compensation included: Thailand, 26.7 million US dollars; Singapore, 8.16 million US dollars; Malaysia, 8.16 million US dollars. – Author's note.

In the 1970s, resource of Southeast Asia accounted for one fifth of Japan's total resource imports, and most foreign trade in countries in Southeast Asia was inseparable from Japan. At this time, Japan with the economic rise had the attitude of developed countries. Japan through the energy diplomacy departing from the US Middle East policy after the "oil crisis", through more economic friction among European countries and by strengthening loan assistance of China, India and Pakistan and other countries, transformed from the economy diplomacy of simple pursuit of interest in the market to seeking international economic dominance, and its political purpose became more obvious.

Economic diplomacy of Germany

Post-War Federal Republic of Germany had almost exactly the same international status and incomplete diplomatic rights doomed by this position with Japan. Therefore, it had to take economic diplomacy as the primary means to achieve its long-term political goals. Unlike Japan, the Federal Republic of Germany promoted their economic foreign policy and the progressively realized strategic objectives by participating in an economic union—the European Economic Community.

The "Paris Agreement" signed on October 23, 1954 declared the abolition of the German occupation regulations, and to end the occupation state, followed by the abolition of the Federal Republic of Germany's economic and trade restrictions. Federal Republic of Germany was accepted into the NATO and the Western European Union. Since then, the Federal Republic of Germany was regarded as a sovereign state, and entered the new period of diplomacy. The Federal German Government led by Adenauer was clear in the diplomatic thought from the outset. They believed that the war made all major European countries lost their former status. Any European country could not play a role in the world economy and politics alone, so they had to unite.

As a country that had not yet got rid of the shadow of being vanquished, the Federal Republic of Germany only had a way out and had the possibility of returning to the world stage and ultimately achieving national reunification by becoming a member of the Commonwealth. Adenauer warned, "We must understand that trust can only be retrieved slowly and step by step, and we must be carefully, avoiding any thing that may cause suspicion of us again". "We must strive to go ahead slowly and carefully. We cannot lose patience at any time, and patience is one of the most powerful political factors".[35]

---

35   Adenauer's memoirs, Vol.1, Shanghai People's Publishing House, 1976, p.277.

Adenauer's patience finally got its result. He saw through the Post-War situation, the US could not leave Germany, France could not leave Germany, and vice versa, so with the premise of upholding the Atlantic alliance, he decided to achieve the French-German reconciliation; he saw that the political status was a very sensitive issue for Germany at that time, evaluating carefully; he saw the importance of economic potential in Germany in an economic union, so he urged the formation of the European Coal and steel Community. Facts had proved that the "European Coal and Steel Community Treaty" signed in 1951 has not only promoted the development of the Federal Republic of Germany's steel industry, but also promoted the development of other industries, and political achievements were extremely obvious. Because the establishment of Coal and Steel Community was equal to announcing serious impediment to the German Post-War economic development, the "Ruhr regulations" that regulated German coal and steel production had expired. Although the Ruhr region was a part of the "co-management" regions , it actually meant that the Federal Republic of Germany had recovered Ruhr's sovereignty.

The Federal Republic of Germany's foreign policy goal was achieved through the economic policy, which could be also confirmed by the development of the European economic integration from the beginning of European Coal and Steel Community. After the 1954 failure of the European Defense Community, Europe generally agreed that economic cooperation was an effective means of achieving political goals. The European Economic Community established on the basis of "Treaty of Rome" in 1957, created a precious condition for the Federal Republic of Germany's economic rise. The rise of the economy also promoted Germany's diplomatic strength. Helmut Schmidt, later served as the prime minister, bluntly said, "For several years, our economic policy was also our foreign policy".[36]

First, through the economic integration, the Federal Republic of Germany completed the process of promoting reconciliation to cooperation between France and Germany, and formed the European integration model with "French-German axis" as its core on this basis.

The relationship between France and Germany was formed because they were in need each other politically and economically. And France and Germany cannot be separated with the development of economic integration, economic interdependence. In the late 1950s, France had become the largest buyer of German goods, and Germany had become the second largest buyer of French goods. By the early 1960s, the Federal Republic

---

36   Alfred Grosser, La IV. Republique et sa Politique exterieure, Armond Colin, 1961, p.7.

of Germany replaced the US as the largest supplier of goods in Western Europe. Meanwhile, no one would forget the role and importance of deutsche mark in the European economy. This meant that, the Federal Republic of Germany established its position in the European Economic Community and the whole Western Europe through economic integration. Secondly, the Federal Republic of Germany, through the European economic integration, basing on "contact countries" system and other common external economic relations channels, expanded the international markets in other regions, so that the economic and political influence spread out of Europe. In the 1970s, there had been more than 70 developing countries established diplomatic relations with the Federal Republic of Germany especially those which the Federal Republic of Germany had given more attention, who had colonial relations with Germany in history. Finally, with the strength of the changes in European economic integration, Germany's policy towards the United States had also undergone subtle changes. It changed from the totally dependent mode to striving for more equal relationship. For example, in the face of the problem with Britain participating in the European Community; it was very difficult for France to reject the application of the United Kingdom if it was not Germany that acquiesced the French opinion about the UK might be the "Trojan horse" in community for the United States; there was another example, in the history of German foreign relations the famous "Ostpolitik" changed the conventional "unilateral" policy of the Federal Republic of Germany towards the United States. However, once this change had understood properly the other two facts needed to be explained clearly. First, European economic integration was initially able to start-up and to develop with the US support. Because Europe that accepted Germany was both the need to against the Soviet Union, but also the need to reduce burden themselves in Europe for the United States. Second, although the policy of the Federal Republic of Germany towards the United States was constantly changing, until the two Germanys reunited, the Atlantic Alliance's advanced position in foreign policy had no fundamental change.

It can be said that, in the 1950s, 1960s and 1970s, the Federal Republic of Germany transformed from an occupied country, its independence lost, into a sovereign and independent country, from a disarmed defeated nation into an important member in the Western military alliance, from a country caught in the economic collapse only depend on relief supplies to survive into a recognized "economic giant", except that the German government's full use of the Post-War situation of the East-West confrontation factors, it also because that the choice of policy which diplomacy served economy first and used economic means to pursue political goals, or say foreign policy was good at transforming economic power into political capital. As Alfred Grosse said in his description of the European international relations of the sixties and seventies, "The German economy seems so vibrant, that cause the change of European competition pattern".[37]

2.2.4 The economic frictions between the United States and Japan

It should be said that Japan's and the Federal Republic of Germany's (including Western Europe) completion of the post-war economic recovery and achievement of economic rise were inseparable with the US support and the economic assistance. In this process, under the absolute influence of the unbalanced political and economic development, there was the competition for economic interests and a variety of economic frictions between the major forces in the capitalist world, the United States, Japan and Western Europe. They only had different features and degrees at different time. In the early 1950s, the economic strength of the United States was far much greater than Japan and Western Europe. The main purpose of Japan and Western Europe was to restore the economy and to meet the minimum needs of the country, which did not constitute a threat to the United States, but in line with the purposes of the US support policy. Thus, even if there was any friction, both sides would tolerate under the politically premise of "unanimous". After the 50s and the 60s, economy of Japan and Western Europe developed a lot, but America's economic strength relatively declined. The tripartite economic friction was prominently showed by the allocation and the possession of resources and commodity markets, with an obvious property of "defending" national interests. In the 1980s, especially after the end of the Cold War, the economic friction between the United States, Japan and Europe was not only the problem of protection and expansion of the market, but a problem of fighting for dominance and control, which had "offensive" nature without compromising.

The US-Japan economic frictions throughout the 1950s

Japan's economic strength was far cry from the United States', and had been in the trade deficit position against the US. The entire Japanese market was flooded with The US industrial and agricultural products. Therefore, even if there had been textile trade friction, the USs hardly considered the Japanese imports as a threat to the US industry and economic interests.[38] Until 1960s, with the rise of the Japanese economy, its modern industrial

---

37   Alfred Grosser, The Western Alliance: European-The US Relations Since 1945, Macmillan Press, London, 1980, p.252.
38   US-Japan Alliance: Past, Present and Future, co-authored by Michael Grim, Patrick Clowning, trans. By Hua Hongxun, Xinhua Publishing House, 2000, p.273.

products continued to flock to the United States. In early 1960s, payment of bilateral trade was balanced. By the time 1965 300 million USD trade deficit appeared in Japan for the first time, which became a turning point in Japan-US trade. Since then, for various reasons, the US foreign trade was tight, but Japanese products hit the US market. To the late 1960s and early 1970s, Japanese products had occupied the US market, while the US product was pushed out of the Japanese market. Japan's trade surplus with the United States was growing, increasing from 1965's $ 300 million to $ 3.9 billion in 1972, $ 12 billion in 1978, $ 16 billion in 1981. Due to the adjustment of energy imports, 1986 was the year that had the highest total foreign trade surplus for Post-War Japan, reaching $ 82.7 billion, of which trade surplus towards the US accounted for $ 58.6 billion. In the 1990s, the surplus still increased year by year, $ 38 billion in 1990, $ 43.67 billion in 1992, over $ 60 billion in 1993.

Japan's exports to the United States were mainly textiles and steel, and also automobiles, household appliances, electronic products and so on. Around these commodities, the "trade war" between the United States and Japan started from the late 1960s and almost had not stopped. In 1968, Japan's trade surplus reached $ 1 billion, and the United States blamed Japan for dumping textiles. The US and Japanese governments had been carrying out several years of negotiations. Nixon not only won the election by his commitment to restrict textile imports of Japan, but also forced Japan signing the "US-Japan Fiber Agreement" in October 1971 with the pressure of normalizing relations with China without noticing Japan. From 1972, Japan limited its quantity of textile exports to the US while expanding imports goods from the United States to quell this "trade war". After the 1973 oil crisis, the US economy kept one way down. The trade dispute around the steel trade between the United States and Japan heated up. Under the requirements of the United States, Japan had "automatically limited" steel exports to the US twice. But because of the downturn in the US steel industry itself, Japan soon restored the level of exports to the United States, which had accounted for 56% of total US steel imports and made the US steel production difficult to maintain the previous level. After several rounds of negotiations between the two sides, they signed the "Agreement of special steel import quotas" in June 1976. Then, in 1977, the United States proposed a prosecution against Japan for dumping a variety of steel products imported.

At that moment, the Japan-US "trade war" opened up a new battlefield. The United States prosecuted Japan for dumping cars and color TV at the same time. In 1978, the United States began to implement a minimum purchase price of steel. Otherwise it would begin dumping investigation, which temporarily limited the Japanese steel imports. But the dispute about car did come to an end until 1981.

The constant trade frictions inevitably extended the dispute to other economic sectors. With the conflicts in the financial sector heating up, the United States opened up financial markets while asking Japan to further open commodity markets, to change monetary and financial system, to internationalize yen, and to soften the terms for foreign access. Japan was also criticized publicly by the United States as the "No.1 unfair trading nation". The US threatened applying clause 301 in the comprehensive trade law to impose sanctions. The US-Japan economic friction not only impacted the economic interests and their relationship of political security, but also hurt the feelings of ordinary citizens in the late 1980s. Every time when the negotiation was held, "bargaining provoked hostile rhetoric in both the US and Japan, news commentary is also full of predictions about the coming of a trade war".[39]

The US said Japan was "a special country, a special race", "an injustice trade partner", "an economic imperialism", and advocated the imposition of economic sanctions. The Japanese said the United States did not work hard to improve their own competitiveness, and advocated using sanctions against sanctions.

The economic frictions between Japan and Western Europe

The economic frictions between Japan and Europe was weaker and happened later than the one between Japan and the US. In the 1950s, because Japan and Europe were in the period of economic renaissance, and they were geographically far apart, so their economic needs and capabilities had not touched the other. The economic connection was very limited. In 1955, Japanese export to the European Community and to the six countries was only $ 81 million, and import was $ 95 million. The export in 1960 was only 175 million and the import was 420 million. In 1958, the trade volume of the six countries of the European Community and the United Kingdom with Japan was merely $ 420 million, only reached 1/7 of the trade between the United States and Japan. After the rapid economic development, the trade between Japan and the European Community grew rapidly. By the time 1974, the trade volume increased to USD. 7.015 billion.

As the level of Japan's economic development was higher than the overall level of the European Community, the trade imbalances put the European Community into a state of long-term deficit which was so difficult to get

---

39   Michael H. Armacost, trans. Yu Tiejun, Friends or Rivals, Xinhua Publishing House, 1998, p.189.

rid of. The deficit increased year by year from $ 50 million in 1968. It was $310 million in 1970, $ 1.345 billion in 1973, $ 4 billion in 1976, $ 11 billion in 1980, $ 22.8 billion in 1988, $ 27.36 billion in 1991, $ 31.19 billion in 1992, $ 28.17 million in 1993.[40]

The economic frictions between Japan and Europe had mostly the same content and problem with the economic frictions between the United States and Japan. For example, steel and manufactured goods (cars, household appliances, electronic products) were the main target of the market. While asking Japan to restrict exports of these products, Europe released the domestic market of agricultural products, aquatic products and leather products. It was also worth noting that, if we compare the trade difference between Japan and Europe with the one between the US and Europe, the proportion of the difference between Japan and Europe was growing greater and greater after the late 1980s.

The economic frictions between the US and Europe

After World War II, Europe became the largest commodity sales market in the US, in which exports to the European Community countries accounted for more than 80%, and Europe was the main area of obtaining trade surplus for the United States. According to statistics, the US trade surplus with the European Community countries was $ 2.126 billion in 1948, $ 0.956 billion in 1955, $ 1.211 billion in 1960. From the mid-1970s, the average annual surplus was nearly $ 8 billion, the figure in 1979 reached $ 12.7 billion. But it needed to be noted that, except for a few years, the Federal Republic of Germany mostly had trade surplus with the United States. Also in 1979, for example, the European Community as a whole had trade deficit with the US, a deficit appeared in eight out of nine member states, the only surplus of $ 900 million occurred in Federal Republic of Germany. With Japan's trade surplus with the US year after year in mind, we can see that Japan and the Federal Republic of Germany had an unusual economic position in trade with the US among the developed countries.

The Europeans thought Europe's position in the US trade deficit was the result of implementation of trade protectionism and dumping agricultural products and advanced technology products of the US, while the US thought the problem lied in the European Community. For example, the European Community kept expanding the scope of the associated countries often in violation of the Most Favored Nation Principle. Moreover, common agricultural policy of the European Community was purely protectionist policy.

---

40   UN, Yearbook of International Trade Statistics; IMF, International Financial Statistics; GATT, International Trade.

With the relative changes in the world economy of the two sides, this friction inevitably got more intensified.

The over-large gap of trade was bound to affect monetary policy and investment policy. The world financial crisis happened in the early 1970s and the late 1960s led to the Economic and Monetary disputes between Europe and the US. In August 1971, the United States announced 10% surtax levied on imports, and the dollar continued to depreciate. In the meanwhile, it decided to formally cancel the "gold standard", and cut the ties between dollar and gold, which abrogated the Western monetary system established in 1944—The Bretton Woods system. This move of the United States was aiming at forcing Europe and Japan to increase their currency value and increased the cost of exports. This approach seemed plausible for Japan and Germany which had trade surplus to the United States in the long term, but for most European countries which had been in a deficit was undoubtedly worsening the situation. Thus, the economic contradictions between the US and Europe brought out the contradictions between European countries. Because the French opposed franc appreciation, announcing the introduction of a dual exchange rate system, while Germany opposed the dual exchange rate system, and advocated the mark to appreciate in free-floating. If the franc did not appreciate, Mark appreciation would incur huge losses. Negotiations were held between the US and Europe and between France and Germany at the same time. The United States strongly requested to raise the value of the European currency, and asked Europe to reduce import tariffs. Europe required the depreciation of the dollar and the removal of import surcharges. Negotiations finally ended in December 1971, an agreement was signed in the Smithsonian Museum in Washington. The United States cancelled the import taxes and depreciated the US Dollar by 7.9%, J-Yen was appreciated by 16.8%, D-Mark appreciated by 13.5%, the the B-Pound and the F-Franc were appreciated 8.6%. In October 1987, Western countries experienced another severe financial crisis.[41]

It began with the fall of stock across the board in the countries, which caused the decline in interest rates and the dollar depreciation. It had a direct impact on the European Monetary System. In 1992, as a result of German unification, Mark exchange rate soared, while the dollar and other European currencies fell, which triggered a new round of financial turmoil in Europe. The UK and Italy quitted the European Exchange Rate Mechanism of the monetary system. The key reason was the parity of the US dollar and the mark.

---

41   It is called "Black Monday" in the world economic history.

The discussion of the economic friction between the Western powers always gave people the impression that the friction between the United States and Japan was greater than the friction between the US and Europe. In fact, Japan was not the largest exporter, but Germany was – it should be noted that it was only the Federal Republic of Germany, but not the whole of the European Community—in the late 1980s, Germany exceeded the US and became the largest exporting country in the world trade for several years in a row. The reason why US-Japan friction was greater, first, was because the European market was relatively open, unlike the Japanese market which was difficult to enter. As a result, Japan maintained a long-term huge trade surplus with the United States, while Europe except the Federal Republic of Germany maintained the long-term deficit. Second, Japan was a unified economic power and the only developed capitalist country in Asia. Before the 1980s, there was no country in Asia which could concern Japan about. Japan could freely revolt against the United States. Europe was not the same, the overall strength of the European Community could compare with the United States, but when it came to national interests, they gave priority to themselves. However, it was hard to fight against the US for individual country except Germany. The German market had always put the focus on Europe, not to mention that Germany was disunited at that time.

2.3 Defeated Power–Economic Power–Political Power

In Western countries, Japan and the Federal Republic of Germany were the largest economy after the United States. After Japan's economic development through the 50s and 60s of the 20th century, in the 1970s, it further consolidated its position in the world economy. From 1967 to 1968, GDP in Japan exceeded the GDP in Britain, France and Japan, accounting for 6.5% share of the capitalist and 6% of world proportion, accounting for 10% in the 80s. In 1989, Japan's GDP was equal to the combination of Britain, France and Germany, which was the equivalent of 60 percent of the United States. Throughout the 1970s, when the world economy trapped in low-speed development as a result of oil and other crises, Japan's economic growth rate remained at a high level up to 5.3%, while the US was 3.3%, the Federal Republic of Germany was 2.7 %, France was 3.9%, and the UK was 2.3%. In the late 1980s, foreign investment of Japan was larger than the United States, not only became the world's number one investment powers, but also became the world's number one creditor country. It also ranked first in the world's foreign exchange reserves, and remained at the world's top row after then. In the 1990s, the the world top ten banks had a branch in Japan and eight out of the world's top ten companies were Japanese. The

Federal Republic of Germany's GDP tripled in the period of rapid economic development, increasing by 7.1% per year from 1950 to 1966. GNP of 1960 exceeded the United Kingdom, and became the largest economy after the United States in capitalist countries. After the economic crisis of 1966-1967, the Federal German economy entered into a stable growth period. The average annual growth rate in GDP from 1967 to 1973 was 4.6%, was left behind Japan and ranked at the third in the capitalist countries, but the industrial exports and gold reserve remained the first. Two such developed capitalist countries with rapidly rising economic strength naturally wanted to play a leading role in the rules of world economic development. At the same time, the respective political hopes and demands that corresponded with the economic status of different stages were also raised.

Japan and the Federal Republic of Germany considered the idea of "defeated power–economic power–political power" as the idea of national development policies. It should be said that there was nothing strange or questionable. Nobody had the right to accuse a nation's aspirations and actions of revitalization and development, even though it had vanquished records in people's memory. Although Japan and the Federal Republic of Germany were vanquished countries in World War II, they had the experiences and lessons learned in the history. They had strong recognized foundation of economic powers, which was the objective requirement of historical and national development in order to become a political power. The key was which kind of political power that a country wanted to have or how to have it.

2.3.1 Japan and the FRG's aspirations for political power

Japan's goal and strategy of becoming a political power

Through the economic development of Japan in the 60s and 70s of 20th century, Japan stood among the world's economic powers. In this process, it was very dissatisfied with the situation that its own international political status was not commensurate with economic development, and continued to ask for more participation in international affairs to enhance the international political status. But at that moment the goal of its becoming a political power was not known by the public. With the rapid development of Japan's economic strength, its economic influence was felt everywhere in the world. It did not feel insecure and there was no sense of loss in exploration and political protection. In the early 1970s, after almost seven years of negotiations, the United States finally returned Okinawa to Japan, and realized the normalization of relations with China, which made the Japanese psychologically feel that they had ended dealing with vanquished countries. By 1975, Japan was officially been accepted into the economic summit meeting of the Western powers, which recognized Japan's economic power in the world. In this context, Japan's request to become a political power was gradually brought into public, and became the country's objectives of external strategy.

It should be said that Japan's political goal became clear in the 1980s. It was Nakasone who formally proposed the goal of becoming a political power. On July 28, 1983, the prime minister Yasuhiro made clear in his speech that, "Strengthening the Japanese voice in the free world and the world of politics not only as an economic power, but also to increase the weight as a political power." This was the first time Japan's ruling politicians proposed political power goals. Nakasone's diplomatic strategy was a global diplomacy. He strived to improve Japan's international status within the range of the whole world. Accompanied by the growth of right-wing forces in Japan and Nakasone's policy of military buildup, his visits to "Grand Shrine", Japan was faced with doubts and objections, particularly in Asia where the political power meant military power. A month later, Nakasone changed "political power" into "international country", which had the same essence and meaning. In 1985, in order to further eliminate the worry of Japan becoming a military power, Nakasone proposed the "four principles of international countries", clarifying that Japan did not want to be a military power, and it would not change the free institutions, and it would began a full range of international cooperation on the basis of strengthening the alliance of Japan, the United States and Europe. On July 29, 1988, Prime Minister Noboru Takeshita said in a speech at the Japanese parliament, "In the future the Japanese should have bold and innovative ideas in politics". In order to meet the aspirations and goals of political power, Japan's diplomatic strategy also made adjustments accordingly, changing from the "the United States lead with Japan followed" to the "full diplomatic"; from the "diplomacy of the middle and small countries" to the "diplomacy of big power".

The unity of Germany and its desire of being a political power

At the beginning of the establishment of Germany, Germany never gave up the political rights of reuniting with East Germany and getting back into the ranks of the great powers. When Federal Republic of Germany became a major economic power, almost every book included an argument that "An economic giant like the Federal Republic of Germany did not want to be a political dwarf anymore". In fact, Germany's desire of becoming a political giant was not only related to whether it was an economic power, but more importantly related to the German reunification. Because it was impossible for a divided state and nation to become a political giant. The Federal Republic of Germany's politicians were fully aware of this. Therefore, the Federal Republic of Germany's goal of being a political giant would always go hand in hand with the German reunification.

Since "the Paris agreement" which took effect on the May 5, 1955 gave the Federal Germany fundamental rights of a sovereign state, the Federal Republic of Germany began try to hold diplomatic activity alone with the Eastern bloc, whereas before, it was usually done by British, the US, France and other countries. At this point, the most prominent event was that Adenauer was invited to visit the Soviet Union and led to the establishment of German diplomatic relations with the Soviet Union. On the basis of establishment of German-Soviet diplomatic relations, the Federal Republic of Germany soon put forward the "Hallstein Doctrine" aiming at unifying the whole Germany with the Federal Republic of Germany at its core. The so-called Hallstein Doctrine, in essence, meant that the German Democratic Republic (GDR) would have no representation other than the Federal Republic of Germany on the basis of insisting "a single representation". It was proposed by the Secretary of State of the German Federal Ministry of Foreign Affairs, Walter Hallstein. It stated that German Government was on behalf of the entire Germany, and did not recognize the German Democratic Republic (GDR), and did not establish or maintain any diplomatic relations with the country which established diplomatic relations with the German Democratic Republic (as one of the four powers responsible for Germany, USSR excluded). Adenauer said, "There are no two Germanys, but only one. The so-called German Democratic Republic is not a country at all. Based on the concept of all public international law, it is an occupied area under Soviet rule, and the people of this area must regain complete freedom."[42] This policy was introduced under certain condition of serious confrontation between the two military blocs, the US and the Soviet Union, and it was full of the sense of the Cold War. Faced with a powerful Soviet Union and its allies, the Federal German Government led by Adenauer merely expressed a desire to become a unified nation, in fact, which was difficult to achieve. By the mid-1960s, under the tense situation of the two military blocs, even the US and the Soviet Union were seeking compromise and temporary cooperation while fighting. The rigid Hallstein Doctrine came to an end.

---

42   Adenauer's memoirs, Vol.1, Shanghai People's Publishing House, 1976, p.417.

If we call the Federal Republic of Germany's previous policy towards the Soviet Union, the East Germany and the Eastern European Group as "Ostpolitik", then when talking about the unity of Germany and its desire of becoming political power, we cannot skip mentioning Germany's "Ostpolitik." In October 1969, the Federal German Social Democratic Party and the Liberal Democrats started to have a coalition. The Social Democratic Party's President Willy Brandt took the post of prime minister, and implemented "small steps policy" of "seeking change by approaching" to improve relations with Eastern countries, namely the so-called "Ostpolitik". The premise of Ostpolitik was the cooperation with the West. In this context, it advocated to recognize the borders status in Europe after World War II, and to improve relations with the Eastern European countries; on the German issue, it acknowledged the German Democratic Republic was a special sovereign country, that it was the second German state. For the Federal Republic of Germany, the East was not a "foreign" country; it advocated the establishment of "one nation, two countries", in order to achieve the unification of Germany. The core of Ostpolitik was the hope that it could end the situation of passively taking orders from other countries on the problem of Germany since the war, and to promote the international position of the Federal Republic of Germany in the process of improving relations with Eastern countries, which created the conditions for the future German reunification.

Germany split into two countries because the defeated Germany was occupied and ruled by the allies. Without achieving a unified nation and the state, regardless of how rich and developed the Federal Republic of Germany was, it would always be difficult to get psychological recognition by political powers. The Brandt's Government of Federal Germany also realized the truth from history and the current situation in Europe: Without the approval and recognition of the Soviet Union and the Eastern European countries, German reunification goal was an impossible political fantasy. Therefore, improving relations with the Soviet Union and the Eastern European countries had become a prerequisite for Germany to be a political power. On August 12, 1970, Brandt went to Moscow to sign the "nonaggression pact of the Federal Republic of Germany and the Soviet Socialist Republics of Union". On December 7th, Brandt also went to Warsaw, and signed the "treaty on the basis of normalizing relationship between the German Federal Republic and the People's Republic of Poland" with Poland ("Warsaw Pact").[43] At the same time, the Western countries

---

43   Before the formal signing of the treaty, Brandt went to Warsaw and visited the Jewish cemetery. When laying flowers to the monument of Jewish war martyrs, he knelt down in

and the Soviet Union carried on a hard negotiation on the status of Berlin. On September 3, 1971, when the Soviet Union made great concession, the Soviet Union, the US, the UK and France signed the four nations' agreement on the issue of Berlin. It played a constraint role to the stability of the West Berlin. Above agreements were signed to further promote the connection between the two German states. In June 1972, two German states held a negotiation on the issue of normalizing relations. On December 21, they signed the "treaty on the basis of the relationship between the Federal Republic of Germany and the German Democratic Republic" (also known as the "basic treaty"). In this process, the Federal Republic of Germany also achieved the normalization of relations with other socialist countries, Czechoslovakia, Hungary, and Bulgaria. In September 1973, two German states joined the United Nations at the same time.[44]

The implementation of "Ostpolitik" by the Federal Republic of Germany not only "was definitely one of the early 1970s eased policy with most amazing results."[45] But also had great positive significance for the Federal Republic of Germany to achieve the aspirations and political power and the future development path. First, the "Ostpolitik" and its achievement successfully demonstrated that the Federal Republic of Germany, as a political independent country, began to implement a major independent diplomatic action. Prior to this, on the major East-West relations, especially on the German question, the Federal Republic of Germany only had "vindicate rights", never "decision-making", it was only a pawn on the East-West contest board. Aspirations and interests of the Federal Republic of Germany could only rely on the three allies, which were the US, British and French, especially the United States to represent and maintain. The Federal Republic of Germany was not only followed them passively and slavishly adjusted its foreign policy every day, but fear of becoming a victim in the trade between the US and the Soviet Union was also at stake. For the Federal Republic of Germany, the implementation of "Ostpolitik" was the way of dealing with the Soviet Union and eastern countries bypassing the United States. Since then, the Federal Republic of Germany could directly have dialogue with

---

front of the monument. This move became a piece of flash news which caused a sensation in the world. In the concept of the West, kneeling down is not valued as in the Eastern world. Asians can kneel down to the venerable, to the elderly, to beg, and to apologize, and the West doesn't have other explanations in addition to repent to God for forgiveness. The key to the problem is that, as an individual, Brandt didn't need to do so. He need not plead for forgiveness, because he was an anti-Fascist veteran, and he actually represented the German government.–Author noted

44   Andre Fontaine, Un Seul lit pour deux reves – Histoire de la "detente" 1962-1981, Fayard, 1981, p.242.

45   Willy Brandt, Meeting and Thinking, The Commercial Press, 1979, p.211.

any country, which expanded the international space of diplomatic activity, and enhanced the Federal Republic of Germany's international status and the voice on the German question. And all of these were indispensable conditions for a political power. Brandt assessed "Ostpolitik" like this, he said, "The first major content of our Ostpolitik is that we are more strongly care for our own business unlike in the past, and we are not just rely on others to speak for us". Then he added, "what we do will raise the awareness in Western Europe, the Atlantic Ocean and international institutions of us. The Federal Republic of Germany will be more independent, and more awakened." Second, the "Ostpolitik" open the gate to the Soviet Union and the Eastern European countries, especially the gate through which we can have direct dialogue with the East of the Federal Republic of Germany and improve the relations with the Soviet Union and East Germany. The mutual understanding and contacts between the two Germany had laid a solid foundation for the future unification of Germany, and its significance was incalculable.

Improvement of relations with Eastern countries eliminated a lot of obstacles for the Federal Republic of Germany to further play an international role. In 1976, the Federal Republic of Germany was elected as the member of the UN Security Council for a term of two years. In 1980, it was also served as chair of the UN General Assembly. In the 1980s, the relationship between the two German states had been further developed. On September 7, 1987, the Chairman of the East German Council of State Honecker paid a visit to the West Germany, and talked with the West German Chancellor Helmut Kohl. The two Germanys' relations had a major breakthrough. In October 1989, against the background of the severe political unrest throughout Eastern Europe, a large-scale mass demonstration for reform and harmonization also took place in East Germany. On November 9, the East German government announced the opening of the Berlin Wall and the border between the East and West Germany. Under this situation, the Federal German Chancellor Helmut Kohl proposed German reunification plan just in time. After the East German government had expressed a desire to unify, the Soviet Union, the US, Britain and France also changed the attitude of opposition or suspicion on the issue of German unification, and decided to take the "2 + 4" program to discuss German reunification, which meant the internal problems of German reunification was left to the two German states to negotiate, and external problems were left to two German state and four countries to negotiate. On September 12, 1990, the two German states signed the "treaty on the final solution to the problem of Germany" with the four countries, which indicated that the reunification of Germany was internationally recognized, unified Germany would enjoy full sovereignty of a country. This was essentially a "peace treaty with Germany" that all parties recognized. On October 3, 1990, the German reunification was declared.

After the reunification, the population of Germany increased to 80 million. If not counting the Soviet Union, it was the most populous country in Europe: land territory increased to 357,000 square kilometers, second only to the Soviet Union in Europe, France and Spain; GNP up to about $ 1.4 trillion, the equivalent to the sum of Britain and France, ranking first in Europe. Of course, the deepest meaning of the reunification of Germany was not lying on population growth and expansion of territory, but on the new German politics. As the division of Germany was linked with the defeat, the reunited Germany got international recognition could be considered as that Germany completely ended the vanquished country position. It was bound to make Germany demand and hope for more in international affairs.

2.3.2 The main strategies of Japan and FRG in achieving political power

After Japan and the Federal Republic of Germany expressed the desire to achieve their own political power and set up the political objectives on the strong economic basis, they began to make policies to achieve this goal. Although the two countries differed in their emphasis on different issues at different times, because of the historical conditions and constraints of the international environment, the main way to seek political power for them was roughly the same.

Change from "master-slave relationship" to "equal relationship" in the alliance

In the Western alliance the United States had the chief role because of the conditions and the objective situation at the time of establishing alliance. For a long time, the inside and outside decision-making power was in the hands of the United States, and its allies barely had the power to decide, especially the vanquished countries like Japan and West Germany. They couldn't have their own voice because their long-term loss of national sovereignty. Since Japan and the Federal Republic of Germany got recognized by the international community step by step and established their position as world economic power, especially in the 1970s after being accepted into the United Nations, due to the shift of the strength and the changes in the international environment, they waned the pressure of following the lead of the United States. They strived to transform the league's "master-slave relationship", "dependence relationship" to the "equal relationship". Even though it was impossible to achieve full equality, they also wanted to expand this equal relationship gradually from every little bit.

The Federal Republic of Germany's "Ostpolitik" which began in the 1960s could be regarded as the attempt to fight for this "equal relationship". The same thing had also undergone in Japan at the same time. Throughout the 1960s, Japan-US relations were at a relatively tight stage. There were three reasons for this tension: First, the high-speed development of the Japanese economy led to the prolonged trade friction between Japan and the US; the second was about "returning" Okinawa. The delay of reaching an agreement between Japan and the US caused a burning hatred among the Japanese people; Third, Johnson administration' of the United States launched the Vietnam War. There was a strong anti-war sentiment in Japan, and the people all worried about being involved in the war. Nixon took office in 1969, although since the solving of the problem of Vietnam War and Okinawa gradually eased the Japan-US conflict, a strategic breakthrough in the Sino-US relations gave the Japan-US relations new pressure.

On July 15, 1971, Chinese and the US governments issued a joint statement declaring that the US President Richard Nixon would visit China before May 1972. This major diplomatic action that could be called as the model of secret diplomacy in world history was like thunder. Japan was the first country affected from that secret diplomacy. Like the other countries of the world, the Japanese government did not know anything about it beforehand. It seemed extremely unusual for Japan. It was "over-top diplomacy". Japan was fooled and deceived. In Japan, the core issue of the Japan-US alliance was involved the Asian and Pacific region. The two countries should carry out prior consultation and communication, which was the basic principle of the Japan-US security system for decades. The move of the United States went against this principle. On the other hand, the strategic transformation of the Sino-US relations impose pressure to Japan's relations with China which remained in a sensitive state for a long time, and made it stay in a passive state. In order to gain the initiative, in 1972, Japanese Prime Minister Tanaka took a "retaliatory action" against Nixon's visit in February. In September, Prime Minister Tanaka signed the "Sino-Japanese Joint Statement" during the visit to China, and announced the establishment of diplomatic relations before the United States. Normalization of relations was finally achieved. This was an unprecedented action independent of the United States in Japan's post-War history of diplomacy.

It needed to be reminded that we should not understand Japanese diplomatic action independent of the United States in a narrow sense. Acting
independently seemed refer to the opposing action which was retaliation. In
fact, in the Japan-US relations, although there were some independent actions for Japan saying "no" to the US, but the most of relations with the US
was not to act independently saying "no" to the United States, but under the
premise of "yes" striving to act as an independent nation. This independent
action was consistent with Japan's special circumstances and its strategy of
seeking political power. It was impossible for Japan to become a political
power while being against the United States because the conditions in Japan
and abroad. Therefore, actively cooperating with the United States and the
superpower in international affairs to make "super action" and shouldering
the responsibility as a big country and as an independent sovereign state
were the major features of Japan's pursuit of a political power position.

The independence manifested by the Federal Republic of Germany had been
fully reflected in the "Ostpolitik", and the requirement of this independence became stronger. If we divide the US and Europe conflicts after World War II into
several stages, then, in the 1950s, it was not mainly directly reflected between
the US and Europe, but reflected within their sphere of influence, such as the
North Korea war, the Indo-China war, the Suez war, the Algerian War, and so
on; to the 1960s, the US and Europe had begun to directly confront with each
other, of which the most representative was the US-French relations, Charles
de Gaulle became a leader in fighting for independence; after the 70s, the US-
European conflict spread to almost all areas, especially with the development
of the European Community, increasing trade disputes, and the differences on
the East-West relations had become increasingly evident, European tendency of
being independent from the United States had been not only showed by France
people. In spite of the different extent in each country, this became a universal phenomenon. Among them, the strategic differences between the Federal
Republic of Germany and the United States became increasingly greater. In
April 1974, following Brandt, Helmut Schmidt took the position of Federal
Chancellor of Germany. Schmidt had been in office for eight years. During that
period, two main characteristics of the Federal Republic of Germany's foreign
relations were: the US-German tensions were about the differences in strategy
and the European alliance motivated by the harmonious relationship between
France and Germany. Schmidt was a strategist advocating balance of power. He
once wrote Western strategy and Strategic Balance and other works.[46]

---

46   Helmut Schmidt, Eine Strategie für den Western (germ.), Berlin, 1986; Helmut
Schmidt, Strategy of Balancing Power: German Peace Policy and Superpowers, trans and
published by Shanghai People's Press, 1975, pp.23-27.

During Schmidt's reign, after the international situation the period of stalemate of reforming arms between the Soviet Union and the US had eased for a moment. Schmidt had serious differences with the United States around medium-range missile problem in the deployment in Europe. The United States advocated negotiations after deployment, while Schmidt advocated negotiations before deployment – there would be no deployment after a successful negotiation, because nobody in Europe wanted to add more nuclear weapons in their own country; Schmidt advocated nuclear deterrence—but it must be global, not just within the European Otherwise it would be difficult to deter the Soviet Union. The important thing was for the United States to control the war in Europe; Schmidt emphasized conventional superiority while advocating nuclear deterrence, and opposed the US policy of nuclear weapons "first nuclear strike" to drag Europe into a nuclear holocaust; Schmidt advocated insisting the dual policy towards the Soviet Union in Europe—could not give up easing Europe because of other regional issues, and opposed the US hard-line policy towards the Soviet Union after the incident of opposing Afghanistan. It was easy to see that, strategic differences rooted from the strategic interests. The essence of the problem was that the Germans, after the French in the 60s, once again raised the issue of whom Europeans took the risk for.

Germany achieved reunification in Drastic Change in 1989. It was no longer a "minors" with guardianship huddled in the European Community and the Atlantic Alliance. After the reunification, Germany's position in Europe, compared with the US position in Europe after the Cold War and Yalta system collapsed, was up, contradicting with the down of the latter. The top issues in international public opinion were whether the United States needed to keep a leading role in Europe, if so, to what extent; and whether it was German's Europe or European Germany. This also showed the special status of the two countries in Europe. After the reunification of Germany. Germany immediately demanded publicly that allied aircrafts should not fly at low altitude airspace in Germany. The German government also summoned national envoys who had troops stationed in Germany to discuss the problem of how to reduce the military exercises of foreign troops in its territory, and called for banning short-range nuclear weapons as soon as possible. Public opinion was that all these were challenging relations with the United States.

Japan and the FRG's active involvement in the international hotspot issues, gradual surmounting of the military restriction

Since the beginning of the world history, any political power must first be a military power. In history, and currently there is no country which has a political power and relevant rights of say in political affairs but does not have proper military power. If there was no strategic breakthrough made related to the bottleneck problem of armaments constraints, Japan and the Federal Republic of Germany would not have the political power to the so because as defeated countries, they were imposed a special status of military restraint.

Since Japan and the Federal Republic of Germany became the members of the US-led Western alliance, the two governments regarded the question of how to break the military constraint as an important agenda. For example, from 1954, the Japanese army developed in the name of Self-Defense Force had become a modern army with a full range of combat capabilities. Germany's military forces sufficiently developed under the name of "NATO obligations". Into the late 1980s, Japan and the Federal Republic of Germany's desire of becoming political powers grew increasingly. They urgently wanted to participate actively in international hot issues and to enhance military strength.

In July 1991, when the three Baltic republics in the Soviet Union, Croatia and Slovenia of Yugoslavia required to be independent, the German government firstly admitted the independence of the three Baltic countries, and later also officially recognized the independence of Croatia and Slovenia and urged other Western countries to recognized their independence. In 1993, the German Federal Constitutional Court broken the "forbidden zone" of sending troops abroad in terms of the Basic Law that ruled Germany can participate in UN peacekeeping operations like other countries. On July 12, 1994, the German Constitutional Court also ruled that Germany could send troops to areas outside the NATO within the framework of the United Nations or NATO with the prerequisite of getting the approval of the Bundestag. Germany believed that, as a member of the United Nations, the international community had reason to expect that Germany after the reunification would unlimitedly involve in the tasks and actions of the United Nations, of course, including military action. Germany joined the charity held by the United Nations in Cambodia and peace military operations in Somalia. By the end of 1995, approximately 3,600 Bundeswehr soldiers joined the NATO peacekeeping force in Bosnia. On January1, 1997, they began to join stabilizing force troops stationed in Croatia and Italy. In 1999,

Germany participated in the NATO war against Yugoslavia as a member of the NATO. This is the first time after World War II that Germany participated in a war against a sovereign state, which indicated that the Germany had great breakthrough in lifting the military constraints of the vanquished countries. After the "9/11", Germany sent 3,900 soldiers to Afghanistan, expressing full support for the US military action against terrorism in Afghanistan.

Germany's move made Japan who always wanted to become a political power by military. If Japan wanted to break the military constraint, the biggest obstacle was the "peace constitution" developed in early post-War. Because Article IX of the Constitution clearly stipulated that Japan "forever gives up the approach of renouncing war as a sovereign state, and the threat or use of force to settle international disputes". "It does not keep the armed forces and other combat forces. The country's right of belligerency will not be recognized". Obviously, an act of giving up war was explicit in Japanese Constitution.[47] Therefore, the Japanese action of breaking the military constraints was preformed simultaneously with the action to amend the Constitution.

Since 1991, Japan had tried to break the constitutional constraints on military actions by sending Japanese minesweepers to the Persian Gulf in the Gulf War. In 1992, the Japanese Diet passed "Cooperation Act of United Nations peacekeeping activities", and sent peacekeepers to Cambodia for the first time. In 1996, under the requirement to further strengthen the Japan-US military alliance system, the new "Japan-US Defense Cooperation Guidelines" was going to be introduced, aiming at expanding the scope of the functions and activities of the SDF. By 1999, Japan's parliament passed a new "Japan-US Defense Cooperation Guidelines", changing the conditions for the exercise of force from "after the invasion by the enemy" to "when under the threat of the enemy". Under the influence of the NATO war against Yugoslavia, Japan also adopted "surrounding situation law", corresponding to "military intervention outside the region" of NATO's new strategy. It clarified that the future affairs of the war in the Taiwan Strait would be included. Not only the scope of the defense could be arbitrarily expanded, but also the support for the US can be provided. In 1999, the Japanese Diet passed the "national flag, national anthem bill", and reaffirmed the legal status of "Hinomaru" and "Kimigayo" which had the features of militarism and had been controversial in the post-war in order to guide the people to confirm the state's actor and to pave the way for becoming

---

47 Concise Japan Encyclopedia by Chinese Academy of Social Sciences, China Social Science Press, 1994, p.137.

a political power. Still in 1999, Japan formally announced its participation in the development of the missile defense system in the US Theater, and substantially increased the defense budget. After 2001, the "9/11" incident, the Japanese Diet passed the Koizumi government's "anti-terrorism bill", including "Special Measures Act towards Terrorist", "Self-Defense Forces Law Amendment", "Coast Guard Amendment". These Acts regulated that Japan could participate in anti-terrorist activities around the world. In June 2003, Japan adopted the "three emergency bill" to confirm the Japanese prime minister could directly send troops to perform military actions without the approval of Congress in emergencies. In December, the Japanese decided to officially send troops to Iraq "to perform humanitarian missions".

In April 2004, with the primary purpose of amending the Constitution, Japan's Liberal Democratic Party (Kempo chosaki) determined the constitutional amendment of Article IX, that Japan might exercise the right of collective self-defense. Then, when "something" occurs the Japanese Diet passed 7 bills including the "National Protection Act". According to these laws, the Japanese government had the right to deploy the SDF directly to the country and to take the necessary military action in an emergency situation. Public thought these bills are an important complement to Japan's "Three emergency bills" passed in the previous year. The bills regulated that when Japan confronted a foreign armed attack or an anticipated attack, the Japanese government and the Japanese Self-Defense Forces would be able fight and protect the Japanese nationals, which meant that Japan's war legislation was thoroughly completed. These related bills continued to be passed, in essence, they paved the way for amending peace constitution "by peripheral legislation to make constitution ineffective" and for becoming a political power. Japan's step to revise the constitution got tighter, and entered the countdown.

Speaking of surmounting military constraints, the international community has more sensitive issue in today's world and that is nuclear proliferation. In the 20th century, since the advent of the atomic bomb, after Japan became the first victim, nuclear confrontation is linked to the "big country", known as "nuclear power"; the country which has the initial possession of nuclear deterrence. Naturally, "nuclear threshold" had become the threshold leading to political power in many people's minds. In fact, after more and more countries had mastered the nuclear capability, the "nuclear power" and the political power would never be the same. Nuclear capability only became a power show in some countries and the leverage of bargaining in international disputes, but did not equal to great power status. After the end of World War II, Japan and the Federal Republic of Germany were restricted in military. Though the restriction decreased as the time passed but the restriction of manufacturing nuclear weapons had never decreased and the restraint of limiting the production of conventional weapons had no longer existed. In October 1954, "the Paris agreement" provided conditions for the Federal Republic of Germany to participate in the NATO. According to additional terms of this Agreement, Adenauer had made a statement that the Federal Republic of Germany would never adopt "ABC" weaponry for German army, and prohibited the production of these weapons on the territory of the Federal Republic.[48] So was Japan. Back in the 1960s, Sato Cabinet had conducted research on this, and ultimately put forward the "three non-nuclear principles": Do not develop, do not possess, and do not apply the nuclear weapons. For a long time in Japan, the issue that whether Japan should possess nuclear weapons or not was prohibited to discuss. But it did not mean that Japan and the Federal Republic of Germany could not afford to develop nuclear weapons and technology, or wanted to show that nobody had a tendency to break the ban. By the end of 1960, the United States proposed multilateral nuclear force plan to NATO allies.

The Federal Germany showed great interest, because this plan would enable the West Germany to participate in the activities of the nuclear club. In 1962, the Federal Republic of Germany suggested the formation of a multinational fleet with nuclear weapons. In 1965, the West German foreign minister Schroeder made it clear that the prerequisite of Federal Republic of Germany's abandoning its nuclear efforts was that preventing the Soviet Union to obstruct the reunification of Germany. This was even more evident in Japan. In recent years, some Japanese ultranationalists required to possess nuclear weapons in public. In 1999, the Japanese Defense Agency Chief Minister Shingo Nishimura advocated the development of nuclear weapons, and called for discussion on this issue. Thus, he was later condemned to resign. In mid 2002, Japanese Chief Cabinet Secretary Yasuo Fukuda said publicly that the Constitution did not prevent Japan from acquiring nuclear weapons, Tokyo Governor Shintaro Ishihara quickly responded. Japan's anti-Liberal Party leader Ichiro Ozawa also said Japan could deal with any threat from China as long as it produced "three or four thousand nuclear warheads".[49]

---

48   "ABC" refers to Atomiques, Bacteriologiques, Chimiques. Andre Fontaine, *Strange Bedfellows – History of 'Detente', 1962-1981*, p.70.
49   Eugene A. Matthews, "Japan's New Nationalism", in *Foreign Affairs*, November/ December 2003.

According to Xinhua News Agency's repost of Japan's Kyodo news on June 18, 2004, the forthcoming memoir of former Japanese Prime Minister Nakasone which would be published on June 25, 2004 revealed that Nakasone had once served as the Japanese Defense Agency's chief (1970-1971), and had ordered Defense Agency officials to carry out a study on the development of nuclear power. In Nakasone's words, he had been against the Japanese development and possession of nuclear weapons, "but if the US withdraws its nuclear umbrella, the situation will be completely different.... In this case, Japan would have to consider all options, including arming themselves with nuclear weapons"[50].

In order to achieve the goal of political power, with the excuse of maintaining its own security, Japan could not be completely ruled out from the countries which had the possibility acquiring nuclear weapons.

As the US key ally, Japan and the Federal Republic of Germany changed their living environment and expanded the place of activities, but also improved the international status by joining alliance. However, any alliance for the purpose of achieving security and competition was not able to escape the shadow of the threat of military and war, and must lead to other countries' suspicion and anxiety, let alone the country which had war misdeeds, such as Japan and Germany. Japan and the Federal Republic of Germany recognized that it was unlikely to depend on the military alliance alone to achieve the goal of political power. Only by taking full advantage of safe conditions provided by the military alliance, participating in as wider range of activities of various international organizations as possible, and shouldering the big powers' responsibilities and obligations, they would maximize their role and influence to foreshadowing a broader basis for achieving the goal of political power. Japan and the Federal Republic of Germany had more advantages than any other country in this regard. First, it was because they are the alliance with the United States. With the support of the US and its allies, Japan and the Federal Republic of Germany almost had all the accesses to any international organizations. Second, it was because Japan and the Federal Republic of Germany had strong economic strength. They provided strong financial support for these international organizations, enough to make the two countries play a greater role. After years of effort, Japan and the Federal Republic of Germany had become important members in many influential international organizations. For example, Japan and the Federal Republic of Germany were both members of the United Nations and they were non-permanent members for many times, acted actively among the permanent members, and were the first to participate in "7 + 1"

---

50   Feature of Xin Hua News Agency, 19 June, 2004.

National summit. Japan was a major member of the Asian Development Bank, which not only played a role in ASEAN "10 + 3" meeting, but also the participant of North Korea six-party talks. Germany was a member of the NATO, the EU, the OSCE and other organizations. So, in many international organizations, where was the Japan and West Germany focused on?

For the Federal Republic of Germany main issue was the strengthening the EU construction. European unity was to strengthen the degree of supranational integration. German unification was to strengthen the strength of independent nations. European Community (predecessor of the European Union) when it is established had a very clear political purpose: to prevent Germany reignited the war in Europe, using a new coalition of supranational institutions. Clearly, a united, strong and unfettered political power, Federal Germany, was inconsistent with this purpose. However, in the decades after the war, Germany's politicians combined the "European unity" and "German unification", the two political goals with contradictory interests. In promoting the European unification Germany achieved unification. Germany searched its "core country" status in the quest of building the European Union into a "super-state" and paved its way for becoming a political power. Did Germany put Europe's interests above the interests of the nation? The answer was no. The only explanation was that Germany integrated national interests into the interests of Europe. Germany adopted the foreign relations guideline of "maximizing German interests against the European interests". Meanwhile, the Federal Republic of Germany also attached great importance to the status and role in the United Nations. When talking about the UN reform, the maintenance and enhancement of the legitimacy and efficiency of the United Nations, the Federal Republic of Germany thought it was necessary to enlarge the number of permanent members of the UN Security Council, which should be expanded to big countries, such as Germany, Japan, India, Brazil and South Africa.

For Japan, regardless of strengthening the assistance and cooperation, seeking support and improving relations in East Asia, it seemed that Japan have a greater interest about its position and its role in the United Nations than the Federal Republic of Germany. Japan joined the United Nations in 1956. It had always wanted to change its "enemy" status in the United Nations and to upgrade its voice. The Ministry of Foreign Affairs of Japan also raised the "UN-centered" approach. Japan established the goal of political power in the 1980s, and from the 90s onwards publicly demanded a higher power in the UN. Although it has been a non-permanent member for the most time today Japan is one of the members of United Nations. Japan bears for about 20% of the dues, only less than the United States.

Japan is the most active country to promote the UN reform and had three key objectives for the reform of the United Nations: First, to delete the "enemy clause" in the "UN Charter" (without deleting this, Japan never felt it has dignity in the United Nations);[51] Second, to adjust the members' contributions ratio; the third was to enlarge the number of members of the UN Security Council–the key was to increase the number of permanent members. In fact, the subtext of the whole "UN reform" was that Japan would become a permanent member of the United Nations. To this end, Japan launched a diplomatic movement thoroughly. The folks set up a "United Nations Reform Insight Conference". The main task of the politicians' visit was to lobby to support Japan becoming a permanent member.

Japan and Germany still making their move to become permanent members of the UN, but it is hard to get a result. Thus, though the desire of Japan and Germany is to have political power rather than being a "normal state" but there is a long way to go, because they have a history of bringing manmade disasters to the world after all. Making people forget this history is impossible; it takes time to make people change their opinion of Japan and Germany. It is more necessary for Japan and Germany to face their history. European neighbors' attitude towards Germany is totally different with Asian neighbors' attitude towards Japan, which also confirmed this point.

---

51   On 11 December, 1995, the UN passed the Japan's, Germany's and Italy's proposal on the UN Charter by majority without revising the constitution, and cancelled the bill of "Enemy Clause". – Author's note.

Chapter III

The Process of Post-War European Integration

The rise of the post-war European integration movement was a new phenomenon in the development of international relations after World War II. As used herein, "Europe", followed a traditional usage. As we all know, the European integration was started with Western Europe, and then gradually expanded to other European places. The EU now has been extended to Central and Eastern Europe. However, the word "Europe" was used when the "European Coal and Steel Community" which is the first institution of the European integration movement that had a supranational nature was founded. Besides, according to articles this was an open institution that "other European countries can join".[1]

Later in the development process of European integration movement also used the concept of "Europe" instead of "Western Europe". In general, the generalized "integration" is "combination of parts into a whole", which means "the process or result of two or more originally independent units combining into a larger unit".[2]

The narrow sense of "European integration" refers to the post-war European Union and unity on the nation-state basis. This integration requires the creation of such "super-national institutions" like "European Coal and Steel Community" and "European Economic Community". The Member States as part of the policy need to transfer decision-making authority to supranational institutions, and are subject to certain constraints

---

1   Pierre Berge, Trans, Ding Yifan, The History and Reality of the European Integration, China Social Sciences Publishing House, 1989, p.102.
2   Chen Yugang, Nations and Super Nations – Comparative Study of European Integration Theories, Shanghai People's Press, 2001, p.5.

of the institution to distinguish from general government cooperation.[3] So the "European integration" mentioned here refers to the joint process of European countries started by Western Europe and featured by establishing supranational institutions after the war, particularly a development process to introduce European integration from the perspective of the state and the relationship between the states, rather than a general process of simple description of the rise and development of European integration.

3.1 French-German Approximation and the Beginning of European Integration

European integration refers to the joint process of European countries started by Western Europe and featured by establishing supranational institutions after the war. According to this definition, the beginning of European integration should be the validity of "the European Coal and Steel Community Treaty" in 1952 and the establishment of its supranational community as "senior agency". However, history is not severed and it is easy to produce. After the end of World War II, the international situation and various dedicated efforts of European integration were crucial for the integration of history.

In the history of post-war European integration, French-German relations have been occupying a pivotal position. French-German reconciliation was the precondition and foundation of European integration. The close cooperation between France and Germany was the important driving force of the progress of European integration, and also the basis for the future European Union. Especially in the early days of European integration, the French-German relationship determined the fate and direction of European integration, so its importance was self-evident.

3.1.1 French-German relations in the early post-War era

Post-War European integration was based on reconciliation and cooperation between France and Germany. But in the early post-War period, the France did not have the intention to make reconciliation with Germany. The main objective of its foreign policy was to weaken Germany, even to dismember Germany to prevent the German comeback in order to ensure its military and economic security. Thus reconciliation and cooperation was not opted by France. Well, how did France and Germany achieve the transition from opposition to detention, from hostility to reconciliation?

---

3   Martine J. Dedman, The Origins and Development of the European Union, 1945-1995, Routledge, London, 1996, p.7.

France's early post-War policy towards Germany

In the early Post-War period, French foreign policy had two characteristics: Weakening Germany and applying neutral policy between the Soviet Union and the US. Reconciliation with Germany and advancing European integration together with the German were not included in the objectives of France's foreign policy.

In November 1944, Charles de Gaulle visited the Soviet Union, and signed the "Treaty of Mutual Alliance" which was mainly aimed at dealing Germany with the Soviet Union, attempting to maintain a balance between the Soviet Union and the US to raise France's international status and restricting Germany as an enemy with the Soviet Union. France's policy to weaken Germany was easy to understand. The Second World War was already the third war between France and Germany for 70 years, and they were all German invasions. These three wars had enormous effects on France. The French nation suffered great losses and humiliation time and time again. Therefore, it was not difficult to understand the post-war French foreign policy found it difficult to get rid of the concerns of German invasion, alert and deep hostility towards Germany.

During the interim government Charles de Gaulle 1944-1947, French policy towards Germany basically followed de Gaulle's view. In August 1945, General de Gaulle said to the US President Harry Truman that three times of the German invasion in France made the French people's lives and property suffer huge losses. Therefore, the French had the right and obligation of requiring to ensure their own safety, that was, in order to ensure safety, they required to dismember Germany and to destroy Germany completely.[4] Early in November 1943, on the Tehran Conference, the "Big Three" (the United States, Britain, and the Soviet Union) discussed and agreed to the division of Germany. On Yalta Conference in February 1945, Roosevelt and Stalin insisted the policy of punishing Germany. Churchill agreed in principle. The details were discussed on the three foreign ministers meeting.

The Soviet Union with the United States' and Britain's insistence agreed on about France to participate in the German occupation. France was also allowed to participate in allies' Control Commission for Germany and occupied the part of Germany, as a vengeance of the failure in 1940. However, Germany was still the scourge of France. The French required participating in decisions about affecting the fate of Germany. On the Potsdam conference

---

4 F. Roy Willis, France, Germany, and the New Europe, 1945-1967, London: Oxford University Press, 1968, p.15.

in July 1945, Truman replaced the former US President Roosevelt who is explicitly opposed the dismemberment of the Germany and claims of obtaining huge compensation. The "Big Three" made a modest change of policy towards Germany. The meeting finally decided that, Germany should be regarded as "a single economic unit" managed by the four military chiefs of the occupation zones; the meeting proposed to set up department of German finances, transportation, communications, foreign trade and industry with a centralized authority.

Charles de Gaulle was not invited to the Potsdam Conference and he didn't have the opportunity to complain to the United States and Britain, Anyway "Potsdam" was not as Charles de Gaulle had imagined it. After the Potsdam conference, French Foreign Minister Bidault notified the United States, Britain and the Soviet ambassador that the French government would not accept some of the terms in the Potsdam resolutions, mainly including: Article 8 (iv), that proposal of the establishment of a centralized administrative departments in Germany, such as the Ministry of Finance, Ministry of Transportation, communications Department, Ministry of Foreign Trade and Industry; Article 14, that was written during the occupation. Germany should be regarded as an economic unit; Article 15 (c), requirement of fair distribution of important commodities among the occupied territories to achieve economic balance in Germany and to reduced demand for imports.[5]

The reason why France was opposed these was that these provisions would re-establish a unified and centralized Germany. In early post-War, the objective of France policy towards Germany was very clear, that was to prevent Germany become a unified, centralized, powerful country once again, to ensure military and economic security of France.

In September 1945, the Foreign Minister of France, the United States, Britain, and the Soviet Union had a meeting in London. France formally put forward their own plan towards Germany, including: First, not allowing the reconstruction of the centralized Germany, opposing the creation of a national political party and central Germany administrative bodies. Second, the Rhineland, the left coastal region of Rhine should depart from Germany. The south of Cologne had used for invading France, it should be occupied permanently by France; north area of Cologne should be jointly governed by the Netherlands, Belgium and the United Kingdom. Third was to achieve the internationalization of the Ruhr and economic integration between

---

5   France, Ministere des affaires etrangeres, Documents francais relatifs a l'Allemagne, 1945-1947, Paris, 1947. Quoted in Roy Willis, France, Germany and New Europe, 1945-1967, pp.16-17.

Saar and France. In addition, Charles de Gaulle also required a large number of claims and the demolition of German factories, in order to compensate for the loss of France's war. These ideas formed the so-called "French program"[6]; the French policy towards Germany after the war. As can be seen, the so-called "French plan" had only one theme, that was to dismember and weaken Germany. A few months after the Potsdam Conference, the French representative in the Control Commission and its subsidiary bodies rejected every proposal trying to rebuild German centralized government, which made the Control Commission off work. Until January 20th, 1946, when Charles de Gaulle stepped down, he had successfully established the French position on the German question. Even after his departure, the French government's policy towards Germany did not change immediately.

Of course, as a visionary statesman, Charles de Gaulle had broader, more ambitious goal. His plan was to "make the countries near the Rhine, the Alps and the Pyrenees a political, economic and strategic alliance and to make this organization become one of the world's three greatest powers; when necessary, making it the arbiter between the two camps; the Soviet Union and the Anglo Saxon"[7].

De Gaulle planned to make Europe the "third force" between the Soviet Union and the US, and to act as balancing the Soviet Union and the US, thus highlighting the great power status of France and restoring the greatness of France.

"The French plan" almost received unanimous support from the extreme left-wing to extreme right-wing political parties in France, but was opposed by the United States, Britain, and the Soviet Union. In July 12, 1946, Soviet Foreign Minister Molotov explicitly rejected the French proposal for the Ruhr and Saar, that the implementation of the internationalization of Ruhr and economic integration of Saar and France; and the United States, Britain, and the Soviet Union considered Rhineland's separation from Germany is unacceptable.

During March 1947, foreign ministers of the United States, Britain, the Soviet Union, and France held a meeting in Moscow. French Foreign Minister Bidault made his last effort for the "French program". He proposed the establishment of a federal system of Germany, and allowing local governments to have great executive powers, and the Ruhr internationalization.

---

6   Roy Willis, France, Germany and New Europe, 1945-1967, p.15.
7   Charles de Gaulle, Memoires de Guerre, Le Salut 1944-1946, Librairie Plon, 1959, p.216.

Molotov rejected the proposal of isolating the Ruhr and Rhineland from Germany, refusing to establish a decentralized federal state and deliberately say nothing about the French request on Saar. Having slighter attitude than the Soviet Union, representatives of the US and British agreed with the economic integration of the Saar and France, and also promised to supply German coal to France.

The Moscow conference firstly marked the failure of French policy towards Germany. France's proposal of to dismembering Germany was rejected by the United States, Britain, and the Soviet Union. So for France it would be hard to do it alone. Secondly, because Molotov opposed French policy towards Germany, France was moving away from the Soviet Union, while moving closer to the United States and Britain on European issues and the German question. It became apparent that the French gave up acting as a balance and an arbiter between East and West. Third, the Moscow meeting was affected by the "Truman Doctrine". The antagonism between the United States and the Soviet intensified. Their relations gradually fell into the Cold Warcrisis, which dissapointed France which expected to act as arbitrator between the East and West.

Changes in French policy towards Germany and the founding of the Federal Republic of Germany

During 1947, French policy towards Germany began to recoil, and a major shift was taking place. It not only gradually abandoned the policy of dismembering Germany and weakening Germany, but tolerated the establishment of the Federal Republic of Germany; at the same time France also gave up acting as a "third force" between the Soviet Union and the US, and stood by the side of the US and Britain.

In 1947 the international situation was quite different than at the end of the World War II. In March 12, Truman read the statement, later known as the "Truman Doctrine" to the joint session of Congress, asking Congress authorization to provide four hundred million US dollars of aid to Greece, Turkey, which got congressional support. Truman explained, "This is the United States answer to the expansion of the communist tyrant tide", it was "a turning point in the US foreign policy". He said, "No matter where if the peace is directly or indirectly threatened than it is the United States safety concern". The introduction of Truman Doctrine showed that the United States would fight against the Soviet Union at any place, and it was a sign of the official start of the Cold War, but also a declaration of the US global expansion strategy. From the standpoint of dominating the world and containing the Soviet Union's global strategy, the United States promoted the policy of reviving Europe and supporting West Germany. On June 5, the US Secretary of State Marshall published a famous speech at Harvard University, proposing "Marshall Plan" to aid Europe. Unlike in the past, the United States stressed that this was not a bilateral aid. The Europeans must agree with each other to develop a list of resources, needs and a common revival program. European cooperation and integration was the prerequisite of the United States to provide assistance. The United States did not accept a divided Europe, a dismembered, poor and weak Germany. As early as September 6th, 1946, the US Secretary of State Byrnes pointed out in his famous speech in Stuttgart that if Germany became a slum, then Europe could not be recovered.[8]

Obviously, the US attitude on the German question run counter to French proposition of dismembering and weakening Germany. France must make a choice. From October to December in 1947, France had received the US emergency aid of $ 337 million, and on January 2, 1948 it received 284 million US dollars. From April 1948 to April 1949, France received $989 million.[9] Relying on the economic assistance of the US, France had to give up acting as a "third force" between the Soviet Union and the US, and chose the side of the US. On the German question, France abandoned their tough policy towards Germany, and no longer mentioned the dismemberment of Germany. It began to re-adjust its policy towards Germany as in the situation of the Cold War.

In Stuttgart speech, Byrnes clearly opposed to separate the left bank of the Rhine from German, and also opposed to place the Ruhr under international condominium. He advocated for economic unity in the United States, Britain, and France, the three occupied territories, and thereby establishing a federal state. He clearly supported the French request to the Saar in exchange for French concessions on the question of Germany. "If the Saar is incorporated in France, then France should reconsider its requirement of German compensation, in order to adapt to changing circumstances".[10]

In addition, he declared: "The US people are willing to return the German government to the German people".[11]

---

8   Kondrad Adenauer's Memoirs, Vol.1, Shanghai People's Press, 1976, p.110.
9   F. Roy Willis, France, Germany, and the New Europe, 1945-1967, London: Oxford University Press, 1968, p.20.
10   Kondrad Adenauer's Memoirs, Vol.1, Shanghai People's Press, 1976, p.105.
11   Ibid., pp 109-110.

On May 29, 1947, Bilateral Economic Commission of the US and British occupation zone was established. The merger of the US and British occupation zone was in full swing. Pressed harder and harder by the US and Britain, France had to admit the progress of double occupied zone, and further considered the possibility of merging the three occupied territories and the establishment of the German government agencies.

On June 27, 1947, foreign ministers of Britain, France, and the Soviet Union held a preparatory meeting in Paris to discuss matters relating to the European Recovery Program.

Because there was a big difference, the Soviet delegation quitted after three days and denounced the Marshall Plan to split Europe into two groups, resulting in dangerous German domination of Europe again. East-West relations deteriorated sharply. In December 1947, on the four foreign ministers of four nations' meeting in London, the Soviet Union proposed to cancel merger of the US and British occupation zones, and immediately establish a democratic government in Germany. It was rejected by the other three ministers. Foreign ministers' meeting in London declared a complete breakdown. East-West relations deteriorated to a greater extent.

In February 1948, representatives of the United States, Britain, France, the Netherlands, Belgium, and Luxembourg discussed the German question in London. Excluding the Soviet Union, it was called the six-nation conference in London. Central theme of the meeting was to set up German government in the Western district, and finally reached a "London Agreement": The west occupation German Constitutional Convention was held in September the 1st to make constitution, in order to set up a federal rather than centralized German government in 1949; also provided the Ruhr coal and steel were controlled by six countries and Germany. "London Agreement" negated almost all the important principles of "French plan": the Rhineland did not receive special treatment; Ruhr industry was still in German hands; so rather than a loose confederation close to France, they were going to establish a German government which would have police, legislative and taxation powers . However, after being satisfied on the Saar problem, France agreed to the terms of "London Agreement". Later the discussion on French National Assembly got extremely difficult, with only eight votes of advantage (297 votes to 289 votes) approving the protocol. The agreement cleared the way for the establishment of the Federal Republic of Germany. On August 20, 1949, the Federal Republic of Germany was proclaimed. On October 7, the German Democratic Republic was proclaimed. Since then, Germany formally split into two countries, East and West Germany was partitioned into two camps, East and West.

France approved the "London Agreement", which marked that it gave up acting as arbitrator between the Soviet Union and the US, and clearly chose the Western camp. On the German question, France agreed to set up the Federal Republic of Germany, marking that it abandoned the policy of dismembering and weakening Germany, relations between France and Germany changed from the opposition to détente, from hostility to reconciliation. As Schumann said, "From 1948 onwards, a constructive cooperation and a policy gradually enhancing the trust replaced the policy of restrained and distrust".[12]

First, the French-German reconciliation was the product of the post-war international situation. Because France and Germany belong to the victors and the vanquished, their statuses were very different, in the course of the French-German reconciliation, the French attitude and policy undoubtedly played a decisive role. The World War II made the old European powers, including France and Germany become a second-rate country, but enhanced the strength of the US and the Soviet Union, expanded their influence, made them have tremendous advantages on politics, economy and military power. Soon after the war, the Soviet Union and the US ended the wartime alliance between the two countries, and opened the prelude to the Cold War. The Cold War pushed Western Europe to the forefront of US-Soviet confrontation. The living environment of the Western European countries deteriorated, and the political situation undergone profound changes. France and Germany became weakened moderate countries in the same camp. They had to survive and develop between the US-Soviet Cold War. Therefore resolving the feud, reconciliation and cooperation had become the common needs of France and Germany. For France, the Cold War made Soviet overtake Germany as the new opponent of France. The main objectives of security and defense of the French turned to the Soviet Union from Germany. On the Soviet threat, Germany after the reconciliation with France would become the security barrier for France. France changed from being in French-Soviet alliance to contain the Soviet Union in the Western camp. Therefore, it was natural that the French policy towards Germany transformed from dismemberment, hostility into reconciliation and cooperation. For Germany, as the vanquished and occupied country, the German economy got trapped in depression after the war. It had lost its sovereignty, and became internationally deprived and frustrated. It was struggling. French-German reconciliation was an important way out of the German diplomatic difficulties and restoring sovereignty and economic renaissance. Only by reconciliation between Germany and France, relying on the

---

12   R. Schuman, Foreign Policy towards Germany Since the War, London, 1953, p.9.

European integration policy, could it achieve the dream of reconstruction and rehabilitation. On November 3rd, 1949, when Chancellor Adenauer met the US "Time" magazine reporter, it was evaluated as an "ice-breaking" interview. He commented: "I am determined to take relations with Germany and France as a fundamental point of our policy. .... The friendship with France will become a point of our policy, because it is the weak link in our policy."[13]

Second, the United States policy towards Europe and Germany had a great influence on France's foreign policy. The US-Soviet cooperation which turned into a Cold War situation was the need for confrontation with the Soviet Union. The United States hoped Europe could be unified to achieve renaissance, and effectively "contain" communism expansion. Meanwhile, the US policy towards Germany had also been eased. The United States realized that Germany which would be part of the integration in Western Europe could not only relieve worries about Germany's nearing to the Soviet camp, but it would also the best constraints for German military expansion. Supporting Germany and making it joining European integration became the integral part of the US policy towards Europe. Therefore, the US spared no effort to support the implementation of the policy of supporting West Germany. France was economically dependent on the US aid, and was supported and protected politically and militarily by the United States, so it was impossible to implement the policy towards Germany that run counter to the US policy. So, giving up the idea of dismembering Germany and achieving reconciliation had become a wise choice for France.

Thirdly, the German division provided a realistic basis for French-German reconciliation and made France temporarily dispel lingering heart towards Germany, which made the French-German reconciliation possible. As Charles de Gaulle said, "After the split, Germany, as a dominating and powerful power, is no longer exist."[14]

At this point of time, the French-German reconciliation had become an irreversible trend.

3.1.2 From French-German reconciliation to cooperation

French-German reconciliation was not only a landmark in the history of bilateral relations, but also a landmark in the history of Europe, because it removed the obstacles for the integration of Western Europe after World War II, and laid the political foundation of the European alliance.

---

13 Ibid., p.287.
14 Charles de Gaulle, Memoires d'Espoir, Le Renouveau 1958-1962, Librairie Plon, 1970, pp.12-14.

European alliance was not a new trend emerged after World War II. Centuries ago, there were some politicians and thinkers had a vision of a united Europe. In the late 1920s, the European Unity Movement developed unofficial activities into inter-governmental activities for the first time. In September 1929, the French Prime Minister and Foreign Minister Briand suggested on League of Nations conference to build "United States of Europe". In May the following year, the French government presented a memo on "organizing the European Union" known as the Briand plan to the European governments of 26, but did not lead to repercussions in all countries. Subsequently, the European unification movement turned into low ebb in the shadow of the war.

In the early post-War period, war-torn Europeans began to reflect on the situation of Europe. The thought of European alliance became popular again. On September 19th, 1946, Winston Churchill delivered a speech at the University of Zurich, Switzerland, entitled "European tragedy", advocating the establishment of "United States of Europe". In May 1948, a variety of European Movements held the first meeting in The Hague, pushing the European unity movement after World War to the climax. On May 5, 1949, 10 foreign ministers from Britain, France, the Netherlands, Belgium, Italy, Denmark, Norway, Sweden, Ireland and other countries signed the Charter of the European Commission in London in October. The European Commission was established in Stella Myers and France was going to carry out cooperation in political and parliamentary terms.

In addition, in March 1948, representatives of Britain, France, the Netherlands, Belgium, and Luxembourg concluded the "Brussels Treaty" to cooperate in military and diplomatic fields. On April 4, 1949, the United States, Canada and the five States Parties of "Brussels Treaty" as well as Italy, Portugal, Denmark, Ireland and Norway signed the "North Atlantic Treaty", a transatlantic alliance that connected America and Europe included European defense under the leadership of the US. On April 16, 1948, with the support of the United States, military commanders of the Netherlands, Belgium, Luxembourg, Britain, France, Italy, Ireland, Iceland, Denmark, Norway, Sweden, Switzerland, Austria, Turkey, Greece, Portugal and West German occupied territories signed a cooperation agreement to set up the organization for economic cooperation in Europe (in 1949, West Germany, in 1959 Spain also joined), which was responsible for the distribution of the total $ 13 billion of Marshall Plan aid, and tried to maintain the Member States' fiscal and monetary stability, export development, modernization of production facilities, coordination of investment and so on, in order to promote trade and economic cooperation among countries. European alliance gradually transformed into reality.

France began to adjust their European policy by changing its policy towards Germany and the development of the European alliance movement. Thus, France actively supported European integration and believed that the European alliance would weaken the influence of major powers and enhance the impact of middle-level countries. France could play a greater role in united Europe and improve their position. On February 13, 1948, French Foreign Minister Georges Bidault announced in the National Assembly that the French now considers that Germany can integrate peaceful into the Europe on condition that Germany should abandon the idea of "ruling Europe".[15]

Bidault declared, "France is an European country first. Our current mission is to enable France to become the vanguard of European integration." In June, 1948, the French finally abandoned the idea of dismembering Germany, and accepted the "London Agreement", agreeing to established the Federal Republic of Germany.[16]

In July, replacing Robert Schuman, Georges Bidault became the French Foreign Minister. Robert Schumann was born in Alsace Lorraine region, grew up in Luxembourg having strong contacts with German culture. His special personal background and experience inevitably had an impact on his thinking. Growing up in geopolitical environment that had been scrambled, Schumann hoped to end the confrontation between France and Germany, and to achieve reconciliation, the reconciliation under a unified framework for Europe. In his opinion, suppressing Germany was not a good way, because "a large country cannot always be constrained by other people. The best way to revive German nationalism is to reject the equality of rights. On the contrary, it should create an environment which will make Germany dynamic and become no threat to its neighbors "[17]. This environment was the European integration.

Schuman Plan and the establishment of the European Coal and Steel Community

In 1948, on the London meeting of the six countries, France made concessions in the establishment of the West German government issues in an exchange for the US and Britain's concession on the issue of Saar. Saar near France was located in the southwest of Germany, rich in coal and

15   F. Roy Willis, France, Germany, and the New Europe, 1945-1967, London: Oxford University Press, 1968, p.20.

16   Pierre Berge, Trans, Ding Yifan, The History and Reality of the European Integration, China Social Sciences Publishing House, 1989, p.64.

17   Ibid., 1989, p 94.

steel, and had always been the object of contention between France and Germany. After World War I, Saar and France established customs union. Its coal mines were owned by France. On January 13, 1935, according to the "Treaty of Versailles", plebiscite was held in Saar. Most of the people were in favor of returning Saar to Germany. After World War II, the economic revival of the French needed a lot of coal, but the imported coal from British occupation of the Ruhr district must be paid in US dollars, and had quota restrictions. French demand for coal was 62 million tons in 1949–1950, but in 1949 the national coal production was only 51.2 million tons. And Saar produced 14.3 million tons of coal in the same year, and its own consumption was only 5 million tons, so it could supplement the coal needed in France.[18] France needed Saar's coal, and required it as a compensation. France-Saar Agreement on March 3, 1950 provides political autonomy of Saar region, but Saar was still subjected to France economically. Although this agreement had a temporary nature, it still caused a strong protest against the Federal Republic of Germany. French-German relations thus worsened. In addition, on April 28, 1949, Ruhr International Control Board composed of representatives of the United States, Britain, France, Belgium, the Netherlands, West Germany, and Luxembourg established the distribution of domestic consumption to oversee and exports of the Ruhr coal and steel production, to prevent German government to occupy the Ruhr resources and to deny neighbors to use these resources. The Federal Republic of Germany also expressed strong dissatisfaction of the International Ruhr Authority because of its discriminatory attitude towards Germany. Germany also required extending the scope of control over to France and Belgium industry.

The Federal Republic of Germany threw a number of recommendations one after another in order to get rid of subordination and to prevent removal a plant and to maintain their own industrial development potential. In early March 1950, the German government published a white paper to protest the "France-Saar Region Agreement", proposing to establish an international commission for the Saar region and a customs union including the southern Saarland state of Germany and Alsace-Lorraine region of France, Lorraine. Since then, the German Chancellor Adenauer in two occasions proposed to establish the French-German economic union. France was reluctant to accept the proposal to avoid being subordinate to Germany, and hoped that they could possess dominant position in the economic union issues. Therefore, the French government's priority was to bring up a plan

---

18   Louis Lister, Europe's Coal and Steel Community, New York: Twentieth Century Fund, 1960, pp.440, 445.

of their own to respond to the German proposal, and to find a new way to implement international controls on German heavy industry. France could not continue to stimulate the Federal Republic of Germany, and prevent possible crisis of the European economy at the same time; it had to ease international tensions, but at the same time to restrict the Federal Republic of Germany in the development of European construction, and include the Federal Republic of Germany in the Western Europe. In April 1950, the chief commissioner of French modernization and equipment, Jean Monnet, drew up a program to establish a French-German coal and steel common market. In the plan, Monet chose coal and steel sectors. France must have the free access to the Ruhr coal for avoiding Germany shut the coal reserves down. Because coal was the "food of industry" and Ruhr coal was of high quality and French and Saar's coal on the other hand were poor quality and not suitable for coking and steeling. Steel was seen as a basic raw material for armaments production and industrial production. The implementation of co-management of steel, almost made a new French-German war become impossible. Monnet also envisaged further expanding of this program to achieve bilateral economic and political integration.

This program was supported by the French foreign minister Robert Schumann immediately. In his view, Monnet plan provided a simultaneous solution for the questions that he had concern to. These problems included the French-German reconciliation, control of coal and steel for peaceful purposes as well as approaching the European integration and the building of a European federal system. On May 9, Schumann wrote to Adenauer to propose the French government's outline of the suggestion, and immediately got enthusiastic support from Adenauer. The plan was in line with his vision, the implementation of co-management could help Germany disentangle from unequal Ruhr International Control Board, and could get it an equal footing with France in coal and steel market; it was also in line with his ideas of French-German reconciliation and the desire of constructing a unified Europe.

In the afternoon, Schumann announced this explosive document to the press. The document declared, "The French government recommends placing all French and German coal and steel production under the management of a common senior agency which other European countries can join. Co-managed coal and steel production will enable establishing a common basis for the economic development of the first phase of the European Union rapidly, and will change the fate of the region which concentrated on the manufacture of weapons of war for a long time yet again became a victim of weapons production. The joint production treaty will not only hinder all future wars between France and Germany, but make them hard to imagine."[19] This was the famous "Schuman Plan".

In this plan, France no longer doubted the Federal Republic of Germany, but to recommend for close cooperation between the two countries. In the field of coal and steel, Germany could achieve equal cooperation with France. In the Federal Republic of Germany, the ruling Christian Democrats fully understood the political significance of the Schuman Plan, and extended a warm welcome to the Schuman Plan. In Italy, Netherlands, Belgium and Luxembourg, Schuman Plan was also welcomed of varying degrees. On April 18, 1951, France, Germany, Italy, the Netherlands, Belgium, and Luxembourg, six countries signed "European Coal and Steel Community Treaty" in Paris which was developed according to Schuman plan. On August 10, 1952, the first organization with supranational nature in the history of European integration was established in Luxembourg. It would directly manage coal and steel production and sales. Coal and Steel Community officially began the operations.

The Schuman Plan and the establishment of the Coal and Steel Community undoubtedly had an epoch-making significance in the history of European integration. It marked the idea of European alliance could become the reality; supranational institution—the creation of "senior agency" and the establishment of the community system marked that the European union was beyond intergovernmental cooperation and opened a new phase of European integration.

On French-German relations, it marked the French no longer implemented discriminatory policy towards Germany. For the first time in the post-War era, Germany received limited equality and sovereignty. The French-German reconciliation turned to close cooperation. As Adenauer said, "For France and Germany, the most far-reaching significance is: after the establishment of a co-production of coal and steel, any war between Germany and France is not only unthinkable, but also impossible in material. Therefore, the conclusion of Coal and Steel Community Treaty first solemnly and eventually ended the state of meeting on the battleground caused by distrust, competition, self-interest between the two countries in the past".[20]

---

19   Pierre Berge, Trans, Ding Yifan, The History and Reality of the European Integration, China Social Sciences Publishing House, 1989, p 102.
20   Adenauer's Memoirs, Vol.1, Shanghai People's Press, 1976, p.486.

The European Defense Community and the French-German relationship

Schuman Plan opened the door to European integration. During 1950–1951, the various plans on sectoral economic integration came out one after another, and became popular at the moment. European integration seemed to proceed along the way of functionalist envisaged by Monnet. But on June 25, 1950, the outbreak of the Korean War dramatically changed the direction of the European construction. The economic plan was shelved, and European defense issue was on the agenda. France and Germany all expressed concerns about the war. German Chancellor Adenauer said, "I believe that Stalin does not only have the action plan against Korea, but also may have the action plan against Germany. What happened in Korea is likely to be repeated in Germany. The same fate is before us".[21]

French independent leader Paul Reynaud believed that although Europe would not be immediately invaded by the Soviet Union, yet again the peace was short-lived.[22]

Since August 1950, the French continued to ask the United States to push the west line of defense to the east as possible. Germany called for the establishment of a police force of 150,000, and the Western troops is increased in the Federal Republic of Germany.

In September, 1950, on the meeting of foreign ministers of the US, Britain and France, the US agreed to supply army forces to Europe, but required the Europeans to strengthen their armament. Meanwhile, the US insisted rearming Germany. France on the other hand rejected the rearming Germany. The French government also understood that if it insisted, the United States might have a direct agreement with Germany and Germany would become a special partner of the US. Therefore, the French had to agree to the principle of German rearmament, but hoped to find a solution that was more conducive to France. After consideration, Jean Monnet developed a European Defense Community plan, and proposed to establish a European army in accordance with the mode and organization of the Coal and Steel Community. He believed that this is not only met the requirements of the US, but also prevent a disaster like the reconstruction of the "Federal German division". It was better to use the Federal German army in the Community than to set up an independent German army. On October 24, 1950, French Prime Minister René Pleven announced this proposal in

21   Jean Monnet, Trans, Sun Huishuang, The Father of Europe – Memoirs of Monnet, International Cultural Publishing Company, 1989, p.150.
22   Pierre Berge, Trans, Ding Yifan, The History and Reality of the European Integration, China Social Sciences Publishing House, 1989, p.124.

the National Assembly. He said, "The French government thought the Coal and Steel plan could be firstly realized to make people of all countries accustom to the concept of a European Community, and then hit the delicate issue of common defense. But things happened in the world do not allow it delaying".[23]

Pleven Plan was welcomed by the Federal Republic of Germany. Gaining the same equal status with other countries in a supranational organization was in line with the policy objectives of the Federal Republic. On February 1, 1952, "European Defense Community Treaty (draft)" was published. Bill passed relatively smoothly in the Federal Republic of Germany's Bundestag. But in the French National Assembly, it only got a slight advantage. On May 27, 1952, France, Germany, Italy, the Netherlands, Belgium, signed the "European Defense Community Treaty" in Paris. The Parliaments of other five countries except France ratified the treaty, but on August 30, 1954, the French National Assembly rejected the treaty. The European Defense Community had failed at the initial phase.

The reason of the failure of the European Defense Community was because it was a premature child in the first place, which was imagined out of the fear caused by the pressure imposed by the Soviet invasion of Europe in the Korean War atmosphere. However, the changes in the international situation were unexpected, and the Korean Armistice Agreement took effect. The European invasion by the Soviet did not happen. After Stalin died on March 5, 1953, the Soviet Union's foreign policy showed signs of adjustment, and the international situation was also increasingly easing. The rearmament of Germany lost its urgency. Secondly, in France, the European Defense Community plan triggered one of the biggest debates since the 1894 Dreyfus case. Many people had doubts about whether European Defense Community could avoid the Federal Republic of Germany's military revival, and they even thought that "the European Defense Community rearmed Germany and lifted the French armed forces".[24] Moreover, since the troops were stuck in the deterioration of Indochina, the French could not maintain balance with Germany after the rearmament. In addition, the pressure exerted by the US to Europe on defense issues had a counter effect. The French who had strong national consciousness disliked the US approach. Therefore, after a heated argument, the French National Assembly rejected the French proposal to implement their treaties. European Defense Community aborted, and associated political community programs also had no result.

---

23   Ibid., p.128.
24   Ibid., p.145.

The failure of the European Defense Community launched a blow to European integration that had just launched. Coal and Steel Community was the only remaining of European integration, European integration suddenly seemed to fall into a downturn. The failure of the European Defense Community was also a hit for French-German relationship that just started. As we all know, the fundamental reason of the rejection of the French laid in the haunting vigilance of France to Germany, the lingering skepticism casted a shadow over the French-German relationship which just got better.

After the failure of the European Defense Community, in 1954, the Federal Republic of Germany was accepted by "the Brussels Treaty" organization, and later renamed as Western European Union. In 1955, the Federal Republic of Germany joined NATO with an equal status. Though European defense was set up through the Western European Union, it was NATO who played a major role in terms of European defense and the Western European Union only had the name. So the real European defense system was not yet set up, but the issue of German rearmament between the Western Europe Union and NATO was resolved.

European Common market and French-German relations

French-German cooperation was just put into practice in the Schuman Plan and the establishment of the Coal and Steel Community, but soon suffered a heavy blow in the failure of the defense community. Could French-German cooperation continue? The establishment of the European Common Market dispelled people's doubts.

Once the problem of the German rearmament was resolved, the question of implementing the European integration was raised. Since the military road was closed, political road was also shut down for Europe and Monnet and others naturally went back to the path of economic integration. He saw the prospect of peaceful use of atomic energy, but also saw the important psychological value it had. So he suggested placing the national nuclear power industry under the supervision of a community to prohibit using it for military purposes. In April 1955, the Luxembourg Foreign Minister Johan Williem Beyen submitted a memorandum to Belgian Foreign Minister Spaak, criticizing the approach of sub-sector integration and advocating a comprehensive integration. He also suggested achieving economic alliance through the customs union. This proposal was quickly responded positively by Netherlands, Belgium, the Federal Republic of Germany and Italy. In June 1955, foreign ministers of the counties in the European Coal and Steel Community met in Messina, Italy, and had a serious discussion on Monnet program and Bain plan. The meeting decided to set up a committee chaired by the Spaak to draft relevant reports. Spaak report introduced in 1956 made a general regulation for establishing Euratom and a common market. In May 29-30, the six foreign ministers' meeting held in Venice, Italy approved the report. Then the second intergovernmental committee chaired by Spark was ordered to draft the treaties of Common Market and Euratom.

In 1956 autumn, because of the Suez Canal and the Hungarian events, international situation became tense, so that the six governments became more determined to accelerate the European integration. On July 20, 1956, Egypt nationalized the sovereignty of the Suez Canal. The oil routes from the Middle East were cut off. Britain and France implemented armed intervention on the Suez, but failed. This made Europeans realize the instability of Europe's energy supply. Therefore, the interest in the development of atomic energy was greatly improved, and the work of establishing Atomic Energy Community progressed smoothly. The failure of the British and French armed intervention made Europeans more aware of the gap between Europe, the Soviet Union and the US and top of it the international tensions led by events happened in Hungary resurged the Europeans' desire to get together to revitalize Europe. The drafting of Common Market Treaty was also progressing rapidly. Although there were differences between France and the Federal Republic of Germany, they still made compromises with each other and achieved a close cooperation under the general principles of European integration. The Federal Republic of Germany who had developed export trade and believed in social market economy, the Netherlands, Belgium, Luxembourg were all in favor of the principle of the common market, hoping to lift tariff barriers to have free trade within the common market. As the Federal Republic of Germany had developed industry and was heavily dependent on import agricultural products, it showed positive attitude towards the establishment of industrial tariffs alliance and apathy for the implementation of the common agricultural policy. On the contrary, French industrially was uncompetitive, but had a developed agriculture and it was badly in need of agricultural export market, so the French felt uneasy towards the establishment of industrial tariffs alliance, but strongly urged to include the common agricultural policy into the Common Market. Germany agreed to implement the common agricultural prices out of the consideration of its industrial interests and political needs of the French-German cooperation, but specific programs was left drafting after the treaty came into force. In addition, France also asked to absorb its overseas territories to participate in the common market, and took it as a condition of accepting the treaty. Chancellor Adenauer accepted the French demands for promoting European integration and seeking equal political status for Germany in Europe.

In Common Market treaty negotiations, France and Germany made compromises on economy, and achieved economic and political cooperation, which removed the obstacles for signing the treaty because they both had the desire of political cooperation and promoting European integration.In March 1957, the six countries signed "EEC Treaty" and "Euratom Treaty" in Rome, the two treaties collectively known as "the Treaty of Rome." In 1958, the "Treaty of Rome" came into effect. EEC, Euratom and the existed European Coal and Steel Community were all set running, European integration had now entered a new phase. The shadow over French-German relations which had been caused by the failure of the defense community faded to some extent. Their cooperation which began from the European Coal and Steel Community was more consolidated too.

The French-German treaty and legalization and institutionalization of the French-German cooperation

The establishment of the common market stimulated economic growth and economic cooperation between France and Germany. From 1958 to 1962, Germany's industrial production grew by 35% and, France's by 23%. In the same period, France's and Germany's trade with the European Economic Community partners doubled, while trade between France and Germany tripled.[25] Common Agricultural Policy was also formulated and carried out with France's insistence, promotion and Germany's compromising.[26]

The Common Agricultural Policy was not implemented in six countries until 1968, which promoted agricultural production and trade in France and Germany.

On March 25, 1959, General de Gaulle said at the first conference after he became president, "Today's Germany is no longer a danger to us. Because Germany has capability, energy and resources, so we see it as an important factor in Europe and throughout the world"[27].

In the fall of 1962, the leaders of France and Germany paid sensational visits. From July 2 to 8, Adenauer's state visit to France was a huge success. Charles de Gaulle gave a warm welcome and highly appreciated Adenauer's visit. On the French-German relationship, he said, "France and

---

25   European Communities, Statistical Office, General Statistical Bulletin, No.3, March 1963,29,68; No.4, June 1984, p.21.

26   Jiang Nan, On the Formulation of Common Agricultural Policy between France and European Community, World History, Vol. 2, 1995, pp.8-17

27   F. Roy Willis, France, Germany, and the New Europe, 1945-1967, London: Oxford University Press, 1968, p.294.

Germany have found that they are complementary, geographically, labor, and abilities"[28].

Germany was very pleased about the statement. Newspapers published articles, arguing that "Feud had ended", "reconciliation between the French and German had been completed. This was a great moment in history". De Gaulle's visit to Germany on September 4 was even more successful. Charles de Gaulle reiterated that "because of the Soviet threat, the joint of French and German people was necessary and because Europe as like the United States needed the basis for power and prosperity." He said, "A new fact, also one of the greatest modern facts, is the friendship between Germany and France".[29] In order to win the heart of the German people, Charles de Gaulle even spoke with skilled German in a public speech, revealing that his ancestors came from Germany and that was a surprise for German.

On January 22, 1963, when the Prime Minister Adenauer visited Paris, he signed the "Treaty of Friendship and Cooperation between the Federal Republic of Germany and France", also known as "the Elysee Treaty". In order to develop cooperation in diplomacy, defense and culture the treaty regulated that heads of the two governments should meet twice a year and ministers met every three months. French and German governments should consult with each other before taking any important decisions on foreign policy. Also a committee should be set up to promote exchanges between young people from the two countries. French-German treaty caused the uneasiness of the US. They hoped Germany could express loyalty to the United States and NATO in the treaty. Within the Federal Republic of Germany, the treaty was not very popular. As a result, the Bundestag added an interpretive resolution in the treaty preamble, stressing the Atlantic Alliance's military integration, cooperation with the United States, respecting the Economic Community and the necessity of accepting the United Kingdom. The resolution greatly reduced the significance of the French-German treaty. It showed that Germany chose Germany-the US relations prior to the German-Franco relations, because at that time the United States was the security guarantor of Germany. On security issues, the United States was more important than in France. Nonetheless, the French-German treaty was still very important to both France and Germany. It reinforced the process of reconciliation and cooperation between France and Germany since 1947, and made friendly relations between France and Germany and this relations were institutionalized and legalized in the form of a treaty; secondly,

28 Ibid., p.306.
29 Ibid., p.306.

the partnership between France and Germany indicated by French-German treaty became the basis of European integration. In later years, France and Germany repeatedly became promoters of integration.

Through the analysis of French-German relations after World War II, we can see that the French-German relations had undergone a shift from hostility to reconciliation and cooperation. The reason was based on the changes of the post-war international situation and the common need of the national interests of both countries. General Charles de Gaulle had done such an elaboration during his visit to Bonn in 1962:

Union, why should we unify? First, it is because we are facing a direct threat. France know that, in the face of Soviet ambition of domination, if the German surrender, the French will be immediately hurt physically and mentally; Similarly, Germany also must know that, if there is no support of France behind Germany, Germany must be at a loose end. Secondly, the reason of the union is the league of the free world, that Europe and the US made commitments that in order to maintain long-term reliability and security, they must build a strong, prosperous core on the old continent, like the United States was the core of the New World. And the basis of the core cannot be anything else but our solidarity. Finally, the reason for the union is to achieve relaxation and international understanding. After discarding the ruling ambitions of antiquated ideological in Eastern Europe, relaxation and international understanding can bring balance, peace and development for the whole of Europe from the Atlantic to the Urals. To achieve this, Western Europe must pursue a vigorous, powerful European Community policy, that is, mainly to pursue a unified policy of France and Germany.[30]

The tense relationship between the East and the West and the formation of the Cold War, as well as the need for the US economic aid and military protection, they all made France have to choose the US side, to accept the US policy of supporting Germany and to abandon dismembering and weakening Germany to achieve reconciliation with Germany. French-German cooperation and European integration were both the need for revival and prosperity of post-War Europe, and the best control and restraint of Germany. It was the best way to eliminate the threat of war in Germany, and was consistent with the interests of the French nation.

At the first meeting with Charles de Gaulle on September 14, 1958, German Chancellor Adenauer had a brief statement about the reason of French-German cooperation; "the existing of superpowers like the United

---

30   Alfred Crosse, Trans. Lu Boyuan, Lu Wen, et al. Foreign Policy of France 1944-1984, World Affairs Press, 1989, p.177.

States and the Soviet Union is, after all, a fact. That is why Europe must be united and why French-German friendship and cooperation should be first strengthened."[31]

For Germany, to end the low status as a defeated nation of post-War era was imperative. Being dependent on the US protection, Germany participated in the European integration as an equal member, which no doubt helped to end the restrictions of the vanquished and achieve some sovereignty and equality that the German dreamed of. This was the wish of Germany and it complied with the national interest of Germany. This was not only the foundation for the reconciliation and cooperation between the two countries, but also the basis of the participation of the two countries in European integration.

3.2 The British-French Relations and Enlargement of the European Community

After the European Community had experienced the initial start-up and development, the United Kingdom applied to join the Community. The expansion of the European Community was a major event in the process of its development. However, France twice vetoed Britain's application to join the European Union, delaying the United Kingdom's accession process for decades, but also postponed the first expansion of the European Community for decades. This had significant impact not only on the post-war British history, but also on the history of the European Community. Why Britain changed the attitude and applied to join the European Community? Why the French opposed the join of the British? The relationship between Britain and France in the process of Britain application was crucial for us to understand the expansion of the European Community and its development.

3.2.1 The United Kingdom missing the opportunities

After World War II, European countries had been severely damaged. In contrast, the UK was not damaged as badly. Britain played an important role in the war against Germany. It was neither a vanquished country, like German and Italian, nor an occupied country, like France, Belgium, and the Netherlands, so it had no painful experience of being defeated. England should have been the best leader in Europe, but Britain rejected the Schuman Plan and the European Common Market, and thus missed the opportunity to become a founding member of the European Community, but also missed opportunity of being the leadership of Europe in the early post-War period.

31   Adenauer's Memoirs, Vol.3, Shanghai People's Press, 1973, p.505.

Britain refused to participate in the process of European integration, which was the result of British policy towards Europe. In fact, after the war, British Foreign Secretary Bevin had pursued an active policy of European integration, envisaging building Western Europe a "third power" led by the British with the core of the Anglo-French cooperation, and also independent of the United States and the Soviet Union. On March 4, 1947, Britain and France signed the "Anglo-French Alliance and Mutual Assistance Treaty" or "Treaty of Dunkirk" in Dunkirk, France. For Britain, on the one hand, "Dunkirk Treaty" laid a foundation for the British and French further cooperation with the aim of preventing the revival of German aggression. On the other hand, the two leaders also noted the threat of the Soviet Union and "communism"; the treaty did not shut the door to the US aid. Therefore, "Dunkirk Treaty '' enabled the British to rely on the Western European Union without having the US making a commitment to Europe, in order to control the situation in Western Europe and the pursue the Atlantic Alliance".[32] On this basis, on March 17, 1948, Britain and France signed the "Brussels Treaty" with the Benelux countries. "Brussels Treaty" was a political, economic and cultural-round treaty of cooperation for Germany and the Soviet Union, with the military alliance as its core.

Marshall Plan led to the division between the Eastern and the Western Europe. In December, 1947, the London meeting by four Foreign Ministers dismissed without contentment on Germany issue. The relationship between the East and the West deteriorated. On February, 1948, representatives from the US, Britain, France, Netherlands, Belgium, and Luxembourg, excluding the Soviet Union, met in London to discuss the issue of Germany, which was called London meeting of six countries. The topic of the meeting was to establish German government in the west occupation zone. Finally, London Agreement was formed which approved the establishment of the Federal Germany. The relationship between the East and the West continued to deteriorate. As Britain had broken the relationship with the past ally, the Soviet Union, establishing the "third power" had lost its meaning. Britain chose to stick to the Western camp and depended on the great economic and military power of the US to prevent the threat of "communism" of the Soviet Union.

On 3 November, 1948, Bevan proposed in the memo to Marshall, "Contracting a regional treaty for aid in Pacific countries should include all threatened countries in the movement of the Pacific, such as the US, Britain, Canada, Ireland, Iceland, Norway, Denmark, Portugal, and

32 Hong Yousheng, The root and Evolution of the British Policy towards the Western European Integration, 1945-1960, Nan Jing University Press, 2001, p.13.

France."[33] On April 4, 1949, the United States, Canada and the five States Parties of "Brussels Treaty" as well as Italy, Portugal, Denmark, Ireland and Norway signed the "North Atlantic Treaty", the US officially involved in European affairs of defense. Britain realized the dream of establishing the Atlantic Union and relying on the Atlantic Alliance's.

The United Kingdom had different opinions than continental Europe and the United States about the nature of the European integration. In continental Europe, the idea of unification had a long history. After the 20th century, the sensational "pan-European" manifesto written by Count Richard Nikolaus von Caudenhove Kalergi in 1923, the French Prime Minister and Foreign Minister Briand proposed "the European Alliance" in 1929 and like post-war vigorous European Unity Movement, a variety of organizations supporting the European alliance emerged in Europe. Especially the federalism was effective in continental Europe. Federalist advocated abandoning this form of nation-states, and to establish a "European Alliance" or "United States of Europe". The US used European integration as a tool to acquire leadership in the Cold War, and spared no effort to support European integration.[34]

While Britain had no interest in political integration, opposing supranational integration, only in favor of intergovernmental cooperation.

On October 9, 1948, Churchill proposed a "three-ring diplomacy" as general policy at the annual meeting of the British Conservative Party. He said, "At this moment of change which is related to the destiny of mankind, when looking forward to the future of our country, I feel there are three large rings in free and democratic countries... For us, the first one of course is the British ring. The second ring is the English-speaking world that the US has played an important role, including my country, Canada and other Commonwealth countries. The last ring is a united Europe.... In fact, we are at the point of connection among three circles."[35]

Clearly, in the mind of Churchill, the united Europe was the last ring. Its position was behind the Commonwealth and the English-speaking world. Not only that, "Although Churchill constantly campaigned for the establishment of the European Union, at that time, for the UK's leading politicians — especially Churchill, EU did not include the UK."[36] Because the British

---

33   Repost from Chen Lemin, The Post-War Diplomatic History of Britain, World Affairs Press, 1994, p.39.
34   The US policy towards the European Integration see Chapter V of the book.
35   Repost from Chen Lemin, The Post-War Diplomatic History of Britain, World Affairs Press, 1994, p.62.
36   Chen Lemin, The Post-War Diplomatic History of Britain, World Affairs Press, 1994, p.65.

thought that the United Kingdom had a power on its territory and throughout the world. If it participated in the European Union as a member state, then it would be disproportionate in terms of Britain's international status. On June 27, 1950, Winston Churchill delivered a speech in the House, said, "As we are in the center of the British Empire and Commonwealth, and have brotherly relations with the United States in the English-speaking world. Therefore, we cannot accept the status of full member states in a federal system in Europe".[37]

Churchill's statements were very illustrative of the British politicians' position in the world affairs in early post-War era and the United Kingdom's opinion of their position in the EU. Britain still wanted to influence and interfere in the European affairs beyond the continent like they did in the 19th century. However, the UK's strength had shrunk. The British Empire went downhill quickly. In the early post-war period, British politician did not see this point. They paid a heavy price for this.

After the transition of seeking to establish a "third force" in the early post-war, and until the late 1940s, British Labor government formed the policy towards the EU with the influence over the 1950s. And to maintain the UK leadership in Europe, which was what the British Foreign Office planners considered to contain the Soviet Union and maintain the British interests with the United States as its core on security, namely wholeheartedly relying on the Atlantic Alliance complemented by the European organizations supporting traditional intergovernmental cooperation, such as the Brussels Treaty Organization, the Organization for economic cooperation in Europe and the European Commission opposing supranational integration.[38] However, the rapid development of European integration let the British down. The British had to make their own choices, and their choice made them lose opportunity to become a founding member of the Community.

After Schuman Plan was proposed by France in 1950, the United Kingdom stated that it would not participate in a plan transferring sovereignty. The UK attitude towards the Schuman Plan was to just participate in the negotiation without making commitments. But France insisted that the negotiation must be held on the promise of accepting the principle of Schuman Plan. Britain must promise to accept the principle of the Schuman Plan, which was to accept supranational institutions of the Coal and Steel Community.

---

37 Repost from Chen Lemin, The Post-War Diplomatic History of Britain, World Affairs Press, 1994, p.66.
38 Hong Yousheng, The Root and Evolution of the British Policy towards the Western European Integration, 1945-1960, Nanjing University Press, 2001, p.69.

The British government feared that the commitment would "entrap" the British, "irreversibly 'sliding' to full-fledged European Union".[39]

British government ultimately rejected the Schuman plan.[40]

In reality, the root of Britain's rejection was not lying on the procedure of whether to make "commitment", but rather on fundamental differences with France on the sovereignty transfer issues. Britain had always supported intergovernmental cooperation, but was not in favor of the establishment of supranational institutions based on "Sovereignty transfer". Therefore, it did not accept the Schuman Plan with supranational colors.

After the Messina conference in 1955, six Western European countries decided to set up the Spaak Committee to discuss the issue of economic integration. Spark Commission proposed to establish a comprehensive common market and the European Atomic Energy Community in Western Europe, which was soon approved by each country. In 1956, the second Intergovernmental Committee chaired by Spark was ordered to draft the Common Market Treaty and the Euratom Treaty. Britain sent observers to the Spark Committee. However, the conclusions of British observers was, "The future treaty you are discussing is not possible to reach an agreement; if it is an agreement, it cannot be approved; if it is approved, it is impossible to implement. Even if it is implemented, it is totally unacceptable for Britain".[41]

Britain wanted free trade and did not want to set up a customs union. Britain advocated that the market did not need to implement the Common Customs Tariff; for instance on atomic Energy Community, while six countries wanted to build a community with a supranational nature, the United Kingdom insisted on bilateral cooperation. Finally, the British withdrew from Spark Commission, and gave up the opportunity to join the Common Market.

Britain's choice was governed by the traditional British policy; the World War II experience and the awareness of sovereignty. British tradition of European policy was detached from the top of the continental European countries, and maneuvered among continental countries to maintain the balance of power among European countries in order to protect their own interests. The British government had been implementing such a foreign

---

39   John W. Yang, Britain and European Unity, 1945-1999, Macmillan Press Ltd, 2000, p.29.
40   Hong Yousheng, The root and Evolution of the British Policy towards the Western European Integration, 1945-1960, Nanjing University Press, 2001, pp.72-114.
41   Roy Denman, Missed Chances: Britain and Europe in the Twentieth Century, London: Cassell, 1996, pp.198-199; Geir Lundestad, Empire by Integration: The United States and European Integration, 1945-1997, Oxford University Press, 1998, p.50.

policy throughout the 19th century. Therefore, the United Kingdom had long been a "maritime country which had the overriding attitude in Europe", "with greater flexibility and wider world than any other European country in the international arena". By this traditional policy Britain try to keep its special status after World War II with the apparent decline in British national circumstances, and refused to join the integration of continental Europe.

Britain did not have the strong desire for European integration as the mainland countries because as a country haven't had the same humiliating experience of being defeated in World War II . After the outbreak of World War II, France, the Netherlands and most other Western European countries had painful experience of being defeated and occupied by Germany. They felt the need to unite for countries. Although it suffered heavy losses with the advantage of English Channel, Britain rejected the Germans at bay. Its psychological feelings were different from continental European countries because it had no historical humiliation of being occupied. Britain was at the center of the meetings held during wartime, planning the Post-War world order together with the United States and the Soviet Union and because of that Britain have had unrealistic fantasies of their own national power, and did not respond the changes of the post-War situation as quickly as the situation required. Thus, it missed the opportunity to participate in the European construction. Because of that they lack of a sense of urgency to join. Therefore, the wartime feelings and experiences was one of the important reasons for losing interest for the integration of super nations.

On the other hand the fundamental reason for UK not to join was laid in the fact that it had very different constitutional system from continental countries. The UK had such a constitutional system which made them spare no effort to defend its sovereignty and autonomy and because of that they had a strong sense of superiority. They believed that the British constitutional system gave maximum freedom for effective activity to democratically elected government and it was considered to be the supreme and perfect and widely respected by Act of Parliament, case law and judicial interpretation of the principles embodied in the rule of law. Britain's constitution and institution withstood the baptism of the war. However, the democratic government of the continent collapsed so comparing two constitutional systems, the superiority of the British constitutional system was obvious. British superiority won their broad support in the UK of defending sovereignty and autonomy and opposing the practice of supranational challenge.[42]

---

42   Chen Lemin, The Post-War Diplomatic History of Britain, World Affairs Press, 1994, p.127.

3.2.2 The UK's application rejected by France for the second time

After exiting from British Council in November 1956, Britain focused on his European project: the "G" plan. The plan recommended setting up industrial free trade zones by the United Kingdom, located in the continental European countries which had established the customs union and other OECD nations. The difference between the customs union and industrial free trade zones planned by the UK was that there would be no implementation of common external tariff in free trade zones, except the trade of agricultural products.[43]

Britain's proposal reflected UK's own economic and political interests. On economy, it adhered to the independent external tariff which enabled it both enjoying preferential tariffs and trade in the Western European market and keeping the "Imperial Preference" with the Commonwealth; excluding agricultural trade was an elimination of competition with European agricultural products in UK market, which effectively protected Commonwealth Preference of agriculture, food and agricultural products of Britain. The reason of this was that Britain was a traditional imperialist country. Its maintenance of economy had long been depended mainly on colonial plunder of cheap raw materials and food as well as exporting industrial product to the colonies. Therefore, the economic ties between Britain and Commonwealth countries were very close, which was very important to the British economy. In 1953, the proportion of the import of raw materials and agricultural products from British colonies took in the import were: 93% of natural rubber, 93% of manganese ore, 81% of copper, 76% of wool, 100% of jute, 81% of wheat, 56% of cream, 54% of meat and meat products, 48% of sugar. In the same period, the proportion of the import of raw materials and agricultural products from British colonies were: 70% of cotton, 46% of wool and wool, 70% of ceramics and glass products, 61% of footwear, 57% of knives, scissors, chemistry, 50% of medicine and dye, 45% of clothing.[44] In political terms, FTA plan was not involving sensitive supranational issues.

It was only a pure trade cooperation program. And it could also merge the Common Market into the Free Trade Area, which was in line with the UK's European outlook. In addition, this program was able to maintain economic and political relations with the Commonwealth, and to improve the UK's position to have a relatively favorable position in Anglo-American relations.

43 Geoffrey Warner, Anne Deighton, British Perceptions of Europe in the Post-War Period, II, pp.51-52, in: Les Europe des Europeens, sous la direction de Rene Girault, en collaboration avec Gerard Bossuat, Publication de la Sorbonne, 1993.
44 Writing group of West European Common Market, West European Common Market, Shanghai People's Press, 1973, pp.161-162.

However, this plan was opposed by six countries. On June 27, 1958, the European Parliament passed a resolution rejecting a large free trade zone plan. In December 1958, a large free trade area negotiation went bankruptcy.

In order to compete with the common market of the six countries, in January 1960, Britain associated with seven countries included Switzerland, Sweden, Denmark, Norway, Austria and Portugal and others to establish the European Free Trade Association, or the "Little Free Trade". Western Europe split into two economic blocs, the "six countries" and the "seven countries".

However, the seven countries were clearly not the opponent of the six countries. The industrial and trade growth rate of the six countries not only were higher than the seven countries but also seven countries were very dependent on trade in the six countries, and its exports to the six countries were greater than the trade volume within the seven countries. For the purposes of the United Kingdom, in 1960, its exports to "EFTA" accounted for 11.9% of total exports, while exports to the Common Market accounted for 15.4% of total exports.[45] The Common Market became more and more important for Britain. Meanwhile, the United Kingdom's and Commonwealth countries' trade stagnated. In 1961, British exports to Europe for the first time exceeded the exports to the Commonwealth. Commonwealth became less and less important to Britain and this forced the British to reconsider the relations with the Common Market. In addition to these economic reasons, political reason was more important within the consideration of the UK. Britain did not want to form continental group with France and Germany at centre and excluding Britain. After the boom of the Common market and the effort by continental countries to build political alliance Britain became increasingly concern about being excluded from Europe. When the time came, the ability of the United Kingdom affecting Europe and the world would be greatly declined. In fact, the British leader had felt the decline of British power and influence. In 1959, the Soviet Union and the US held the first summit meeting. When Eisenhower and Khrushchev met, they left Macmillan alone, isolated, who wanted to intermediate. However, the balance of power between Britain and France and Germany at this time had shrunk compared with the situation in 1950.

In 1950, its gross domestic product twice as big than France and West Germany altogether, the UK was undoubtedly the second largest Western powers after the United States,. Its armed force in the North Atlantic Alliance was also second only to the United States. After ten years, West Germany was entered the period of "economic miracle", the economic

---

45   Ibid..

growth rate was three times the growth rate of the Britain in 1950s. In 1954, West Germany got a chance to re-arming. France's economic growth rate was also higher than the United Kingdom. The strength of the armed forces of France in 1958 surpassed the United Kingdom. In 1960, France also became the world's fourth nuclear power.[46]

Even the West German leader Adenauer mocked the British side "as a rich person who lost all property without knowing".[47]

In addition, because the United States strongly supported the European integration, if the UK kept long-term alienation from European integration, the UK-US relations were bound to be affected. In February 1960, the British Foreign Secretary Selwyn Lloyd McMillan reminded the Prime Minister that the US would consider the six-nation community as the group in which they had dialogue in Europe, and Eisenhower also warned McMillan by himself that if Britain did not join the community, then, the Anglo-American special relationship would be declining.[48]

The factors above prompted the British to change its European policy, and Britain decided to join the process of European integration.

On August 9, 1961, the British formally applied to join the European Economic Community. On February 28, 1962, it also proposed to join the European Coal and Steel Community and the European Atomic Energy Community.

Britain was especially concerned about agriculture and its relationship with the Commonwealth countries. As mentioned earlier, Britain was a traditional imperialist country, and it had very close economic ties with the colonies. Although colonies became independent in the 1960s, Britain was still concerned about the Commonwealth's "Imperial Preference" and its maintenance.

Since 1880s, the British import of agricultural products from colonies enjoyed tax exemption. In this context, the British traditional agricultural policy was to take on approaches of direct subsidies and paying for the difference to the producers of certain categories, which was very different from the Common Agricultural Policy, that advocating price support in the European Union. And the implementation of the Common Agricultural Policy was very negative for the food-importing country, Britain. Therefore,

---

46 Geoffrey Warner, Anne Deighton, British Perceptions of Europe in the Post-War Period, II, p.59.
47 Repost form John W. Yang, Britain and European Unity, 1945-1999, Macmillan Press Ltd, 2000, p.63.
48 John W. Yang, Britain and European Unity, 1945-1999, Macmillan Press Ltd, 2000, p.66.

the British were very concerned about whether their own interests could be protected in agriculture. France was a big country of agricultural production and exporting. Because of that it could benefit from price support policy and agricultural export subsidies in the common agricultural policy, thus France was a staunch supporter of the Common Agricultural Policy. France was very clear that letting the United Kingdom join the Community undoubtedly increase an opposition faction in developing common agricultural policy when the common agricultural policy had not been formed completely.

In six countries, the Netherlands, Belgium, Luxembourg and Italy were in favor of the application of the United Kingdom, while Chancellor Adenauer and General Charles de Gaulle seemed less enthusiastic, but did not oppose it. In January 1962, the six countries reached agreement in the financial and the main content of the Common Agricultural Policy due to the threat of France not transforming to the second stage of the customs union. Because France stressed the need to develop a common agricultural policy before Britain joined, so this agreement seemed to calm French. There was no reason to reject the United Kingdom. Britain's participation seemed to be inevitable. However, after President Kennedy proposed a "grand plan" to revitalize Atlantic Alliance, the situation changed.

President Kennedy proposed the establishment of open trade alliances between the US and European economies, a large free trade zone. In August 1962, "Trade Expansion Act" got passed in the US Congress. The bill was established on the basis of the assumption that the United Kingdom joined the European common market. The United States wanted Britain to join the Common Market, using the "special relationship" with Britain to revive the Atlantic Alliance and to achieve their leadership role in the Atlantic Alliance. In defense, Kennedy proposed the establishment of "multilateral nuclear force" of NATO, controlling the British and French nuclear forces in hands of NATO, or say in the hands of the United States.

However, Charles de Gaulle insisted to develop independent nuclear forces of France, thinking that the French could not hand out its own defense to someone else, and must relied on itself. France must have a "strike force", of which he believed the main part was nuclear weapons. For the establishment of NATO's "multilateral nuclear force" recommended by Kennedy, Charles de Gaulle considered it as a hoax, as a means to control the British and French nuclear weapons for the United States. The multilateral force participating in the NATO would deprive France of its independent strike force.[49]

---

49   Pierre Berge, Trans, Ding Yifan, The History and Reality of the European Integration, China Social Sciences Publishing House, 1989, p.272.

Therefore, on January 14, 1963, Charles de Gaulle stated on the reporter conference that France refused to sign the "Nassau agreement". He also rejected the British application to join the Common Market. He first emphasized that the six countries on the mainland were "mostly the same in nature" in economy. He pointed out the economic differences between Britain and the mainland countries, with particular emphasis on that the United Kingdom's agricultural policy "is obviously incompatible with the system that six countries have naturally established themselves". After citing economic reasons, Charles de Gaulle also cited political reasons to show the attitude of refusing Britain. He believed that after Britain joined the Community, other countries would also join the FTA, such as the Common Market was completely different from the Common Market the six countries established:

It is expected that such a complex group with so many members, will not last long. Finally, a large Atlantic community depends on the United States and is led by the US will soon swallow up the EC.

For some, this may be a reasonable assumption, but it is not what the French want to do, nor has done. what the French are doing is basically realizing its wish to build an authentic Europe.[50]

Britain's first application to join the Common Market failed.

The British Labor government that came to power in 1964 made an application to join the Common Market for the second time on May 11, 1967. This time, the British compromised substantially. It did not only agree on the common agricultural policy it compromised in many other ways. On May 30, at the summit of celebrating the tenth anniversary of the signing "Treaty of Rome", General Charles de Gaulle also promised that the French would not obstruct the Community for UK's application. However, on the reporters' conference on November 27th, Charles de Gaulle once again rejected the United Kingdom. He criticized that the economic situation in the United Kingdom was incompatible with the provisions of the European Economic Community. He thought that the British could negotiate with the six countries after settling the economy. Charles de Gaulle commented: the permission of British participation "is allowing for the destruction to the structure that is built with effort and hope but is covered by those machinations and infinite delays for the six countries". Because if the UK joined the Community, the economic system of the six countries could be replaced by a free trade zone including the whole Western Europe, which would require "repealing Community, and disbanding its institutions".[51]

---

50 Institute for International Relations, The Memories of Charles de Gaulle (May, 1958-January, 1964), World Affairs Press, 1964, p.411.
51 Pierre Berge, Trans, Ding Yifan, The History and Reality of the European Integration, China Social Sciences Publishing House, 1989, p 301.

The reason of De Gaulle's rejection of Britain was of course partly it wanted to oppose the US control and it feared that the UK would become a "Trojan Horse" for the US. There was real economic and political considerations.

De Gaulle's European integration goal was to establish a Europe independent form the United States. He hoped to create a "European Europe", a Europe no longer closely linked with the United States and could have an equal dialogue with the Soviet Union and the US, a "third force" which could help to store the world balance. Because of the special relationship between Britain and the United States, Charles de Gaulle worried that the participation of the United Kingdom would benefit Atlantic, would make European Economic Community melt into the Atlantic community, and the US would dominate Europe.

In the existing European Community, France and Germany was the core of European integration. Charles de Gaulle thought that France could take advantage of the vanquished status of West Germany, and achieve leadership in the Community. Britain was a traditional power. The participation of Britain was bound to change the pattern in the Community. Charles de Gaulle was afraid that Britain would become the center of Community, and would have the risk of being isolated and becoming a minority.

In addition, France did not want Britain to join before the establishment of the Common Market for agriculture. Because of the complexity and sensitivity of the agriculture issues, "Treaty of Rome" did not provide a specific embodiment of the Common Agricultural Policy. After the "Treaty of Rome" came into force in 1958, the development of a common agricultural policy began. There were the twists and turns in the development of the Common Agricultural Policy due to the delay by the West Germany and other countries so the progress was slow. Before the complete formulation and implementation of the common agricultural policy, the French did not want Britain to join.

3.2 The third application by the United Kingdom and further negotiations

In April 1969, French President Charles de Gaulle resigned from office, Georges Pompidou was elected president. Pompidou had a more relaxed attitude towards Britain's participation in the Community, changing the hard-line policy of Charles de Gaulle towards Britain. At that time, West Germany's strength was markedly enhanced, coupled with the implementation of "Ostpolitik", the sphere of foreign relations was greatly expanded, and its position in international politics was improved. This was a stimulus for France. Pompidou decided to absorb the British into the European Economic Community in order to balance the forces of West Germany. On the other hand, the Common Agricultural Policy had the basic shape after 10 years of arduous and lengthy effort. On July 1, 1968, the EC six countries abolished trade restrictions on most agricultural products between Member States. They developed a uniform price and established common external tariff barriers of agricultural products and achieved the completion of the Common Agricultural Market of 18 months ahead of schedule. France's concern about the possibility of Britain's interferences with the Common Agricultural Policy has no longer valid. In December 1969, in the six-nation European Economic Community Summit, French President Georges Pompidou proposed to expand community, which removed the biggest obstacle for the United Kingdom's participation.

In 1970, Britain's Conservative Party led by Heath came to power. Heath seized the opportunity to submit an application to join the European Economic Community for the third time. Britain was willing to accept the status quo of EEC, including the Common Agricultural Policy.

In the negotiations, agricultural issues and financial problems became the focus of discussion. Common Agricultural Policy was a direct intervention to production, sale, import and export of agricultural products of each country in the Community. Until national agricultural policies was replaced by a common policy, the old agricultural policies would be coordinated. The "Treaty of Rome" Article 38 stated "The Common Market will be expanded to agriculture and agricultural trade"[52] EC formally decided to establish the Common Agricultural Policy. On July 1, 1968 after the process up to 10 years, six countries of the EC finally achieved the goal of establishing the common agricultural market.

The main feature of the common agricultural policy was first, the implementation of the common price based on price support policy and intervention mechanism: Community preformed the price support for agricultural products. When the price of agricultural products dropped to the level of the intervention price (also called support price), the Community's intervention agencies began to purchase at the intervention price. Therefore, the price of agricultural products would have never dropped below the intervention price. This was the main way of the community to guarantee farmers' income levels. Second, the Community implemented agricultural trade policy

---

52   Treaty Establishing the European Economic Community and Connected Documents, Publishing Services of the European Communities, 1962, p.47.

featured by import taxes and export subsidies. It imposed import duties on foreign goods outside the agricultural community to exclude them from the market, while providing subsidies to export of the Community to dump the agricultural products in the world market. The main purpose was to limit the import of agricultural imports from the third country by imposition of import duties, to encourage imports of agricultural products from within the Community; and to encourage and support the export of agricultural products from the Community. Third, the implementation of the Common Agricultural Policy required joint finance. The difference on the taxes levied on the import should be included in the common finance. And expenditure of intervention and export subsidies should be paid by the co-finance.

One consequence of the Common Agricultural Policy was the transfer of income from net importer of agricultural to exporting countries. This transfer was realized through the Community's financial and trade practices. According to the Community's principles of budget and foreign trade policy, agricultural importer of agricultural products needed to pay import duties to the Community budget when importing from outside the Community; and exporter of agricultural products could get the export subsidies provided by the Community budget when exporting to the world market. In other words, the community was actually transferring the budget from importers to exporters. Another situation was that if the community's importers directly imported agricultural products from the Community's exporters, they did not need to pay import duties, but the price was equivalent to the world price plus import duty. The price that exporting country got was equivalent to the world price plus export subsidies. In this way, income directly transferred from consumers of one country to producers of another country. Both cases were essentially the same, transferring income from importing countries to exporting countries.

Since the 1880s, the traditional imperialist country, Britain, made full use of the status of the World's largest net importer of food to import duty-free agricultural products from the colonies. Its traditional agricultural policy was to perform the payment of difference and direct subsidies to certain categories of producers, which was very different from the price support policy of the common agricultural policy. According to the previous analysis, as the United Kingdom imports large quantities of agricultural products and exports less each year, and therefore, it paid more and earned less in the Community budget. Implementation of the Common Agricultural Policy was bound to make an importer, in this case is the UK, as a net spender but this was not beneficial for UK.

Therefore, in the negotiations began in June 1970, although the United Kingdom accepted the Common Agricultural Policy of the Community and abandoned the traditional British system of direct subsidies and payment of the difference, it required the industry have a three-year transition period, while agriculture should have up to 7 years of transition. The French government strongly opposed to this practice, thinking that the British was going to enjoy the benefits of industrial Common Market first, and but it would be bound by the agricultural market. On the ministerial meeting on December 8, British European Affairs Minister Geoffrey Ripon announced its acceptance of the Commission proposed five-year transition period, but said that it was difficult to implement the Common Agricultural Policy within 5 years. France insisted on the Committee's recommendation, while the other five countries agreed to extend the transition period to 8 years. Financial share proposed by the UK was also considered to be too little by the six countries.

There were also different opinions on British purchase of sugar and butter from Commonwealth. Britain always purchased sugar from the British Antilles, Mauritius Islands and Fiji Islands and bought butter from New Zealand butter. France hoped that the British reduce its purchase of sugar and butter from Commonwealth countries, and buys it from the Community instead. The French government also raised the problem of the difference of pound and using pound as the reserve currency. From the prospects of the European Monetary Union French government worrying about the difference of the pound and the reserve currency status of pounds would affect the establishment of the European Monetary Union.

During the negotiations, the French side displayed the most hard-line attitude. But the relationship between Britain and France did not develop into irreconcilable, because France did not oppose the join of the British, but to bargain on specific issues in order to protect their own interests. After consultations, the British government promised to freeze pound difference. In agriculture, the British made a concession on share of the Community budget. France also made concessions on butter issues. So far, the obstacles of Britain's participation in the Common Market had been ruled out.

On January 22, 1972, the United Kingdom, Denmark, Ireland and Norway signed the European Atomic Energy Community and the European Coal and Steel Community Treaty for joining the European Economic Community in Brussels. The transitional period was five years. Treaty came into effect on January 1, 1973. Because Norway's referendum did not agree to join the community, so the expansion of the community this time only included the United Kingdom, Denmark and Ireland. Britain finally got what it wished after applying for joining the European Community more than a decade ago.

Taking a look at the first expansion of the European Community, we can see that the contradictions and conflicts between Britain and France ran throughout the process; particularly in the first time and the second time when the UK was applying to join the community. General de Gaulle vetoed Britain's application twice, which epitomized the differences between the two countries on the interests and outlook of Europe. France's rejection to Britain was not only because it concerned about that Britain, a traditional European power, would threat the central role of France and Germany in the integration and becomes an obstacle of the common agricultural policy but because of the British and French relations was closely related to the United States: The French feared that Britain would use its special relationship with the United States to make the European Community a tool for US to control Europe, and made Europe loss of its independence.

3.3 France, Germany, and Britain and the Development of European Integration

In the 1960s, the European Union had gone through the "empty chair crisis" and France twice vetoed Britain to join the Common Market and other events. The development of the Community was in an unprecedented difficult period. From the late 1960s to the early 1990s, countries in the Community held The Hague conference, started with the European Monetary System and the European Council mechanism, issued a "Single European Act", and signed the "Treaty on European Union" so by all these European integration gradually moved towards the road to recovery. France and Germany played a pivotal role in the critical period of rejuvenation of the Community, with promoting the progress of integration and made important contributions. Britain after joined the European Community in 1973 appeared as a "bad partner" and "troublemaker" for European countries. In addition to the lack of interest in establishment of the single European internal market, British influence on integration could only be described as "disruptive", but not "constructive". This section will discuss the role of the most important countries of the European Union in the process of European integration, the United Kingdom, France and Germany.

3.3.1 The United Kingdom and European integration

British "re-negotiations" and the referendum

On February 28, 1974, the second year that the United Kingdom joined the European Community, the Labor Party won the election. The majority of party members of Harold Wilson-led Labor Party had no objection to the British join in the community, but for Conservatives the condition that Community offers was not satisfactory enough; especially it was difficult to shoulder the burden of sharing the Community budget for the United Kingdom, therefore it advocated the revision of these conditions. It could not join under the conditions provided by the Conservative Party. In the Labor Party, the left-wing Labor Party which opposed European integration imposed great pressure on Wilson. On the General Assembly of Labor representatives in October 1972, the left-wing put forward a provision that once Labor Party returned to power, it should begin to withdraw the British from the Community. Although Wilson managed to avoid voting on the proposal, however, he had to ensure "to renegotiate" on the treaty. In 1973, the Labor Party's annual meeting decided that if the Labor Party came to power, the Labor government would renegotiate with the Community about agricultural policy, budget assessments and other issues, and then decided whether the United Kingdom should stay in the Community by holding a referendum. Because Wilson won by a slight advantage in the election, so re-negotiation was brought on the table. The support of public opinion was very important to him. On April 1, 1974, British Foreign Secretary James Callaghan proposed "a fundamental renegotiation on joining the treaty". Other eight countries of the Community wanted Britain to remain in the Community. Besides, the "renegotiation" mainly involved not the revision itself but the examination of the actual consequences of the Treaty and the measures that should be implemented. Therefore, the eight countries decided to empathized Labor party's domestic difficulties, and tolerated British approach which was an approximated blackmail.

Re-negotiation mainly included related issues of Common Agricultural Policy and financial arrangements, without any requirement of industry and taxation, only hoping that necessities would not be taxed when adjusting VAT in the future. Wilson asked a "major modification" in the Common Agricultural Policy: when pricing, it should give more consideration to the interests of consumers and avoid excess; it should reduce the automatic nature of the intervention; it should provide subsidies to the agricultural producers in the most backward areas. France resolutely defended the principles of the Common Agricultural Policy, but agreed to the requirement of re-examining the German way of implementation. On giving Commonwealth countries preferential subsidies, States also made concessions. Labor government required to defend the interests of the Commonwealth better, especially to safeguard preferences of sugar in British Antilles and dairy products in New Zealand. On February 28, 1975, the European Community and altogether 46 of African, Caribbean and Pacific countries signed the

"Lome Convention" so that almost all products in these countries could enter the Community without paying customs duties. There were 21 of former British colonies included these countries. The sugar issue in British Antilles was resolved. The Community also made concessions about New Zealand's dairy products. Labor government also called for the establishment of the European Regional Development Fund, in order to offset Britain's burden in Agricultural Policy. This requirement had also been met. In 1975, due to the absence of a mature regional development policy of the Community, limited funds were available for regional development, consequently the EEC had started an experimental period for the regional development funding. Other members believed that Britain gained more than it sacrificed for the EEC project and Britain was totally ineffective on reducing the budget expenses of the Common Agricultural Policy. Please notice that, at that time, almost 70% of the EU budget was spent on the Common Agricultural Policy (CAP).

During the negotiations on financial arrangements, Wilson proposed to reduce the contribution share of the UK to the common EEC budget. He argued that by 1978, Britain would pay 24% of the Community budget, and would get only 10% from the total budget expenditures, while Britain's GNP would only amount to 14% of the Community's total GNP (19% in 1974). For Wilson, this unfair situation should be changed.[53]

France and other member states accused Britain of asking for "rebates" which was incompatible with the spirit of EEC's traditional "Own Resources" concept and the conception of common budget. On the Paris Summit in December, 1974 since this was the main content of the UK's request and an important necessity for Wilson government of UK to guarantee domestic public support, the other eight members decided to establish some kind of "correction mechanism" which is called the "UK rebate policy", as a concessions to UK to include it into the economic integration process.

Finally, the EEC decided to establish a system of compensation for the member states which were in an "unbearable situation", but this compensation would not exceed 3% of that year's budget. This financial mechanism would be applied in the seven-year pilot phase. In Dublin Summit held on March 10 to 11 in 1975, Wilson government gained more concessions, that is even if there was surplus in UK's balance of payments (referring to the North Sea oil), it would still receive rebate as long as the standard of living in UK has not improved significantly.

53   Pierre Berge, Trans, Ding Yifan, The History and Reality of the European Integration, China Social Sciences Publishing House, 1989, p.344.

Wilson considered the concessions achieved in the re-negotiations as a victory of his Labor government, but the re-negotiation did not lead to modifications in the treaty, or damage the outcome that the European Community had made. In referendum held on June 5, 1975, British, electorate expressed significant support for EC membership, with 67.2 % in favour on a national turnout of 64%.

Issues and challenges around the common budget issues and the common agricultural policy

Although Britain had reached a tentative agreement to receive a rebate for its contributions to the common budget, Britain's share of total financial resources of the Community had still increased from 8% in 1973 to 18% in 1979. According to a treaty signed by the Community countries on April 21, 1970, the Community decided to gradually establish the "own sources" conception for the common budget revenues of the EEC. The "own resources" are taxes raised on behalf of the EU as a whole, principally import duties on goods brought into the EU. These are collected by the state where import occurs and passed on to the EU. States are allowed to keep a proportion of the revenue to cover administration at a rate increasing every year from 1971 to 1975.

Treaty began to regulate this "own sources" conception from 1971 onwards, 90% of the taxation of agricultural products should be passed to the EEC's "own resources".

As another "own sources" we see VAT-based own resources are taxes on EU citizens based on the proportion of VAT levied in each member country, this would start with the year 1975, comprising a percentage (around 0.3%) of each member state's standardised value added tax (VAT) rate, although VAT rates and exemptions vary in different countries, so a formula is used to create the 'harmonised tax base', upon which the EU charge is levied—the upper limit being max.1%—. The starting point for calculations is the total VAT raised in a country. This is then adjusted using a weighted average of VAT rates applying in that country, producing the intermediate tax base. Further adjustments are made where there is a derogation from the VAT directive allowing certain goods to be zero-rated. The tax base is capped, such that it may not be greater than 50% of a country's gross national income.

The "own resources" conception system would also cover the United Kingdom. On January 1, 1979, the "own sources" system gained a stable basis as a concept, but now a new problem had emerged. With the progress of the preferences of the Community system, the agricultural tax was reduced. Besides, with diminishing import tax rates and constant import tax cancellations to many world countries outside the EEC, import tax revenues had also decreased. Reduced budget incomes has forced the Community to raise revenue or save from EEC expenditures, or increase the VAT rate to be transferred by the member states, thus the original 1% upper limit was revised.

On May 3, 1979, after Margaret Thatcher was elected as the UK prime minister, she immediately demanded to revise the budget system and reform the Common Agricultural Policy. Firstly, here we need to talk about the relationship between the common agricultural policy and member state contributions to the EEC budget. The Common Agricultural Policy had been formed, in June 1970, when the four new applicant states implemented negotiations with the Community, the UK was outside these negotiations or ineffective. The expenditures regarding the Common Agricultural Policy had accounted for two-thirds of the total budget of the Community for a long time after establishment. Between 1967 and 1980, the European Agricultural Guidance and Guarantee Fund[54] expenditures has increased about 10 times, and the proportion of EOGAF (The European Agricultural Guidance and Guarantee Fund) in the EEC total budget had never been less than 70%.[55]

This made Britain have a larger share in the Community. The British governments argued that they provided 20% of the common financial resources, but only got 10% from the Community's expenditures.[56]

For the British side, this situation was, of course, unfair, and it should be changed. On March 11, 1975, during the Dublin Summit, nine countries reached an agreement to start re-negotiations with Britain about the condition of its joining and other members made some concessions towards the United Kingdom. But the agreement in the Dublin Summit only temporarily improved Britain's demands regarding its contribution (expenditures) to the Community. During 1976, the United Kingdom's expenditure for the Common Agricultural Policy had raised sharply. In turn since the UK had a small agricultural sector meant that the UK gained few receipts under the EEC's redistributive policies.

---

54 The European Agricultural Guarantee Fund, finances direct payments to farmers under the Common Agricultural Policy (CAP) and measures to regulate agricultural markets such as intervention and export refunds. The EAGF and the European Agricultural Fond for Rural Development (EAFRD), which finances the rural development programmes of the Member States, were set up on 1 January 2007 and thus the European Agricultural Guidance and Guarantee Fund (EAGGF) was replaced.

55 Agricultural Situation in the European Community: 1975-1981 Reports; Court of Auditors, Annual Reports 1977-1981.pp 4-5.

56 Pierre Berge, Trans, Ding Yifan, The History and Reality of the European Integration, China Social Sciences Publishing House, 1989, p. 371.

It is estimated that in 1979, the UK's net spending on the Common Agricultural Policy was 1.106 billion pounds, while another big net spender, West Germany had spent only 5.9 billion pounds. Consequently, the British GNP had decreased to 0.59 % as a result of agricultural expenditures, while the figure of West Germany was only 0.17%.[57]

After Margaret Thatcher came to power, she firmly proposed to establish an effective and permanent rebate mechanism, and demanded return of all the UK's net contribution to the EEC, and urged a thorough reform of the Common Agricultural Policy to solve the problem of Britain bearing an excessive contribution burden for common agricultural policy. After more than six months of arduous negotiations, on May 30th, 1980, the Council of Ministers reached an interim agreement, agreeing that Britain would be handed back the two-thirds of its net contribution, it made to the EEC in 1980 and 1981, on the other side, in exchange, Britain agreed to raise the EC agricultural prices by 5%.

But this interim agreement of May 30th, 1980, could not solve the problem of Britain's net contribution to EEC. The Council believed that Britain's problem should be resolved through structural reforms, and entrusted the Committee to come up with a solution on agriculture and budgetary questions. On May 30, 1980, the European Commission issued a famous warrant. The Committee therefore issued three documents: "Reflections on the Common Agricultural Policy" ("EC Gazette", Supplement 6/80), "Report on the Warrant" ("EC Gazette", Supplement 1/81) and "European Agriculture Guidelines" (COM [81]608 final).

The Commission stressed the need for the application of this new principle of "common responsibility" in the document of "Reflections", and regulated that "(agricultural products) financial responsibility is divided into two phases: the EC was in charge of the first phase, and the European Community and producers shared responsibility of the second stage by a certain percentage."[58]

In other words, the price guarantee system of the Common Agricultural Policy was no longer infinite. The producers should also be accountable for their own production. But at the same time, the Commission emphasized the shared responsibility of the tax should not challenge the basic objectives of the Common Agricultural Policy, especially the protection of

57   B.E.Hill, The Common Agricultural Policy, Past, Present and Future, London: Methuen & Co. Ltd, 1984, pp.74-75.
58   "Reflection on the Common Agriculture Policy", see Bulletin of the EC, Supplement 6/80, 13.

farmers' income and the contribution of agriculture to the trade balance. Commission clearly stated in the warrant, "the objective of the Treaty of Rome, which is to ensure the safety of the food supply, satisfy consumers, improve productivity and increase farmers' income, has been achieved", so "we cannot abondon nor want to abandon the mechanisms of common agricultural policy ...... "[59]

In order to carry out the report, the Executive Committee proposed to break the upper limit of 1% VAT rate to increase the "own resources", thus revitalize the European economic integration project which was strongly opposed by the British government. Britain thought it should carry out the reform by reducing agricultural expenditures, not by increasing the rate of value-added tax to be given to the common budget. France insisted that rebates given to Britain should be diminished, and EEC expenditures to support the agricultural product prices, should not be reduced . The Federal Republic of Germany has been another net contributor in the EEC, which provided nearly 30% of the financial resources of the EEC in 1980, but only got 23% of the total expenditures. So, its attitude has been similar to the attitude of the United Kingdom.[60]

In 1982, budget issue further deteriorated the relationship between Britain and other member states. In the European Council held in June 1983, the British representative proposed to connect the problem of solving the rebates of Britain's contributions, with Community's other financial problems such as the issue of raising the limit of 1% VAT. Thatcher government declared that unless a lasting solution was found to solve the problem of Britain's unfair high contributions, it would not agree to any common resolution.

The European affairs meeting held in December in Athens stuck in an impasse, ended up with no communique for the first time in the history of the European Union summit. The summit held on March 29, 1984 in Brussels still failed. After the meeting, the British government decided to terminate all payments to community until the issue was resolved. At that time, the EC was facing a serious financial crisis. If it did not break the ceiling of 1% VAT, it would announce fiscal exhaustion in 1983. In addition, there were Spain and Portugal, the two new members which would soon join the Community, so the original budget structure would undoubtedly be challenged. These factors had contributed to the EEC's determination to

59   "Report on the Mandate", see Bulletin of the EC, Supplement 1/18, 11.
60   Jiang Nan, On the Formulation of Common Agricultural Policy between France and European Community, World History, Vol. 4, 2002.

solve the budget problem and the problem of UK's financial contribution to the EEC budget.

After more than a year of negotiations, the countries finally reached a compromise in the Fontainebleau meeting on June 25, 1984: the EC gave back 1 billion ECU (European Currency Unit) to the UK in 1984, extracting 66% of the UK's annual net contributions at a fixed ratio and gave it back to the United Kingdom as a rebate from 1985; at the same time, the decision of increasing the limit volume of the VAT of the EC's self-financial resources from 1% to 1.4% was passed. So far, the quarrels on contribution to the EEC budget between the UK and the Community was over.

It should be noted that this contribution was not only a problem of Britain, since it was related to the common agricultural policy and budget system, it was indeed, as Margaret Thatcher said, an "European problem". However, the different opinions and contradictions and the negotiation that the United Kingdom experienced with the other members of EEC , for example the on the issue of "contribution to the EEC budget" has also promoted and facilitated the development of the European Community. To a certain extent, the United Kingdom had brought a lot of trouble to the Community in the 1970s and 1980s, and was even considered as a "half-hearted member" of the Community. Britain had posed great challenges for the European integration.

3.3.2 The French-German "axis" and the revival of European integration

After the "French-German cooperation treaty" was signed in 1963, France and Germany had agreement on a range of issues. They promoted the development of the European Community, and were called "axis" and the "engine" of European integration.

The Hague Conference

Due to Charles de Gaulle government's "empty chair crisis" and de Gaulle's twice vetoes on British application of joining the European Community, the European Community's activity was once deadlocked. The failure of the referendum on April 27, 1969 led to the resignation of Charles de Gaulle. On June 15, Georges Pompidou was elected as the President of France. The new president seemed to be more flexible than Charles de Gaulle on the issue of European alliance. He expressed determination to continue the construction of the European Community, and finished building a common market at the end of the transitional period in 1970, advocating further development in many areas, such as energy, transportation, currency and others; he said, "there is no objection of the participation in the Community of the United Kingdom or any other countries under possible conditions in principle"; he also suggested to hold meetings of the heads of state or government to promote the construction of Europe.

On July 21, 1968 at the European Union foreign ministers' meeting, the French Foreign Minister Maurice Schumann formally proposed French government to hold the heads of state and heads of government meetings in The Hague in autumn 1969. France thought that the Community should be first built, and then it develop deeper, finally expands. On September 8th and 9th, the President Pompidou and the Chancellor of Germany Kissinger met in Bonn, recommending other member states to participate actively in the Summit. On September 15th, six foreign ministers reached an agreement on the date and agenda of the summit, and the agenda for the meeting was about building, deepening and expanding the Community and the general policy of Europe. France proposed the option of "build–deepen–expand" and no longer veto expansion, which made the Community see the hope for revitalization. On October 21, the German Social Democrat Willy Brandt was elected Chancellor of the Federal Republic of Germany. Willy Brandt especially concerned about the open policy to the east, but also hoped to strengthen the construction of Europe. He chose to stand close to the French on European issues. The congruence of France and Germany created favorable conditions for revitalizing European integration.

The EC summit was held in The Hague from December 1, 1969 to December 2, 1969. Some important decisions made on building, deepening and expanding the Community and other issues. The French government was ensured that the common market would be built by January the 1st, 1970, which meant the basic principles and implementation program of the Common Agricultural Policy that would be beneficial to France were finally established. In deepening, Pompidou proposed the establishment of economic and monetary union. Brandt supported Pompidou's proposal. Other countries also agreed to develop a phased plan in 1970. All countries agreed to negotiate about the expansion.

The success of the Hague Conference made the European Community ruled out the impasse, and promoted the development of the Community again. However, due to the impact of the international monetary crisis like the 1973 oil crisis and the recession of 1975, the goal of establishing economic and monetary union made by the Hague Conference was failed to achieve. However, it was because of a series of economic and financial crisis that made the voices of the European Community to establish economic and monetary union rise up again.

European monetary system

Since the 1970s, the dollar crisis affected the stability of the European currency more and more seriously, and had adverse impact on the economy of the European Community and the common policy. First of all, every time when dollar crisis happened, countries threw a lot of dollars to buy one kind of European currency or more which was considered to be more stable than other currencies. This led to the fluctuation and widening differences of exchange rate between the European countries, which had an impact on the European economy. Therefore, it was essential to establish a stable currency area in Europe in order to get rid of the impact the dollar fluctuation had on the European economy. Secondly, the mutual trade of the European Community countries accounted for half of the total foreign trade. Foreign trade was an important factor in promoting economic growth in the nine countries. However, the currency fluctuated, the outbreak of the economic crisis and the emergence of trade protectionism made mutual trade rate decrease among the nine countries, which influenced the national trade and economic growth.[61] In addition, the implementation of the Common Agricultural Policy also required a stable currency as a basis. In the late 1960s, the financial turmoil of the devaluation of the French franc and deutsche mark appreciation happened. According to the Common Agricultural Policy's requirement of uniform price, when currency devaluated, the price should be raised in order to maintain the unity of agricultural prices, but the French government feared that raising agricultural commodities' price would cause a chain reaction, and therefore refused to raise prices, and still chose to use the exchange rate before depreciation; when the currency appreciated, the price should be lowered, but the West German government feared the price would lead to dissatisfaction of the farmers, and therefore, followed the French approach. In this way, a dedicated exchange rate of agricultural products, "green exchange rate" was formed by detached from the actual market price,. Green exchange rate made agricultural prices actually deviate from the common price. In order to safeguard the common price and to prevent traders to speculate, the European Community adopted a monetary compensation approach, which was levying taxes or providing subsidies when agricultural products were transiting, and raising or lowering the price to a uniform price level.[62] Green

---

61 Wu Yikang et al, European Economic Community, People's Publishing House, 1983, pp 210-211.
62 Ibid., p.172-173.

exchange rate and monetary compensation were only the temporal ways to maintain the common price. Without a stable currency, it was impossible to carry out a real common price. The factors mentioned above all made voices of establishing a stable currency gradually rise.

On October 27, 1977, the President of the European Commission Roy Jenkins delivered a speech at the University of Florence, calling for re-launching economic and monetary union. He stressed the role of the monetary union on ensuring foreign exchange stability, revitalizing investment and promoting economic growth. Commission insisted the revival of economic and monetary union, and developed a program of action in March 1978. The action of the Committee received enthusiastic support of France and Germany. DM was a powerful currency. The effect of a wave of speculation caused by the dollar always fell on the deutsche mark first, especially since 1978, the dollar kept falling, the deutsche mark continued to appreciate, which made West Germany's foreign trade suffer a great loss. Thus, West Germany actively advocated the establishment of European region of stable currencies which was independent from the dollars. For France, as the frequent exchange rate fluctuations directly affected the consolidation of the Common Agricultural Policy, it was also eager to enhance the stability of the exchange rate. France and Germany agreed on stabilizing the currency, the two countries jointly promoted the establishment of the European Monetary System.

On April 8, 1978, a political decision of setting up the European Monetary System was made at the European Council meeting in Copenhagen with the joint efforts of France and Germany. On Bremen summit on July 6, France and Germany formally proposed to establish the European Monetary System. After the meeting, the Community institutions were authorized to review the recommendations and to develop specific programs of the European monetary system. From December 4, 1978 to December 5, 1978, the European Council held in Brussels adopted a resolution on the establishment of the European Monetary System. Britain refused to participate, but ensured the stable currency exchange rate of pound to other common currencies. Italy and Ireland agreed to participate, but their condition was to increase community's support to their region. On December 25, 1978, France suddenly said that only by abolishing the monetary compensation of the common agricultural policy, it agreed that the European Monetary System came into force.[63] The program of European Monetary System which was originally planned to implement on January 1, 1979 was for-

---

63   See Wu Yikang et al, *European Economic Community*, People's Publishing House, 1983, pp.174-175.

ced to delay. After repeated consultations, France and Germany made compromises by gradually reducing monetary compensation, until it was finally canceled. France accepted the plan. On 13 March 1979, the European monetary system formally came into effect.

Monetary compensation is targeted at France and other countries whose green exchange rate exceeds the exchange of market, which means importing subsidiaries and exporting tax are beneficial for importing but not exporting. France is a big exporting country of agricultural products, and has a large amount of agricultural products to export. Therefore, monetary compensation is bad for France.

The establishment of the European monetary system made the EC a relatively stable currency zone, and it was an important step forward towards economic and monetary integration.

The European Council

President Pompidou adhered on Charles de Gaulle's view on "States' Europe", opposing the transfer of national sovereignty to Community supranational institutions, but advocating the development of joint actions of governments. Therefore, he put hopes on the summit, advocating determining the fundamental direction of the European Community by national politicians. He believed that the Hague Conference was a successful case, so he proposed to convene a new summit. After getting positive response from countries, a summit of nine countries including Britain and other new members of the European Community was held in Paris between 19–21 October, 1972.

The summit in Paris adopted a broad range of program: At the latest by the end of 1980, the economic and monetary union would be realized; the regional development fund would be established; the social action program would be formed; the industry, science, technology policy would be formulated; environmental protection program would be made; energy policy would be developed; the Community's policy in the GATT negotiations would be produced; political cooperation would be strengthened and so on. Finally, in accordance with the recommendations of the Pompidou, nine countries set up "an important goal of integrating the relationships between the Member States and a European alliance in full compliance with the signed treaty before the end of the 1970s". However, due to differences between doctrines of federalism and confederation, the program did not give specific instruction of the nature and organization of the alliance, and there were also different opinions on the question of how to achieve these massive programs. Willy Brandt claimed to entrust the Community institutions, while Georges Pompidou thought it should be left to intergovernmental cooperation to deal with. Some of the "European School" hoped that the Commission would become the prototype of the future joint government to implement these programs.

At this point, Jean Monnet once again contributed his wisdom for the construction of Europe. He disagreed with transforming the committee into the next European government, thinking that the committee was for European economic affairs and it was unable to exercise the powers of governments. He had little hope on the European Parliament. He believed that if people wanted to promote the development of the European Community, they could only pursue the root of power from governments. In the summer of 1973, Jean Monet proposed to let heads of state and government form a "provisional government of Europe" in a draft to oversee the implementation of the Paris agenda. The task of the provisional government was to pass a European alliance draft of having one European government and one elected European Parliament. The meeting of the provisional government was held quarterly in each year to issue instructions to Council of Ministers.

Georges Pompidou and Willy Brandt were interested in Monnet's suggestion. In September 1973, Pompidou recommended regular meetings with the top leadership of the countries and the development of political cooperation among the nine countries. In October, he announced that the French Government proposed to "determine the principles of the regular meetings attended by only the heads of state and heads of government within the scope of political cooperation to compare and coordinate their attitude" and proposed the first meeting should be held before the end of 1973. But Pompidou did not adopt the suggestion of the European alliance proposed by Monnet. Brandt immediately expressed support for the proposal of resolving issues through regular meetings of the league. He thought this was a necessary step towards political union.

There was no significant progress on this issue in Copenhagen meeting on the 14th and 15th of December 1973. The communique issued and just pointed out that the heads of state or government would generally hold more regular meetings, but did not set a specific time for the summit. However, the change of the heads occurred in 1974 made significant progress for the summit. And on May 14, 1974 Helmut Schmidt took the position of Federal Chancellor of Germany. On May 19, Valery Giscard d'Estaing was elected President of the French Republic. They had forged a friendship when they were finance ministers. They reached an agreement on promoting European construction. Jean Monnet thought this was a good opportunity, so he repeated his idea of establishing European provisional government, and soon got the response from the two sides.

Giscard d'Estaing was convinced that there must be a European power, the Community institutions could not be weakened, and these two approaches of the community and the government should be combined. But he always said, "The Commission cannot become the prototype of the European government. The transfer of sovereignty enables the European construction to start, but cannot let it go further. When such transfer touches only individual areas, people will tolerate it. But when it touches an important issue, it will immediately cause a self-defense reaction of administering sectors and governments. What we should do is to organize regular cooperation among governments, and to ensure that national policies converge under the premise of respecting the privilege of each country".[64]

Based on this idea, Giscard d'Estaing made use of the good opportunity when it was France's turn to be the chairman on duty; he held a summit meeting in Paris on December 9th and 10th in 1974 to study economic issues. At this meeting, they agreed to establish Economic and Monetary Union and the European Regional Development Fund required by the United Kingdom and Italy, and to withstand against inflation and protect jobs. Countries also agreed to have meetings of heads of state for political cooperation three times a year, in order to solve those pressing problems. This was the origin of the "Council of Europe".

The Council of Europe played an important role on European Community's affairs. The Community's important political and economic problem was its main topic, such as the decision of the election of the European Parliament since 1973, the UK renegotiation in 1975, the establishment of the European Monetary System in 1979 and the decision on the British share of the budget since 1980 were made by the European Council, which gave the Community institutions instructions. The "Single European Act" in 1987 formally incorporated the European Council into the organizational structure of the European Community, "EU Treaty" further confirmed the role of the Council of Europe was that it "should provide the impetus needed for the development of the alliance, and determine the overall political policy"[65]. In the course of development of European integration, the European Council had played an increasingly important role.

---

64   The History and Reality of the European Integration, by Pierre Berge, Trans, by Ding Yifan, China Social Sciences Press, 1989, p.390.
65   The Collection of the Treaties of the European Community by Dai Bingran, Fudan University Press, 1993, p.386.

3.3.3 From the "Single European Act" to the "Treaty on European Union"

In 1984, at the Fontainebleau meeting, the two temporary committees were set up and they soon started to work. "Dodge committee" led by the Irish expert James Dodge assumed responsibility for the institutional affairs, Italian Pietro Adon-nino led "Adon-nino committee" was responsible for affairs of "the people's Europe". On January 1, 1985, Frenchman Jacques Delors took the position as the new Chairman of the Community Board. Delors-led Community Committee, Mitterrand-led France and Chancellor Kohl-led Germany actively promoted the progress of European integration, but the United Kingdom remained reluctant.

"Single Market" plan and the "Single European Act"

With the effort of the Italian European federalists Altiero Spinelli, in February 1984, the European Parliament adopted the "Establishment of the European Union Treaty (draft)". The "Draft" proposed to amend the "Treaty of Rome" and to develop a single treaty for establishing the European Union, and it also proposed the reform of the Community's decision-making process while remaining the three existing systems of the Community to improve decision-making efficiency and to eliminate the "democratic deficit". "Bill" also proposed "subsidiary principle", which caused a big stir a decade later in the community, which was, only when the community was more suitable than the member states to complete a transaction, the implementation of this transaction could be in the charge of the Community.

Mitterrand expressed support for the institutional and political reform in his speech in the European Parliament not long after "Bill" was adopted. Kohl also held the same attitude. France and Germany signed an agreement on phasing out the control of transit personnel between two countries in July 1984. Britain was only interest to the establishment of the single common internal market. On the eve of Fontainebleau meeting, Margaret Thatcher mentioned nothing about the reform of the system in a letter to heads of countries entitled "Europe's Future". In Dodge Committee, French representative nominated by Mitterrand, Maurice Darfur was a loyal supporter of European integration and a contractor of the "Treaty of Rome", while the British representative nominated by Margaret Thatcher, Malcolm Rifkin was an active advocate of the deregulation and of market liberalization, a staunch defender of national sovereignty. This showed that the British and French leaders had different attitudes towards the reform of the Community's institutions.[66]

---

66   Desmond Dinan, Ever Closer Union: An Introduction to European Integration, 2nd Edition, The Macmillan Press Ltd, 1999, p.114.

However, the United Kingdom and France and Germany unanimously supported the proposal on the establishment of the internal market position. Therefore, the progress of the internal market went smoothly. In December 1984, at the Dublin European Council, the Community once again stressed the goal of "improving the internal market". In March 1985, the European Council held a special meeting in Brussels, deciding it should be the Commission to develop specific agenda for completing the internal market by 1992, and formally accepted the goal of achieving a single market in 1992. Delors designated a committee member, Sir Arthur Koch Rumsfeld, who was responsible for the internal market and financial institutions affairs, to be responsible for developing specific programs. Sir Arthur Koch Rumsfeld had served as trade minister in Margaret Thatcher's Cabinet, and he was an ardent supporter of the single market program. Under his leadership, a specific implementation measure and a precise timetable for the completion of the single market were soon developed. On June 15, 1985, the Commission formally issued the white paper entitled "improve the internal market". This was the famous "Branch Wakefield report". The White Paper divided obstacles that hindered the establishment of a real single market into physical barriers, technical barriers and tax barriers, requiring to eliminate these barriers by 1992 for the latest, and to form a truly unified internal market. White Paper provided an important basis for the European leaders to make a final decision at Milan meeting.

On June 29th, 1985, the European Council meeting was held in Milan, focusing on the issue of the single market program and community reform. The meeting confirmed the "White Paper" status as a programmatic document of great marketing plan and instructed the Council of Ministers to develop specific implementation measures after the meeting. However, the British were against the contents of eliminating "barriers of taxation" and unifying national VAT rate system in the white paper. Because of Britain's opposition, Milan meeting temporarily did not include it in the scope of the implementation of marketing plan.

The views on the system reform were not unanimous as on the single market program. After the start of the meeting, France and Germany jointly issued a document entitled "EU Treaty" advocating European political cooperation. They supported for using a single treaty to define the reform undergoing. Continental countries generally supported French, German opinion, and hoped to develop a unified file through the convening of an intergovernmental conference. However, Thatcher was strongly against the proposal of continental countries. She also insisted that the idea to convene an intergovernmental conference was unnecessary. Denmark and Greece agreed with the British point of view. Facing the dispute between the two factions, the Italian Prime Minister Craxi held a majority vote on whether an intergovernmental conference should be held with the support of France and Germany. As a result, the six founding members of the Community together with the Irish voted, while Britain, Denmark, and Greece vetoed. UK was helpless after the voting result of 7 to 3. Milan meeting approved the "White Paper" about internal market plan, and decided to convene an intergovernmental conference to modify the "Treaty of Rome", so that the revitalization of European integration had taken a decisive step.

On September 9, 1985, the first official "intergovernmental conference" (IGC) in history of the European Community was held in Luxembourg. The meeting had lasted for months. The attended representatives were foreign ministers and other officials from the Ministry of Foreign Affairs who were responsible for the daily agenda. The community committee was also formally invited to attend the meeting. On the problem of qualified majority voting and enlarging powers of the European Parliament, countries shared great differences. About the form of the future new treaty, continental countries led by France and Germany still adhered to combining the modification of the original treaty and the new provisions of the Foreign and Security Policy into one treaty, while the United Kingdom was opposed to the merger.

The European Council was held in Luxembourg on the 2nd and the 3rd of December, 1985. The meeting decided to implement qualified majority voting in most areas related to the single internal market; the decision included the "European political cooperation" mechanism which was independent in the scope of activities of the Community, but was not included in the formal treaty of the Community. A formal "common Foreign and Security Policy" would not be formed temporarily.

In the middle of the month, the last meeting of the Intergovernmental Conference decided to combine the original modified treaty and the new treaty about diplomatic and security cooperation together, known as the "Single European Act." The "Single European Act" included the following main elements: The first, it reiterated the ambitious goal of establishing the European Union, "it is determined that on the basis of each community's own regulations, and on the basis of cooperation in the field of foreign policy among the signing countries, the European Union could be established, and the necessary means of action can be endowed".[67]

---

67   Dai Bingran, The Collection of the Treaties of the European Community, Fudan University Press, 1993, p.353.

The Second, "we are determined to improve the economic and social conditions by extending common policies and seeking new goals. We would ensure that each community can function more smoothly by providing the most desirable conditions to the various agencies for the interest of the Community to exercise their powers"[68].

One of the most important elements was formally including the big market plan of 1992 into the Act. It was regulated that an internal market with "no internal borders" which could ensure the "free flow of goods, personnel, services and capital" would be built gradually before the end of 1992. The Act also provided a new reform about the reform of the institutional system. Third, a formal mechanism was added to help coordinating views and cooperation in the field of diplomacy and security within the Community.

The "Single European Act" was signed by The Hague and other 12 countries including the two new members, Spain and Portugal in Luxembourg between February 17 -28, 1986. On July 1, 1987 the Act came into effect. The "Single European Act" provided another legal document for the European Community integration process. The birth of this Act marked the revitalization of the European integration in 1980s.

The "EU Treaty"

The EC countries decided to build the European Union before 1980 at the Summit in Paris held from October the 19th to 21th in 1972. The Summit held from December the 9th to 10th in 1974 instructed the Belgian Prime Minister Leo Tindemans to draft a complete report on EU issues. A year later, Tindemans submitted the report: He was convinced that establishing the European Union was necessary, he did not only regard the EU as a terminology, but as a stage towards the reunification of Europe; he was not in favor of providing a constitution for the future European Union, but advocated strengthening the Community's institutions without amending the treaty to protect the existing accomplishments of the Community; he initiated to establish a common foreign policy for exchanging views on defense issues, and to create an office of European equipments; he suggested enlarging the executive power of the Commission and the authority of the European Court of Justice; he also believed that the European Parliament should be elected by general election; the powers of the European Parliament should be expanded to enable it to participate in legislative affairs". Tindemans Report" was unpopular at the time. Many countries believed Tindemans had gone too far. The report also did not receive enough attention. The European Council meeting held from the 29th to the 30th November, 1976

---

68   Ibid., p.353-354.

The Hague only issued a statement of consolidating and developing the accomplishments that the Community had already achieved.

With the creation of the Council of Europe in 1974, the European Parliament elections in 1979 and the progress of the European political co-operation, other countries felt it was necessary to reform and improve the decision-making capacity of the Community to solve the problem of ex-panding to the Mediterranean Sea and the budget crisis. The Commission insisted on strengthening political cooperation without strengthening in-ter-governmental cooperation. It advocated strengthening the role of the European Parliament. The Council of Ministers should delegate more aut-hority to the Commission, and made greater use of qualified majority vo-ting in decisions making, and so on.

In October 1981, the EC Council of Ministers of Foreign Affairs held in London passed the "London Report", calling for strengthening and ex-panding the "European political cooperation" mechanism established since 1970. On November 18th, the Foreign Minister of West Germany, Genscher and Italian Foreign Minister Colombo proposed a "European Act" program jointly to the Parliament, known as "Genscher–Colombo plan". The report repeated the shelved target of establishing "the European Union". It neit-her involved in the treaty, nor the mandatory legal documents. It only re-commended developing the three existing communities and strengthening European political cooperation mechanisms to exploit new areas; the plan also proposed to strengthen the decision-making capacity, to expand the powers of the European Parliament, and to perform institutional reform in the Community. The countries had different opinions about the plan, and the discussion and the differences continued for a year and a half. On June 19, 1983, at the European Council held in Stuttgart, the Federal Republic of Germany took the advantage of its status as a Presidency to force the meeting adopted the "Solemn Declaration on European Union". Germany pointed out that the EU's goal was to "consolidate and continue to develop the Community. The EU wished to "develop and strengthen the political co-operation within the framework of the "Treaty of Paris" and the "Treaty of Rome" by deepening the existing policies and establishing new policies.[69]

Although the Declaration not out of the intention of France and Germany and the result of Germans and Italians plan, the French-German axis still played a major and decisive role in the process of establishing the European Union. On the path towards the establishment of the European Union, such

---

69   Pierre Gerbet, La Construction de l'Europe, Nouvelle edition revisee at mise a jour, Imprimerie Nationale, 1994, p.407.

as the process of starting the European Monetary System and establishing the European Council and the European single market, the French-German axis had played an important role.

In the process of implementing the single market program, both the business community and the administration had found that if the currencies, the economic and the monetary policies in each country were not the same, then it was impossible to have a real single big market. Therefore, the establishment of the "economic and monetary union" came back on the agenda. But this issue was too sensitive and the British boycotted it. Britain believed that the monetary and financial policies were related to national sovereignty, and not allowed others to get involved. What Britain most concern about was that the disappearances of the international status and role of the pound in the monetary union. When the European Monetary System was established in 1979, Britain refused to participate. Britain only ensured that the exchange rate between the pound and other common currencies could remain stable. In addition, the West German Federal Bank also opposed the EMU program because of the fear about the German mark's status.

But most of the continental continental countries, especially France, Germany and the heads of their governments all actively supported the Economic and Monetary Union program. French and German leaders were the proponents of the European Monetary System, and now they still had to act as the bearer of the Economic and Monetary Union plan. The two governments both expressed support for the existing European monetary system, for the future establishment of the European Central Bank and for the ultimate realization of the single currency. In June 1988, at the Council of Europe in Hanover, it was decided to set up a Committee of Experts led by Delors and attended by the presidents of each country's central bank of the member states, specializing in the implementation of the Economic and Monetary Union plan. In April 1989, it was recommended by the research report from Delors Committee that economic and monetary union plan should be divided into three phases: The first phase was cooperation of national currencies, including the strengthening of the existing European monetary system, for deeper integration; the second stage was to establish a "European system of Central Banks", the prototype of European Central Bank in the future; the third stage was the eventual establishment of a unified European Central Bank and the realization of a single currency. A month later, the community committee led by Delors introduced another important document, "Social Charter about the Fundamental Rights of Workers (Draft)", referred to as "Social Charter".

On June 26th to June 27th, 1989, the European Council was held in Madrid. The Economic and Monetary Union started from July, 1990 and for the preparation of Economic and Monetary Union an intergovernmental meeting was convened. Margaret Thatcher declared that Britain will only accept the first stage; she also strongly opposed "Social Charter" and the conference was unsuccessful. In December, Strasbourg European Council decided to approve "Social Charter" raised by the Commission, but it did not have legal effect and decided to convene a new intergovernmental meeting on the establishment of Economic and Monetary Union at the end of 1990. Thatcher voted against both resolutions, she is the only opponent among 12 member states.

In 1989, the situation of Eastern Europe changed dramatically including government alternation of Eastern European countries, unification of the two German was inevitable. Western European countries, especially France, worried about the unification of Germany. France decided to leash Germany in a more closely integrated way, and to make Germany a "European Germany" instead of making Europe a "Germany Europe". Germany also made commitment to dispel the doubts of each partner country, then to clear away obstacles of unification. On November 2, 1989, a few days before the opening of the Berlin Wall, Mitterrand made it clear to Kohl in the French-German summit: "The situation of Eastern Europe prompted us to accelerate the pace of integrating and strengthening the community." Kohl agreed, saying that "unification of Europe is a must, so that Germany issue will not be a problem."[70]

On November 5th, Mitterrand put it more specifically to presidential adviser: "A united Germany will bring Europe double jeopardy. The reason lies in its strength, it will also lead to alliance of United Kingdom, France and Soviet Union. A war will certainly outbreak in 21st century. In order to eliminate the hazard from the reunification of Germany, we must create Europe quickly." He also said, "We hope to build a European Union which is strong and has common currency, only in this way can we control German." Kohl was also clear that some misdeeds in the Germany history have caused a strong sense of fear towards Germany, and only a common European house could eliminate this fear.[71]

Therefore, both Mitterrand and Kohl had a positive attitude towards European integration. On April 19, 1990, Mitterrand and Kohl proposed a new intergovernmental meeting on behalf of the two governments, whose

---

70   Zhang Xichang, The Biography of Mitterrand, World Affairs Press, 1997, p.319.
71   Ibid.

purpose was strengthening democratic legitimacy of the union; making organizations more effective through Most Resolved System of Council of Ministers; ensuring the solidarity of alliance in fields of economy, currency and politics; formulating and implementing a common foreign and security policy.[72]

On April 28th, 1990, the European Council discussed the French-German initiative in Dublin. Thatcher attacked that the political union would make the community a single country that British would not welcome. In June 1990, the second Dublin European Council decided to convene an intergovernmental conference on "political union" in December. England made reservations again.

On October 27, 1990, the European Council held a special meeting in Rome, decided to start the second stage of Economic and Monetary Union in January 1994. Britain refused to implement "single currency", and advocated the combination of "common currency" and national currency. On December 6th, Mitterrand and Kohl sent a letter to the member states, elaborating their vision of the future political union which was "strong and united, close to the citizens, committed to the mission of the federal". It also made specific recommendations to efficiency of decision-making, common Foreign and Security Policy, strengthening democratic legitimacy of the Community and other aspects.[73]

French-German axis once again provided impetus for the European integration movement, and formulated a specific and consistent progress and development model.

On December 16th, 1990, two intergovernmental meetings opened in Rome at the same time. After tough negotiations, the European Council was held in a Dutch city Maastricht on December 9th, 1991. Each member state decided to sign a treaty for establishment of European Union. The meeting reviewed outcome of the two intergovernmental meetings, and reached the following agreements based on "Treaty on European Union (draft)". Following "pillar" model, member states decided to establish a European Union who had three pillars. The first pillar was the three existing Community, the European Community (European Economic Community replaced), the European coal and Steel Community and the European atomic Energy Community; the second pillar was the common Foreign and Security Policy; the third pillar was cooperation of justice and home affairs.

---

72   The History and Reality of the European Integration by Pierre Berge, Trans. by Ding Yifan, China Social Sciences Press, 1989, p. 450.
73   Ibid., pp.452-454.

Community agencies continued to reform, endowing European Council a mission that "providing necessary impetus for its development, and determining general political guidelines", making it the highest decision-making body.[74]

Including economic and monetary union, the first pillar made a clear timetable, and formally established "Union citizenship" in order to protect the rights and interests of citizens in member states.[75]

In the Common Foreign and Security Policy, "Western European Union was regarded as a unified part; Western European Union was required to formulate and implement Union Decisions and Actions who had defense implication",[76] it was demonstrated for the first time that the community itself should acquire defense ability and defense means. The "subsidiary" principle that Britain insisted on was formally included in the alliance treaty as a decision-making principle. Special provision made Britain and Denmark have the right to not join the third stage of Economic and Monetary Union. "Social Charter" was not officially included in the treaty, just as a protocol attached to the treaty, and does not have the equivalent legal binding as the treaty. Britain did not join in this protocol.

On February 7th, 1992, 12 member states signed the "Treaty on European Union" in Maastricht, so the treaty was also called "Maastricht Treaty" ("TEU in short). On November 1st, 1993, "TEU" came into effect, and it created the European Union and led to the creation of the single European currency, the Euro, thus the European integration entered into a new phase.

The conference between France and Germany held in the Hague, the establishment of the European Monetary System and formation of mechanism of European Council played a pivotal role in promoting the "Single European Act". Establishing European Union made irreplaceable contributions on revitalizing European integration in the 1980s. However, another European power United Kingdom was still conflicting with the community for re-negotiation and "its excess financial contribution". During the operation of the European Monetary System and the development from European Community to European Union, the United Kingdom stayed aloof or openly opposed, or showed indifference. Compared with the contribution to European integration made by France and Germany, Britain's share was cast into shade.

---

74   The Collection of the Treaties of the European Community Dai Bingran trans, Fudan University Press, 1993, p.386.
75   Ibid., p.385.
76   Ibid., p.490.

Throughout the European integration–the history of the European Union, major West European countries play a role which was positive or negative, of promoting or impeding and had a crucial impact on the development of integration. In the beginning, reconciliation and cooperation between France and Germany constituted the premise and foundation of integration. But for the consensus and common action, European integration could not become reality from a concept and just become castles in the air, and in this way the success of European Union would be impossible. France and Germany not only promoted the birth of integration with the other four countries, but also became the axis and engine of integration with reconciliation and close cooperation. In the critical period of the integration expansion, the conflict between France and Britain and two vetoes of French President Charles de Gaulle's made Britain wander outside the community more than 10 years, which had a significant impact on the development trend and the scale of European Community. In the 1980s, for the revitalization of European integration, France and Germany played an important part, promoted the progress of integration on a range of issues, and made contribution on transformation from European Community to European Union. Whereas, during the same period, Britain often acted as a troublemaker and opponent, that constituted a stark contrast with the positive image of France and Germany.

As we can see from the process of European integration, sovereign states especially large countries had great impact on integration. No matter promoting or impeding, sovereign states always controlled the direction and rhythm of the development. In the decision-making framework of community, Commission on behalf of the Community was the main proposal and implementing agency. And policy maker was the Council of Ministers on behalf of the interests of different countries. Such decision making process meant that each country held the final decision of integration. It was always in the control of sovereign countries. Meanwhile, European integration was a voluntary choice; sovereign states sometimes had to make some concessions for the progress of integration. Community had progressed through a history of more than fifty years, dealing with the tough contradiction between the European integration and state sovereignty, and would be further involved with this contradiction as its moves forward.

Chapter IV

The Western Alliance and the Unexpected Challenges Posed by the National Liberation Movement

Ever since there is oppression, there is resistance and fight for national liberation and independence. After World War I, as the proletarian revolution made a great step forward and would further expand, new content and features were given to the national liberation movement of the colonies and semi-colonies; at the end of the World War II, the emerging national democratic forces that had grown and developed during the anti-Fascist war soon became one of the main themes of the world's development. This new round of national liberation movement featured by opposition to colonialism, hegemony and power politics, and the liberation movements of the colonies and semi-colonies not only destroyed the last line of defense of the old colonialism, but also greatly impacted the newly formed post-war Western alliance.

4.1 The Western Allies and the Colonial Issues

In the later period of World War II, the anti-Fascist war was about to succeed, the major countries of the anti-Fascist alliance began the negotiations for the post-war arrangement. They discussed not only how to deal with the vanquished, but also a very important issue that was how to divide and gain their respective spheres of influence. The first thing they discussed was about the sovereignty over the old colonies which had been invaded by German, Italian and Japanese Fascists. This problem sparked a blatant type of altercation among the Western allies and continued to influence the internal relations of the Western Union for a long time in the future after the Western allies have transformed from one wartime alliance into another alliance against the Soviet Union.

4.1.1 The "Mandate" doctrine of the West

After the end of World War I, the victors adopted a "Mandate" approach towards the colonies originally belonged to the vanquished, that was, the League of Nations would appoint the colonial of the defeated to a particular country. For example, the former German territories in Africa and Asia and the former Ottoman Empire's territories in the Middle East were appointed by the League of Nations to Britain, France, Belgium, Japan and other countries. In fact, this was a new way for the victors to re-divide the colonial through the National League and to implement a new round of dominating the colonies. Around the end of World War II, Britain, the US and other countries began planning to own the colonies which had been occupied by the Fascist. The so-called "Mandate" problem was one way to solve the ownership problem of the post-War colonies raised by the United States; the colonies which should have been mandated were delivered to the countries. Those countries- were in charge of the appropriate international institutions (UN) to implement the "International Management".

The problem of "Mandate" was first proposed in October 1943 in the meeting of the foreign ministers of the Soviet Union, the US and Britain, which was a preparation meeting for the Tehran conference. During the meeting, the US government submitted three documents: "the German Issue Memorandum", "Declaration on Guiding Economic Relations" and "the Declaration of Mandating the People of the Dependencies". The declaration was drafted by the US President Roosevelt personally, which advocated the establishment of an international institution for custodian in the future. The international organizations should change the ruling of the colonies by one-country to an international trusteeship. The declaration was rejected by the British Foreign Secretary Eden face to face.[1]

During subsequent meetings in Tehran, Roosevelt told Stalin that he had a discussion with Chiang Kai-shek in Cairo about "the possibility of implementing trusteeship regime in Indochina, whose task is to let the people prepare for the future independence within a period of time, perhaps in two to three decades". According to the US record of the Tehran meeting, Roosevelt and Stalin both mentioned that the trusteeship must be implemented on the military bases and the strategic points near Germany and Japan at a dinner held by Stalin on December 29th, 1943. At this time, Churchill

---

1 Cordell Hull, Memoirs of Cordell Hull, vol.2, Macmillan, New York, 1948, 1305. Hull attended the meeting of foreign ministers in Moscow as the US secretary of the state, Eden who also attended the meeting did not write about the meeting in his memoirs. See Anthony Eden, the Memoirs – The Reckoning, Cassell Company Ltd, London, 1965, pp.410-418.

said, for the UK, they did not want to get any new territory or base, but they intended to keep everything they already had. He said they could not take away anything from the United Kingdom without starting a war. Churchill mentioned Singapore and Hong Kong in particular.[2] Churchill's strongest response to the issue of the mandated territory happened during the Yalta Conference. On February 9, 1945, the three leaders from Soviet Union, the US and Britain heard about the report of the foreign ministers' meeting. When the US Secretary of State Stettinius reported that the exchange of views on the trusteeship would be held before the United Nations General Assembly, Churchill interrupted emotionally, saying that he did not agree with even one word in the report, because no one had ever discussed with him or had reported to him. He asserted that he would not let the forty or fifty countries join the negotiation on the destiny of the British Empire. As long as he reigned, he would never concede even a small bit from the legacy of the British Empire.[3]

Churchill was extremely sensitive about the "mandated territory". It was naturally an instinctive reaction of a representative of the old colonial empire. As the world's largest colonial empire, Britain saw the hope of the triumph over Fascism but still worried about their international status after the war. To be honest, besides the strength accumulated in the industrial revolution, the main reason of calling Britain a "big country" in the history was that Britain's colonies. In the eve of World War II, despite the impact of the national democratic movement after World War I, the British Empire accounted for a quarter of the world's total land area, its population also accounted for a quarter of the world's population, which made Britain still a genuine colonial power. However, the impact brought by the war to the colonial empire was unstoppable, which imposed a direct threat to the interests of the British Empire or to the interests of Britain as a big power–because if there was no interest of the empire, there would be no interest of Britain as a big power. The threat of war faced by the British Empire mainly included four aspects, as will be discussed below:

First, the war had greatly awakened the aspirations of the colonial people to fight for their independence and put their aspirations into reaction. The classical writers of Marxism had many brilliant expositions on the relationship between war and revolution which were fully conformed in the First World War. The World War II not only continued to prove the regularity of

---

2   The State Department, The US Foreign Relations, Foreign Files (the Cairo Conference and the Teheran Conference in 1943), 554. However, Churchill did not mention it in his memoirs, see Winston Churchill, The Second World War, vol.5, the Commercial Press, 1975, pp.568-570.

3   Ibid., p.560.

these expositions, but also showed new features. The most notable features were: The proletarian revolution and the national democratic revolution were combined to fight against the Fascism with the colonial rulers, which made the national democratic movement not only have the right leadership and direction, but also have the maximum space for development and save the strength and condition for getting independent after the war. Second, on the contrary, the war once again severely weakened Britain, making it feel difficult to maintain the old empire. In this regard, the United Kingdom had both the historical experience and the real difficulties. In World War I, Britain had been weakened severely. In the national democratic movement in the colonies, the British had to allow some of the colonial countries to have independence, such as Afghanistan and Iraq; Britain also had to endow greater autonomy and independence to the autonomous territories, like Ireland, Australia, Canada, South Africa and New Zealand. Now, the British politicians bearing the tradition of the empire felt the history was about to repeat itself. Because although the war was not over, they had felt that the burdens of war and the difficulties after the war was far weigh out the ones in the First World War. The "Empire faction" represented by Churchill was determined to defend the empire's last line of defense. They kept alert to the possibility of delivering the British colonies to "international trusteeship". Third, during the war, although the colonies had provided strong human and material resources for the British anti-Fascist war, the war limited the effective contact and exchanges within the British Empire. Britain was worried about those colonies that had been occupied by the enemies, such as Malaysia, Singapore, Hong Kong and Myanmar. If Britain could not recollect those lost colonies after the war, it would not only lose a foothold in East Asia, but also might bear a chain effect. Fourth, with the United States' international status in the war was recognized, the British worried that the US would take advantage of the period. Early in the war, because the British were busy taking care of themselves, many British colonies and autonomous territories turned to the protection of the United States. Britain worried that this would become a fait accompli after the war.

Thus, in order to safeguard the interests of the big countries after the war and during the war, Britain gradually formed a post-war policy that it must "stick to the colonial interests". For the same interests, the old colonial powers, such as France, the Netherlands and Belgium and others, like Britain, were all trying to take all means to continue the old colonial rule.

At the Yalta Conference, Churchill reluctantly agreed to the idea about the mandate doctrine when getting a clear promise by the United States that the institution of the United Nations trusteeship would not include the

British Empire, it was only responsible for the disposal of the subsidiary region of the enemy. On April 25, 1945, the International Organizations' meeting was held in San Francisco as a preparation for the UN. When discussing international trusteeship system, the United States and Britain put forward their own programs. The United States proposed to divide the mandated territory into strategic one and non-strategic one; it should be the Security Council to strengthen the management or set up a Trusteeship Council to do it. First, the US proposal must ensure they could keep on "managing" the important territories for strategic use that were gained from Japan. The second was to use the "international trusteeship" as a way to infiltrate the territories of Britain, France and other old colonial countries. English program was designed to oppose the division of strategic and non-strategic areas. The British opposed the establishment of the Trusteeship Council. The UK program gained the support of France. After some dispute, in the terms of the trusteeship system the Charter was finally included. It was regulated that the territory which could be mandated contained three parts: The non-independent territory under the rule the former League of Nations, the subsidiary territory of the former enemy and the territory delivered by the colonial countries to be mandated. The mandated territory was managed by one or more countries. The Trusteeship Council was set up to be responsible for the specific tasks. The country managing the strategic mandated territory should be responsible to the Security Council. The country managing the non-strategic mandated territory should be responsible to the General Assembly.

Although there were provisions in the UN Charter, it was not easy to implement them. The first thing on the agenda was the ownership problem of the Italian colony. At the end of the war, the Italian colonies in Africa, including Libya, Eritrea and Italian Somaliland, were all under the British occupation. The United States, as well as the Soviet Union, also hoped to occupy some of the territory. The United States proposed to implement ten years of international trusteeship on the Italian colonies, while the Soviet Union proposed to implement a single trusteeship directly on a part of Libya, which was rejected by Britain. As France was worried about the chain effect in French colonies in Africa, France even advocated that Italy could still host itself. This problem remained unsolved both after the foreign ministers' meeting in London in September 1945 and later the foreign ministers' meeting in Paris in April 1946. The treaty towards Italy signed in February 1947. Until November 1949, the UN passed a resolution: Libya got its independence in January 1952; the Italian Somaliland would be hosted by Italy for a decade and merged with the British Somaliland in 1960 to become an independent Republic of Somalia; Eritrea would merge with Ethiopia.

With the end of the war, the differences on the colonial problem that the United States, Britain, France and other old colonial powers had became more acute.

4.1.2 The contest for colonies in Southeast Asia

In the first few years after World War II, the most influential events for the Western alliance were the colony problems than Indonesian independence and the French return to Indochina.

Dutch had ruled the colony in Indonesia for three hundred years, but fell into Japanese hands during World War II. After the war, the Dutch tried to re-implement colonial rule in Indonesia with the support of the British. The Republic of Indonesia that had declared its independence twice in 1947 and in 1948 launched a war of aggression, which was resolutely resisted by the Indonesian people. Still at the end of 1945, the United States kept an eye on Indonesia, waiting and looking for the most suitable opportunity to squeeze out and replace the Dutch position in Indonesia. When Indonesia's national independence forces prevailed, the United States was seemingly neutral; when the army of Britain and the Netherlands launched armed attack, the United States helped mediate, calling for a ceasefire; when the Indonesian government was at a disadvantage with leaders arrested by the Dutch army, the United States was forced by both internal and external pressure to intervene publicly. It should be said that the US government felt very embarrassed at the beginning. On the one hand, the Netherlands was the US ally in Europe—it was one of the sponsors of the "Brussels Treaty" and the North Atlantic Alliance under construction.

On the other hand, the United States had to take into account their consistent assertion of distinguishing the autonomy from the old colonialism, and the public opinion in particular. On December 23, 1948, the US secretary of the Congress of Industrial Organization Philip Murray said, "I express the hope on behalf of the CIO members that the US government should continue to take all possible measures in the diplomatic and economic fields, helping to end the Dutch aggression in Indonesia and to ensure the agreement on recognizing the legitimate rights and interests of the Indonesian people for democracy and autonomy".[4] On January 28, 1949, the UN Security Council adopted the US proposal for a cease-fire in Indonesia, the release

---

4 Alfred Grosser, The Western Alliance – the US -European Relations since 1945, p.92.

of the Indonesian leaders and the restoration of the Republic of Indonesia's government. But the Netherlands still insisted to set troops in Indonesia infinitely, and did not agree to restore the Indonesian government. In order to impose pressure on the Netherlands, the United States suspended its Marshall plan to aid the Netherlands, and formally notified the Netherlands that the United States was ready to provide military assistance to the allies in the North Atlantic Treaty Organization under construction, but did not want to offer military assistance to the Netherlands which still had the problem of the colony unsolved. Finally, the Dutch made concessions, signed the "roundtable agreement," and agreed with the Indonesian independence. Thus, the US gained another effective market for investment and exports in Southeast Asia except the Philippines, which would make up for their shortage of rubber and petroleum resources. Although the Netherlands still retained a variety of real power in Indonesia according to the agreement at that time, the Dutchmen felt bitter. It was almost happened at the same time when the NATO was founded, but it made the Dutch send a lament, what were the benefits for establishing the North Atlantic Alliance?

Indochina became a French colony from the mid-19th century. In the World War II, with the fall of France at the hands of Hitler in June 1940, Japan which had occupied more than half of China expanded into Indochina. The US attitude towards Japan's military expansion in Indochina became gradually certain just as its opinion of the entire war. The US announced the Japanese to withdraw from Indochina, and finally to take over Indochina and opposed the French returning to Indochina. In January 1943, Roosevelt and Charles de Gaulle had the first meeting in Casablanca by the arrangement of Churchill. According to the recollections of Roosevelt's son, Charles de Gaulle had clearly told Roosevelt that he hoped the allies would return the French colonies to France immediately after the liberation of France. But after the meeting, Roosevelt said, "I am not even sure that returning the colonies to France is right." "For what logic, what habits, what law of the history, these lands should belong to France".[5]

Since then, Roosevelt repeatedly expressed his will to deliver Indochina to the international trusteeship in different occasions with different people. According to Charles Bohlen, during the Tehran Conference, when talking about France with Stalin, Roosevelt said he would not stand for restoring the rule of the French in Indochina through the sacrifices of allies', because after a century of colonial rule, the living standard got worse in Indochina

---

5   Elliot Roosevelt, As He Saw It, Duell, Sloan and Pearce, New York, 1946, 114-115. But Charles de Gaulle did not mention this requirement, only stated his willingness to establish French regime domestically and in the empire. See Charles de Gaulle, War Memoirs, vol.2, p.98.

than before.[6] He also said the same thing in his memo to Hull. He said, "It is true that I think Indochina should no longer be returned to France, but should be placed under the international trusteeship. It has been a year since I had expressed this opinion. France which possessed thirty million inhabitants has existed for almost a hundred years, but people's living situation is worse than the initial occupation period....France has squeezed Indochina for centuries. The people in Indochina deserve a better future".[7]

Roosevelt also instructed not to argue about this issue with the British, because the British were afraid of hurting their own empire.

However, Charles de Gaulle was determined to protect the interests of the French Empire at that time, no less than Churchill's determination to protect the interests of the British Empire. Still during the war, Charles de Gaulle argued or even put up a fight with Britain and the US for the French "unity and integrity". In the summer of 1941, he had a quarrel with Britain on the ownership of two mandated ruling regions Syrian and Lebanese; by the end of 1941, he ignored the warnings and opposition of the United States, and deprived French Saint Pierre Island and Miquelon Island in the Western Hemisphere from the hands of the Vichy regime with forces. From 1943, the French National Liberation Committee under the leadership of Charles Charles de Gaulle began its activities for returning to Indochina. De Gaulle's idea was very clear. France's armed forces must be involved in the fighting against Japan for the liberation of Indochina. "Well, the French bloodshed in Indochina will become the most powerful authority" Otherwise, everyone would have required for French withdrawal from Indochina by then. In the latter part of the war, Roosevelt had repeatedly instructed the State Department that they should not associated with any French resistance force related to Indochina. In March 1945, he also told the US general Wedemeyer who was in charge of military affairs in China to prevent all British and French activities in the Far East and did not give any support to the French. On March 9, 1945, the Japanese army struggled in Indochina by taking over all the French colonial institutions in Indochina through forces. Charles de Gaulle held negotiations with the United States, hoping to ship the French army in Africa and Madagascar to the Far East, but the United States did not agree. The French troops had asked for the US air support in China. Churchill also came forward to ask Roosevelt about changing the attitude of the US and, hoping he could support France in the war against the Japanese in Indochina, but it was rejected. The United States not only

6   Charles E. Pollen, Witness the History, 1929-1969, p.140.
7   The State Department, The US Foreign Relations, Foreign Files (the Cairo Conference and the Teheran Conference in 1943), p.872.

did not support the French to maintain the ruling in Indochina, but also thought there were other proposals for the British support. The US attitude angered Charles de Gaulle. He said, "I have already seen this, so there is nothing strange about this dark psychology. But once we won, until the moment we are no longer bound by any allies, I must make France return to Indochina".[8]

Now, the problem was what kind of contradictions and differences there had been between the United States and its European allies on the issues of the old colonies. Did the United States really oppose colonialism?

4.1.3 Did the United States really oppose colonialism?

On October 15, 1999, an article entitled "Britain's Cold War and the general plan of President Roosevelt: East Theater, 1943-1963" wrote by Michael Billington was posted in the United States' Government Chief Information Review. The author was an The US veteran studied the modern history of Southeast Asia. The author believed that one of the most precious legacy left by Roosevelt was his tireless devotion to end the colonialism by Portugal, the Netherlands, Britain and France. He also said that Roosevelt insisted when he was alive that all forms of colonialism must be ended, especially that Hong Kong must be returned to China. There were similar sort of views among the West politicians and academics. For example, Charles Bohlen said, "Roosevelt's remark on Indochina reflects two of his views, which I have heard for many times in the next few years. The first was that he has intense hatred towards colonialism. There are many occasions in record that he expressed his opposition to the colonial rule, which often irritated the British. The second is that he seemed keen to emphasize the benefits of a mandate system. This was often his solution for those who do not yet have the requisitions to be independent".[9] As for the French, they had their own opinions. Alfred Grosse said, "The attitude of the United States—both disgust of the British Empire and dislike every colonial empire—was out of two motivations at least. Primarily, it was because of the specific material interests: to open up new markets and eliminate exclusive rights over any market secondly, the immoral aspects of colonialism.".[10]

It was superficial to regard the contradiction between the United States and the old colonial powers of Europe at the end of World War II by indicating that the United States' opposed to the colonialism. This was just a one-sided

---

8 Charles de Gaulle, War Memoirs, vol.3, p.201.
9 Charles E. Pollen, Witness the History, 1929-1969, p.140.
10 Alfred Grosser, The Western Alliance – the US-European Relations since 1945, p.18.

conclusion ignoring the nature of the problem. For many Westerners, only the United States was the model of modern democracy. They believed that the United States followed a progresssive path different from the old continent of Europe—it established the US-style freedom and democracy under the British colonial rule through the War of Independence, thinking that the nature of the United States was so different with the nature of European colonialism. In fact, as a new type of country built by the Europeans; the United States did not wash away the traces of colonialism brought by the old continent of Europe. From a historical viewpoint, it was the pioneer settlers of the US who firstly deprived the local indigenous people from their homelands who lived there for centuries long, and after these pioneers won independence from the the old colonial masters, they attempted to invade Canada by fighting against the British (1812-1814), and after this war, they started a second war—plunder—campaign against the Indians, with the pretext of developing the West. In 1846, the United States declared war against Mexico and conquered Texas, New Mexico, California and other places, accounting for half of the land territory in Mexico; in 1898, the United States declared war against Spain and won the Spanish colonies, the Philippines, Guam, Cuba and Puerto Rico, and annexed Hawaii; in 1903, it occupied Midway, controlled the Panama Canal. Moreover, the United States proposed the "open door" policy, asking for the "equal opportunity", "equal access to interests in colonies", and the joint partition of China with the European powers. Such action could not be counted as anti-colonialism in any case.

Of course, the United States had certain differences from the old European colonial powers as a brand new nation although its people came from the old continent of Europe. The biggest difference on the issues related to the colonies was that the United States did not have many colonies or heavy burden as a newcomer, so it could benefit from the conflicts between the colonial people and the old colonial power. Although the old European colonial powers had benefited from the colonies for many years, with the awakening of the colonial people, their resistance, their burden within and out of the countries became heavier. The old colonial rule was difficult to maintain. This was the background of the quarrel between Roosevelt's America and the old colonial powers around the end of World War II. Having seized the opportunity of the fall of colonialism's reputation, the US showed the gesture to keep divided from the old European colonialism and to express sympathy for the people in colonies out of its need for strategic and practical interests, so that it could prepare a public environment for its replacement.

Two things were worth noticing here. First, the United States opposed the European colonial powers to return to the colonies to resume colonial governance. The fundamental purpose of the US was to meet the needs of expanding the US capital and to reach the overseas sphere of influence possessed by the old European colonial powers for many years. Even Western scholars saw this point clearly. We have already quoted Grosse before. He believed one of the motives of the United States was "to open up new markets and break the exclusive barriers". At the same time pointing out this motive, Grosse also cited the US State Department of Commerce's adviser's words, "The great the US nation will never allow the British and the Dutch to dominate the purchase price of tin and rubber". Later, when it came to the US policy in Indochina, the scholar who was quite well known in France and in Europe said explicitly, "it has been the US suggestion to the French for more than seven years that they should respect the independence of South Vietnam, so that they can unite all nationalist forces against the North Vietnamese Communist Party. But once the US military advisers in South Vietnam replace the French, the US government did not do what they said about the independence of South Vietnam.. The US anti-colonialism is just an excuse to replace the presence of Europe in the former colonies. This view—is very popular at least in France—therefore has been confirmed."[11] Second, there was disagreement of interests on the issue of colonies between the United States and the old European colonial powers and as the colonial people's resistance increased their disputes became more intense.

This was a fact. But this was only one side of the fact, which was not even the main aspect. The main aspect was that they connected, cooperated with each other and suppressed the national democratic movement of the colonial people for the most of the time to avoid losing the traditional benefits in colonies. This was determined by the common desire of expanding capital and the international environment during the Cold War era.

4.2 National Liberation Movement and the US-European Relations

After World War II, the national liberation movement almost swept all the colonial and semi-colonial territories throughout the world with an unprecedented momentum. The vast movement of people took the leadership of the new political party and the armed attack as the main form, became a touchstone to expose the nature of the Western alliance, and destroyed the colonial ruling system which had lasted for hundreds of years at the same time.

---

11   Ibid., pp.136-137.

4.2.1 The US-Europe cooperation to suppress the national liberation movement

The differences of interests between the US and the old European colonial powers on the colonial problem could not comprise their cooperation out of their common interests to crackdown the national liberation movement. On the Potsdam Conference in July 1945, the new US President Truman approved European countries' going back to their Asian colonies. The United States agreed to return Hong Kong to the United Kingdom, Burma was also placed under the management of the Southeast Asian headquarter of the British Army. The Dutch East Indies and the French Indochina no longer belonged to the US occupation plan. After the Japanese surrendered, the British immediately occupied Burma, Singapore, Malaysia and Hong Kong, the Netherlands and France soon returned to Southeast Asia. Although the US Truman government, like Roosevelt, said they could not use the US aid to help rebuild colonies, in fact, the acquiescence and the help of the United States delivered the European colonial army back to their colonies and supported them to continue repressing national liberation movements. For example, in Vietnam, during the Battle of Dien Bien Phu in June 1950 to May 1954, the United States provided $ 2.6 billion to France through the Marshall Plan, accounting for 80% cost of the French war in Vietnam. The US aid to the Netherlands was also transferred to the national liberation movement suppressing the Indonesian people. The typical examples of the cooperation between the United States and European countries to suppress the national liberation movement included; the Korean war waged by the United Nations forces with the lead of the United States and supported by the European countries and secondly the civil war supported by the United States to suppress the Chinese revolution, but the most typical one was the Anglo-American suppression of the people's revolution in Greece.

Greece was a traditional sphere of influence of the British Empire. Before Hitler occupied Athens in 1941, the Greece King George II and his government fled to Britain. The Greek people despised the king and the government for their irresponsible escape. They began to resist the Fascist aggression, and set up the Greek National Liberation Front and the People's Liberation Army led by the Communist Party of Greece, which turned out to be the most powerful military and political force in the war of anti-Fascism. In October 1944, the Greek gained its liberation. Under the protection of the UK, Greek government in exile returned to Athens. Britain had long been premeditating to use military power to force the Greek National Liberation Front to hand over the army. It mobilized and gathered the military forces from the battlefield in Italy and India, and launched a massive attack to the Greek People's Liberation Army. With the influence of an existed "hand over guns" and the ambiguous attitude of the Soviet Union, only a few people still stuck to the fight, while the Greek People's Liberation Army was disbanded, the revolutionary forces were repressed. The revolutionary forces were unwilling to be oppressed, so they were gathered again in Greece in the second half of 1946 and founded the Democratic Army of Greece, which gave a heavy blow to the government forces. The Greek government stuck in the economic and political crisis, and turned to Britain for rapid and massive aid. But at this time, Britain was too exhausted to take care of itself in the war, so it had to resort to the United States.

Initially, the US did not support the British interference in Greece, which seemed a little "quasi-colonialism" for the public. But the UK only wanted to maintain its long-term influence in Greece. Of course, the United States was just despising the things it could not reach, so it had to hold this attitude towards the things it could not directly intervene. But now there was an opportunity to replace Britain. In February 1947, after the British government raised its request, the US President Truman issued a statement in March 12 which was called "Truman doctrine" later. In the 20-minute long statement, Truman's words included Greece, Turkey, and the United States' responsibility to lead the world, the meaning of supporting Greece and Turkey, and the determination to curb the expansion of "totalitarian". He asked Congress to authorize $ 400 million to provide assistance to Greece and Turkey before the end of June 1948, and sent civilian and military personnel "to help the reconstruction"[12]. The Greek took $300 million of $ 400 million, and said $149 million would be used for military assistance. By June 1949, Greece received $ 648 million aid from the US, of which about $ 500 million was used for the repression of domestic revolution. The US soldiers also directly involved in the repression. They are not only established a joint US-Greek General Staff, but also involved in the training to teach the use of the US weapons. In October 1949, the helpless Democratic Army of Greece was forced to stop by the powerful attack of the United States and the Greek nationalist army.

During a decade from 1940, the Greek national democratic movement experienced a heroic struggle against the German and Italian Fascists as well as the British and the US colonialism and imperialism, and left a glorious page in the world history. Greek people defeated the German and Italian Fascists, but were frustrated by the bloody crackdown produces by

---

12   Arthur M. Schlesinger, The Dynamics of World Power, A Documentary History of United States Foreign Policy, 1945-1973, Vol.2, New York, 1973, pp.309-313.

the Anglo-American colonialism. It should be noted that the Greek national democratic movement was repressed jointly by the UK and US under the slogan of of "opposing communist expansion".

Since Churchill's "Iron Curtain" speech in 1946 unveiled the Cold War, a strange phenomenon appeared in international politics: Almost all the leaders of the national liberation movement fought for independence and democracy, from Indonesia's Sukarno to Bourguiba of Tunisia, from Guzman of Guatemala to Egypt's Nasser, were almost said to be communists or communist sympathizers by the Western countries. Britain, France and other European countries with tradition of possessing colonies asked the United States to support the suppression of the national democratic movement in the colonies with the excuse of "opposing communist expansion"; the United States took the opportunity to replace the British and French position with the same excuse, and expanded its sphere of influence. Then, "opposing communist expansion" had become synonymous with suppressing the national democratic movement of the Western colonialism and imperialism and became the guise for the United States and the European colonial countries to maintain colonial interests and fight for spheres of influence together.

4.2.2 The national liberation wars shook the US-European cooperation and differences grew

Armed struggle was the main form of struggle opted by the peoples of colonies and semi-colonies in their fight for national independence and liberation after World War II. In these armed struggles, the Korean war against the United States, the Vietnamese war against French colonialism in Indochina, the Algerian war of national liberation against French colonial rule, and the Egyptian war of Suez against the Anglo-French invasion, the Vietnamese war against the United States for its national salvation and the struggle of the Palestinian people to return back to their homeland supported by Arab countries, all had a significant impact on the EU-US relations after the war.

Due to differences of interests between the US and the old European colonial powers they could not comprise and fully cooperate in suppressing the national liberation movement, their conflicting interests made it impossible to avoid political conflicts caused by the national liberation movement.

On June 25, 1950, the Korean War broke out. In order to control the enti-re North Korea and further threaten the new China, the US manipulated the UN to send troops to interfere in the internal affairs of North Korea, which expanded a civil war to the first major local international conflict after the war. The US aggression was hit by a powerful resistance of the Korean and Chinese people. The plight of the United States in the Korean War not only triggered a debate on the Korean War policy in the United States, but also relation between European allies. During the Korean War, the United Kingdom had three basic measures. First, they sent a small scale military expeditionary force to the United Nations to do something for the US agg-ression in Korea; second, they persuaded the United States to keep balan-ced, so that it would forget the European strategic location; third, they de-termined to prevent the United States to use nuclear weapons and to expand the war to China. On November 30, 1950, the US President Harry Truman issued a statement advocating the expansion of the Korean War, and in-tentionally mentioned the atomic bomb threat in his answer to a reporter. The nuclear threat did not and could not frighten the Chinese people, but the US European allies were much frightened. Nearly a hundred of British members of Labor Party sent a letter to Prime Minister Attlee, protesting the United States' attempt to use the atomic bomb against China. Under domestic pressures and Europe, Attlee talked with Truman on December 4th in Washington: "In the UK, this is known as a decisive action to stop President Truman to use the atomic bomb in the Korean War. The war is not well received by the people in Britain, not only by the left-wing forces."[13]

The differences between Europe and the US in the Korean War indica-ted that the newly established North Atlantic alliance lacked full accord. Although the UK's concern was out of its special interests about regional issues of Hong Kong, but the differences between Europe and the US regar-ding global strategic priorities and policies became obvious.[14]

When the Korean War began, the Indochina war had been ongoing for three and half years. The United States already had suspected France's re-turn to Indochina. France also kept alert to the United States' interventi-on in the problem of Indochina. France believed that the Indochina war was France's domestic dispute, and prevented the US intervention at the beginning. However, the situation got increasingly unfavorable for the France. The Vietnamese People's Army had gained the control of more

---

13　The Western Alliance - the US-European Relations since 1945 by Alfred Grosser, Routledge Press, p.121.
14　The differences between the US and Europe in the Korean War can be seen in 1.4 part of this book. – Author's note.

than half of Vietnam and most parts of Laos and Cambodia by 1953. The heavy burden of war and the severe situation put the French domestic politics into chaos and caused France to ask more direct support from the US. On the one hand, the US was afraid to lose Indochina after the victory of the Chinese Revolution and failure in the Korean War; on the other hand, they did not want to support the French military operations in Indochina to maintain French rule in Indochina. So the United States decided to be not directly involved, waiting for an opportunity and creating the conditions for eventually taking over Indochina. Took advantage of the support of the US Marshall Plan to the French in Indochina, the US strengthened the economic and political penetration of Indochina and fostered the pro-The US political forces. The United States sent economic, political and military intelligence agents continuously to Indochina. Wu Tingyan who was supported by the US later became the US puppet to control the South Vietnamese. In 1954, before the Geneva meeting on the political solution of the Indochina War, the French army and the Vietnamese People's Army all bet the victory of the Battle on the battle of Dien Bien Phu. Starting from February, the Vietnamese People's Army concentrated superior forces to attack the last largest stronghold of the French army. In order to keep the Dien Bien Phu, the French had repeatedly asked the US to dispatch bomber support, but was rejected by the United States. In July, China, Vietnam, the Soviet Union, France and other countries cleared the interference of the United States and South Vietnamese puppet regime, and finally announced the Joint Declaration which included the ceasefire in Indochina, the withdrawal of all foreign troops and the respect to the independence of the three countries of Indochina. But the United States saw no benefits from the ceasefire, so it refused to sign the declaration together with the South Vietnamese puppet regime. The victory of Indochina war undoubtedly deepened the mistrust between France and the United States.

The victory of Indochina greatly encouraged the struggle of the Algerian people against the French colonialists rule. On November 1, 1954, the Algerian national liberation war broke out, but was repressed brutally by the French colonial army. For the French, this war, which nearly lasted for eight years, not only made the cabinets fall one by one, but also put colonists into a condemnation because of the heinous repression. Because of the heroic struggle of the Algerian people, the French Charles de Gaulle's government had to sign the "Evian Agreement" in 1962, and Algeria gained independence. Despite being "cruel" and "painful", but after removing the "colonial burden," Charles de Gaulle dedicated to dealing with domestic and foreign affairs, he felt "fortunate" after all. However, this fortune could not hide his discontent with the US on the problem of Algeria, because the United States condemned France at the United Nations, demanding an end to the Algerian war and the independence for Algeria as soon as possible; Britain and the US continued to transport weapons to countries which they support Algeria in spite of the opposition of France, and a considerable part of these weapons could be re-exported to the hands of the Algerian National Liberation Army. On November 15, 1957, the news that a group of the US weapons arrived in Tunisia irritated the French. The French delegation attending the meeting of NATO announced their withdrawal from the meeting. They believed that "the efforts made by all the participants for their wish to unite the Atlantic are meaningless"; and the United States "secretly" received representatives of the Provisional Government of the Republic of Algeria without consultation with France. Thus, France's dissatisfaction with the United States deepened again, because just as the United Kingdom, France still held the grudge for being "abandoned" and "humiliated" in Suez in 1956.

In July 1956, the United States contradicted itself, and canceled the loan originally promised to provide to build the Aswan Dam in Egypt. Then the United Kingdom and the World Bank also canceled the loan. This made Egypt which already had economic difficulties suffer great loss. Egypt asked for compensation from the Suez Canal, but was rejected. The Nasser government decided to nationalize the Suez Canal Company controlled by the British and the French. Egypt's tough stance was out of the expectation of Britain and France. After several negotiations without real progress, Britain and France instigated the Israeli to launch a war of aggression to Egypt on October 29, and then they sent troops to interfere, trying to regain the control of the Suez Canal by force and overthrow the Nasser government. The aggression in Egypt received almost unanimous opposition of the world. The United States regarded the Suez crisis as a great opportunity to get involved in the Middle East and to replace Britain and France from the outset. The US did not cooperate with the economic sanctions against Egypt imposed by Britain and France, did not freeze the overseas assets of Egypt, and expressed its willingness to pay shipping fee as the compensation for Egypt. However, France disregarded that the US had repeatedly warned Britain and France "not to resort to force", and "not to resort to force before the US election on November 6" the warning, which was out of the US expectations. At the special session of the UN General Assembly on November 1, the resolution No. 997 in which United States called for an immediate cease-fire was approved by 64 votes (including the Soviet Union), 5 vetoes from Britain, France, Israel, Australia and New Zealand, 6 abstention votes (including NATO allies Canada, the Netherlands, Belgium, Portugal). On November 6, Britain and France, and Israel were forced to agree to a ceasefire and began to withdraw in disgrace on December 3rd.

The British against the US policy in the Suez Crisis

When the Western scholars analyzed the reasons for the British and French failure in the Suez war, they generally had little mention of the heroic resistance of the Egyptian people and the massive support of the people around the world, but thinking it was mainly because the US, which was a one-sided conclusion. However, the problem could also be reversed: if the United States did not oppose, while the Soviet Union got caught in handling the Hungary incident, there would be a different outcome of the Suez war. Alfred Grosse wrote, "The main reason for making the British and French governments yield is not the opposition of the British Labor Party, or the ultimatum issued by Marshal Bulganin, but the relentless pressure imposed by the US government on the pound". He quoted the words of the British Chancellor of the Exchequer and the US Treasury Secretary in the book as evidence. McMillan said, "If we get the money that we deserve from the IMF, or even better, to get temporary loan assistance from the United States, I would not be so worried. It can be understood that the United States does not want to provide aid, but it is unforgiveable that the US obstructed the IMF to offer assistance... The answer I got is that the US government won't agree to make specific arrangements until we agree to a ceasefire...... This is a shameless way to exert pressure". George Humphrey told the British ambassador face to face that, "Before you get out of Suez, as long as I am able to stop, you'll never get a cent from the the the US government!"[15]

Thus, we can see the sharp contradiction between the United States and its major European allies on the Suez issue. Therefore, from the impact of the national democratic movement after the war on the Western Union, the Suez war in 1956 reflected the contradictions between the United States and Europe in their post-war competition for spheres of influence. It was the first reveal of an internal large-scale conflict in the post-war Western Union, and also showed the centrifugal tendency of the European countries inside the Western alliance to ignore the will of the United States in the decision-making process of major issues for the first time.

As the well-known French journalist André Fontaine wrote, the aggressive US intervention war to hinder Vietnam's unification was an "ill-conceived war"[16].

---

15   The Western Alliance – the US-European Relations by Alfred Grosser, Routledge Press, p.144.
16   Andre Fontaine, Un Seul lit pour deux reves – Histoire de la "detente" 1962-1981, Fayard, 1981, p.39.

The United States obstructed the elections held in Vietnam according to the "Geneva Agreement" in order to support the puppet regime it fostered. Facing the growing demands of reunification of the Vietnamese people, the United States sent troops to Vietnam in November 1961. With the heroic fight of the Vietnamese people, the United States continued to expand the scale of war, and implemented "special war" in South Vietnam to brutally repress the Vietnamese people's fight against the United States for national salvation. The US dropped bombs and used napalm and other biochemical weapons in North Vietnam. The US became extremely brutal, implementing every form of attack. The invading army also increased from several thousand to 540 thousand in 1969. In the West, few of the European allies supported the US invasion policy towards Vietnam. Except Federal Republic of Germany supported due to its internal relations, and Italy expressed its indifferent attitude, it was difficult to hear any remark of support from Britain.

But Britain had repeatedly expressed its opposition to the bomb attack in Hanoi and Haiphong, and tried to communicate between the two sides to bring an end to the war as soon as possible. In February 1965, British Prime Minister Wilson called to suggest the US President Johnson to meet with North Vietnam, but was rebuked by Johnson, "If you want to help us in Vietnam, then send some people here to deal with the guerrillas, and announce that you are going to help us in the press". Wilson could not conceal his anger facing the arrogant intransigence of the United States. In his memoirs, he doubted whether people from the US wanted to drag him on the pirate ship, whether the US hawks began to rise, or the White House was in extreme confusion.[17]

For the US, the most embarrassing thing during the Vietnam War was to face the French.

The problem was simple, because the trouble that the US involved was exactly the same trouble the French had; the things the US were doing in Vietnam were exactly the something the French had done in Vietnam; the US humiliated the French because of the colonial problem, but now it was French turn to ridiculed the US.

France almost completed the main task of "decolonization" after Charles de Gaulle had taken care of the Algeria event in 1962. Thus, France seized this opportunity to criticize the United States because of its experience. On May 31, 1961, shortly after taking office, the US President John F. Kennedy

---

17   Harold Wilson, The Labour Government, 1964-1970: A Personal Record, London, Weidenfeld and Nicolson, 1971, p.80.

visited France. During this visit Charles de Gaulle personally warned the United States as follows: You can never get away from this area if you intervene. After the nation awakened, any foreign force is untenable, no matter how clever it is. You will see this later. Even if you can find a few local leaders who choose to stand by your side for their own benefit, but the people do not agree, they still have to oppose you. Even more advertisement of your ideal won't work anymore. In addition, the locals will judge by mix of power and the ideal. Therefore, the more you are anti-communist, the more the communists are shown as the defenders of national independence, the more help they can get from the people, especially the help from the hopeless people. We French have learnt our lessons. You Americans used to want to replace our position in Indochina. Now, you step our footsteps, and re-ignite the war fire that has gone out. I remind you, you will be stuck in a military and political bottomless pit step by step, no matter how much you spend or how much sacrifice you make there. What you, we and others should do is this is not replace Asian state power, but to give them something to get rid of poverty and humiliation, while poverty and humiliation are precisely the things generate totalitarian. I am taking to you on behalf of the entire West.[18]

On August 29, 1963, Charles de Gaulle made a statement about the Vietnam issue, stressing that the future of South Vietnam should be decided by the Vietnamese people rather than anyone else. France not only refused to follow the US lead in international organizations to sign a joint statement condemning the Vietnamese people, but also kept in contact with the Vietnamese government, especially with the President Ho Chi Minh. On September 1, 1966, Charles de Gaulle delivered a speech at the Phnom Penh stadium in Cambodia, condemning the US intervention in Vietnam. He said the US action in Vietnam made the war broke out again in Vietnam, "although the US military force is unlikely to be destroyed, on the other hand, the Asian people can never obey the strangers' laws from across the Pacific". He believed that the negotiations depended on the US decision and commitment to withdraw the troops within an appropriate period of time. He hoped the United States would do so, because "it will not damage its dignity, will not violate its ideals, and will not harm its interests". On the contrary, "how will the world cheer for the United States"? If the United States did not make such a decision, "the possibility of the success in any mediation would be very hard".[19]

---

18 Charlles de Gaulle, Memoires d'Espoir – Le Renouveau, Librairie Plon, 1971, pp 274-275.
19 Charlles de Gaulle, Discours et Messages, V, Librairie Plon, 1970, pp 75-78.

However, Kennedy and Johnson both refused to listen to the advice of Charles de Gaulle. In March 1968, the United States declared a unilateral cease of bombing and sought for the mediation of France. However, the war continued swinging between cease fires and relaunches.

It was until the Nixon–Kissinger era in January 1973 that the United States accepted the reality of the Vietnamese people's victory, and signed an agreement to end the war and restore the peace.

It should be noted that Charles de Gaulle expressed support for the independence of Indochina, and opposed the US intervention in the Vietnam War, which was consistent with his opposition to US hegemonic control of Western Europe and the strategies of sticking to independence and maintaining the status as a great power. This was a new feature on the international political arena by the end of World War II after the 1960s. How to safeguard the national independence and sovereignty became a prominent and complex problem in international relations after the war. Because this issue not only involved a wide range of things, almost all the major issues of international relations were related to this, and it not only existed among different countries or rival groups, but also existed among internal allies even with more intensity. This showed that the post-War struggle to safeguard national independence and sovereignty was not only reflected in the struggle for defending national independence and sovereignty of newly independent nation after the war, in the colonial and semi-colonial struggle for national independence and sovereignty, but also was reflected in the struggle for national independence and sovereignty caused by dissatisfaction to hegemony in the US-Soviet system. Whether people were aware of it or admit it or not, most countries were facing a problem of how to protect national independence and state sovereignty in that period, except for the two superpowers, the Soviet Union and the US. This was the international background against the impact of the national democratic movement on the Western alliance.

4.3 The Middle East Issues and whether they were connected to Western Alliance

When talking about the relationship between the national democratic movement after the war and the Western alliance, we cannot avoid mentioning the Middle East. Because the problem of Middle East had existed for a long time, it was complex and had some impact on the Western alliance, especially that after the Iraq war in 2003, many Western media put their hopes of repairing the relationship within the alliance on the joint solution of the Middle East issue by the United States and Europe, so we must analysis the impact of the problem in the Middle East featured by the Arab-Israeli conflict on the Western alliance by separately putting it into a certain historical background.

In history, Jews and Arabs both had occupied Palestine. The Jews had established the Kingdom of Israel and Hebrew here in the 13th century BC; the Arabs took over Palestine from the Romans in the 7th century. In late 19th century, Zionism escalated among Jews who scattered around the world. A lot of them immigrated to Palestine. The dispute began thereafter. Jews continued to have bloodshed conflicts with Palestinian Arabs. In November 1947, the United Nations adopted the resolution 181 (b) which required the establishment of the nation of Jews and the nation of Arabs in Palestine, and the holy city Jerusalem was internationalized. Israel was proclaimed in May 1948, while the Arabs failed to set up a Palestinian State because of their dissatisfaction with the resolution. Israel had five times of large-scale war against the Arab countries after its founding, and occupied a large part of land where the Arabs lived and in Jerusalem. Millions of Arabs were expelled from their homes as refugees. In May 1964, the Palestinian Arabs formed the Palestine Liberation Organization (Al Fatah), and began their armed struggle in order to return to their homes and restore national rights.

Generally speaking, the US and European allies shared basically the same strategies in the lengthy process of the Arab-Israeli conflict after the war. The US always supported Israel. It utilized the complex relationship between the Arab countries to maintain a peace-and-war situation in the Middle East, in order to exert its influence in the Middle East. Although the European countries led by Britain and France were dissatisfied with being excluded by the United States in the Middle East, they were powerless, so they had to compromise. In addition to the restrictions of the Western alliance's strategy against the Soviet Union, European countries had to follow the US Middle East policy. However, this follow-up wasn't equal to total agreement or total contradiction with European countries, but meant that they began to pay particular attention to development and changes of the Middle East policy.

As early as during the First World War, Britain ruled by its real power and implemented a "divide and rule" policy of pleasing both sides in the Palestine. On the eve of World War II, in order to keep oil supply and the strategic location in the Middle East and to prevent certain Arab elites choosing Hitler's side, Britain intentionally made its policy favorable to Arabs, promised them ten years of independence, and limited the amount of Jewish immigrants.[20] This worsened the relationship between the United Kingdom and the Jews. The Jews turned to the United States, which was exactly what the US wanted. Gradually, a Jewish "pressure group" was formed which was influential enough to change the US policy in the Middle East. In the early post-War period, the United States obviously inclined to support Zionism, which sometimes went against Britain which hoped to maintain its national interest in Arabs. For example, the United Nations regulation that it was the United States who promoted the resolution No. 181 (b), while the United Kingdom supported the Palestinian Arabs to oppose this resolution. When the first Middle East war began in May 1948, the British encouraged Arab countries to send troops to Palestine, which led to the "anti-British campaign" that had been rarely seen for many years in the United States. But there was something worth noticing, at this time the Soviet Union just as the United States, was an active supporter of Israel.[21]

In October, 1956, Israel, together with Britain and France, launched the second Middle East war (the Suez War) to invade Egypt, and put aside its relations with the United States. After 1960s, the hegemony of the Soviet Union and the US was already established, the Soviet Union further expanded its own forces in the Middle East and the Arab countries, and the Israeli military force and economy had developed rapidly. The pressure from pro-Israel department of the US strengthened. Israel had become an ally that the US needed to maintain because of the global need for the strategy towards the Soviet Union. On the contrary, the US European allies expressed disagreement on the US policy favoring Israel in dealing with the Arab-Israeli conflict, but preferred a policy that was neither against the existence of Israel nor to offend the Arab countries, which distanced them from the United States.

The Arab were defeated miserably in the third Middle East War in 1967 (the "Six-Day War) with the support of the United States and the Soviet Union on the sidelines. The Israel-occupied territory has expanded four times, and Palestinian refugees had increased by 410 thousand. This situation eventually led to the fourth Middle East war in 1973 (the "October" War, also known as "Ramadan War" or "Yom Kippur War"), which influenced the world history exceedingly. Due to the application of the Arab "oil weapon", the entire Western economy was endangered. The two sides of the conflict and their supporters realized that it was difficult to solve the

---

20   See Britain's White Paper on Palestine. Institute for International Relations, References of Palestinian Issues, World Affairs Press, 1960, pp.14-22.
21   The Soviet Union's reason for supporting Israel, see Pan Guang, Yu Jianhua, Wang Jian, The Road to Jews' Revival, Shanghai Academy of Social Science Press, 1998, pp.186-188.

fundamental problem in the Middle East by force, and it was necessary to seek a path of peace. The war further established the US position and influence in the Middle East, which also further expanded the differences between the United States and its allies. Europeans complained, "A serious crisis threatened the whole world: some part of the crisis was solved on the battlefield, some other part was solved by the US-Soviet dialogue, but Washington and Moscow did not expect to ask the opinions of Europeans from the beginning to the end". Meanwhile, the US were also complaining, Kissinger said, "What makes us worried is that whenever the United States was going to make some major decisions, the Europeans was always doing its own thing, like the alliance has never existed. They show more interest in fishing for small benefits rather than cooperating with the United States".[22]

In October 1973, nine countries of the EC formally wrote and proposed the "European-Arab dialogue" to the Arab League. In November, the EC foreign ministers' meeting in Brussels put forward suggestions on solving the problem in the Middle East, expressing that Israel should withdraw from the Arab territories occupied by force since 1967, and should respect the sovereignty and the territorial integrity of all countries with considerations of the legitimate rights of the Palestinian Arabs. In June 1980, the European Community asked Israel to withdraw from occupied territories in the "Venice Declaration", recognized the self-determination of the Palestinian people and opposed any unilateral change in the status of Jerusalem and in the immigrant settlement construction in the occupied territories. Compared with the US attitude, the EC's political attitude of supporting Arab countries was very obvious. By the end of 1987, the EC imposed economic sanctions against Israel due to Israel's bloody repression of the Palestinian people's uprising in the occupied territories. In October 1991, the Middle East meeting was held in Madrid, thus, the arduous journey to achieve the peaceful Middle East began with the Arab-Israeli peace talks as its center. In the ten years from October 1991 to "9/11" incident in 2001 , Palestine and Israel signed the peace treaty at the basis of "land for peace" principle and the Israeli prime minister Rabin was assassinated. The new round Israeli-Palestinian conflict was provoked by Israeli Prime Minister Ariel Sharon. Soon, Palestinian people's resistance was included in the list of "terrorism" by President Bush. The United States and Israel jointly launched a "striking Arafat movement" in 2002. President Bush declared that only a new Palestinian leader who would make "no compromise to terrorism" could lead to a Palestinian State; while Israeli Prime Minister Ariel Sharon used tanks and bulldozers to put Arafat under "house arrest".

---

22   Andre Fontaine, Un Seul lit pour deux reves – Histoire de la "detente" 1962-1981, Fayard, 1981, pp.333,334.

EU countries found that the peace process in the Middle East stuck in a hopeless situation. Although they still strongly protested Israel's military action, they understood that the key was still the US "unilateral" policy. EU countries asked the United States to change its position and solve the conflict with justice and reason, which required imposing pressure on Israel first to make it withdraw its troops and restore Arafat's personal freedom.

The Iraq War that the United States launched in 2003 torn apart the Western alliance. After the military occupation of Iraq, the United States decided to push forward the Middle East peace process. It began to put the policy of "founding first, negotiations second" into practice to resolve the Israeli-Palestinian conflict, in order to change its hegemonic image and improve the endangered relationship within the alliance. At the same time, the Western media came up with some ideas because their concerns about the outlook of the alliance. They put their hope to make up the rift in the Western alliance joint resolution of the Middle East issue. By the end of 2003, Brzezinski published an article entitled "The Potentially Danger of Hegemony" in the US "National Interest" Winter Quarterly. He called the Eurasian subcontinent panhandle where most of the countries were Muslim as the "Global Balkans", thinking that the United States could count on only one true partnership of Europe to cope the "Global Balkans" problem with it. Almost at the same time, an article entitled "Bound to Cooperate? Transatlantic Policy in the Middle East" was published in the Washington Quarterly, claiming that although the United States and Europe had common interests in the Middle East, it did not mean that they would cooperate with each other naturally. The US and Europe should take the initiative to cooperate. "The US-European cooperation should make some breakthrough in the Middle East"[23].

On November 28, 2004, the Spanish El Pais published an open letter wrote by the former French President Giscard d'Estaing, the former Italian Prime Minister Giuliano Amato, and the former dean of the London School of Economics Dahrendorf to US President George W. Bush, in which they recommended that the United States should sign a new transatlantic agreement with Europe. They put particular emphasis on the cooperation of Europe and the US in dealing with the Middle East issue, predicting that "the Middle East will become the key to geopolitics within the next decade". In the special issue of News Week in 2005, Brzezinski called for the recovery of the cooperation between the US and European Union, and emphasized again that they should cope with the core of—the Middle East

---

23   Dalia Dassa Kaye, "Bound to Cooperate? Transatlantic Policy in the Middle East", in The Washington Quarterly, Winter 2003-2004.

issue. On these issues "the most appropriate ally for the United States is the EU"[24]. By the end of 2004, with Israel's unilateral withdrawal from Gaza and the death of the Palestinian leader Yasser Arafat, the Israeli-Palestinian conflict became the primary focus of the relationship between Europe and the US. Could the Middle East problem become the adhesive for the Western alliance?

In general, the reasons for the different attitudes of the European countries and the US on the Middle East problem included the following aspects. First, from the perspective of the strategic thinking and values, the European countries were dissatisfied with the United States' practice of handling all the Middle East affairs alone since the Suez War in 1956 and its exclusion of Europe. They wanted to improve the EU's position and influence by being involved in major international issues such as the Middle East problem; Meanwhile, European countries began to pursue a fair, reasonable and peaceful solution to international conflicts due to their history and tradition, which was inconsistent with the US policy of admiring military forces in the Middle East and the policy of favoring the Israeli military action. Second, from the perspective of geopolitical interests, the importance of the Middle East with the majority of Arab countries to Europe was no greater than the importance of Mexico to the United States. Three points were particularly important.

Firstly, as the Latin America has been the "backyard", of the US, the Middle East could be seen as the "backyard", of Europe. This was not only because the Middle East was geographically located adjacent to Europe, but also because many countries of the Middle East were included in the traditional sphere of influence of Europe. History could not be severed. Secondly, unlike the United States, Europe was very dependent on oil supplies and delivery of the Middle East. The lessons of history should not be forgotten. In 1973, the Arab countries of the Middle East have caused an economic crisis by decreasing oil production and using this as a weapon to defend their economic interests.. The first victim of this struggle was not the United States, but its allies; Japan and European countries. Europe would not allow this event repeat itself. Third, there has been a pressure group on behalf of Jewish interests in the US, whereas the African originated Muslim population was two times more than that of European Jews. This was an important domestic political factor that Europe could not ignore. Besides these reasons which could be placed on the table to discuss, there was a reason that could not be easily spoken out, the "anti-Semitism" in European history and the "anti-Americanism" as a realistic interest conflict,

---

24   Zbigniew Brzezinski, "A Grand Alliance", in News Week Issues 2005, Dec.27, 2004.

which can be regarded as the background of the special relation between the US and the Israel.

However, it seemed not easy to overcome or circumvent these factors that negatively influenced the alliance between the United States and Europe and strike a compromise within the alliance. Even though they could strike a compromise that could adjust their interest relations, probably the best interests of the Israeli and Palestinian people, two issues would be doubtful: who could guarantee that the Middle East would enjoy lasting peace and that it would forever avoid a future split in the Western alliance?

Chapter V

The Changes of Japan's and the Federal Republic of Germany's International Position

The U.S.' post-war attitude towards the European integration has been positive in general. But the U.S.' goal was to put the integrated Europe within the framework of the Trans-Atlantic Alliance which was led by the U.S. In terms of the relations between the U.S. and U.S.' attitude towards the European Integration the historical process can divided into several stages: In the immediate post-war years, the US played an important role in supporting and pushing the start of the European Integration, and the European Integration started within the framework of the Trans-Atlantic Alliance; in the 1960s, Europe represented mainly by Charles de Gaulle became a challenge to the US, and the US foreign policy towards Europe became weak within the framework of the Trans-Atlantic Alliance; in the 1970s, the US adjusted its foreign policy towards the European Integration, but its principle of supporting the European Integration remained the same; in the 1980s, with the further development of the European Integration and changes in the international situation, the positive and supportive attitude of the US towards the European Integration gradually changed into conditional support. A series of changes appeared in the traditional alliance between the U.S. and Europe.

5.1 The United States and the early integration process of Europe

Started in the 1950s, the Europe's integration has gone through an half a century of history and has made great achievements, which attracts many researchers' interests. However, there are few researchers and studies of the

US attitude and policy towards the European Integration. In fact, the US as the important alliance with Europe and strong supporter of the European Integration had played a key role especially in the start of the European Integration and its early stage. It could even be seen that without the support from the US, the success of the European Integration could not be imagined.

5.1.1 The supportive policy of the US towards the European integration

At the later stage of World War II, the US government was still skeptical of the European integration. In March 1943, Richard Coudenhove-Kalergi, leader of the "Pan-Europan Movement" who was then living in exile in the US, prepared a draft memo calling for establishing the European Union and sent it to President Roosevelt, who denied it immediately. In August the same year in the draft charter for building the UN organization, the US did not suggest any kind of regional organizations for the post-war Europe either.[1]

These facts reveal that in President Roosevelt's plans of the post-war world, the European integration was not on the agenda. This was on one hand because an integrated Europe, whether it was led by the UK or led jointly by the UK and the Soviet Union, would mean to push the US out of Europe, which was something that the US was unwilling to see. On the other hand even more importantly, Roosevelt thought the US could continue its partnership with the Soviet Union, and the US foreign policy should be based on the cooperation between the US and the Soviet Union. Roosevelt had expected to explore cooperation opportunities with the Soviet Union by recognizing its spheres of influence in the Eastern Europe, instead of confronting the Soviet Union directly. For the Soviet government, both in order to control Eastern Europe and for the sake of Soviet security interests, any kind of European integration was worrisome. Roosevelt was clear that the European integration would face immediate opposition from the Soviet Union and would thus deteriorate the relations between the two big powers, so he remained skeptical of the European integration.

Affected by this thought, Roosevelt, like Stalin, insisted on punishing Germany severely at the Tehran Conference and the Yalta Conference, and the UK was in agreement with that approach. However, Roosevelt died on April 12, 1945 and Truman became the next president of the US, which

---

1   Max Beloff, The United States and the Unity of Europe, London, Westport: Greenwood Press, 1976, p.2-3.

marked a significant change in the US foreign policies towards the Soviet Union and Europe. In July 1945, at the Potsdam Conference participated with the US, the UK and the Soviet Union, the US changed its Yalta Conference policy of punishing Germany severely and favored a moderate policy of supporting the rebuilding of Germany. Besides, Truman opposed the Soviet Union's policy of dismembering Germany and that Germany should pay a heavy war indemnity, which constituted an irreconcilable gap between the U.S. and the Soviet Union.

After the US dropped two atomic bombs on Japan and the Soviet Union declared war against Japan, Japan was forced to surrender, and the Second World War was finally over. The Second World War has changed the whole world strategical pattern significantly. The US's influence had grown unprecedentedly during the war. It was the only country without any war-torn region among the warring countries. Besides, munitions deliveries by the US to the Soviet Union, the UK and France had made the US an ordnance factory of these countries, plus its sole monopoly of the atomic bomb, the US became a military superpower. The US had prevented the economic depression during the war and made unprecedented economic progress. By the end of WWII, the US was able to produce the 60% of the total industrial output, 1/3 of the foreign trade and 3/4 of the gold reserves in the capitalist world, and had become the largest capital exporting and creditor country of the world. For Europe, WWII had completely broken the Europe-centered world pattern that had lasted for several centuries. The defeated Germany and Italy left the imperialist contest stage for supremacy. The UK and France, although they were the victors of the war, were also severely weakened because of the war, and their colonial rule was tottering. They had left the contest stage for supremacy as well. At the same time, the military power of the Soviet Union had grown unprecedentedly, and its military force as well as political influence had expanded to Central and Eastern Europe along with its Red Army deployments in these countries. The US and the Soviet Union had become the two superpowers on the stage of world politics.

Its huge economic and military power extremely expanded the US political ambitions. After Truman took office, he claimed repeatedly that the US would lead the world and all the world should adopt its systems. However, it was not easy for the US to become the sole dominator of the world. For from the US, the major obstacle was the Soviet Union, which had won a high international prestige during the Anti-Fascist War. In the early postwar period, with the direct impact and support of the Soviet government and the Soviet troops stationed there, the communist parties of the Eastern

European countries had strengthened their public support and forces, with several steps they changed the former multi-party political systems of their countries, and finally became the absolute leading political forces by the end of 1948. Within the Soviet orbit Eastern Europe became its sphere of influence. In 1945, the Soviet Union also signed mutual aid agreements with Poland, Romania, Hungary, Czechoslovakia, Yugoslavia, Bulgaria, Albania and others, which also aimed to isolate Germany. The US and Western European countries were extremely sensitive about the Soviet moves in the Eastern Europe, they regarded every action of the Soviet Union as the expansion of the communist ideology and socialist system and as a greedy interest seeking. Therefore, the US policy towards Europe soon turned from the full burial of the Fascist forces to "containment" of the Soviet Union. The "containment" theory of George F. Kennan which was first declared in February 1946, had soon received the attention of the US statesmen. In 1947, he was appointed as the director of Policy Planning Staff of the State Department, and assigned to design the US global strategy including the the containment of the SU. By the end of 1945, Truman began to replace most of the members of the Roosevelt cabinet, including the finance minister Jr. Henry Morgenthau who advocated punishing Germany ruthlessly and commerce minister Henry Wallace who advocated continuing cooperation with the Soviet Union. Thus Truman was arranging the new leadership that would implement the new US global strategy.

Truman delivered a report to the joint session of the US Congress on March 12, 1947, which was later referred to as the "Truman Doctrine" in which he requested the Congress to authorize an aid worth four hundred million US dollars to Greece and Turkey and later managed to pass the bill. He explained, "This is the US reply to the expansion wave made by communist tyrants" and is "the turning point of the US foreign policy". He said, "Both direct and indirect attempts to threaten peace in any place of the world involved the security interests of the US." The introduction of the "Truman Doctrine" revealed the America's intention of confrontation with the Soviet Union in all aspects, which marked the official launch of US-Soviet Cold War and meanwhile reflected the global expansion strategy of the US.

The Cold War exerted a far-reaching influence on the European policies of the US. Similarly, its attitude towards European integration changed as well. The possibility that Roosevelt had been concerned over, namely, the US support of European integration would be opposed by the Soviet Union and accordingly harm the US-Soviet relations, had become a reality with the outbreak of the US-Soviet Cold War. In fact, the US-Soviet relations transformed from cooperation into confrontation, and meanwhile the war-ridden countries of the Europe began to lobby for a united and strong Europe rather than a divided and weak one. In US eyes, as long as Europe became united, it could be able to resist the expansion of the Soviet Union and "curb" the spread of communism. Moreover, the US leaders began to realize that Germany's promotion towards Western European integration would not only prevent the possible German-Soviet Union, but also constrained the Soviet military expansion effectively. In a word, they had designed an optimal solution to the issue of Germany through European integration. In addition, only by a firm integration, could the European countries terminate the wars among themselves, forever. Conflicts among the European countries had caused two world wars and also drifted the US into war. European unity was the only way to diminish and avoid military and economic obligations of the US towards Europe, in the long-term. Therefore, as far as the US was concerned, the recovery, revival and integration of Europe were inseparably linked with the US aid to this continent.

The US bore a clear political intention in its support of the European integration. A memorandum released in May 1947 by a group which was authorized by the Foreign Aid Commission pointed out that there had been a long-term goal for the US foreign policy, namely, to "achieve a strategic advantage (over the Soviet Union)" and "gain the chance of winning the possible war against the Soviet". Playing a vital role in the general world situation, Western Europe should be allied with the US or at least remain neutral so that the US could fulfill its strategic goals. Furthermore, Western Europe should achieve the the recovery and revival as soon as possible, since its current weakness was detrimental for the US aiming to gain absolute superiority over the Soviet Union. Meanwhile, the US had defined its short-term foreign policy goal as resisting against the so-called expansion of communism. To accomplish this goal, to merely offer financial aid to Western Europe would be far from enough, and more important was "to help non-communist Europe in maintaining its ideological and spiritual vacuum". And the only feasible solution to realize these aims would be the integration of European countries. The US politicians thought only this idea could bring the West Europe and the US together and enable "resisting against the communist attack". A report delivered to the Congress shows that the economic factors behind the US policy of the European integration was not ignored at all: "with the advent of peace, economy may possibly fall into recession again. One important tool to avoid recession is to increase the foreign trade. However, if other regions in the world nationalize their basic industries or close their markets, the US will no longer be able to compete in the world markets." The U.S.' major trading partners,

European countries, were faced with a severe economic recession after the war, they lacked US dollar reserves and were unable to service their loans. For the upcoming future the US was extremely worried of losing the European market and the continuation of the turmoil in Europe. As a result, the revival of Europe via the transatlantic alliance was of great significance for the economic development of the US. Under Secretary of State William Clayton who was responsible for economic affairs suggested that President and Secretary of State called on "The US people to sacrifice their interests and tighten their belts a little bit to save Europeans out of hunger and unrest (rather than Russians) and meanwhile to protect the glorious heritage of the US for ourselves and our children". How to achieve the revival of Europe? Under Secretary of State Acheson gave a speech in Cleveland, Mississippi, on May 8th, 1946, saying "Only when various parts of European economy work together as a harmonious whole can the revival of Europe be complete. Making European economy cooperative is a basic goal of our foreign policy." In May 27 this year, Under Secretary of State William Clayton submitted a memorandum to the Secretary of State and pointed out "If European economy continues to be divided into many small airtight pieces, it will never be reconstructed and recover from wounds of the war."

On January 19, 1947, John Foster Dulles, foreign policy expert of the Republican Party and the bipartisan spokesman of foreign policy declared that the support of European unification was an indispensable attempt that was about to be made by the US. On March 1, Senator Fulbright presented a bill to the Congress, in which he illustrated his backing for the establishment of United States of Europe within the range of the United Nations. During April and May of 1947, executive departments of the US took political and economic integration of Europe into serious consideration. A large number of people in the State Council, mainly young officials, firmly believed that European integration was the only way to accomplish the world's security and prosperity and kept urging for the European integration with the use of the US diplomatic and economic power. In this case, European integration turned to be one of the foreign policy goals set by the US, so European integration policy was easily combined with the financial aid issue.

Since the end of the war, the US had provided Western Europe with financial assistance of 9 billion dollars through UNRRA, IMF and WB as well as a special loan to Britain. Yet, the economy of various European countries still failed to get out of the vicious cycle in the spring of 1947. Moreover, most of them suffered devastating natural disasters in winters from 1946 to 1947, with their people living in extreme hardships, workers going on strike frequently and society being trapped in unrest. The

US politicians feared that the Communist Party and the left-wing force won power in Western Europe and the so-called communist expansion in Europe became a reality under such circumstance. After participating in the council of foreign ministers held in Moscow in March 1947, Secretary of State Marshall delivered a speech on the radio: "The patient is painful, but doctors are still discussing endlessly…" Being deeply convinced that Stalin was awaiting Europe to fall into his hands, Marshall insistedly emphasized the extreme urgency of the aid to Europe.

Marshall made a famous speech at Harvard University on June 5, 1947, pointing out that Europe's current economic, social and political situations deteriorated severely and needed help urgently and meanwhile asked European countries to make a program together. This is the well-known "Marshall Plan". G. Marshall elaborated that Europe was immersed in crisis, which would be more terrible without substantial foreign aid. At that time, its people would fall into desperation and unrest, which was bound to bring serious consequences to US economy. Therefore, the US must render great support to Europe in recovering. He emphasized that this assistance didn't target against any country, but against poverty, hunger and chaos and for promoting Europe to create political and social conditions in which free institution could be sustained; European reconstruction was the business of Europeans, so the initiative and program must come from Europe itself and then the US offered assistance in accordance with its actual needs; the US aid should not be assigned to individual countries in a scattered manner, but instead European countries, at least some European countries, jointly proposed a general plan for the basic consideration of the US. Different from the past, the US stressed this was not a bilateral aid and Europeans ought to agree with each other and formulate a list where resources and demands were written as well as a common program of revival. Only when this condition was met, the US would provide an essential assistance. In other words, the US desired to connect financial aid with European integration together. Cooperation and integration of European countries were the prerequisite of the US assistance. It is clear that Marshall Plan is not only the foundation of the US-European Alliance, but the initial ticket of European integration—European Union.

The US government's policy about European integration had been crystallized through Marshall Plan, which was the US first time to declare its attitude towards European integration in public and also its first time to exert influence for the purpose of the unification of European countries. Since then, the US had supported European integration openly and often promoted the process of European integration in the early stage.

5.1.2 The United States and the European Community

Under the support of the US, the Netherlands, Belgium, Luxembourg, Britain, France, Italy, Ireland, Iceland, Denmark, Norway, Sweden, Switzerland, Austria, Turkey, Greece, Portugal and the military commander of Western occupied area of Germany signed an agreement on April 16 of 1948 and founded the Organization for European Economic Cooperation (West Germany and Spain joined in it respectively in 1949 and 1959) that was responsible for allocating the13 billion US Dollars aid offered by Marshall Plan. Furthermore, the Organization for European Economic Cooperation strove to make each member ensure its fiscal and monetary stability, developing export, modernize producing facilities and coordinating investment. This organization stimulated economic cooperation and trade among European countries, but played a limited role in the process of European integration. From 1947 to 1950, Europeans did not establish any customs union (except the alliance by the Netherlands, Belgium and Luxembourg which was beyond the expectation of the US); free trade volume among European countries didn't develop as desired and a lucrative common European market didn't come into being yet. The US commentators who used to have high expectations for the Western European integration were greatly disappointed.

To promote the development of European integration, the US elaborated to seek a variety of solutions. The first step was to determine the leadership of the European integration. During the early post-War period, Germany and Italy were defeated countries and France's performance in the war affected its status; accordingly, Britain naturally became the leader in the eyes of the US. However, British leaders possesed a policy of their regarding the continental Europe. According to the "Three-circles Diplomacy", Britain believed relations within the British Commonwealth of Nations as well as its special relation with the US mattered much more than its relation with continental European countries. With a sense of superiority of its constitutional system, Britain opposed European integration by claiming it had a supranational nature and rather advocated the transatlantic cooperation involving the US. It was not until the year of 1949 that the US finally recognized that Britain cherished no interest in European integration at all and thus could not serve as its leader.

The US had no choice but to accept the reality that Western European Integration didn't involve Britain, but this plan must continue forward and it must also be led by a European country. Under such circumstance, the US began to take France into another consideration. Yet, France also bore its own series of ideas about a joint Europe. To restore its position as a big power in the world, France initially tried to implement a balanced policy between the US and the Soviet Union. Charles de Gaulle visited the Soviet Union in November 1944. During his stay there, he signed France-Soviet Treaty of Friendship which aimed at treating the hereditary enemy of Germany jointly with the Soviet Union (the long-term feud between France and Germany made itself known to the whole world) while making a balance between the US and the Soviet Union and improving its international status. In the council of four-country foreign ministers held in 1945, France insisted on dismembering Germany so as to get rid of this old enemy once and for all. Due to strong opposition of the US, Britain and the Soviet Union, France had to abandon the proposal, but suppression of Germany remained the center of its foreign policy during the early post-war period.

After the Cold War opened its prelude, the US pressed ahead with policies of propping up Germany for the sake of fighting against the Soviet Union. Demanding economic and military assistance from the US, France could not seek a balance between the US and Soviet Union any more. After Charles de Gaulle left office, the government of the Fourth Republic of France gradually changed the initial policy and stood on the side of the US for an active support of the European integration which could both give effective play to its role and restrict Germany at the same time. Accordingly, the French policy on Germany had to change also. In fact, it was too risky to seek balance only with Germany, so France hoped to ally with Britain. Nevertheless, Britain was not interested in any supranational organization, and in this case, France had to take the issue of reconciliation into serious account. Georges Bidault urged the National Assembly to choose between isolation and cooperation which included joint work with West Germany. In June 1948, France eventually abandoned the idea of dismembering Germany and agreed to establish Federal Republic of Germany by accepting London Agreement.

European integration turned out to be a second-to-none choice for the US, while it intended to support Germany against the Soviet Union, on the other side restricted the strenghtening of Germany to avoid the resurgence of nationalism among its people. On October 19th, 1949, the US Secretary of State Dean Acheson warned: "the familiar signs of dangerous nationalism" "the familiar signs of dangerous nationalism" arose in West Germany and "its danger lies in the fact that the time for preventing and reversing this trend is very limited". Acheson noted that France should assume the leadership responsibilities "quickly and decisively" and they could no longer wait for Britain. He believed that the process of European

integration was in the grasp of French people who were capable of incorpo-
rating Germany into West Europe. The US leaders had two great worries:
potential nationalism in Germany and the Soviet Union dominating Europe
or its ascendance to a leading position. Acheson pointed out that to avoid
that becoming a reality France was supposed to grab the final opportunity.
The US ambassadors had a brief meeting at Paris from October 21 to 22
with significant European countries and during the meeting the statement
"without Britain the European integration including Germany couldn't be
achieved" by Acheson created a doubt, since France would never be allied
with its old enemy. Although Acheson agreed "France is unable to serve
as the leader…and Britain's influence and help are of great significance",
he still insisted on his basic point of view and reiterated that France had to
perform the responsibilities of leadership. He said to Schumann on October
30, "It is time for France to integrate the Federal Republic of Germany
into Europe rapidly and decisively", and France should agree to provide
West Germany with more right of independence and self-determination and
bring it into relevant international organizations as well; otherwise, the democratic forces in FRG would be undermined which would lead to the rise
of extremism and to the increase of Soviet influence.

To seek a breakthrough, officials of the Truman administration racked
their brains. On April 25, 1950, John McCloy, Chairman of the US High
Commission to Germany, first proposed that the West must change its original thinking to abandon the Ruhr International Control Board and set up
an international agency for the purpose of controlling coal and steel industries in Western Europe while endowing Germany with a member status
at NATO. Merely two weeks later, France came up with Schuman Plan
that requested the foundation of a coal and steel community in Europe,
which happened to coincide with the idea of the US people and thus won
their enthusiastic support. On May 9, 1950, according to the plan of a joint French-German coal and steel market made by Jean Monnet, General
Commissioner of French Modernization and Equipment Plan, French
Foreign Minister Robert Schuman gave German Chancellor Adenauer a piece of advice, which was immediately taken by him.

The Truman administration held that this was an effective way to solve
the issue of Germany and realize French-German reconciliation. Germany
would blend into Europe with an equal status and therefore could never be
pulled into the camp of the Soviet Union. Meanwhile, France would not
hinder Germany from reviving and integrating into Europe and the reconciliation between the two countries would be achieved soon. However, the
US coal and steel industries objected to the foundation of European Coal

and Steel Community, in fear of the increasing competitiveness of Europe. The US government also had scruple in this regard, full of worries about the carte nature of this community. Nevertheless, for political reasons, the US almost approved of the French proposal completely. Acheson made it clear in a statement in August 1952: "The US supports the Coal and Steel Community strongly because it plays a crucial role in the political and economic unification of Europe."

The U.S.' support for the European Coal and Steel Community was by no means an empty talk but sincere and concrete. During the negotiation on Treaty of European Coal and Steel Community, the US encouraged Europe to establish a community with the least restriction and meanwhile advocated complete free trade of products covered in Schuman Plan. It even insisted that transitional rather than permanent preferential measures should be given to the coal industry in Italy and the steel sector of Belgium whose costs were relatively high, in order to facilitate European integration. The Netherlands, Belgium, Luxembourg, France, the Federal Republic of Germany and Italy signed Treaty of European Coal and Steel Community at Paris on April 18, 1951. On August 10 of the following year, Advanced Organization, the first unity with the supranational nature in the history of European integration, was set up at Luxembourg, which marked Treaty of European Coal and Steel Community came into effect. In 1952, the US announced that it would contact the Coal and Steel Community directly in matters relating to coal and steel instead of dealing with any individual country. The US also provided 1 million US Dollars loan to the community in 1954 to help it obtain concession in GATT negotiations.

The outbreak of the Korean War on June 25, 1950 forced the US to immediately cherish a keen interest in European defense, and therefore the demand for arming West Germany grew increasingly urgent. During the council of foreign ministers of the US, Britain and France which was held at New York in September 1950, The US Secretary of State said bluntly, "I want to see Federal German in military uniforms in the fall of 1951." He suggested that an integrated army should be established in Europe with the involvement of dozens of divisions from the Federal Republic of Germany and there should be no autonomous German army. Under the pressure of the US, France must take the initiative to seek a proper solution. Jean Monnet put forward the European Defense Community Program, in which he proposed the foundation of a European army in accordance with the mode and organizational system of the European Coal and Steel Community. French Prime Minister René Pleven published this proposal in the National Assembly on October 24 of 1950. In fact, France prepared inadequately for this program and European countries other than the Federal Republic of Germany didn't develop a strong appetite for it yet. Satisfied with France's agreement to rearmament of Germany, the US required enlisting soldiers before the establishment of the defense community and setting up two divisions of Federal Republic of Germany before the end of 1951, but such impatient idea was abandoned for the strong opposition of France. The US supported the program of European army, because it was the only way for everyone to accept German involvement in European defense. President Truman and Secretary of State Acheson both expressed the same meaning respectively. Secondly, European army would promote the unification of Europe, which was an effective solution to all hardships plaguing Europe now. The US was actually the one to be blamed for the current situation. Furthermore, expecting Europeans to protect themselves and thus reduce the US' economic and military burden, the US leaders nurtured the hope of troop withdrawal from Europe.

The US officials regarded the establishment of the European Defense Community as a breakthrough in the US foreign policy. In January 1953, General Eisenhower who was the US president then looked forward to this joint work. Secretary of State Dulles was also impatient about it and even threatened that if France was unwilling to set up a coalition force in Europe, the US would severely reconsider whether it should get involved in the joint European defense. Yet, the US pressure on Europe took a counterproductive effect. French disliked being imposed. In August 1954, France disliked being imposed, consequently, in August 1954, the French National Assembly rejected the draft for the European Defense Community. With this rejection had displayed that the French leaders had damaged their own status among the allies.

The US had continued rendering its support to the European Atomic Energy Community and the European Common Market. In order to maintain superiority the West enjoyed over the Soviet Union in the use of nuclear energy and also boost the advancement of European integration, the US was agreeable to see its European allies taking advantage of nuclear energy peacefully and thus approved of the establishment of the European Atomic Energy Community. Learning a lesson from the rash mistake in the issue of European Defense Community, Secretary of State Dulles instructed the US ambassadors to Bonn that they should "found federal agencies and conduct necessary sovereignty transfer in Europe", but the State Council hoped the US ambassadors to "encourage and support German people and Europeans to advocate this view" without any pressure imposed from the US. Although the ultimate status of the European Atomic Energy Community was not the one expected by the US, although it neither prohibited the military use of nuclear energy nor prevented the proliferation of nuclear weapons, it helped the European integration and accordingly the US was still satisfied and continued to support it.

The US corporates were critical towards the European Customs Union, especially towards the protectionism in European establishment of a Common Agricultural Market Program, but the U.S. government did not give up its support of European common market plan due to the agricultural issue.

United States said the issues caused by common market, including agricultural issues, should be the negotiation issue within the frame of General Agreement on Tariffs and Trade (GATT). And in order not to disturb the approval of the treaty Department of States decided all the negotiation on economic issues should be conducted after the approval of Treaty of Rome by six nations. There were two reasons: Firstly, it believed that the common market would potentially be the strong rival of the US, but it may also conform to the economic interests of the US, i.e., "Economic community may strengthen and modernize European economy, improve productivity and consumption. All these will enable Europe be a better export market of the US". The US was confident that European Economic Community would not pose a threat to its own economy, because a strong, united European economy would have more possibility to conduct free trade with the US to ensure the trading benefit of the US than a weak and low efficient European economy. Secondly, the U.S. leaders thought that "close economic cooperation would greatly promote the communication between European nations". To the US, economic factors should be put at the second place while the political profits brought by the united Europe at the first place.

5.1.3 US' motives for promoting European Community

As we have discussed above the US has sometimes displayed even more positive attitude than the Europeans in promoting the development of the European community after since it emerged. Below, we will analyze US' motives.

First is a political consideration, which was the need to the "Dual Containment" of the Soviet Union and Germany. From the late war to the Post-War, the US changed from indifference to support. Therefore, the analysis of the US political change of European community should be put into that period during which the largest change of the US foreign strategy was its policy to the Soviet Union. Roosevelt's thought of co-operation with the Soviet Union determined the mild basic policy of the US to the Soviet Union. However, with the confrontations getting fiercer, the situation of Cold War gradually formed. It became the top priority of the US to contain the Soviet Union. In the eyes of the US, European Community was beneficial to contain the Soviet union, which was the most fundamental political reason for supporting European Community and also the basic reason for making economic concessions; such as taking risk and supporting Europe to realize its economic recovery and implementing Economic Community. Europe is of great strategic interest to the United States. The United States had to protect the Western Europe in order to dominate the world and contain the Soviet Union. They lost Eastern Europe, if Western Europe would eventually fell into the Soviet sphere of influence due to its economic dislocation and face with the political unrest or revolution this would have been the most nightmares of the US Therefore, the US with huge amount to money helped the Western Europe with its economy at the risk. For the US, promoting the European Community was not only US' important strategy to contain the Soviet Union, but also targeted the FRG. Therefore, there is the conclusion: European Community is beneficial to European Renaissance and prosperity which is beneficial to contain the Soviet Union, so the US should support European Community.

European Community is not only the US most important strategy to contain both the Soviet Union and Germany. People often tend see the US' helping hand to Germany and US efforts to integrate Germany into Europe, but ignore that the US also aimed to contain Germany. In fact, the US citizens were afraid to be involved into the internal wars of the Europe. These wars had already pulled the US into fight twice and these two wars were launched by Germany, so the US had vigilance to Germany. How to eliminate German extreme nationalism in and threat to peace and how to contain Germany became the crucial thing. The US saw the hope of European peace in European Community, especially France and Germany. The US should neither discriminate Germany nor indulge it, so integrating Germany into European Community was the best way to restrict Germany. In addition, in the special circumstances of the Cold War, the US was afraid that Germany would side with the Soviet Union at the beginning and later they worried it would take a neutral position between the US and Soviet Union and thirdly, Western European Community would keep Germany in the Western camp. Therefore, it was believed that European Community would solve the "German" issue, which was an important reason for the US to support European Community.

The second is the economic considerations. The US has huge economic interests in Europe and the US economic prosperity was closed to the economic renaissance and prosperity of the Western Europe. The policymakers of Truman government believed that the US economic vitality required rebuilding Europe as the major trading partner and integrating it into the multilateral system of world trade. To the US, European economic renaissance could only be achieved through joint Europe. They also believed the vast market and free trading system was the key to economic prosperity while European economy was hard to revive because trading protectionism in its split market. Europe needed to break protectionism to realize economic prosperity to implement free trading within Europe and form a united common market. Prosperous Europe was not only an indispensable trading partner of US, but also reduced its aid and commitment to Europe. They deeply believed a prosperous Europe with developed economy would be in accordance with the US interest.

The third factor was US' self-confidence in its systems. Many US leaders believed, that the US model, including federalism, stable political democracy, economic freedom and open markets was a successful model worth following. Senator Alexander Smith said "We all know the centuries of splitting Europe affected people's motivation for development. In the US, we have successfully solved the difficult problem with political system and financial and economic unity. Our experience can have profound influence on a responsible Europe or at least on the unity of European countries."

Dulles once claimed: "US public viewed the divisions in the Europe as the result of constant national wars in the history, so I think the Europeans should take the initiative to get united so as to eliminate wars and develop peace. Paul Hoffman, leader of Organization of European Economic Cooperation (OEEC), also believed the US experience is worth reference for Europe. In his speech delivered at OEEC, he mentioned, "In the US, we had a single market of 150 million consumers, which is indispensable to maintain our economic power and efficiency." In general, to the US, their federalism was a marvelous antidote to European perennial war while the united market in the US was the foundation of European economic prosperity. This is another important reason of their supporting to European economic and political Community.

5.2 Charles de Gaulle's challenge towards the US

After Charles de Gaulle resumed power in 1958, there was a series of disputes and conflicts between France and the US on the issues of European political unity, nuclear policy and Britain joining in the European common market, which brought some trouble to the US and aroused a flutter in the North Atlantic Alliance. Due to the challenges to the US put forward by de Gaulle, the US policy to European Community was affected and the process of European Community was slow down due to the conflicts between France and the US as well as some factors of European Community. Therefore, the dispute between the European Union—North Atlantic Alliance led by the US and European Community came into existence.

5.2.1 Political integration process in the Europe

The contradictions between France and the US originated from many historical and realistic factors, one of which was the dispute on European policy between Charles de Gaulle and the US. The premise of the US support for European Community was that "it should develop within the framework of North Atlantic Alliance (NATO)", i.e., within the leadership of the US, and it would be helpful to realize the US strategy of containing the Soviet Union. Therefore, the integrated Europe should be included into a broader Atlantic Framework. The US assisted the economic renaissance of Western Europe through Marshall Plan and OEEC, which seemed to have no relationship with Atlantic Framework but it was the first step to establish the Atlantic Framework. Of course, the more important strategy was to set up NATO, through which to include European Defense Community (EDC) under the leadership of the US and made it in accordance with the US Atlantic Framework. Acheson, the Secretary of State said, "We can discover the specific expression of North Atlantic Framework in NATO. Accordingly, within the Framework, we seek maximum common action for the same objective of North America and Western Europe." Later, GATT also became one part of Atlantic Framework to enforce the economic relation between the US and Europe. The US support for early European Community was because, it's not threatening Atlantic Framework. For instance, the US didn't emphasize Atlantic Framework when supporting European Coal and Steel Community (ECSC) because ECSC was the only organization dealing with coal and steel issues which would not threaten Atlantic Framework. The US support for EDC was because the US took EDC as subordinate to NATO. Acheson said, "We will support this plan (Plan of EDC) as long as it is a part of and protected by NATO." One of the reasons the US supporting for European common market was the Western European economic power was unable to threaten the US economic power, which would not pose threat to Atlantic Framework.

What Charles de Gaulle wanted was "Europe belonging to the world" and "Europe belonging to Europeans". The former refers to "Supranational Europe". Charles de Gaulle advocated to organize European organizations through cooperation between nations but opposed to setting supranational European united organization. He opposed the opinion of supranational country for many times, emphasizing, "Cooperation between nations is the only solution to realize European unity to any degree." "It is only an illusion to set up some effective action mechanism and gain people's support beyond the nation or above nation." "Europe belonging to the Europeans" refers to the influence and leading role of the US, "Europe belonging to the Europeans" is related with "Europe belonging to the world" which means Europe belong to Europeans when it is belonged to the world but supranational Europe only depended on the US. At the Press on May 15, 1962, Charles de Gaulle accused in public that the advocators of supranational Europe were on the side of the US. His ideal Europe was the "third power" independent from the US and Soviet Union because only such kind of Europe could "become a powerful opponent to Soviet Union and can solve the problem of the relation between Eastern and Western Europe as well as the issue of unity of Germany". In fact, de Gaulle's assumption was set up on the basis of "Europe belonging to the Europeans" with France and Germany as the core, France as the leader and excluding the influence of the US and Britain, whose purpose was to regain the France's status as the super nation in Europe and even the whole world.

The disputes over the two Europe related issues: between cooperative Europe and integrated Europe, between Europe belonging to Europeans, and the Atlantic Alliance and also conflicts between France and US were intensified. But since the beginning, the US did not fully understand the intensions of Charles de Gaulle. Gaulle's desire for the political integration of Europe was the point which the US had understood well.

Charles de Gaulle supported the EEC (European Economic Community), considering the economic interests of France, and insisted on formulating common agricultural policy to make contributions to common market. Furthermore, Charles de Gaulle also believed, "If Europe is not built on politics, then economy group itself will never be solid." Therefore, in the late 1950s and early 1960s, Charles de Gaulle proposed the assumption of establishing Western Political Union of Europe which had two features: Firstly, he opposed to political community of supranational Europe but advocated the cooperation between nations. For instance, he regarded cooperation was the only solution in foreign policy. Community would never been achieved when it became the threat to its sovereignty. All the responsibility should be taken through consistent determination of all the nations. He had always believed that supra-nationalism was a threat to the independence and existence of national states and should be prohibited before development. Secondly, Charles de Gaulle desired to establish "Europe belonging to the Europeans" which meant a federal union of European states federal which could enjoy a relation of equal footing with Soviet Union and the US and enjoy independence from the US; Europe should be a "Third Power" which could act as a balancing force in the world. These ideas formed the core content of Charles de Gaulle led France's political union plan.

In the beginning, the US was not skeptical about de Gaulle's proposal, because the US believed that it would be easy to include his plan into the framework of US plan and targets. President Eisenhower had been supporting "a stronger and more independent Western Europe" and he even mentioned that he would like the strong Europe be "the Third Power" which, of course, was not neutral. What he expected was the strong Europe could be the powerful partner of the US rather than a weak nation waiting for the US assistance or an ally keeping distance from the US Kennedy government was more aware of de Gaulle's plan than President Eisenhower, but he supported Western European Political Union at the start. They believed the political union could closely link Western Germany with the West, which was undoubtedly what the US concerned most during the Cold War.

It was European countries who were skeptical about de Gaulle's plan first. Britain and Holland worried this plan would exclude the US and Britain from the issues of European continent and they also worried he would seek for the hegemony of France in Europe. These two nations continuously reminded the US of the potential danger, but they did not receive the same opinion from the officials of State Department. The officials persuaded them to be more positive. Adenauer government was on the same side as these nations to this point, worrying the Western European Political Union would isolate the relationship with the US and Britain. However, Adenauer also realized the positive significance of de Gaulle's plan in reinforcing the political unity of Western Europe. Therefore, Adenauer supported Charles de Gaulle on the issue of political union and also realized they need to prevent his replacement of the existing Europe and NATO with political union to broadening the gap between Europe and the US.

On July 29-30, 1960, during the Rambouillet Talks between the leaders of France and Germany, Charles de Gaulle clearly explained his opinion, "A united Europe will be an organized, ethnic and national union and it will be a giant federal union. The existing community will be integrated in and yield to the leadership of political power, because community doesn't represent any political power. Defense will be one of the themes of cooperation, so NATO should be reformed according to Europeans' proposal to end the situation of community because it does not give any responsibility to Europeans on the issue of defense." De Gaulle's suggestion aroused great disturbance. On the one hand, Adenauer suspected the possibility of repelling the US from Europe, on the other hand Italy, Holland, Belgium, and Luxembourg agreed to oppose any challenge towards the US commitment for the European defense, they proposed that Britain should join the political union, hoping to contain France and Germany in this way, besides they rejected any change in the status of NATO.

The US also sensed de Gaulle's ambitions. In early October, Eisenhower mentioned in his letter to Adenauer that if the six European nations destroyed NATO with Charles de Gaulle suggestion, the US would reconsider the whole European plan. He encouraged Adenauer to protect NATO and the supranational European Community. But Eisenhower government still hoped to change the negative elements in the Political Union Plan into positive and insisted that Germany and other members of European Community should try to contain de Gaulle, the US still did not opt to involve in the European disputes.

After the leaders' conference of European Community in Feb. 1961, the six nations resolved to set up a committee consisting of representatives from the government of the six nations to propose specific suggestions on political union to the next conference. This committee was anchored by a French diplomat Christian Fouchet, and called as "Fouchet Committee". On Oct. 19, France proposed a draft of setting up "Union of States" (as the first Fouchet Plan) to the committee, suggesting adopting common foreign policy and defense policy and cooperation in science and culture. It did not mention economic administration in National Union, which gave the impression that the National Union had nothing to do with the offices in community. This enabled this draft to be the discussing basis to other nations who had different opinions with France on supranational nature, defense and Britain's joining and required some changes.

On Jan. 18, 1962, France proposed a more disappointing file (i.e. the second Fouchet Plan) to Fouchet Committee. In this file, the powers of "Union of States" was extended to economic fields; all the statements giving the hints of NATO on the issue of defense were cancelled; the powers of the Union in setting and administrating the organs were were too weak and it did not have an independent secretariat.

Belgium, Holland and others rejected to follow the road of "Third Power" led by France; they also argued that the political union issue should be considered after integrating Britain into the Community. Italy, Western Germany and France still wanted the US to persuade Belgium and Holland to move on to future negotiation. In April, the second Fouchet Plan came into a deadlock. Although US Ambassador to Western Europe informed Washington about the negative developments, and especially Belgium and Holland's resistance the US government still did not want to get involved in the dispute of European Political Union, but the US government began to realize its plan on Western Europe was fundamentally different from the French plan. The US aimed that European Community should be integrated into the broad framework of Atlantic alliance and Western European Political Union should be integrated into the irreplaceable NATO. However, France would like to keep distance with Atlantic Alliance. In early May, the US Secretary Dean Rusk said, "de Gaulle's opinion of Europe opposed the real community and the Atlantic Alliance, also his true aims is to to paralyze the NATO alliance."

Failed to gain the support of the European Community members, de Gaulle was angry. On May 15th, 1962, he launched a strong blow to the idea of supranational power in the press, pointing out: "during the process of building Europe, "only the union of states solution is the effective, legitimate and possible way. I have mentioned and I have to mention that Europe is an entity consisting of different nations and it cannot exist in other forms which are only myths, fancy." He openly accused: "the advocators of supranational Europe (under the American design) are working for the US, may be this group will follow some other nations out of Europe. In this way, the federator (for Europe) would not be a European". French Foreign minister had similarly said that it would be an "Atlantic Europe, not a European Europe.

Thus, the US' and other European leaders' previous doubts about Charles de Gaulle that he would replace Western European Political Union with union of states and would distance Europe from the US, were verified. Kennedy and most of his aides quickly accepted Rusk's viewpoint and expressed their deep distrust for Charles de Gaulle. Moreover, what dissatisfied the US occured in January 1963, de Gaulle signed the Treaty of Cooperation between France and Germany and refused the US' plan of "Multilateral Nuclear Power" under the framework of NATO and opposed the British application for joining the common market. This worsened the relations between France and the US and led to a complete distrust. Since then, the US government gave up its hopes for the European political union and seldom mentioned "the Third Power". US believed that Charles de Gaulle wanted to be the powerful leader of Europe and aimed to exclude Britain and the US from European issues. The Western European Political Union exposed the disputes and differences between France and the US, but their disputes and differences were much more than that.

5.2.2 Independent nuclear policies of France

France and the US had also conflicts on nuclear policy in addition to the disputes and conflicts on European Political Union. The US advocated the control of the spread of nuclear arms, regarding it as a crucial step to minimize the risk of nuclear war. For the US, the most effective and secure protection of nuclear arms was US's control over nuclear power. However, Charles de Gaulle insisted on developing the independent nuclear power of France, believing the defense power of France should not be handed to others but controlled by France itself.

He mentioned: "French defense power is the business of French people. If France is involved in a war, it should be its war and the effort should belong to it. Undoubtedly, once the war starts, France will resist to the end with the cooperation with other nations, but we should fight by ourselves with our own power and in our way... so, in recent years, we should have a power used by us. It is generally called "attacking power" which should launch attack at anytime anywhere. Of course, the main part of this power is nuclear arm."

Charles de Gaulle believed that the international circumstances in 1958 was totally different from those when NATO was founded. Western nations moved out of post-war setback and the Soviet Union was unable to conquer Western nations but hoped to mitigate the international circumstances. The chance of a breakthrough in world conflicts was slim. Furthermore, the nuclear power of the Soviet Union developed very fast and reached such a level which was enough to wipe out the US. If there was an alternative, the two nations would not fight, but it was possible for them to drop bombs on in between, i.e., Central Europe and Western Europe. In this way, NATO could not ensure the safety of Western Europe. Based on this analysis, the plan proposed by Charles de Gaulle was: France broke away from NATO military integration but not from NATO; mitigated with the Oriental group—the Soviet Union and China; and finally, set up nuclear power to protect France from an attack of any nation. In the first negotiation between the Secretaries of the US, John Foster Dulles came into power in June 1958, he made it clear that he would like to develop the nuclear power of France.

Dulles persuaded Charles de Gaulle giving up the plan of research French nuclear arms, but Charles de Gaulle replied, "If you agree to sell us your atomic bomb, we are willing to buy but it should be completely controlled by us with no restriction." The US surely disagreed and the disputes couldn't be settled. In February, 1960, regardless of the US disagreement and persuasion, France tested its first atomic bomb successfully.

Unable to stop France developing its nuclear arms independently, the US turned to the second best—trying to control the nuclear power. In December, 1962, the US and Britain held a meeting in Nassau, Bahamas, and reached agreement on the plan of building "Multilateral Force" (MLF). According to the Agreement, the US offered Britain "Polaris" missile and assisted Britain in manufacturing matching nuclear submarine and nuclear warhead. Britain should allocate this nuclear submarine team to NATO and within the control of General Headquarter of European Allies, but Britain reserved the right to retreat and re-allocated the nuclear power when its "highest national right" was under threat. The US also allocated the equivalent power to NATO. The US and British nuclear power would become parts of the NATO "MLF". J. Kennedy wrote to Charles de Gaulle that France would enjoy the same arrangement as Britain and suggested him to buy "Polaris" missile which could be used within NATO area. But Charles de Gaulle regarded it as a trap which was the US way to control the nuclear arms of Britain and France. Joining the MLF would make France unable to have its own independent attacking power. On January 14, 1963, Charles de Gaulle claimed at the Press that France would never join in the MLF plan. Accordance with French defense policy to integrate French military means to MLF which was controlled by foreigners would not be acceptable by France. France refused to sign the Nassau Agreement. Then, the Soviet Union, the US and Britain signed Partial Nuclear Test Ban Treaty on August 5, aiming at preventing China and France from developing nuclear arms and protecting the US's and Soviet Union's monopoly of nuclear power, which was certainly denied by China and France. Charles de Gaulle said, the US and Soviet Union, who had conducted hundreds of nuclear tests and had been qualified with the nuclear power to destroy the whole world, asked other nations to make commitment not to conduct nuclear test forever. This is not an agreement which could be agreed upon. Or else, a new hegemony would be set up.

5.2.3 Britain's becoming the "Trojan Horse" of the US

Another attack on the European plan of the US was Charles de Gaulle's opposition to Britain's joining the Common Market. As early as during the negotiation of Fouchet Plan, Belgium and Holland proposed to let Britain join in the negotiation on European Political Unity, hoping to contain France in this way and let France be affected from the relationship between nations along the Atlantic Ocean in order to prevent it becoming the power leader in Western Europe. However, the US officials were not in full support to this proposal, believing the other five members in European Community could contain France and they did not want Britain to join in. Furthermore, Britain opposed to any supranational power. Letting Britain join in might lead to powerlessness of the six nations in political area. Out of this consideration, the Eisenhower administration was not enthusiastic about allowing Britain join the European construction.

However, during the time of negotiation of Second Fouchet Plan, the US gained a further understanding on de Gaulle's intention, and it began to change its mind and to believe that France was unworthy of trust. The US lost its hope as to whether the other five nations could contain France or not and believed it was necessary to let Britain contain France. The US hoped Britain could be helpful in balancing the status of France in Western Europe and hoped Britain could help the US stop de Gaulle's implement of "Third Power". Therefore, the Kennedy administration showed more enthusiasm in Britain's entry into the European Union. Kennedy mentioned in a policy instruction in April 1961, "As long as Britain maintains the connection among the six nations, we should encourage its joining without too many requirements." Firstly, it was because the US hoped Britain could reinforce the common values of Atlantic nations and secondly it hoped to "establish 'special relationship' with Europe based on its 'special relationship' with Britain".

Within the six nations, Holland, Belgium, Luxembourg and Italy held a positive view towards British joining into common market but Adenauer was not enthusiastic but at the same time he was not opposed to it. In January, 1962, France threatened to not moving into the second phase of Customs Union, forcing the six nations reach agreement on finance of Common Agricultural Policy and its main content. France emphasized on making Common Agricultural Policy before British joining, so this agreement made France relieve and it had no other excuse denying British joining. It seemed inevitable for Britain to join. However, a huge change occurred after Kennedy proposed the "Significant Plan" of revitalizing Atlantic Union.

Kennedy proposed to set up an open business union between the US and Europe in order to form a large free trading zone. In August, 1962, the Trade Expansion Act was approved in the US. It was established on the assumption of British entry into the European Common Market. The US would like to reinforce its fancy of revitalizing the Atlantic Alliance to lead Atlantic Alliance with the help of its "special relationship" with Britain. In the area of defense, Kennedy proposed to set up "MNP" to control European nuclear power. Charles de Gaulle found it was unacceptable. He refused to join in "MNP" and denied the British application to join in the EU common market. When British Labor Party came to power in 1964, it proposed its application of joining the common market for the second time on May 11, 1967. This time, it was still strongly opposed by France although Britain agreed to accept Common Agricultural Policy and made concession in many aspects.

Obviously, de Gaulle's opposition to Britain joining in European Community was not only out of the economic and political consideration, but of its dissatisfaction of the US policy to Europe. His two denials were not only towards Britain but also the US control of Europe and the US strategic assumption to Western Europe. In the eyes of Charles de Gaulle, Britain undoubtedly had become the "Trojan Horse" of the US. He believed Britain had long been controlled by the US. He would never forget Churchill once he said to him during the war time, "You should be aware that if I have to make choice between European Continent and Ocean, I will always choose the latter. And you should also be aware that if I have to make choice between you and Roosevelt, I will choose the latter again."

Taking into consideration that Britain had long stood by European issue, Charles de Gaulle believed Britain "re-launches the attack because they could not stop the European Community, so they decide to destroy this organization from internal". Britain could not join in the common market as the US had expected, which frustrated the European Policy of the US again.

Charles de Gaulle stood on the opposite side from the US on the issues of European Political Union, MNP, and Britain joining into common market, which disappointed the US several times. In addition, France established diplomatic relationships with China in 1964 and quit from NATO military integration in 1966. It opposed to the Vietnam War and the internal relationship of Atlantic Alliance was in danger, which ran oppositely to the quick development of European Community at this stage. All of these cause a headache for the US. Its European Policy suffered from frustration due to de Gaulle's challenge, but it could do nothing because of French international status under the leadership of Charles de Gaulle and his domestic prestige. Washington claimed more than once, hoping France would be friendlier when Charles de Gaulle finished his term.

The European integration plan of the US was attacked because of the disputes and differences between France and the US. However, the US still supported European integration, because the US believed that integration would be beneficial. It would not only strengthen the Western European power, reduce the burden of the US, but also helped the US realize its purpose of containing the Soviet Union. And it could inter-contain the nations of Western Europe. It could prevent German from re-launching of war and prevent France from dictatorship.

5.3 Readjustment of European policy by the US

During late 1960s and early 1970, world political and economic trend changed significantly. The equivalent power between the US and the Soviet Union and the quick economic development of Europe enabled the power between the US and Europe to change and Europe started to seek the equal status as the US. The disputes between the US and Europe were intensified in politics, economy and defense. The US faced the increase of Soviet Union's power. Faced with the European economic pressure, political requirement and world's appealing of anti-hegemony, the US adjusted its European policy while seeking for peace with Soviet Union to protect its global strategic benefits, hoping to make it better suit to the power between the two nations.

5.3.1 The background of US' policy adjustment

In 1969, Nixon government hoped to ease the relation with the world globally when forced by the change of international trend. In May 1972, the US and Soviet Union signed Anti-Ballistic Missile Treaty (ABMT) and Strategic Arms Limitation Talks (SALT), limiting the anti-ballistic missile bases, number of missile and number of intercontinental ballistic missile respectively. In August, 1972, the US Senate passed ABMT with 88 votes to 2. Then, a joint session of Senate and Congress approved the ABMT. These were two very significant treaties the US and the Soviet Union signed during the ease period.

The intense situation between the US and the Soviet Union towards Western Europe eased too. The Minister of Foreign Affairs of the US, Britain, France and the Soviet Union signed the final protocol on the Western Berlin issue in June 1972. And to make "Four Parties Protocol" of

Western Berlin issue signed in March 1971 come into effect. The three great powers led by the US admitted that West Berlin was not a part of German Federal Republic; and the Soviet Union admitted the connection between West Berlin and German Federal Republic which could consul the residents in West Berlin and represent West Berlin residents in international organization and international conference. The issue of West Berlin had always been the focus during the Cold War between the US and the Soviet Union and aroused fierce disputes. Therefore, the reconciliation on this issue marked the ease of the fight between Soviet Union and the US in Europe.

The reconciliation between the Soviet Union and the US in 1970s was caused by various reasons, but one of which was the US lost the advantage over the Soviet Union in militarily, especially strategic nuclear arms with each had own merits and becoming equivalent. The strategic arms owned by the US were superior to the Soviet Union in many aspects, for instance, the technology of intercontinental ballistic missile and the ballistic missile of submarine; the technology of carrier of anti-ballistic missile and MIRV returning into atmosphere. However, the strategic arms of the Soviet Union started to own some advantages, for example, its quality and category were over the US; the throwing weight carried by its intercontinental missile was heavier than that of the US; its air defense system was larger and stronger than that of the US.

In economy, Europe posed an ever-increasing threat to the US in 1950, payment deficit showed up in the US for the first time and increased during 1958 to 1959. In April 1961, Kennedy told Douglas Dillon, Secretary of Treasury two things bothering him: "nuclear war and payment deficit". Since the foundation of European Economic Community, there had been inevitably increasing number of economic frictions.

The disputes between the US and Europe were significant in agriculture. After the foundation of European Economic Community, the six nations, according to the rules in Treaty of Rome, started to make up Common Agricultural Policy with intensive protectionism. In 1958, agricultural products occupied one third of the total exports of the US. The US would like to expand it to improve its financial balance. Although its agricultural export to Europe increased, the portion in the total amount decreased, which was meaningless to improve its financial balance. Furthermore, the influence of the US agricultural profit group was large to affect the Congress, which resulted in the US attention to the making up of the Common Agricultural Policy of European Community.

Another disputing area of the US and Europe was the courtesy to the former colonies given by the Community, especially when Britain joined in the Community, the courtesy would expand to mass colonies of the Great Britain. After denying British application by de Gaulle, it was undoubtedly a disaster politically, but financially, it might be profitable. According the analysis on the first meeting of Homeland Security Committee of the US on January 31, 1963, the Common Agricultural Policy might not be implemented immediately; the issue of colony was eased with the denial of British application because the requirements from French colonies were not met. But it was proved to be wrong soon. The formulation of Common Agricultural Policy was different but still required, and it was put into force gradually; the Community reached agreement on the courtesy to the former courtesy.

In March, 1962, President Kennedy who cared about the international payment issue improved the tax on carpet and glass in the US. The Community also delayed the decrease on input tax on polyethylene, polystyrene, varnish, painting, clothing and other products. The US further took new measure on the wool and chemicals. The Community revenged on the input of fowl. This was the serious trading war between the US and the Community for the first time.

The US did not oppose to the European Community but was eager to change the situation of payment balance. Therefore, the US started to actively promote the negotiation on General Agreement on Tariffs and Trade (GATT).

In order to break the tariff wall of the Community and expand its export of commodity, the US took reducing tariff as the bait, putting forward the slogan of "trade liberalization" to reduce and even break the tariff wall of the Community through multilateral trading negotiation of GATT. The Community also attempted to let the US reduce tariff through multilateral trading negotiation of GATT to gain advantage of expanding export. Therefore, the two parties bargained fiercely. In the Dillon Round during 1961 to 1962, they reached agreement to reduce 25% tariff respectively. In the Kennedy Round during 1964 to 1968, the US proposed that all the nations reduce 50% tariff and reached the agreement that industrial products reduced 35% tariff in average within five years. After the tariff decrease, the export tariff of the Community was 6%, the US was 7.1% and Japan was 9.7%.

In 1970s, the status of the US in world economy was declining while Community was increasing. The world gross output of the US was decreased from 70% in 1950 to 66% in 1960s and even below 50% in early 1970s. Meanwhile, the proportion of the US in the West trading declined from 1/2 to 1/3 and even 1/4. Europe was no longer the weak one during the early post-war stage who was in need of assistance from the US. The European Community enjoyed a superior status in trading. From 1950 to 1970, its proportion in the world export increased from 15.4% to 28.8% while the US decreased from 16.7% to 13.7%; the proportion of the Community in international reverses increased from 6.1% to 32.5% while the US decreased from 49.8% to 15.7%. in 1959-1969, the average increase of labor productivity of the Community was 5.4% while the US was 2.6%.

Since 1970s, crisis appeared in US dollar which had been served as the world currency since the WWII and the international payment deficit was increasing. In August, 1971, Nixon government had to announce to stop the exchanging rate of 35 U.S. dollars/ounce of gold as in the Bretton Woods System. The US dollar was devalued. The leading role of US dollar was reversed and the leading role of the US in Atlantic Alliance was attacked.

The equal power of the US and the Soviet Union as well as the large gap between the US and European economic power made the US status decline. The comparative decline of the US and the comparative increase of Community enabled Europe to seek for the equal status as the US. The General Minister of Western Germany, Schmidt said, "During the past years, the US were conditioned to German's obedience to them. They knew we could not leave them, but Germany is different. Germany has been rebuilt and the economic energy has been recovered, so has our dignity. We should let the US know we won't listen to their order anymore." Heath, the British Minster clearly pointed out at the banquet celebrating Britain joining in the European Community that the target of the Community was to make Europe "the genuine partner of the US"; when admitting Europe could not be independent from the US. French President G. Pompidou emphasized that Europe should be united. He said, "The US is the nation with the most powerful economy. The eight nations formed the alliance of Atlantic Treaty. We have such close relation with the powerful nation. It is ridiculous for use to be united to oppose any idea of the US. However, it is the close relation which requires unique character of Europe from the US. The freedom of Western Europe is the result of the determining interference of the US soldiers at that time; Western Europe was rebuilt with the help of the US and seeks for security with the ally with the US; Western Europe has taken US dollar as the main currency of foreign currency reserve; Europe cannot depend from the US, but Europe should also keep its independent entity."

The words of the leaders from the powerful nations within European Community reflect their view of the status of Europe and the relation between the US and Europe. On the one hand, they clearly realized that Europe needed the US, especially in the US protection in security; but on the other hand, they opposed to the European's completely dependent on the US, wishing Europe would be more independent.

5.3.2 From "European Year" to deep disputes

Facing the new changes in the relation between the US and Europe, Henry Kissinger who later became the National Security Advisor proposed in 1968 that the US should adjust in its European policy. He pointed out that the US garrison had been in Europe for over two decades, which lowered the European fear of Soviet Union attack and retreating of the US. A new and stronger Europe would be different from in 1949, so "the US cannot count on the fancy to take the occasional European situation of being exhausted after war to an eternal international relation". He also believed "A united Europe will hold a special European opinion towards world affairs—in other words Europe will challenge the hegemony of the US Atlantic policy". This maybe the price which should be paid for the European unity, but the US would not admit the price because of the weak policy it."

On February 23, 1969, Nixon visited Europe after being inaugurated for one month. Before that, Europe had just suffered from the fierce fight on the future of Europe between Britain and France. On February 4 and 14, President Charles de Gaulle and British ambassador to Paris mentioned the future of Europe in his private talk with Christopher Solms that Europe first of all should set itself free from NATO "designed and controlled by the US ". It should depend on the cooperation between the super nations of Britain, France, Germany and Italy. Its core was the forgiveness and cooperation between Britain and France. Secondly, it should change the structure of Common Market. He lacked the confidence of the future of the EU Common Market, wanting to replace it with some extensive free trading zones, especially agricultural product free trading zones. Thirdly, because the relation between France and Britain was the footstone of the plan, Charles de Gaulle planed to have a bilateral talk on economy, currency, politics and financial issues with Britain. Although Britain held different opinions with Charles de Gaulle on the issues of NATO, the relation between the US and whether they should set up a Four-nation Leadership Institute in Europe, Britain still believed de Gaulle's suggestion was useful and was willing to take a further negotiation.

Britain informed member nations of NATO including the US the conference highlights, which aroused a great disturbance within NATO and the US. The court and the commonalty in the US suggested government refuse de Gaulle's proposal of setting up special guiding institute of European super nations. However, Kissinger had his own opinion. The day before visit, February 22nd, Kissinger proposed to President Nixon in his memo on the Western European policy of the US:

Making sure our responsibility of the NATO; making sure our support to European Unity, including British joining the EU Common Market; but making it clear that we are not willing to be involved in the debate about the development of European unity and its form, methods; when and how to take step.

The former two points followed the European policy of the post-war US, but the third point was different from the traditional The US policy. Before Nixon government, all previous the US governments had supported the supranational European unity but Nixon government gave up its support to supranational nation and turned its attention to the Atlantic cooperation. Kissinger believed, "What we focus is the Atlantic relation, and making up the internal arrangement is the business of Europeans, which should be left to be solved by them. In the long run, this attitude is the most beneficial to British joining in Common Market." The US should "let Europeans solve the internal development of European unity and propose a new form of Atlantic cooperation with the US wisdom and influence".

In 1973, President Nixon defined 1973 as "European Year" as suggested by Kissinger. This was their ambition to re-define and strengthen the relationship between Europe and the US within the Atlantic Framework. After retreating from the Vietnam and establishing the new relation with China and the Soviet Union, Europe became the focus of Washington again. However, the US still asked for the leadership in the area of defense. In 1974, Nixon even claimed that if Europe was not willing to be in the leadership of the US, the US would not keep the current position in the defense in Europe.

In June, 1974, the US and European Community signed the new Atlantic Charter and the 15 NATO nations, including eight nations (except Ireland) in European Community and the U.S. signed Declaration of Atlantic Relation which re-declared that the "common defense between the US and Europe is integrated and indispensible" because the Soviet Union was still the only rival of the Atlantic Alliance; member nations should keep friendly, equal and united spirit; they should be "devoted to eliminating the root of conflicts on economic policies and encourage economic cooperation in between."

It should be said the equality between the US and Europe was only orally while the nature was protecting and being protected; leading and being led, especially the subordination on the issue of defense. What was different was the US emphasized politically the Atlantic Framework of European Integration rather than promoting the supranational nation of European Integration or interfering in the specific form, method and time arrangement of European Unity.

Charles de Gaulle represented the Europe political challenge of Atlantic Framework led by the US while another challenge to the US was the economy. On this issue, political target overweight economic target. To the US, British joining into European Community worsened economy but political target was more important than economic target. And most policy-deciders believed generally, European Integration was beneficial to The US economy, for instance, Marshall Plan. To the US, a sound European market was beneficial to expand the US export market; another instance was European Integration. Even though its powerful economy it is the rival of the US and the European protectionism was adverse to the US, but all the economic departments of the US believed a stronger and more modern European economy could offer a better export market to the US. However, due to the decline of economy, the U no longer took the tolerant attitude to Europe but paid more attention to economic profits and protection of its market. In 1974, the Congress passed new trading law whose biggest feature was asking for the protection of the US market and made rigid limits on the concession made in the GATT during Tokyo Round. This showed that to some degrees, the US admitted that the economic status of European Community became equal with the US. The US took European Community more as its rival and paid more attention to protect its market.

The background of adjustments of European policy by Nixon-Kissinger leadership

Firstly, they believed in the past, the US over-estimated the influence of European Integration. Kissinger was clear that "there is a group of scholars, ex-officials and journalists along the Atlantic Ocean who believe the European Union Movement will fail only if the US offers motivation, especially when the fear mostly motivation and Russian disappear". He wrote to oppose the opinion as early as before he served as the National Security Advisor in 1968. "Rather than saying that the future of a more united Europe depends on the blame from Washington, it's better to say it depends on the development of London, Paris and Bonn." "Our influence fails to realize our ideal plan but more than enough to stop the things we don't like." He insisted that "we refuse to join in the fights within Europe, which reinforces our relation with Europe and Atlantic nations"

In economy, Nixon government believed that US was declining while the super nations in other areas were uprising, so the US had no reason to over-estimate its influence. Nixon believed in terms of economic issue and potential, there were five centers, i.e., the US, the Soviet Union, Western Europe, China and Japan. They should cooperate more but order less due to the strength declining of the US.

Secondly, the basic benefits of the US and Western Europe were in accordance in the past, but Nixon government realized that this assumption was not fully correct. In fact, it was most possible that Europe took some policies the US disagreed. Kissinger analyzed that "we try to combine supranational Europe with the more united Atlantic Union which is under the leadership of the US, but these two objects may be proved to be incompatible," because with the increase of strength, Europe went on its own way. Some US officials worried that a supranational Europe would become the third power which taking France as a center and may even became like anti-Americanism. Politically, Charles de Gaulle's challenge to the US enabled the US citizens feel the complex emotions of the Europeans towards the US Financially, the US may have a deeper sense of the disagreement of the European and the US profits, for instance, the ever-bothering agricultural trading issue, the disputes of GATT in Tokyo Round Talks. Not only the economic department but also the Congress and President concerned about these issues. In the analysis of Nixon and Kissinger, the defense cooperation between the US and Europe was not bad, but the economic area was far from satisfied. On the one hand, Europe depended on the US military and defense power. On the other hand, it stood at the opposite side as the US, which aroused the dissatisfaction of the US.

Thirdly, supporting the in-depth European Integration may affect the friendly relation between the US and Britain. Since 1960s, the US had changed its attitude and supported British joining into European Community (see 5.2 of this chapter). Not soon, the US discovered that the close relation between Britain and the US could not be maintained if Europe developed into a united federal. Otherwise, the special relation between the US and Britain could be kept in a loosely tied European federal. Then, Britain also opposed to supranational power, which was an important reason for Britain to be kept away from European Integration at the early stage. Also, the US attitude towards British joining into the European Integration had negative effect (see 5.2 in this chapter). Therefore, Kissinger said, "Our 'low profile' on the issue of European Unity gives a significant improvement of the future of Britain."

The US adjusted its policy of European Integration according to situation, but it didn't change its basic attitude towards European integration. It still actively supported the progress of European Union. Kissinger suggested in his letter to President Nixon that "I think, although it may be difficult in the short term but setting up a more united Europe is in accordance with our basic profit in NATO,... In the long run, it is acceptable if we can take Europe as a real and more equal partner." The reason was "a stronger and more united European will improve the more equal and fruitful partner relationship." Obviously, the US foothold was still Atlantic relation. Since the end of war, the US had focused on the situation that Europe was too weak to take the responsibility of being "the US partner". The US would like to see a strong Europe and a powerful European Unity, which was the basic motivation of the US to support the progress of European Integration. The US would not oppose to the strong and united Europe until Europe could be strong enough to stand on the equal ground and pose threat to the leadership of the US. As for equality, it was in red-tape and could only be tested when Europe was strong enough to be as equal as the US.

Therefore, at the initial stage of the European Integration, through Marshall Plan the US give the first motivation to influence the issue of leadership, but also showed enthusiastic support to promote the progress. Undoubtedly, it played an important role in the process of post-war European integration. From another angle, Europe had been the world center for centuries, but in the initial stage of post-war, Europe because it lost its status had to depend on the economic support and military protection of the US. As one of the two super nations of post-war, the US enjoyed the undoubted impact on Europe and the world. With such uneven strength, it was unimaginable that the US had not supported European Integration. From this sense, the US support to European Integration was indispensable. The US policy and attitude towards European Integration has affected the European Integration to a certain degree.

With the establishment of European Community and quick development of European economy, the European economic strength became obvious gradually. Its independent consciousness was strengthened and it showed the wish to seek for the equality as the US. However, due to the decline in politics and economy, the US adjusted its European policy. Financially, it took Europe as the rival rather than the partner who needed assistance and paid more attention to protect its economic profits. Politically, it adopted a freer attitude rather than interfering in the specific form, method and time arrangement of European Unity. In the areas of defense and security, the relation between the US and Europe was still subordinate. Europe still depended on the protection from the US and would not be independent from the protection of the US due to its weakness. Generally, in the 30 years of post-war, the US adopted supportive attitude towards European Integration. The adjustment at 1970s did not change its basic principle of supporting European Integration. It was a partial and slight adjustment rather than a huge reversion.

The Soviet Union attacked the global strategy in 1980s. Regan government halted the easy progress and re-containment of the Soviet Union. In order to stop the expansion of the Soviet Union, the US continued its bipolar confrontation. On one side, it was still active for European Integration because it was clear that a united Europe benefited not only the US itself but also its global strategy. On the other side, the independent feature of Europe developed with the in-depth of the development of European Integration. The disputes between the US and Europe were in-depth, which enabled the US refused to support European Integration at a cost. In 1980s, the disputes between the US and Europe were shown from two aspects. One was the in-depth economic friction. The US worried that with the expansion and deepening of European Integration, European Community would gradually have negative impact on the US profits financially. The other was that Europe kept away from the US on the issue of the relation with the Soviet Union politically. Europe advocated the easy policy while the US advocated containing, which led to the strategic mind divergence of the Western Alliance whose influence still exists today.

Ultimately, the US support of European Integration was for its own national profit. It did not support the European Integration at any cost. "The US should continue its support for European Economic Integration, but we should lead it move along the road as we expected with our influence." These words describe the US mind exactly. On the one hand, the US hoped Europe would be independent to reduce the responsibility it took in the Europe. On the other hand, it did not want Europe to be fully independent, but wanted it to be integrated into the Atlantic Framework which was in the leadership of the US. To the US, Atlantic Framework meant the leadership. The US support to the European Integration was based on the precondition that Integration would not threaten Atlantic Framework. In other words, the US leadership over Europe was undoubted. Its support for European Integration aimed to integrate Europe under its leadership.

Chapter VI

The End of Cold War and the Western Alliance

Beginning in the late 1980s, a series of epoch-making changes have been taking place in the world situation. After the US and the Soviet Union adjusted their global strategies and turned to détente and dialogue from confrontation, sudden changes of political institutions took place in European countries. Then two Germanys reunified, the Warsaw Pact and COMECON dismantled themselves, and the Soviet Union disintegrated, and consequently the Cold War ended. And subsequently, the Yalta System which formed at the end of World War II and in which two military blocs led by the US and the Soviet went in confrontation collapsed. Before a new system of international relations was established, the world situation went into a turbulent period of transition. In the transition, it became a focus in the struggles in international relations that what kind of system of international relations should be built and what were the principles on which to build it. The characteristics of the transition were almost all developed, developing and new emerging developing countries were involved in the struggles. Moreover, it inevitably shook the foundation of the Western alliance, which demanded a re-assessment of the relations between major Western powers.

6.1 The New International Situation in the post-Cold War era

6.1.1 The End of Cold War— Collapse of the Yalta System

In the world history, the Cold War was a special phenomenon in international relations after the World War II. It referred specifically to the state of antagonism between United States and The Soviet Union and between the blocs of countries both represented in nearly half a century without direct military engagements by the two powers, following the framework of the Yalta System agreed upon in the final stages of the war. The formation of the Cold War had gone through a process. George Kennan's 8,000-word-long telegram in February, 1946, Winston Churchill's speech at Fulton in March, and the release of the Truman Doctrine in March 1947... were all the preludes to the Cold War (some maintain that the events mark the start of the War). The foundation of NATO and establishment of two Germanys in 1949 formally launched the War. Its ending also lasted for a period. It began with the Revolutions of 1989, went through the German reunification and the dissolution of the Warsaw Pact and the Council for Mutual Economic Assistance (COMECON), and ended up with collapse of The Soviet Union.

The Revolutions of 1989 began in Poland, Hungary and Czechoslovakia, where the liberal tradition were strong. On January 16, 1989, the Central Committee of PZPR (Polska Zjednoczona Partia Robotnicza) passed two resolutions. One was to build social institutions based on parliamentary democracy and civil society in Poland and implement the Tripartite system, and to introduce suffrage and competition into the administrative mechanism of the party; the second was to, under a pluralistic political system, reinstate legitimacy of the Solidarity Union which was banned in 1982, and abolish the order of prohibition to new trade unions. As a result of a series of elections from June 1989, the opposition including the Solidarity held the rein of government and PZPR suffered from heavy failures and fell into a crisis and chaos. On January 27, 1990, PZPR held its last congress and announced the cessation of all its activities. Transformations in Hungary took place almost at the same time. In January 1989, a great debate began in Hungary regarding the nature of the Hungarian Revolution of 1956 and appraisal of Imre Nagy . On February 11, Socialist Workers' Party of Hungary (MSZNP) issued a communiqué saying the Hungarian Revolution of 1956 was a people's uprising and announced to implement a pluralistic political system and multi-party system. On October 6, MSZNP was renamed as MSZP (Magyar Szocialista Párty), but it still failed to keep on rule and was excluded from the government after the election in March 1990. In Czechoslovakia, January 16 was the day for celebration of the protesting against the Soviet Union's invasion in 1968.[1]

On that day in 1989, the commemoration quickly became demonstrations. Under pressure from incessant demonstrations, Komunistická strana Ceskoslovenska (KSC) promised to re-establish free election and multi-party system. By the end of November, the Federal Parliament of Czechoslovakia passed an amendment to the constitution, deleting the provisions concerning the leading role of the KSC. And, on November 30th, KSC confessed it had lost leading position in the country. The same thing also happened in such countries as Bulgaria, Romania and East Germany. In Romania, armed conflicts broke out because demonstrations were cracked down by the Ceausescu government, while the political upheavals in East Germany ultimately resulted in reunification of two Germanys. Then the unified Germany became a member of the Western alliance (for the German reunification, see Section 2.3). The Revolutions of 1989 showed a fundamental change has occurred in one of the two military blocs in antagonism, and its collapse is well in sight. On March 31, 1991, the military establishment of the Warsaw Pact declared to withdraw, which was closely followed by the summit meeting of the Warsaw Pact on July 1, approving the protocol for dissolution of the pact; and two days before, the member states of COMECON had ratified an accord to announce its dissolution.

Nowadays, politicians, ideologists and historians have different explanations for the end of the Cold War. Although there have been debates on the causes and on the key reason, it is an undeniable historical fact that the perestroika and glasnost promoted by Gorbachev, General Secretary of the Communist Party of the Soviet Union (CPSU), had triggered the revolutions which finally resulted in the break-up of the Soviet Union, letting the US-led Western alliance win the Cold War without even a struggle. Gorbachev's "new thinking" advocated the "free choice" of political future and social systems by Eastern European countries. Under his instigation, the long repressed discontentment and rebelling emotion in these countries has led to explosions, one after the other. Faced with the rapid political changes in these countries, Gorbachev not only acquiesced and welcomed, but also brought them into the Soviet Union which was already in numerous

---

1 On Jan. 16, 1969, Jan Palach, a college student, walked onto Wenceslas Square, Prague, doused himself in gasoline and set himself alight as a protest against his country's invasion by the Soviet Union on August 20, 1968. Since then, Jan. 16 was set as a memorial day dedicated to Palach.

hidden crises. In December 1989, Gorbachev-led CPSU Central Committee proposed to amend the constitutional provisions concerning CPSU's leading status and role. In March 1990, the Congress of People's Deputies of the Soviet Union passed a resolution to remove the leading role of the CPSU in the political and social life of the country, and Boris Yeltsin, in the name of Russian president, issued a decree banning all Communist Party activities in Russia. In the period, the Baltic States (Lithuania, Estonia and Latvia) also declared independence. Not long after that, the other republics of the Soviet Union one after another issued statements proclaiming the sovereignty of the republics above everything. In 1991, in order to maintain the union, the Soviet Union proposed to promulgate a new "Union of Sovereign State Treaty" designed to recognize and expand the sovereignty of the republics. The new treaty, however, had not been signed before the 1991 Soviet coup d'état attempt.[2]

Yeltsin, who gained fame for quelling the attempt, announced a freeze on the activities of the Russian Communist Party on August 23rd. On that same day, the office block of CPSU was closed. The next day, Gorbachev resigned as CPSU general secretary and recommended CPSU to dissolve itself. On August 25th, CPSU Central Committee and its secretariat announced dissolution. On August 29th, the Supreme Soviet of the Soviet Union decreed the termination and banning of all the Party activities in Russia and the confiscation of all CPSU's properties and all propaganda facilities. On December 1, 1991, Ukraine declared independence. On December 8, after the Minsk summit talks among the three largest republics, Russia, Ukraine and Belarus, they declared "The Soviet Union officially ceased to exist as a subject of international law and a geopolitical entity" and signed an agreement to establish the "Commonwealth of Independent States." On December 21, leaders of the 11 republics signed a series of documents for the commonwealth at Almaty, and formally announced the dissolution of The Soviet Union. Gorbachev was excluded from the Almaty meeting, but he received a letter with the signatures of the 11 heads of republics asking him to hand over the nuclear button and military control. On December

---

2   On August 19, 1991, in order to preserve the integrity of Soviet Union and oppose to the new union treaty, eight high-level officials within the Soviet government, led by Vice President Gennady Yanayev, including Premier Valentin Pavlov, Defense Minister Dmitry Yazov, Chairman of KGB Vladimir Kryuchkov, and Interior Minister Boris Pugo, etc. organized the State Committee on the State of Emergency taking the opportunity of Gorbachev's going on holiday in Crimea, announcing that due to health reasons Gorbachev could not continue to perform the role of President, named Yanayev as acting president. They declared the state of emergency in some regions and tried to take control of the country. The committee collapsed in only three days under the strong deterrent force of Russian President Boris Yeltsin.

25, Gorbachev delivered a televised public speech declaring his departure from office. The Soviet flag was lowered for the last time over the Kremlin, marking the end of the Soviet Union.

The Cold War after World War II was an overall international situation characterized by the comprehensive confrontation and rivalry between the US-led Western alliance and the Soviet-led Eastern alliance. Confrontation and rivalry between the Soviet Union and the US, although being comprehensive, mainly relied on two military blocs: NATO and Warsaw Pact. Therefore, military confrontation and competition were key aspects. Since post-war Europe was split into spheres of influence by the Soviet Union and the US and Germany was partitioned to be occupied, Europe, especially Germany, became the forefront of confrontation and contention. As the confrontation and rivalry mainly took place between the Soviet Union and the US, especially when it evolved into vying for hegemony by two superpowers, the situation is named "bipolar structure." Because the confrontation and rivalry was carried out based on the principles and tacit understanding reached by the US, Britain and the Soviet Union at the Yalta Conference in the final stage of the war, hence the name "Yalta System." Today, two Germanys have reunified, former divided Europe has moved towards integration because of Eastern European nations' return one after another, the Warsaw Pact has been disbanded, ending its military rival with NATO, the dissolution of the Soviet Union concluded the Cold War, and United States became the world's only superpower. The Cold War was over, the bipolar pattern was terminated, and the Yalta System collapsed.

The end of the Cold War—collapse of the Yalta system—came at the cost of the disintegration of the socialist camp and dissolution of the Soviet Union, the first socialist country in the world. No matter how to appraise the socialism in these countries and what reasons are attributed to the collapse, what has been recorded in the history is that, after contest for several decades, the Communists lost their rule and socialism failed as well in these countries. And this fact made the US-led Western alliance and even the capitalist world on the whole fall into a state of fabulous hilarity. What the new international situation would be? How would major powers adjust their international strategies to the new situation and deal with the relationships between them. Would the world engage in another war to build a new system of international relations? Those were the new issues, world faced soon after the Cold War ended.

6.1.2 New International Order and the New System of International Relations

It has been a hot topic how to establish a new international order and a new system of international relations after the Revolutions of 1989, end of the Cold War, and collapse of the Yalta System. The discussion has been running through the whole period of transition towards establishment of a new system, and it has not yet ended. The so-called "international order," in essence, refers to the guiding principles and the codes of conduct for handling international affairs and dealing with relations between countries; and the so-called "system of international relations" ought to be the concrete forms of power configuration and mutual relations between different forces—especially major powers—in the world under the constraints of an international order or certain principles and norms. With an international order, there would be a corresponding system of international relations. The former is rational generalization, while the latter can be seen as perceptual expressions, and both are two sides of the same issue.

New International Order During the several decades after the end of World War II, the nature of the international order was the dominance of hegemonism and power politics pursued by superpowers in world affairs. Its manifestation was the bipolar rivalry and the state of Cold War under the Yalta System. In the old order, regional hegemonism and regional power politics also became rampant, which gave the whole world no respite. To establish a new international order, it is naturally targeted at the old one. However, it is too naïve to assume that since the old international system has collapsed, there would be no grounding for the old order to rely on and "it will be inevitably replaced by a new one." In fact, the end of the rivalry between two superpowers doesn't necessarily mean disappearance of hegemonism and power politics. Instead, both still exist and are trying to continue in new forms.

For a "new" international order, it should first and upmost mean negation of the old one. In particular, for those who formulated the old order, if they kept on talking about the "new order" without completely denying their past, it would absolutely be impossible for them to propose a truly new order in accordance with the trends in the world development.

After the end of the Cold War and collapse of the Yalta System, major powers in the world has stepped on the stage to offer their ideas about how to establish a new international order.

The US and the new international order

On August 7th, 1990, the Gulf War broke out. The US, while busily en-gaged in the fighting in the war, took the opportunity to publicize their ideas about "building an international new order" on every occasion. On September 11, 1990, President George H.W. Bush officially elaborated his proposal to establish a US-led new international order at a joint session of the Congress. He portrayed a new world blueprint under the new internati-onal order and said that "An era in which the nations of the world, East and West, North and South, can prosper and live in harmony. A hundred gene-rations have searched for this elusive path to peace, while a thousand wars raged across the span of human endeavor. Today that new world is strugg-ling to be born, a world quite different from the one we've known, a world where the rule of law supplants the rule of the jungle, a world in which nations recognize the shared responsibility for freedom and justice, a world where the strong respect the rights of the weak." On October 1st, Bush delivered a speech at the UN General Assembly, and claimed that establish-ment of a new international order is the responsibility of United States. On January 29th, 1991, Bush addressed before a joint session of the Congress on the State of the Union, emphasizing "in a rapidly changing world, The US leadership is indispensable," and "Among the nations of the world, only the United States of America has both moral standing and means to back it up."On March 5, Bush, when taking about the just-concluded Gulf War at the Congress, said that "We have before us the opportunity to forge for ourselves and for future generations a new world order." According to sta-tistics, as of that day, Bush has mentioned "new international order" for 42 times. On April 13, in the remarks at Maxwell Air Force Base, Bush propo-sed a set of principles for forging a new international order: "peaceful sett-lements of disputes, solidarity against aggression, reduced and controlled arsenals, and just treatment of all peoples." On August 13, when submitting Statement on the 1991 National Security Strategy Report, Bush stressed that the US should "build a new international system in accordance with our own values and ideals."

To put it simply, the nature of the new international order advocated by United States is one under the US' leadership and taking their values as gui-ding principles. It is deemed to have to include the following basic elements:

Firstly, to establish the US' leadership in building the new international order, in other words, the coming new order should be led by the US In the order, it is not allowed to challenge the leadership of the US, and no other superpower will be allowed to emerge capable to compete with it.

Secondly, there is only one set of recognized values, namely, the US values, ideology and capitalist economic and political models founded on the Western values, and based on the values, to advance globalization.

Thirdly, the most powerful guarantee for establishment and maintenance of this new international order is existence of the unique military strength of the US, and it would not hesitate to use force to safeguard its national strategic interests. Therefore, for the US new international order is nothing more than turning hegemonism and power politics—in which both the Soviet Union and the United States dominated the world — into the dominance of the world by United States alone, namely, from a bipolar world to unipolar world. And nothing in the nature of hegemonism and power politics of the old international order has been changed.

Japanese and European proposals for the new international order

On January 9, 1990, Toshiki Kaifu, Japanese Prime Minister, wrote a letter to the US President George H.W. Bush, making it clear that "we must forge a new international order by adopting the 'three-polar' strategy of Japan, US and Europe." In the Fall issue of Foreign Policy in the year, he published an article titled "Japan's Vision", claiming that "Japan intends to participate whole-heatedly in the process of creating a new international order, one that will offer bright prospects for all humankind."[3]

He described the goals of new international order Japan advocated comprehensively: first, ensure peace and security; second, respect freedom and democracy; third, guarantee world prosperity through open market economies; fourth, preserve an environment in which all people can lead rewarding lives, and fifth, create a stable international order founded upon dialogue and coordination. However, as one important power in the Asian and Pacific region, in addition to active participation in international new order, Japan pays more attention to the new order in Asia, striving for a dominant role in the regional new order.

European nations' stand on new international order is somewhat complex. On one hand, they agree with the United States to promote Western democracy through the Western values promoted by the US, and therefore they followed the US in the Gulf War, providing financial and logistic assistance; on the other hand, they also they were also worried against the threat of US's ambition for "a unipolar world," and hoped to establish an autonomous new regional order in Europe by taking the opportunity that emerged by the end of the Cold War and by the return of "Eastern Europe"

---

3   Toshiki Kaifu,"Japan's Vision," in Foreign Policy, Fall 1990, p.27.

to Europe, and to create a family of European nations. European countries also expressed their dissatisfaction with the US version of new international order. French President Francois Mitterrand believed that a new international order could not impose Pax Americana onto other nations. In the 1990 New Year Address, he said "It is obvious that Europe will no longer be the one we knew for half a century. Yesterday, it was still attached to the two superpowers; but in the future, it will be back to its own history and geography like returning home." "I'd like to see the formation of a veritable European confederation which is peaceful and secure, co-organized by and unifying all the nations of our continent for permanent mutual exchanges in the 1990s." [4]

Dissonance emerged even in the most reliable allies of the United States. Douglas Hurd, British Foreign Secretary, said that no one could claim that a country had the ability to decide everything. Both Pax Americana and Pax Atlantica were unrealistic. Hence, European countries on the one hand actively accelerated building their independent defense force, and on the other hand speeded up the construction of the monetary and economic union during their integration process.

China's proposals on the new international order

As early as in September 21, 1988, the Chinese leader Deng Xiaoping pointed out that "a foreign policy China firmly pursues is to oppose all forms of hegemonism and China is determined to safeguard world peace. It is now necessary to establish both a new international economic order and a new international political order." [5]

After the end of the Cold War and collapse of the Yalta System, in response to the US version of new international order, China soon proposed a clear approach for a new international order. The core of China's proposal was the Five Principles of Peaceful Coexistence, to serve as the basic principles in building the new the order. The core of China's proposal was the Five Principles of Peaceful Coexistence, serving as the basic principles for establishing the order. The Five Principles, which involved the fundamental principles of correct handling of international relations, were in line with the purposes of the Charter of the United Nations. Since its first formal codification in 1954, it has stood up to the long test of history and has been widely accepted in the international community. On February 28, 1972, the Joint Communiqué of the United States of America and People's Republic of China approved the Five Principles, declaring "there are essential

---

4   Le Monde, January 2, 1990.
5   People's Daily, September 22, 1988.

differences between China and the United States in their social systems and foreign policies. However, the two sides agreed that countries, regardless of their social systems, should deal with their relations on the principles of respect for the sovereignty and territorial integrity of all states, non-aggression against other states, non-interference in the internal affairs of other states, equality and mutual benefit, and peaceful coexistence." The Sino-Soviet joint communiqué also solemnly declared to develop bilateral relations based on the Five Principles in May, 1989. China has been firm in its attitude, and it always opposes hegemonism, infringement upon the sovereignty of other countries and interference in other country's internal affairs in the name of building a new international order.

It is a battle and a contest among powers in the world what kind of and how to build a new international order. And it has become a demand in our time to establish a new international order that is peaceful, stable, fair and rational. In the contest for establishment of a new international order, it is first and upmost to reveal the turmoil and unrest brought by the old international order to the world, and to be vigilant of potential turmoil and unrest. Only on this basis can a new international order be built compliant with global trends, in the interests of all the countries and accepted by the majority of countries. Nevertheless, it is not easy to forge a new international order that is peaceful, stable, fair and rational. Since the international order can be understood as the guiding principles for handling international affairs and dealing with relations between nations, then different versions of new international order will represent the interests of different countries. Nation state, which is more inspiring than anything else for a people, was bred and gradually came into existence in the medieval Europe. As a great historical initiative, Engels hailed it as "one of the most important levers for the progress in the medieval ages."[6]

Despite the fact that capitalism has existed for centuries and socialism for nearly a century, both will turn into vacuous preaching devoid of practical impact if they are detached from national interests. During the transition period from an old international order to a new one, it was predicted that the subtle difference in national interests would have huge impact on the entire international order, and it was asserted that "national interest priority" would become the mainstream of international relations.

---

6   Friedrich Engels, "On the Decline of Feudalism and the Rise of Nation State," A Complete Collection of Karl Marx and Frederick Engels, Vol. 21, Beijing: People's Publishing House, 1957, p.452.

New system of international relations

International order and international relation system are complementary to each other. An international order is accompanied by a corresponding international system. Therefore, the struggle to establish a new international order after the end of the Cold War and collapse of the Yalta System synchronized with the fight for a new system of international relations.

Since the world came into the modern times, establishment of every new system of international relations has been brought about by a war, and every international order has been maintained through a balance of powers. The Thirty Years' War taking place in 1618-1648 was the first large-scale war during the transition from the feudal age to the capitalist one in Europe. The protracted war was concluded by the signing of the Treaty of Westphalia in 1648, which defined the diplomatic status of independent sovereign countries in international relations, set a precedent for settlement of international disputes and ending international wars by signing a treaty at an international conference, and laid a relatively balanced system of international relations in Europe. In 1815, the victory of the Sixth Coalition against France brought about the end of the Napoleonic Wars. The Final Act of the Congress of Vienna altered European political atlas. Several European powers restored to some extent the balance of power broken by the wars through intense bargaining in and outside the meeting, resulting in the Vienna System. In 1918, upon the conclusion of World War I, the imperialist powers were busy marking off spheres of influence at the Paris Conference regardless of the interests of small peoples and countries, and the Versailles-Washington System came into being. The prototype of the Yalta System had been fixed by US, Britain and the Soviet Union before the powder smoke of World War II disappeared. Since, the original balance was greatly abondoned with the end of the Cold War and collapse of the Yalta System, It was imperative to form a new system of international relations to maintain the world order. However, the Yalta System did not perish by a war, but by a form of "peaceful competition" under the shadow of huge weaponary. Thus, in the 1990s, during the early stage of collapse of the Yalta System, the West generally stressed the success of "peaceful evolution." While emphasizing the role of "economic interests" and other factors in international relations, the whole world hoped to establish a new international order and a new system of international relations by peaceful means.

However, the real changes of the world situation broke the alluring fantasy. The reality facing the world now was that United States was trying to build a US-led new international order and system of international relations through a series of wars and military alliance contracts by relying on its unique military and economic strength. Since the Yalta System became shaking and in collapse, the United States directly led and participated in the Gulf War (1990-1991), Bosnian War (1992-1995), Kosovo War (1999), Afghan War (2001), and Iraq War (2003). And during the period, it signed agreements including such military alliances as redefinition of the Treaty of Mutual Cooperation and Security between the United States and Japan and built the system of missile defense. The United States has demonstrated to the world its strategic intention to establish a US-led new international order and a new system of international relations which was fixed by military strength.

Therefore, when the world came to the end of the 20th century, despite such ideas and sayings as "common interest of the mankind," "common values," "globalization," "human rights overrides sovereignty" sound beautiful and tempting, the reality was still what decided the fundamental principles of a new international order and a new system of international relations were national interests, power politics, and strength. At the turn of centuries and during the transition period from an old system of international relations to a new one, while many kind-hearted people were campaigning for a new international order and a new system of international relations which was fairer and more rational, the United States had started to build a new international order and a new system of international relations through a series of wars—from the Gulf War to the Iraq War. The problem now, in front of the reality taking shape, was whether various forces and powers in the world would accept it or not and how to accept it if they did.

After the end of the Cold War and collapse of the Yalta System, discussions and debates centering on definition of the new international order and the new system of international relations never stopped. There were such sayings as "one superpower and several powers," "powers juxtapose," "one globe, several systems," "unipolar pattern" and "multipolar pattern", just to name a few. They reflected the ideal of people for a fairer and more rational world and the hope of countries for greater national interests. However, ideal or hope was not reality. In the discussions, the public opinion often attached too much importance to definitions and names of the coming new international order and new system of international relations, was keen to the debate what it was called, while ignoring what it was. In front of a series of wars the United States launched, people had to re-think the reality. In terms of the past systems of international relations, in fact, they were objective beings under certain historical conditions instead of the products of ideals and hopes. As to their names, there had been neither definite names nor universally accepted definitions. The Vienna System, the

Versailles-Washington System, and the Yalta System were all summaries and conclusions in history by later generations. It should also be left to history to decide what the system of international relations in the 21st century should be properly defined: "uni-polar world" "multi-polar world" "US-led multi-polar world" or anything else. In fact, the definition of future new international order or the system of international relations is less important than what it really is. The nature of the system of international relations was reflected in that under what principles, by what means and in what forms international forces, especially major powers, dealt with international affairs. The Yalta System, for instance, was based on the principle of hegemonism, using the means of threat of force, and adopted form of fight and compromise between two superpowers to deal with international affairs during the Cold War. Only when people captured the nature could they properly position themselves and make the right judgments and decisions under the new international situation.

6.1.3 The Status and Role of Major World Powers

Since the commence of the history of international relations, the status and role of major powers or alliances of nations had always been the key factors in a system of international relations. In the post-Cold War era, especiallly in the last decade of 20th century, the status and the role of major powers in the new system of international relations became more and more clear.

The dominant status of the United Sates in the world basically established.

After the collapse of the Yalta System, the United States became the only superpower. Its political, economic and military capabilities were unparallel in the world. Against the background, the US as a whole was enveloped in an atmosphere of joy, by the victory of the Cold War. Meanwhile, the US aspiration to become the "world leader" has inflated rapidly, which had evolved into some strategies and tactics embodied in their power politics and "unilateralism" in international affairs. The IMF and World Bank were under its control. You had to seek support and assent from the US before you could obtain aid from the institutions; if you wanted to join the WTO, you had to accept the terms that the US set; if you refused the claims and rules made by US, you might face sanctions and force threats. In the last decade of the 20th century, the US had established its dominant status and role in international affairs by waging a series of wars. Although there were some doubts about its role as "the world leader" in and outside China and some scholars had analyzed the constraints of the US, they could only make their analyses of the extent to which and how long the US could keep the status and play the role, and could not deny the fact that it had established its dominant status and role in international affairs. Of course, "dominant status and role," which could be understood as one can influence and master a situation, were still something different from "leading status and role." Above all, the US could not handle international affair in the way similar to a top administrative leader ruling a nation.

The status of Japan and Europe continued as "minor partners"

In the post-Cold War era, being worried that it would be harder to cope with the US control, both Japan and Europe have actively adjusted their policies in an attempt to seek a more favorable position and role for themselves in the new system of international relations. In particular, Europe tried to take the opportunity of the "returning" of Eastern Europe to accelerate the construction of European Union by promoting the establishment of the Eurozone and promoting the relations with the rest of the world, especially Asia and Middle East. Just for the reason, more attention in the world public opinion was paid to the frictions and contradictions between the US and Japan and between the US and Europe. For instance, some saw the following as the examples of their frictions and contradictions: "automobile war," "beef war," "banana war," disputes on several trade sanction acts, quarrels over attacking with bombs or sending ground troops in several military actions, over the sharing of the military expenditure and how many forces should be sent, etc. In the Chinese academy, there was even such judgment: the contradiction between the Western countries would be the principal contradiction in the world. However, it was not easy for Japan and Europe to enhance their international status and role rapidly by taking the opportunity of the transition to a new system of international relations. During the Gulf War in 1990-1991, Japan and Europe felt abashed and annoyed as they only provided some military expenditure without bringing their military strength into play. Therefore, although Europe had tried to solve the Bosnian crisis by its own, only with the intervention from the US could the war fire there be eventually extinguished. And the financial crisis in 1998 showed Japan's indifference and powerlessness. Therefore, Europe was not able to handle the crises in Europe on its own, and Japan also was not able to handle the crises in Asia on its own. Neither could handle significant international affairs without the participation of the US. In the Western alliance, the relation of subordination between Europe and the US and between Japan and the US had not been weakened. Instead, it had been reinforced by a series of wars led by the US.

Russia: still not negligible

As a consequence of the Soviet Union's disintegration, political upheavals and a series of wrong economic decisions, Russia has given a feeble image. From Yeltsin to Putin, Russia has not yet gained acceptance by the West, though it had become politically pluralistic and economically privatized. A big turn of its foreign policy to the West had taken place and the former communist party had to compete in elections. NATO and the EU not only excluded Russia, but also squeezed its sphere of influence through expansion of the EU to include Eastern Europe. To further weaken Russia, the US pursued a squeezing strategy. It seemed that the strategy would continue in the 21st century. Russia, beset with troubles both internally and externally, was still not let off by the US. That was enough to justify two points: first, it was enough to show that Russia still had enough weight, especially its military might and economic potential, and was still an actor not to be negligible in the new system of international relations, though it has been weakened. Second, that the US did not let off Russia which had changed its ideology and social system showed that the US would try to ruin any major power not entirely because of difference or rivalry in ideology and social system, but mainly for their strategic need to keep itself on the position of the sole superpower.

China's peaceful development strategy and its

China sought to continue to strike an optimum balance between "keeping low profile" and "concentrating on capacity building up".

In the period after the end of Cold War and the collapse of the Yalta System, China succeeded to withstand the pressure caused by the comprehensive setback in the world socialist movement and experienced the roughest time with the "political disturbances" in 1989 and succesfully faced the Asian financial crisis. China took the path of peaceful development in accordance with the policies outlined by Deng Xiaoping and made epoch-making accomplishments in socialist modernization. As a developing country in the critical time for deepening reform and a nation with considerable political, economic and developmental potential, China had neither the intention nor the capability to be in rivalry with the Western powers led by the US. What it needed was peaceful development and "keeping low profile." However, as a regional power, China shouldered the responsibilities she should do for both regional and global developments. It should also enjoy the corresponding status and role in the world. When it comes to the matters and affairs concerning her vital and long term interests, China was obliged to "make some difference." Such a status and role China played would be

difficult to be changed in a short time-frame, which implied that the US would continue its "hybrid of containment and engagement" policy towards
China in the coming new system of international relations and China would
continue to strike a balance between "keep low profile" and "concentrating
on building up".

6.1.4 Ideological Reasons behind the Western Alliance in the post-Cold War Era

By a careful analysis, we can see that different systems of international
relations in different periods of the world history had also ideological grounds for their formation and existence, although means of coercion such
as wars, were the main factor behind the new international patterns. The
Vienna System formed after the Napoleonic Wars was based on the ideological groundings of "orthodoxy" and "balance of power." "orthodoxy",
which was generally recognized—though with different interpretations—
on the "musical dance" at Vienna, met the interests of European powers
to share the loot and maintain the feudal autocracies, and it began a new
structure of balance of powers in Europe. In the Versailles-Washington
System established after World War I, the ideologies concerning systems
of international relations were in a perplexed state of confusion because
the October Revolution took place in Russia and Europe had been weakened by the war. Although the US offered "Wilsonianism" with "Fourteen
Points" as its core, it had not been able to get recognized in and outside
the US because the country had just stepped on the arena of international
politics. Henceforth, the Versailles Sub-System was dominated by "revanc-
hism" and "retaliation". Although the Washington Sub-system re-divided
spheres of influence in Asia, Versailles-Washington System as a whole was
constructed on a fragile basis. The Yalta System, which came into existence
after World War II, was based on the "Iron Curtain" divison as mentioned in
Churchill's speech at Fulton and the subsequent "Two Camps" (socialism
and capitalism) in light of the fact that Europe—which had further weakened after two World Wars—had to rely on the US. And numerous new
states had to rely nations on the Soviet Union. With the end of the Cold War
and collapse of the Yalta System, then, what would be the ideological basis
on which the new system of international relations would be established?

In the late 1980s and early 1990s, the drastic changes in the politics in
Eastern Europe resulted in disappearance of even the form of the socialist
camp, which had ceased to exist except in name for long. As an enterprise,
the world socialist movement laid in ebb. Before the rapid changes and
heavy pressure, the movement ran into a quandary in ideology. Except for a

very few countries which continued to go on the socialist road and had offered some theories in accordance with their own conditions, the movement as a whole had not been able to offer a novel ideology or theory suitable to the new historical circumstances and in accordance with the need to lead the whole enterprise out of the present predicaments. On the contrary, in the Western alliance led by the US, a large number of scholars and ideologists had advanced the ideologies of global capitalism to a brisk period of unprecedented expansion to justify the ideal and enterprise they pursued and practice were right. As far as the ideas and theories about the new system of international relations were concerned, they were related with many disciplines. In 1989, Francis Fukuyama published an essay entitled "The End of History?" in the Journal of National Interest (Summer issue).[7]

Fukuyama argued that the end of the Cold War symbolized triumph of the Western political and economic system and ideology, and that Western liberal democracy which achieved predominance prevailed over communism. Liberal democracy evolved as "the end point of human ideology" and "final form of government." He hailed the Western triumph of the Cold War as "the end of history." Once it came out, the thesis evoked heated discussions which evolved into both vehement criticism and arguments in favor from international academia. Soon, the thesis was recorded as the most eminent theory in the annual history at the end of the 20th century when great transformation took place.

Francis Fukuyama, a US sociologist and political scientist, once served as Professor of Public Policy at the School of Public Policy at George Mason University, and as a senior researcher in the RAND Corporation. He had also been vice director of the Policy Planning Staff of the Department of State. His publications included The Great Disruption: Human Nature and the Reconstitution of Social Order and Trust. In 1992, Fukuyama expanded the essay "The End of History?" into a book entitled The End of History and the Last Man, which becomes his representative work. The book was subsequently translated in to more than 20 languages, was a hit to international academia and political circles and successively ranked the top of the best-sellers.

Despite his emphasis on the originality of the thesis, the end of history thesis did not begin with him. In 1988, when two great superpowers were at the culmination of confrontation, former President Richard Nixon published the book 1999: Victory without War in which he predicted that the

---

7   Francis Fuknyama, "The End of History?" in the Journal of National Interest, p.12-29, Summer 1989; The End of History and the Last Man, New York: Free Press, 1992.

US would prevail in the Cold War without resorting to war and the Soviet Union would collapse in 1999.[8]

For Nixon, the most significant event of the 20th century would be the "rise and fall of the communism" and now, Marxism and Leninism had exhausted tricks and had little effect on the world. His envision of the future world was a monopolistic one, without the presence of communism and challenges to capitalism. The only way to achieve the great goal was through "subduing the enemy without fighting." He admonished that containment should be integrated with negotiation and competition. Then it is possible to defeat the rival. Less than a year later, Zbigniew K. Brzezinski, an US strategist and former National Security Advisor to President Jimmy Carter, published the book Grand Failure: The Birth and Death of Communism in the Twentieth Century [8] in which he argued that socialism in Eastern Europe was imposed and it was bound to be abandoned by Eastern Europe in a way similar to rejection of the organ by human bodies. Based on his analysis of the data and materials gained, he believed The Soviet Union would collapse at any time, and China would still be ruled by communist party in the 21st century, but no longer a state on the basis of public ownership. He coined the phrase "commercial communism" to make the point.

Nixon's and Brzezinski's forecasts were highly precise, though not as renowned as Fukuyama's "end of history" thesis in the academia. The reason, first of all, is Fukuyama witnessed the demise of communism, while Nixon's and Brzezinski's forecasts were nothing more than envision of the future, not solidly founded on reality. Secondly, Fukuyama elevated the thesis to human history and social development, while the formers' argument was seen in light of two distinct political and ideological systems.

Starting his research on Marx and Hegel, Fukuyama claimed that the universalization of world history and the end of history were mainly propelled by "modern natural science" and "the struggle for identification." The former could explain the advent of modernization and globalization, while the latter could explain the inevitability of liberalization (equalization) and democratization, which were the final destiny of human history. Authoritarian regimes, Fukuyama believed, were bond to collapse as they failed to meet the challenge of innovation required by modern natural science. "Desire for recognition of equality" would inevitably make it be displaced by "liberal democracy." "The legitimacy of liberal democracy as a

---

8   Richard Nixon, 1999: Victory Without War, New York: Simon and Schuster, 1988; Zbigniew K. Brzezinski, Grand Failure: The Birth and Death of Communism in the Twentieth Century, New York: Collier Books, 1990.

system of government had emerged throughout the world over the past few years, as it conquered rival ideologies like hereditary monarchy, Fascism, and most recently communism." More than that, however, he argued that liberal democracy may constitute the "end point of mankind's ideological evolution" and the "final form of human government."

The end of history thesis, therefore, carried two implications: one referred that the antithesis to liberal democracy ideology and political system having failed, being failing and ordaining to fail, all of which stood at brink of history. That was the end of history. The other referred to the proposition that Western liberal democracy signified the end point of mankind's ideological evolution and the universalization of Western liberal democracy as the final form of human government.

Regardless of whether "end of history thesis" conformed to the rule of history or not, it represented a certain idea in the study of history. Unfortunately, in the argumentation of thesis, Fukuyama reasoned and argued philosophically without qualifying the argument with experimental analyses. Therefore, some of the criticism centered on the inadequacy and mistakes of proofs and facts in Fukuyama's thesis. Undoubtedly, the "end of history" thesis was the product of naïve optimism of the West when it was joyfully celebrating the triumph of the Cold War and abreacting political sensitivity. History did not end in Fukuyama's way. It repeated itself in the rest of the world. Not all of the countries were willing to choose the social system of the West, which obliged the US to impose with force. Human society was more replete with rampant conflicts rather than promised equality and freedom.

The Clash of Civilizations?", an article by Samuel Huntington published in Foreign Affairs in 1993, triggered a heated debate immediately in the studies of international relations.[9]

Because Confucian civilization was mentioned in the article, it evoked much discussion and comments in Chinese academic circles, which is a rare phenomenon.

Huntington was an authoritative scholar in the studies of contemporary international politics in United States. In 1950s, he began to teach at Harvard. He was appointed as an assistant to Brzezinski, National Security Advisor to President Jimmy Carter. As a frequent guest of the US Department of State, Department of Defense and CIA, Huntington was famous for his conservative political stand and incisive academic views. When the article of "The Clash of Civilizations?" was published, he was director of John M.

---

9   Samuel P. Huntington, "The Clash of Civilizations?" in Foreign Affairs, Summer 1993.

Olin Institute for Strategic Studies at Harvard. His publications include: The Solider and the State; Political Power: USA-USSR; Political Order in Changing Societies; No Easy Choice: Political Participation in Developing Countries; The US Politics: the Promise of Disharmony; and The Third Wave: Democratization in the Late Twentieth Century.

Huntington's main ideas in "The Clash of Civilizations?":

The clash of civilizations will override all other conflicts and even dominate global politics.

Huntington has argued that, the end of the Cold War manifested that the world had entered in a new stage of development, and the theoretical models for observation and analyses of international politics in the Cold War no longer met the requirements of the new stage. It was one of his objectives to provide a new theoretical model for the stage. He divided history of international relation in modern times into four periods. The international conflicts before the French Revolution and Napoleonic Wars were the struggles for "orthodoxy" and territories among autocratic monarchs. It was the second period from then to the World War I. During the period, most of international conflicts were those over national interests, military struggles involving economic interests, sphere of influence, sovereignty or territories. It was the third period from the October Revolution in Russia to the dissolution of The Soviet Union. In this new period, the national interests far prevailed over ideological conflicts. And in Huntington's opinion, after the end of the Cold War, opinion, the world system it has entered into the fourth period, that is, the "post-Cold War Era." He claimed that it was inevitable that international conflicts would still exist in the new period in history. However, in the new context, the fundamental sources of conflicts were contradictions among different cultures and civilizations, rather than ideological oppositions and conflicts over economic interests. Huntington did not deny the role of national states in international affairs, and claimed that the global conflicts in the new stage would not simply happen between and be demarked by countries. Although the boundaries between different civilizations were not obvious, there were indeed different zones of different civilizations playing their roles in the world. The world should be divided according to differences of cultures or contexts of civilizations instead of differences of political and economic systems or levels of development as in the period of the Cold War. The distribution of political power in the new world would largely depend on the result of interactions between major civilizations in the world, because global political conflicts in the future would happen among nations and blocs of different civilizations. The clashes of civilizations would dominate global politics, and the boundaries between civilizations would be the lines of demarcation in the future conflicts. Huntington divided the world into a number of zones of civilizations, including Western, Confucian, Japanese, Islamic, Indian, Slavic-Orthodox, Latin American and African. In the long term, he believed, the axis in human history was still civilization. The West had always been seeing national state as the key actor in international politics, which, in fact, was just a section of world history.

The clashes between heterogeneous civilizations is inevitable.

Huntington offered six reasons for the inevitability of clashes:

First, the differences among civilizations were not only real, but also fundamental and difficult to be coordinated. Civilizations were differentiated from each other by religion, history and tradition. The differences were product of evolution for centuries and would not disappear easily. They were far more fundamental than those between political ideologies and different levels of economic development. Rich might become poor and vice versa. One person could possess two nationalities; however, it was far more difficult for him to become both Catholic and Islam believer. Over the centuries, differences among civilizations had generated the most prolonged and the most violent clashes.

Second, the world was becoming smaller and smaller, and interactions between different civilizations were increasing. The increasing interactions both intensified awareness and identities of civilizations and increase long-enduring disagreements and hostilities.

Third, economic modernization and social changes all over the world were separating people from longstanding localities. While weakening local identities, they also weakened the awareness of nation state as a source of identity, and religious move in to fill the vacuum.

Fourth, the dual role of the West boosted the growth of civilization consciousness in other parts of the world. On one hand, the West was at the peak of power, and on the other, the phenomena of "localization" and "returning to the fundamentals" spread in the regions of non-Western civilizations. The confrontation between the West at the peak of power and the non-Western nations with increasingly strong desire, being more and more determined, and with more and more resources, to shape the world in their own ways became more and more serious.

Fifth, unlike political and economic characteristics which could be diluted and removed easily, cultural characteristics and differences were less easily changed. Sixth, economic regionalism intensified conflicts among different civilizations. The role of regional blocs of economies became more and more important. Economic regionalization could succeed only based on homogeneous civilizations and successful economic regionalism would reinforce consciousness of civilization.

When conflict occurred among different civilizations, the common character of a civilization—"kin-country" syndrome—would replace political ideologies and the traditional spheres of power and become the critical basis for cooperation and alliance in the post-Cold War era. Then, it was natural that nations of homogeneous civilizations would support each other. Although it was possible for the conflicts between the nations to take place, however, neither their scale nor their intensity was comparable to the conflicts between different civilizations.

With the end of Cold War, a new situation of confrontation between the West and non-West has occurred.

Huntington reminded us of "the axis in the coming world politics," that was, clash between the West and the rest or non-Western countries. In other words, we should pay attention to the reactions of non-Western civilizations to the power and values of the West which had arrived at the peak in the world. He felt that there had been three reactions. The first was the extreme attitude—for example, that taken by a few self-isolated nations, such as Burma and North Korea—to refuse both Western penetration and participation into the sphere of influence controlled by the West at heavy cost. The second was the attitude of the nations which had tried to join in the West and accept its values and political institutions. The third alternative was to attempt to strike a balance with the West by developing economic and military capabilities and cooperating with other non-Western countries against the West, while keeping indigenous values and institutions, that was, to modernize, but not to Westernize.

In Huntington's opinion, due to differences and conflicts of civilizations between the West and the non-West, and the struggles for power and position in international system, most of non-Western nations did not wish to be integrated in the Western civilization or it was impossible for them to get integrated in it, they were trying to get knowledge, technologies, equipments and weapons from the West and confront the West through cooperation among them. Huntington specially demonstrated the challenges to the Western civilization from the Confucian and Islamic ones. He claimed: historically, Islam has bloody borders, and in the new era, those nations which belong to Confucian culture are developing their military power in large scale and have proliferated sophisticated weapons, even those of mass destruction; and in the meanwhile, they actively supported Islamic nations to confront with the Western civilization. Here, Huntington notably mentioned China. He believed that a connection between Islamic civilizations and Confucian ones had come into existence, which challenged the Western power, interests and values. Therefore, a new form of arms race emerged between Islamic-Confucian nations and the West. He claimed that "a central focus of conflict for the immediate future would be between the West and several Islamic-Confucian states."

What should be the West's response to the challenges arising from the non-West?

As to the challenges, Huntington said, the West should first integrate itself and pay special attention to the cooperation between Europe and North America, the two largest regions of the Western civilization. On the basis, Eastern Europe and Latin America whose civilization was close to the West should be incorporated into the latter. The cooperative relations with Russia and Japan should be maintained and promoted. The escalation of clash of civilization between different regions into war should be prevented. The military strength and expansion of Confucianist and Islamic states should be contained. Reduction of military capacities of the West should be delayed and its military superiority in East and Southwest Asia maintained. Differences and conflicts among Confucian and Islamic states could be exploited. Those non-Western nations inclined to the Western values and interests should be supported. The international institutions that served and legitimized the Western interests and values should be consolidated and non-Western nations should be encouraged to join these institutions.

Although Huntington reminded us that there would be no unified civilization in the future world and different civilizations should learn to co-exist with each other, but the arguments throughout his article are based on the West-centrism, and all non-Western civilizations seen as "heretic". He made suggestions for the maintenance of the Western (in essence, Americanism) dominance in the world, which inevitably evoked opposition and criticism.

Michael W. Doyle's Theory of Democratic Peace

In 1983, an article entitled "Kant, Liberal Legacies and Foreign Affairs" was published in Philosophy and Public Affairs which was written by Michael W. Doyle, a Princeton professor.[10]

---

10 Michael W. Doyle, "Kant, Liberal Legacies and Foreign Affairs," in Philosophy and Public Affairs, Vol.12, Nr.3, 1983 (Summer); Bruce Russett, Grasping the Democratic Peace, Princeton University Press, 1993; John M. Owen, "How Liberalism Produces Democratic Peace," in International Security, Fall 1994.

The key argument in the article was that "there has never been war bet-ween liberal democracies." The judgment was a summary of the history of relationship between democratic nations, and also an inference for the future international relations, which caused a stir in academia.By the early 1990s, with the end of the Cold War, a number of scholars, such as Bruce Russett from the Yale University and John M. Owen from the Stanford University , have developed this idea further and in more detail,10 which was called as the "democratic peace theory".

Democratic peace theorists have argued that they inherited the thoughts and theories of Immanuel Kant through his seminal book Perpetual Peace published in 1795. Kant thought that republicanism was the only one of several necessary conditions for guaranteeing individual moral autonomy, something which could be sublimated into a kind of harmonious social or-der. A unified law could be generated among liberal democratic republics to guarantee perpetual peace. Kant also predicted that democratic republics would enjoy perpetual peace on the basis of the principle of liberal democ-racy. By inheriting Kant's ideas, democratic peace theorists asserted that there would be no war between democracies. In their sight, of course, "de-mocracies" were only referred to the Western democratic nations, such as the United States and Western European countries. They did not admit the existence of liberal democracy in any other form.

Why would there not happen war between democracies? First of all, said democratic peace theorists, there had happened no war between democra-cies for two centuries in the world history, except for few individual cases. Second, the attributes of democracies decided that there would be no war between them. The attributes, in their opinion, were what Kant's moral au-tonomy means. On the issue of war, moral autonomy endowed democratic nations with dual constraints on themselves, i.e., constraints of institutional mechanism and constraints of cultural norms. The so-called constraints of institutional mechanism referred to the pluralistic political systems (multi-party system, tripartite political system and suffrage) in Western democra-cies, which forced government to seriously consider opinions of all poli-tical forces and the public opinion in decision-making and avoided going into war indiscreetly. The so-called constraints of cultural norms referred to a set of norms or codes for actions, such as mutual recognition, respect and compromise, which came from the connotation of liberal democracy and made conflicts more easily to be solved. Even there emerged conflict, it would not be escalated to a solution by force.

Since there would be no war between democracies, according to the democratic peace theorists' logic, two inferences would be natural: the more democratic nations in the world, the larger zone in peace, the more possible for our world to be peaceful; the world can be divided into two parts: "zone of democratic peace" consisting of Western democratic countries and "zone of non-democratic turbulence" of the rest world. In the latter, the extremist and non-democratic nations in transition were the most possible to trigger war, and they were source of threats to world peace. Therefore, it was reasonable for Western democracies to export their democracy, even by force. Because the two constraints in democracies had no effect on non-democratic nations when conflicts between democratic and non-democratic states took place, democratic states needed not to restrict themselves and it was necessary to adopt more serious codes of international actions for the non-democratic "heretic" states, which was a "lofty mission".

Democratic peace thesis also evokes heated debates currently. It became a hot topic for the discussions among political scientists whether the differentiation between democracy and non-democracy was rational or whether democracy was the principal reason for peace, not to mention whether or not historians might agree the judgment that no war taking place among democratic states for two centuries. The most important was that the final inference of democratic peace thesis exposed its nature of hegemonism, that was, democratic peace theorists would spread the Western values over the world without hesitating to use force.

The description above is only several representative theses. There are also other theories, such as "convergence theory," "competition between different styles of capitalism" and "the Third Way." The intention to give a short introduction to the theories here is to remind us of the fact: at the critical juncture of changing systems of international relations in the world history, Western ideologists had come to justify the universality and rationality of their political institutions and values in different perspectives. On the two battlefronts – military and ideology – and together with politicians and military strategists, they were spreading their values and identification with their political institutions based on the values in the world. Based on the theoretical and practical efforts, they were trying to build a new system of international relations which could fit to the new era and provide a theoretical foundation for maintenance of the Western alliance. However, neither Fukuyama's triumph of Western liberal democracy nor Huntington's theory of superiority of Western civilization, and "democratic peace theory" as well, could undermine and solve the contradictions and conflicts arising in the new historical context inside the alliance, though they both highlighted the similarities and affinities of the West.

6.2 The Reorientation of the Western Alliance

6.2.1 The Issue of who would lead Europe after the great changes in the European landscape

In the post-Cold War era, the dominance of the US and the Soviet Union had already come to an end. In fact, although the former dominant forces desired to continue the old status quo but were in a disadvantegous position to do so, on the other hand, other major powers or European countries were not prepared or strong enough to replace the status of the US and the Russia in Europe. After the great upheaval in the world situation and important changes in Europe, the issue of who would be the leader of Europe has attracted great concern.

The trend of New Atlanticism in the US

The US and European political ideologists had already sensed the political consequences of the European turmoil in 1980s, consequently they began to design new strategies for their position towards Europe after the events. The US aspired to maintain its sole leadership in Europe, while the major countries represented by the EC wanted to take the chance to share with or take the leadership role in Europe from the US when the Soviet Union fell down and Eastern Europe united. The so-called Atlanticism was a foreign policy of the US after World War II. It was based on the US-led Europe-the US alliance. Its purpose was to fight against the Soviet Union to secure the US and European allies. During the decades in the late 20th century, Atlanticism was the embodiment of the US policy towards Europe, as well as the major guideline in maintaining the Europe-US alliance. Therefore, during the several decades after the war, whenever there was conflict and argument in Europe-US relationship, there was the dividing line between the Atlanticist and the European faction in Europe.

In the early Post-War era, under the guidance of the Atlanticism, the US provided European allies Economic aid and security because of the specific historical condition, and European countries accepted the US leading role. The economy of the major European countries developed rapidly in the late 1950s and the early 1960s whose status became comparable to the economy of Europe and the US represented by the European Common Market. European economy no longer relied on the US aid and became a competitor for the US economy. From the respect of security, although Europe still needed the umbrella of the US nuclear weapon, but it did not worried about the threat of the Soviet Union like it did in the early Post-War because of the balanced power of the US and the Soviet Union in Europe. Anyway European countries would not bet their security all on the US. In addition, Europeans were discontented about the US posture of being a savior, so the alliance under the guidance of the Atlanticism was influenced by European independent tendency represented by France's Charles de Gaulle. Thus, the US president Kennedy took the opportunity of visiting Britain, the Republic of Germany and Italy in 1963 to illustrate the Atlantic partnership, and promised to stand with Europe no matter what. He accused the people who split the alliance as "they make friends suffer while enemies benefits" and tried to revive the Atlantic alliance. The economic friction between the US and Europe got intensified in the age of Nixon. In term of security issues, the reason of the difference attitude towards the Soviet Union connected to the influence of de Gaulle; Germany's Ostpolitik (East Policy) revealed the European characteristics. Besides, the differences between the US and Europe was beyond the issues related to Europe; there was other important international affairs. For instance, European countries directly accused the US favoring Israel's policy in the Middle East policy. This suggested that Europe, as an entity, began to fight for its status in all directions in front of the US. Facing with this situation, Kissinger handed out a memo on Europe- US relations to Nixon in March 1970. In the memo, Kissinger firstly emphasized that the US leadership within the alliance must not be changed, which was decided by the US strength and Europe's deficiency. Meanwhile, he pointed out that the US should not rush to apply its policy towards the Soviet Union and reduce its army in Europe in order to keep the "unity of the alliance", in case of forcing European allies turned to Moscow.[11]

On 15 March, 1973, Nixon announced the year of 1973 as the "year of Europe", expressing that he would do everything to improve its relationship with Europe. On 26 June, 1974, with the US advocacy, the NATO member Brussels' head meeting passed the Declaration of Trans-Atlantic Relations called as the New Atlantic Charter which focused on the friendly, equal and unified relationship between the US and Europe.

On 4 December, 1989, facing the turbulent European situation, President George W. Bush delivered a speech on the US future principles and policies in dealing with the relationship with the Atlantic alliance under the updated situation at the special NATO meeting of leaders in Brussels, which was named as the New Atlanticism. Not long after this speech, the US Secretary of State Becker made a speech entitled "A New Europe, A New Atlanticism: the New Structure in New Era" in West Berlin on 12 December, elaborating the New Atlanticism.[12]

---

11   White House Years – Kissinger's Memoirs, by Henry Kissinger, trans by Chen Yaohua, Vol. 1, World Affairs Press, 1980, pp.509-510.
12   European Documents No.1588, 15 Dec. 1989.

Becker has argued that Europe was experiencing an unprecedented peaceful revolution which proposed a new task to the US which was how to consolidate the achievements of this revolution with the allies. The US thought it was necessary to provide a new structure of allies to secure this revolution, so that the split state could truly end and the unity of Atlantic could be achieved during this process. Becker firstly emphasized the necessity of the US military existence in Europe despite the changing European situation. Then, he pointed out the role that NATO, the EC and the European Security Council played in the future Europe in terms of structural security. Given the consequence of European peaceful revolution, the US thought it should make some strategic adjustments and reconstruct the structure while performing the military function of NATO. The US wanted to enlarge the NATO's function, and made it a political organization within the new framework of European security and made it take the initiative in the development of political and economical relationships with oriental states. Thus, the US-led NATO could influence and control the future Europe from the perspectives of military, politics and economy, so that the US leading role in Europe would be secured. For the EC, the US could not possibly ignore its development and importance. Under the new circumstances, the US said it would unite with Europe on the fresh foundation. The US admitted that the EC was a "economic pillar" for the Atlantic alliance and was playing an increasingly crucial role in politics in new Europe. The US hoped that the EC would further open to the United States and established legally binding institutional relationship with the US. Obviously, the US not only wanted the EC to assume more responsibility in Europe, but also wanted the EC to play its role within the limited framework under the guidance of the US. As for the European Security Council, the US also wanted it to expand its function in order to become a useful tool for improving the change of the Soviet Union and the Eastern European countries towards the Western political and economic system, because it was composed of oriental countries.

European countries expressed their welcome to the US New Atlanticism with caution. They appreciated the US enthusiasm expressed in the European turmoil towards the Soviet Union and the Eastern European countries, so they would like to make further negotiation with the US for the future of Europe. However, they were still cautious because of America's attempt to dominant European affairs. On 23 November, 1990, the US issued the Declaration of the European Community-the US Relations after its meeting on the US-European relations with the EC.[13]

---

13 European Commission, Bulletin of the European Community 11,1990; Europe Documents No.1622, 23 Nov, 1990.

The declaration firstly affirmed the contribution of the US-European alliance to the world democracy and economic development, especially to Europe, stating that it would keep maintaining and developing NATO and the EC and strengthen their relationship. It also pointed out that under the updated situation the coastal allies of the Atlantic were facing the same task. They all needed to support the political and economic transformation of developing countries, especially of the Middle East countries, and to promote permanent development of the world economy; they should shoulder the responsibility of preventing armed conflicts, fight against the terrorism and drugs dealing, strengthen the environmental protection and stop the spreading of weapons of mass destruction. In order to better perform these obligations, the declaration set the mechanism for negotiations and communications between the US and Europe which included a common reporting system, the joint summits, and regular the foreign ministers' meetings.

This declaration was the accumulated outcome of the evolution of Europe-US relations since World War II .Within the transatlantic alliance, Europe had long been regarded as a partner depending on the US, led and protected by it. The annunciation of a formal declaration on comprehensive and cooperative partnership showed that the US had already placed Europe at an equal status when evaluating and handling international affairs, and the US had recognized the major partner status of the EC as a matter of fact. Even though everything in the declaration did not equal to the things in reality, it still stabilized the Europe-US relations, at least in the early period of the post-Cold War era, they built a foundation for the mutual support and cooperation of Western allies in dealing with some of the major international issues. Due to the complexity of the European and world situation until 1995, the US again proposed the strengthening of the transatlantic-Europe-US partnership.[14]

On December 3rd, the US and the European alliance held a summit in Madrid, and they signed the New Guidelines for Transatlantic Relations. Compared to the declaration in 1990, this new guideline did not have much new content and wording. Its significance was that it was necessary to demonstrate the stability of the transatlantic alliance to the world when the US-Europe differences got more and more deepened and publicized.

A new round of competing for Europe's dominance; Although the US and Europe gave people an impression of being a maintainer of transatlantic alliance relationship, this would not cover their differences in reallocating the interest in Europe after the upheaval.

---

14   European Commission, Bulletin of the European Union 12, 1995.

The special summit of European Security Council was held in Paris from 19 to 21 November 1990. Altogether 34 heads of member states of the European Security Council included the members of NATO and of the Warsaw Treaty Organization attended the summit. Paris Charter was signed at the meeting. The full name of the European Security Council was the Conference on Security and Co-operation in Europe.[15]

The Paris Charter announced that the Europe after the Cold War should be democratic, free, equal and safe, demanding the members becoming the market economy countries which respected human rights, democracy and legal system, and stressed that every state had the right to make its own decisions regarding security. The special summit of the European Security Council in Paris in 1990 was held with the promotion of European countries and the Soviet Union. The instability and uncertainty increased in Europe because of the upheaval in Eastern Europe and the reunification of Germany. European countries and the Soviet Union were not only worried about whether NATO and the Warsaw Treaty Organization, the institutions built in the Cold War era, could handle the new situation, but also wished that the European Security Council could be the international institution enabled the European countries to decide their own fate, so that they could weaken the US power in Europe. Because of the same reason, the US resisted this summit at the beginning. It worried that the European Security Council would impair the NATO's function. The US did not support the summit until it sensed that its New Atlanticism was not rejected in Europe, the Soviet military strength declined dramatically, and the status of NATO was not in danger. The European Security Council made few decisions because each country had its own agenda. Although the US and Europe had different attempt in this meeting, they reached an unprecedented agreement on imputing Western democracy and economic structure to Eastern Europe.

Not long after the Cold War has ended, the competition for the dominance in Europe has most obviously surfaced with issue of Bosnia and Herzegovina.

---

15   The first European Security Council was held on 30 July, 1975. On August 1, the attending states signed the Last Document in Helsinki. The European Security Council was renamed as the Conference on Security and Co-operation in Europe from the 1st January, 1995. The European Security Council as well as the European Security Organization had a meeting without any legal binding among the regions and states to maintain European political stability and to peacefully settle the conflicts. It was positioned as a regional institution of the UN. It was regulated that the European Security Council could perform peacekeeping operation both among the all member states and within the single member state. – Note by the Author.

The issue of Bosnia and Herzegovina emerged with the disintegration of Yugoslavia. The intense political changes in Eastern Europe triggered the national conflict concealed in Eastern European countries for many years. The Socialist Federal Republic of Yugoslavia which composed of six republics was a multi-national country. Because of historical and practical reasons of policy, the national issue of Yugoslavia had not been solved. In 1988, the opposition of Yugoslav republics of Slovenia and Croatia first proposed their requirement of being independent. In 1990, the opposition of the two republics won the election, announcing the introduction of the capitalist system. On June 25, 1991, the Republic of Slovenia and Croatia declared formal independence, which was intervened by the federal government's military force. Large-scale armed conflict was triggered. The United States and European Union countries were still cautious this time for they all feared that the situation throughout Europe would get out of hand and would have an impact on regional security and national transformation. The United Nations and the United States both required not rushing to recognize the two republics' independence. The European Community showed up to mediate. Thus, the two sides were temperately out of the military conflict, but the root of the problem still remained unsolved. The EC attached great importance to the issue of Yugoslavia, and actively mediated the crisis. From the beginning of the crisis, the European Union was trying to reflect their important position in dealing with the crisis, trying to grasp the single initiative of solving the Yugoslavia crisis.

Initially, the EC countries still wanted to maintain the unity of Yugoslavia for the maintenance of stability and security throughout Europe. However, Germany just after the reunification caused an opposite effect. After the reunification, Germany had become the strongest country with the largest population in the European Union. Germany, a country eager to show its strength, is pivotal in the EU. Germany had long been dissatisfied with the European Union's policy which supported the unity in Yugoslavia, complaining that the EU should defend the national self-determination of nations trapped in the socialist Yugoslavian Republic , and announced that if the EU did not change the policy, Germany would act alone. And Germany would be the first to support the independence of Slovenia and Croatia.[16]

---

16 Slovenia and Croatia had historical connections with Germany. Slovenia and Croatia belonged to the territory of Austro-Hungary before the end of World War, and their populations mostly believed in Catholicism. Catholic Church supported the Fascist forces to establish puppet occupation regimes during the World War II.–Note by the Author.

Germany's demands and actions have caused great shock in the EU, and caused high doubts among the political elite who already had doubts about the German reunification, they have become even more uneasy. However, Germany was adamant. After a heated debate, the EU recognized the independence of Slovenia and Croatia on January 15, 1992. This move has promoted the separation of other Yugoslav Republics of Macedonia and Bosnia and Herzegovina. Yugoslavia was thus disintegrated, and the Bosnian civil war broke out.

Bosnian civil war finally broke out caused by different claims and demands towards the independence of the three main ethnic groups in Bosnia and Herzegovina Republic of Yugoslavia. European Union countries' and the United States' view of the Bosnian civil war was quite the same; they all recognized the Bosnian independence on April 6th, 1992. Both sides hoped that Bosnia and Herzegovina could become an independent sovereign state to completely undermine Yugoslavia with which they did not want to seek refuge at all, and in order to further squeeze the main successor of the former Soviet Union, the Russian state. Therefore, European countries were basically supportive to the dissidents and fighters against the Federal Republic of Yugoslavia and Serbian state in the Bosnian civil war. Although they had almost identical opinions towards the civil war in Bosnia and Herzegovina, they had important disagreements and struggles about the question of who would be the one to lead the implementation of these ideas. During the beginning of the civil war in Bosnia and Herzegovina, France, Britain and other European Union countries were all ambitious, believing that this was a great opportunity to show the strength of the European Union and to realize "United Europe Dream" They opposed NATO coming forward to solve the problem of Bosnia and Herzegovina, and they would rather opted for the EC assisting the UN-led mediation efforts. At this point the United States took a position of watching on the sidelines, and even refused to send peacekeeping troops. The Bush administration believed that the national issue in the Balkans had a long history. It had intricate contradictions, but it did not yet pose a direct threat to the US interests in Europe. Consequently, the US intended to hand the task of intervention to its European allies. If successful, it would benefit the United States; if it turned out unsuccessful, the United States would gain a more irreplaceable role when being asked for help. Development of the situation exactly proved the expectations of the United States. The EU lacked a common foreign and security policy, particularly lacked a unified and strong military force, the practice had proved that the EU did not have the ability to operate and solve such a major European affair alone. In 1993, after a series of solution proposals which all failed to be implemented, France, Britain, Germany and other EU countries felt that they were unable to control and reverse the situation in Bosnia and Herzegovina. In order to prevent the worsening of the situation, they strongly urged the United States to intervene. The Clinton administration naturally took over the leadership of dealing with the conflict in Bosnia and Herzegovina from the hands of its European allies, and was authorized to use NATO military forces by the United Nations. On November 21, 1995, with the after the notorious NATO air strikes and the military attacks by the Bosnian Muslims and supported by the Croatian army, the Bosnian Serbs were forced to sign the "Dayton Agreement." The US's strength of military intervention and power politics was further confirmed in the issue of Bosnia and Herzegovina.

6.2.2 Nato and EU's Eastward Expansion

At the end of the Cold War, Henry Kissinger has pointed out: "The current task of the allies is to adjust the two basic organizations which carried forward the transatlantic relations, NATO and the European Union (with the old name of the European Economic Community), and to adapt them to the post-Cold War world", "NATO is still the main connection between the US and Europe." But he also made clear that, "the premise of the establishment of these two organizations is shaken by the collapse of the Soviet Union and the reunification of Germany."[17]

NATO's status and its nature

The North Atlantic Treaty Organization, as the name implies, it is a regional organization of the countries located along the North Atlantic. When being established, it aimed to establish a collective defense, to "maintain and develop their individual and collective capacity to resist armed attack through self-help and mutual aid methods." That was to say, when a Member State suffered any armed attack or was threatened, it would be regarded as an attack or a threat to all Member States. Thus, all Member States were obliged to "take the necessary action." Such as NATO showed to the world that it was a regional military bloc; its strategic goal was to perform "collective defense"; its scope of defense was within the areas of the North Atlantic allies, and the focus was "forward defense." Therefore, we could say that "Atlantic" military bloc feature of NATO was very obvious.

17　Diplomacy by Henry Kissinger, trans. by Gu Shuxin, Lin Tiangui, Hainan Publishing House, 1997, pp.760,761.

In the Cold War era, NATO had made several military strategic adjustments based on changes in the situation and the development of the balance of power. By the end of 1949, NATO had discussed the report on the "strategic concept of defending the North Atlantic region," and formally adopted the "forward defense strategy" in September the following year; in the 1950s, NATO adopted the Eisenhower's "massive retaliation strategy", claiming that it "would pay back a serious large-scale nuclear revenge for every violation of NATO's territorial integrity." By the 1960s, NATO had proposed a "strategy of flexible response", trying to cope with the allies' various forms of multiple-scale war by strengthening conventional forces, tactical nuclear forces and strategic nuclear forces; in the 1980s, NATO proposed the "deep-strike strategy," stressing that it should quickly and effectively take advantage of advanced weapons to attack the enemy's rear zones in depth after the Warsaw Pact Group launched the attack. All these adjustments were adjustments of "collective defense strategy" within the Atlantic allies". There was no fundamental change in NATO's "Atlantic" military bloc feature.

NATO after its establishment has experienced the Korean War, the Berlin crisis, the Cuban missile crisis, the U2 aircraft incident, the 1968 Czech event, the Afghanistan events, etc. Despite the escalating arms race, a confrontation in the form of large scale war between the two military blocs' was once evaluated as on the verge of eruption But due to the balanced power relations, the possible war that people worrisome about did not occur in Europe. Although the peace in Europe was merely a "peace under the bayonets," in terms of its endurance, NATO had basically achieved to prove its value as a collective defense organ of the trans-Atlantic alliance.

After great upheaval of the Eastern Europe, and the disintegration of the Soviet Union, the dissolution of the Warsaw Pact, NATO's value, purpose, attributes, status and role as the opposite party was naturally questioned and stirred controversial ideas which mainly included three aspects; .

Firstly, doubts on the existence of NATO as a tool of Western alliance.

The reason behind establishment of the NATO was the so-called Soviet Union and the Eastern European military threat to the West. Now, this major threat ceased to exist. NATO and European alliance had lost the reason to exist. The future EU-US relations were no longer the alliance built on the basis of political and military alliance with the same rival of the Soviet Union. Although the main form of their alliance – NATO would not immediately announced its dissolution, its state of being caught in the confusion and bickering was sufficient to show that the original NATO also ceased to exist. NATO was likely to have to keep running, but only performed the role of coordinating or cooperating between Europe and the US when dealing with certain issues instead of carrying out the allying action of the original sense.

Secondly, people questioned whether it was still necessary to maintain the alliance through the tool of NATO.

After the Soviet Union has disintegrated as a huge political and military superpower, there remained no country or group of countries which could compete with the United States or Western Europe from the aspects of politics and military, let alone compete with the US-European alliance. As for the possible regional conflicts and dangers that might arise, if one still wanted to solve the problem through NATO, not only it was unnecessary in terms of military aspect, but also ineffective to solve the problem. The difference between the US and Europe during the Gulf War and the Yugoslav civil war was the proof. From the mainstream of international relations which became prominent, the trend of "peace and development", the necessity of maintaining the NATO alliance, has become irrational.

Thirdly, people questioned the possibility and feasibility of maintaining the alliance through NATO.

Constrained by the terms of NATO, it was the central motive force for the US-European alliance for decades to deal with the Soviet threat and to suppress the contradictions between each other. Now, the centripetal force did not exist, but the centrifugal force increased. Various conflicts covered by the contradiction between the US and the Soviet Union in the past now emerged. Conflicts of interest deepened the conflicts between Europe and the US, which was bound to shake the foundation set by NATO to maintain the US-European alliance.

The questioning and controversial debates did not last long. After Western countries had experienced a period of joy and self-satisfaction about the Cold War victory, but soon they began to realize that, despite the Warsaw Treaty Organization had perished they could not afford to dissolve the NATO. The reasons were: first, though there was no military bloc being antithesis of NATO, this did not mean that the force on behalf of the group's interest completely "disappeared in the history". It might just become a potential rival instead of a public adversary. People still had to take preventive measures. Second, since people thought that they could use NATO to beat the opponent, they could also use NATO which was a practical and useful tool to implement and to realize the Western democratic system. Third, the alliance between the United States and Europe must continue to maintain because of their common strategic interests and needs of their respective strategic interests, and NATO was currently the only form to maintain this alliance. Fourth, the former Eastern European countries all requested to "return to Europe" out of their suspicion and fear towards Russia, and they asked to join NATO and the European Union. This enriched both the existences of NATO and the European Union.

However, the reason for the existence of NATO could not only depend on the Eastern European countries' request of "return" or on the basis of obvious Russian threat. There should be new contacts to be included into the strategic objectives of the NATO and only after then the existence and development of NATO would have proper reasons. Consequently, several adjustments and revisions were made regarding NATO's strategic concepts in the post-Cold War era.

On July 6, 1990, the NATO summit in London officially announced the end of the Cold War, proposing the strategic adjustment of NATO. It decided to transform NATO from a political organization with military forces into a military organization with political powers to highlight NATO's political attributes and functions, and and declared its aim to end the former confrontation with the Soviet Union, and declared its will to start political and military cooperation with East European countries including the Soviet Union. The meeting proposed to establish cooperative relations with the former Warsaw Pact countries for the first time. The NATO Summit in Rome was held on November 7-9 in 1991. The meeting adopted the "NATO's new strategic concept" document. Its core content was to expand the role of NATO, of which the most important two points were: First, the main function of NATO changed from the collective defense to the Warsaw Treaty Organization's armed attack into a "conflict prevention and crisis management"; Second, the "forward defense strategy" (one-way defense) that NATO had followed for years was transformed into a "comprehensive defense strategy." On June 4, 1992, it was the first time that NATO could perform tasks outside the defending zone of NATO. It decided to assist the CSCE to implement peacekeeping mission in Europe. On October 2, in the same year, NATO decided to formally establish a rapid response force according to its new strategy. The force was composed of troops from 12 member states of NATO. Its mission was to assist member countries in dealing with an urgent crisis. At the end of the year, NATO also decided to carry out peacekeeping mission outside the defending zone in the future according to the authority given by the UN Security Council. On April 12, 1993, NATO began to implement the "no-fly" operations in Bosnia and Herzegovina, and carried out large-scale air strikes in Bosnia in the subsequent two years. On July 8, 1997, the NATO summit in Madrid decided to re-design the new strategic concept of 1991. NATO had discussed and amended the draft of the new strategy preparing for the 21st century for many times since May 1998, and was ready to hand it in to the summit in Washington in remembering of NATO's 50th anniversary. In order to show the feasibility and the necessity of this new strategy, NATO's multinational army led by the US carried out a large-scale air strike in Yugoslavia without the permission of the UN on March 4, 1999. This was the first time that NATO attacked a sovereign state since its foundation. NATO held a summit in Washington from April 23 to 25 in the same year, adopting the concept of the new strategy facing the 21st century.

According to the communiqué issued at the Washington meeting, the main content of the new strategy of NATO in the 21st century was to build a stronger and broader transatlantic alliance, making NATO become "more large-scale, stronger in military and more flexible in action." Regardless of geographical location, NATO would open its door to all European democracies; it clarified NATO's mission in the new era—"deterring and defending against any invasion in the member states of NATO," being ready to actively participate in the prevention of regional conflicts and in the crisis management; it declared NATO had the obligations to protect the "common values" and the "common interest" of the member states, so NATO could take military action when the member states were not directly threatened, which enabled NATO to attack outside the scope of the alliance; because of the rejection of France and other states, the United States and Britain failed openly abandon the "authority endowed by the UN", but admitted that the United Nations was the essential part in maintaining peace and security issues. It also stressed the feasibility of "voluntary joint action" within the Union, allowing voluntary joint military action without the constraint of "consensus principle".

NATO's Secretary General Javier Solana said, "It marks that NATO has changed from an alliance focusing on collective defense into an alliance which will protect the European security and the democratic values inside and outside the Union." Obviously, NATO's new strategy had made NATO a "global" tool, instead of "Atlantic-oriented" and, "offensive" instead of being "defensive."

In order to gain a deeper understanding of this significant change in NATO's nature, we should also notice the other two basic characteristics that remained unchanged in NATO's new strategy:

Firstly, NATO remained to be an international military organization.

NATO was a product of the Cold War, which was one of the main military tools served for the confrontation in the Cold War. After the Cold War, in order to find a reason to continue to exist, NATO repeatedly required to play greater political functions, transforming from a military organization into a political organization. However, since NATO insisted that achieving political goals must have the backing of military strength, thinking that military force was an important means to achieve political goals, plus there was still an adversary and its accessing conditions different from other national political organizations, therefore, NATO only became a larger national military group.

Secondly, the US's leadership in NATO has not changed.

NATO was under the US control since its foundation. Over these years, NATO's strategy was essentially the US strategy. Despite the growth and decline of the power of Europe and the US, since the 1960s, there used to be the crisis of France's fighting for independence, a dispute about the military spending, a controversy about the Southern European commander's duties, a dispute about the characteristics of European independent defense, but the United States never allowed other countries sharing the leadership. With the implementation of NATO's new strategy, its members and functions would further expand, while the US leadership in NATO could not be replaced like always. Of course, it should be noted that, although NATO repositioned to adapt to the new situation and development, it could not be avoided that the new situation would inevitably bring new contradictions, the prospect for the North Atlantic Alliance was not optimistic.

NATO's eastward expansion

The Warsaw Pact had gradually phased out its activities since March 1991. Then NATO began to focus its efforts to fill the possible vacuum in Eastern Europe. It started to prepare the conditions to fill that vacuum.

Shortly after the upheaval in Eastern Europe, almost all former Eastern European countries belonged to the Soviet Union and Eastern Europe applied to join NATO and the European Union influenced by the slogan "return to Europe". This requirement was soon expanded to the original post-Soviet republics. In fact, "return to Europe", the slogan of the moment did not belong to a geographical concept, nor a complete concept of history or culture, because in term of geographical concept, it was not "return" at all. No one had ever said that the Eastern European countries did not belong to Europe, so "return" to where? From the historical and cultural perspectives, this saying was far from the logical perspective. Eastern and Western Europe were the two tributaries of European civilization, whose origin was the Greek civilization and Roman civilization. If we generally say that Eastern Europe should "return to Europe", then it meant the Western civilization was the true civilization of Europe, which even Eastern European countries themselves would not buy it.

Secondly, even though Eastern Europe "returned to Europe", it was difficult to believe that Eastern Orthodox Christians and Muslims could "return" to Christianity in Western Europe from the religious and cultural point of view.

Thirdly, Russia should also be one part of the European civilization, if the "return to Europe" made sense, Eastern Europe, Western Europe, or the United States should all agree to accept Russia's "return to Europe". However, they not only did not show any enthusiasm for that, instead, they regarded the "return" as an effective action to get rid of and isolate and suppress Russia. Therefore, the "return to Europe" slogan could only be a political concept, a political statement that the Eastern European people would chose the Western democracy and join the European defense system, and disgust from its past and hope for the future. After the primary stages of frenzied catharsis, NATO and the European Union began to solve the problem of Eastern European countries' participation in the EU gradually, and step by step, because any drastic action might irritate Russia and re-aggravate the tensions in Europe.

On July 6, 1990, the NATO summit in London raised the issue of establishing political and military cooperation with the Warsaw Pact countries for the first time, while deciding to make strategic adjustments in NATO. The NATO countries' foreign ministers' meeting was held in Copenhagen on June 6–7, 1991. The conference stated that they would strengthen the political and military relations with the Eastern European countries and "establish a constructive partnership." In November, the proposed establishment of the North Atlantic Cooperation Council was adopted at the NATO Summit in Rome. The meeting said that the representatives of the former Warsaw Pact countries could participate in a series of NATO officials' meeting by passing the "Rome Declaration on Peace and Cooperation". On December 20th, NATO and the former Warsaw Pact countries' foreign ministers attended the meeting for the establishment of the North Atlantic Cooperation Council in Brussels, and adopted the "Statements of Dialogue, Partnership and Cooperation." By June 1992, members of the North Atlantic Cooperation Council reached 37 countries-16 former NATO countries and the 21 former Warsaw Pact countries and the former Soviet republics. From January 10-11, 1994, the NATO summit in Brussels approved the US proposed plan of establishing "partnership for peace" with former Warsaw Pact countries. This was an important strategic step for NATO in expanding the organization. Its purpose was to appease Eastern European countries eager to participate in NATO, to prepare for their participation as the next step, while not immediately accepting them in order to avoid incurring a strong reaction of the Russia. This meant that, in this period of time, the United States did not favor the immediate participation of Eastern European countries to NATO. When Clinton explained why the United States originally opposed Poland, Hungary, the Czech Republic and Slovakia which handed in their application at the very beginning to join NATO, Clinton claimed that the transatlantic alliance could not stand "drawing a new boundary between the East and the West and the prophecy of future conflict. I want to inform the people in Europe and the US who advocated the United States' eastward expansion in Europe and a new dividing line that we should not block the possibility of achieving a best prospect of Europe, and that is democracy everywhere, market economy everywhere, all peoples of Europe should cooperate for common security. "[18]

The Organization for Security and Cooperation in Europe didn't sign "the European Stability Pact" in Paris until March 1995, and after Russia officially joined NATO's "Partnership for Peace" program on May 31 after several rounds of negotiations, NATO officially raised the strategy of eastward expansion.

The NATO Council adopted the "Report on Feasibility of NATO's eastward expansion" on September 20, 1995. In October 1996, the US President Bill Clinton proposed the plan of NATO's admitting new members in 1999 in his reelection. In May 1997, the Atlantic Partnership Council replacing the North Atlantic Cooperation Council and aiming at strengthening the security relationship between NATO and the non-NATO member states in Eurasia was formally set up. On July 8-9, 1997, the NATO summit in Madrid officially announced the list of the first batch of the countries involved in the eastward expansion of NATO, and decided to invite Poland, Hungary and Czechoslovakia to negotiations. This marked the implementation of NATO's eastward expansion plan that had been brewing for years. Poland, Hungary, and the Czech Republic officially joined the North Atlantic Treaty Organization on March 12, 1999. On November 21, 2002, NATO's Secretary General George Robertson announced at the NATO

---

18 Diplomacy by Henry Kissinger, trans. by Gu Shuxin, Lin Tiangui, , Hainan Publishing House, 1997, pp.760,761.

summit in Prague that NATO decided to invite 7 of the 10 candidate countries to participate in NATO and to start concrete negotiations. The seven countries included Latvia, Estonia, Lithuania, Slovakia, Bulgaria, Romania, and Slovenia. This was the broadest expansion since its foundation. The seven countries submitted the formal legal texts for participating in NATO on March 30, 2004, and became new members of NATO. So far, NATO had 26 member states.

The EU's eastward expansion

Although the European Union had different opinions on the whole international situation and the strategic actions to be taken with the United States in the post-Cold War era, it shared similarities in the full use of the opportunity to occupy the "intermediate regions" and additionally in the expansion of Western democracy, the EU was more ambitious for the Eastern Europe's "return" even EU was more enthusiastic than the United States. After the upheaval of Eastern Europe, the EU adjusted the political and economic relations with Eastern European countries in time in order to prepare for accepting new members. The EU greatly expanded the original system of partnership agreements which was signed with Turkey, Malta and Cyprus in the 1960s and 1970s. On April 28, 1990, the European Union Special Summit in Dublin decided to begin to establish the system of neighborhood (partnership) agreements with Eastern European countries. The European Community had done so with Poland, Hungary, the Czech Republic and Slovakia, Bulgaria, Romania, Latvia, Estonia, Lithuania and other countries since the end of 1991 to 1996. The neighborhood (partnership) agreements mainly involved free trade, economic and technical cooperation, financial aid, and political dialogue. It laid the foundation for the official launch of the EU's eastward expansion. The EC held a summit in Copenhagen in June 1993, making a commitment in public that it would accept the existence of Eastern European countries in the union, and announced the accession criteria called "Copenhagen criteria". It included the political criteria for democratic institutions, the legal system and human rights, the economic criteria for competitiveness in market economy, and legal standards that all legal systems of the EC should be followed. After the EU Treaty came into effect on November 1, 1993, the EU developed the Strategy of Central and Eastern European Countries to Join the EU. On December 9-10, 1994, the Essen summit of the European Union approved the strategy of pulling Central and Eastern Europe closer to EU after discussion, requiring the use of a variety of tools to help the associate country achieve the access to the EU as soon as possible. The EU carried out the fourth expansion in history on January 1, 1995 by accepting Austria, Finland and Sweden, so the EU had 15 member countries. In addition, Turkey (April 14, 1987),

Cyprus (July 4, 1990), Malta (July 16, 1990), Switzerland (May 2, 1992), Norway (November 25, 1992), Hungary (April 1, 1994), Poland (April 8, 1994), Romania (June 22, 1995), Slovakia (June 27, 1995), Latvia (October 27, 1995), Estonia (November 28, 1995), Lithuania (December 8, 1995), Bulgaria (December 14, 1995), Czech Republic (January 17, 1996), Slovenia (June 10, 1996) also made an application to join the EU. The majority of the applicant countries were Eastern European countries, except that Norway and Switzerland temporarily abandoned the application due to referendum.[19]

The EU enlargement is was also known as eastward expansion, like NATO's expansion.

The EU summit in Madrid on December 15 -16, 1995 proposed the schedule of negotiations on joining the EU with Central and Eastern European countries for the first time. The European Commission President Santer submitted an important document named "Agenda of 2000" to the European Parliament on July 16, 1997 to show the world the prospect of the EU's enlargement and its blueprint of the 21st century. In order to help the countries achieve the access to the union as soon as possible, the documents approved 21 billion Euros for this special purpose. On December 13, 1997, the EU summit in Luxembourg reached an agreement on the fifth enlargement, decided to launch "a comprehensive enlargement process," and agreed to have negotiations with Poland, Hungary, the Czech Republic, Estonia, Slovenia and Cyprus, and the negotiation began on March 31, 1998. In order to accelerate the process of eastward expansion, on December 11, 1999, the EU summit in Helsinki also approved the negotiations with Malta, Slovakia, Latvia, Lithuania, Bulgaria and Romania, and the negotiations began from February next year. The EU's principle was the country which had mature conditions could be admitted first. It held the negotiations with the applicant countries within dozens of departments involved in. After two years of arduous negotiations, the EU summit in Seville on June 22, 2002 confirmed that the negotiations with Poland, Hungary, the Czech Republic, Slovakia, Slovenia, Estonia, Latvia, Lithuania, Malta and Cyprus would be finished at the end of 2002. On December 13, 2002, the EU announced at the Copenhagen Summit that they had accomplished the negotiations with the 10 countries mentioned above, and the EU formally would invite the 10 countries to join the EU in May 1, 2004. On that day, the EU achieved the largest enlargement in history as an alliance organization of states with 25 members joining the union, with the highest degree of integration.

---

19   The 1st enlargement (Denmark, Ireland, and Britain) was in 1973; the 2nd enlargement (Greece) was in 1981; the 3rd enlargement (Portugal and Spain) was in 1986. – Author noted.

The new epoch after the eastward expansion

In the spring of 2004, Europe was pushed again to the forefront of the international political and economic stage. A large-scale integration in European history had become a reality, almost simultaneously with the eastward expansion of NATO and the EU. This integration included the Eastern European countries with advertisement of the idea of "return to Europe" in mind as the main character, and was carried out in a peaceful manner by the the two institutions with different properties. It was the largest expansion that the two unions had been through, which lighted the hope for the future of Europe and stirred the thoughts about common, collective international policy for the EU.

The eastward expansion of NATO recruited seven new members, namely Bulgaria, Romania, Slovakia, Slovenia, and the three Baltic states of Estonia, Latvia, and Lithuania. If the Baltic countries are evaluated as an eastward expansion, then we can say that NATO has accepted seven Eastern European countries, the figure would add up to ten, if Poland, Hungary and the Czech Republic which were recruited in the fourth expansion round of NATO in 1999. . The eastward expansion of the EU has recruited a total of 10 new member states. If we do not include Cyprus and Malta, there are eight Eastern European countries including Poland, Hungary, Czech Republic, Slovakia, Slovenia, Estonia, Latvia, and Lithuania. We can see the vigorous effect of the expansion, since so many Eastern European countries have almost simultaneously joined NATO and the EU. Of course, the expansion of NATO and the EU did not end with these "achievements" , and we cannot say that the "return to Europe" is completed, because some other Eastern European and some republics of the former Soviet Union are still working hard to join the union.

But anyway, the large-scale eastward expansions of the two organizations can be considered as the success in "return to Europe" after the great upheaval of Eastern Europe.

NATO and the European Union naturally regarded the successful eastward expansion as a great spiritual affirmation of their system, ideology and culture. Through the expansion, NATO's sphere of influence was extended to vast regions including the Baltic to the Black Sea regions, while the EU's sphere of influence was also extended to the Baltic Sea and the eastern Mediterranean. The simultaneous expansion of two alliances produced a resonant effect: the expansion objectively showed the world that NATO and the European Union could not be substituted in the current international situation and the Western liberal democratic principles supporting them have become quite attractive. It avoided the doubts about the necessity of NATO's existence which had emerged after the dissolution of the Warsaw Pact and provided an empirical evidence for the transformation of NATO from an Atlantic to global alliance, from a purely military organization to a political one. It also showed that the contradiction between expansion and deepening not only impeded the development of the EU, although it is difficult to tell what would be the future of Europe like, after all, it demonstrated the possibility of a "united Europe" in a proper form to the world. Meanwhile, the new member states achieved the political objective of "return to Europe", so that the countries' political systems got stabilized on their way to Western liberal democracy. They not only got double security guarantees from NATO and the EU and economic benefits from the EU, but also got the chance to show up on a variety of international arenas with the new identity as new allies. Of course, "return to Europe" achievement by the eastward expansion brought not only positive effects, but also new problems and troubles due to different circumstances of new members within the union, such as the distribution of interests, the problem of its costs and of the internal mechanism reforms, etc. However, its most negative effect was delivered to sphere of international relations.

First, it was Russia which showed its uneasiness. Russia had been on high alert towards NATO since the dissolution of the Warsaw Pact. It also had the temptation to join NATO, hoping to go with the "return to Europe" trend. Once it was hopeless, Russia began to list the reasons for which NATO should not exist, and resolutely opposed NATO's eastward expansion, especially against the participation of the former Soviet republics and CIS countries in NATO. NATO's eastward expansion made Russia have a direct military border with NATO. Besides the eastward expansion was not over yet, there were Ukraine and the Caucasus, the former Soviet republics in Central Asia which asked to join NATO, so Russia worried about being surrounded without a way out. Since seven former Soviet republics were involved in the EU enlargement which provided a common political and economic border between Russia and the EU, the tension and pressure surged in Russia. Eastern European countries gained a sense of security by the police of eastward expansion, but Russia was the loser from it. It was imperative for Russia to make military strategic adjustments and enhance its military defense capabilities.

Second, the goal of NATO's and the EU's enlargement can be evaluated as consistent if we look from the perspective of "return to Europe". NATO's and the EU's enlargement aspired to realize the values of Western liberal democracy and to promote democratization and civil society in the Eastern

European countries. The substantial overlap of the new members in the eastward expansion of NATO and the European Union also proved this point. NATO and the EU were the two pillars for the stable development of the post-war Western Europe. NATO provided military security, while the EU provided the economic foundation. The two together constituted the political stability of Western Europe. However, the US and Europe had extremely different opinions on how to understand the liberal democratic values, on how to implement liberal democracy and a number of specific issues since the end of the Cold War. Therefore, they had different policies towards Russia and in dealing with the status of NATO and the EU. When NATO completed the eastward expansion and Russia was restless, German Chancellor Gerhard Schroeder and French President Jacques Chirac went to Moscow in early April 2004. Someone said they were going to "comfort" Russia, some others said they went for counteracting the influence of NATO's eastward expansion the Europeans and for showing their confidence.[20]

In order to protect its own strategic ideas could be effectively implemented, the United States tried to compensate for the inadequacy of NATO's political property, while Europe endeavored to compensate for the EU's lack of military property. Thus, NATO and the EU developed a new function unknowingly, being used by the US and Europe to influence and press to each other. And the comments on the rivalry between the United States and Europe with the tool of NATO and the European Union were constantly seen in newspapers.[21]

6.2.3 The Strengthening of the Military Alliance between the US and Japan

The Post-Cold War era and the US-Japan alliance

The doubts and questioning about the NATO, triggered by the end of the Cold War and breakdown of the Yalta system also effected the US-Japan alliance.

The Treaty of Mutual Cooperation and Security between the United States and Japan which was in force since 1952 was an unequal treaty signed by Japan as a defeated nation by the United States. The treaty said that Japan by the United States. The treaty said Japan only had the obligations of providing military bases and logistical supply to the US, but no authority to

---

20   Laure Mandeville, "Les relations entre Paris et Moscou au beau fixe", Le Figaro, Lundi 5 Avril 2004.
21   David P. Calleo, "Transatlantic Folly: NATO vs the EU", in World Policy Journal, Fall, 2003.

interfere in military operations. In 1960, Japan and the United States made modification and supplementation on the Treaty of Mutual Cooperation and Security between the United States and Japan, clarifying that the US had the obligation to protect Japan and they should discuss before the US military took action. The US troops could not be invited to suppress the "rebellion" in Japan. It announced the first time that the obligation of the US military in Japan was not just to maintain Japan's security, but also for the security of the north of the Philippines, the security in the Far East, including China and South Korea. In 1978, Japan and the US specified the security treaty and developed the US-Japan Defense Cooperation Guidelines. This guideline not only made clear of the specific tasks and cooperation program of the Japanese and the US military forces in wartime, but also intentionally motivated Japan to accelerate the pace of military buildup. In the context of the Cold War and the specific historical and realistic conditions in Asia, the US-Japan Security Treaty contained the content and nature of the military alliance just from the outset. However, due to the special status of Japan as a defeated nation and all the constraints, the Japanese political and media circles did not want to use the term "military alliance" for a long time. It was until late 1970s and early 1980s was "the US-Japan alliance" officially used for the Japanese official conversations. The Japanese Prime Minister Suzuki visited the US on May 4-9, 1981. He and President Reagan issued a joint statement with the term of "the US-Japan alliance". As a result, when a reporter asked him the specific meaning of "the US-Japan alliance," the Prime Minister Suzuki denied the implication of military alliance, which was different from the interpretation of the Foreign Ministry and caused a public outcry. On May 16, the Foreign Minister Ito therefore resigned. The Japanese public gradually accepted "the US-Japan alliance" only after Yasuhiro Suzuki had succeeded in November 1982.[22]

It was not accidental that the "the US-Japan alliance" had been gradually accepted. Vietnam sent troops of 100,000 to invade Cambodia with the Soviet Union's support on December 25, 1978, occupied Phnom Penh on January 7th, the following year, and set up a puppet regime. In February 1979, Islamic revolution broke out in Iran. The religious leader Khomeini overthrew the Pahlavi dynasty and announced the establishment of the Islamic Republic of Iran. On November 4 the same year, Iran seized the hostage of the US embassy. Thus, the US-Iranian relations deteriorated drastically. Meanwhile, the Soviet frequently warned the United States not to interfere in Iran, and rejected the United States' proposal to impose sanctions on Iraq at the United Nations. The Soviet Union sent troops and

---

22   Ibid.

invaded Afghanistan on December 27th, 1979, to support the pro-Soviet Afghan government, which regarded the United States as the main enemy. The Iran-Iraq war broke out on September 20, 1980. The United States sent troops to Salvador and published the papers about the Soviet Union's intervention in the internal affairs of Salvador on January 22nd, 1981. On March 26th, President Reagan warned the Soviet Union not to interfere in Polish affairs. A series of international events made the United States and its allies feel the pressure of the Soviet Union's expansion of influence and power. Under these circumstances, the US-Japan alliance was increasingly accepted and recognized by the Japanese media. It also had undergone a qualitative change, changing from the defense of Japan and East Asia to the fight against the Soviet expansion and active cooperation with the US.

Nakasone after taking office, stated: "the US-Japan alliance of course includes military alliance." Nakasone visited the United States in January 1983, and committed to strengthen the US-Japan strategic cooperation. Specifically, Japan would built it an "unsinkable aircraft carrier" to resist Soviet's Backfire strategic bombers, and would blockade Soya, Tsugaru, and Tsushima Strait in order to stop the navy ships from the Soviet Union, increase military spending and maintain an annual growth rate of about 7%; and in turn the US should provide newly developed advanced military technologies to the Japanese side; Japanese SDF ships would defend the United States when a threat occurred. In December 1984, the two countries established a joint operational plan. Their strategic cooperation was strengthened unprecedentedly.[23]

This trend of cooperation continued in during Takeshita and Kaifu Cabinets. However, although Nakasone cabinet had endeavored to strengthen the US-Japan alliance, the US-Japan alliance was inevitably effected by the general situation.

The upheaval in Eastern Europe, the unification of Germany, the end of Cold War and the breakdown of the Yalta system has also shaken the US-Japan alliance which was developed and nurtured on the basis of fighting against the Soviet expansion. The specific objective of the alliance no longer existed, so its foundation collapsed naturally and the centripetal force decreased accordingly. On the contrary, the accumulated conflicts and differences aggravated day by day.

---

23 Concise Encyclopedia of Japan by Chinese Academy of Social Sciences, China Social Sciences Press, 1994, p 617.

It was the heyday of Japan's bubble economy after Cold War. During December 1986 to September 1991, 58 consecutive months of economic growth was known as the "Heisei boom." By 1990, Japan's GNP was equivalent to 60% of the US GNP, and per capita GNP was 10% higher than the United States. The entire Japanese society was intoxicated by the economic pomp, believing that the 21st century would be the century of Japan. Because of economic and trade imbalance between the United States and Japan, the contradiction between them stirred by economy got deeper and wider. The US-Japan economic contradiction was difficult to eliminate and their friction got deepened gradually, which would have direct impact on political exchanges, people's feeling, national psychology and cultural differences between the two countries. In the 1980s with the further expansion of the US-Japan trade deficit, the gap in the area of investment was also growing. Only in 1988, for example, Japanese direct investment in the US amounted to15 billion US dollars. On the contrary, the US direct investment in Japan was only $ 1.8 billion. The influx of Japanese capital to the United States and a large number of acquisitions of the US companies by Japanese monopolies were called as "Buy American hot", which caused the uneasiness in the administration of the United States. In 1989, Japan's Sony Corp. bought the Columbia Pictures Entertainment in the US; Japan's Mitsubishi estate company spent $ 800 million to buy Rockefeller Center building in New York, and finally sparked the outrage in the United States. The US sadly thought that the Japanese "bought the soul" of the US, and were "advancing to the heart." Many the US officials were worried that if this went on, the most US companies would belong to the Japanese. With the growth of Japan's economy and its political desire, the sentiment of Japan's ultra-nationalist forces represented by Ishihara had also risen. They not only dissatisfied with their unequal status in the US-Japan alliance, but also produced an ethnocentric feeling and contempt to the United States. Ishihara's Japan Can Say "No"—Strategies for the New Japan-US Relations was published in 1989.[24]

The US was seen as a country without history in this book. It said that the US history was very short, and the US hadn't experienced major turning points in history. The United States replaced Europe in the mid-20th century and became the world's superpower, but now it already began to go downhill. Ishihara believed that the dominant position of the United States, was already being replaced by the "negro Japan" He added: "this

24   Akio Morita, chairman of Sony Corporation; Ishihara has long served as a is the Diet member and as the governor of Tokyo. He published numerous political commentary collection among others, which included Japan Will Still Say "No" and Japan Will Determinedly Say "No" and so on. Western media wrote much about his racist ideas.

was is exactly the reason why the US officials are uneasy, their frustration regarding Japan's economic policies originates from the race prejudice". He held that the US "have a historical tradition of being self-conceit" which turned into arrogance later. He believed that history was at the big turning point, and Japanese responsibility given by the history called the Japanese to abandon the memory of being subservient to the US in post-war decades and had the courage to say "no". Japanese should act as the protagonist of a new world history. Ishihara's idea in the book was an embodiment of Japanese politics after the Cold War. It profoundly exposed Japan's distorted national ambition of rushing from a political power to an economic power after the Cold War. Its repercussions were great in both Japan and abroad.

During the Gulf War began in August 1990, the United States formally request the cooperation and joint action with the allies. On August 29, the Japanese government provided financial assistance 1 billion US dollar to the multinational force led by the US which increased to 2 billion US dollar on September 14th. Meanwhile, the Japanese government also provided 2 billions of development assistance to the damaged neighboring countries in the Gulf War. After the outbreak of war, the Japanese government provided 9 billion US dollar again to the multinational force on January 24th, 1991. In addition, the Japanese government gave unequivocal support to the multinational force in other various occasions. However, Japanese material assistance and moral support were not praised by the United States from the start to the end of the Gulf War. The United States' accusation of Japan continued to overweight. In the US public's opinion, Japan's financial aid was forced and intentionally delayed. The US expressed its dissatisfaction especially with Japan's not sending military support. It blamed Japan that it was not a true friend, but just a "paper ally" "lacking of international responsibility." Facing with US accusations, Japan felt it was undertreated for all its efforts. Japanese media said the troop-contributing was constrained by the Constitution. They spent huge amount of money but only be accused. Japan thought the US did not have reasons and compassion. All of a sudden, the two countries launched an oral attack towards each other. The public of the both countries became so emotional that President Bush cancelled his visit to Japan which was originally planned March 1991.

After Miyazawa formed his cabinet, Japan had even tough attitude towards the relations with the US, pointing out that the US companies were shortsighted, and stressed that the US economic downturn was because of its own reasons which had nothing to do with Japan. In January 1992, the Japanese House of Representatives Speaker, former foreign minister

Sakurauchi publicly pointed out that "the problem of the US economy rooted in the inferior quality of the US workers," "The US are not doing enough work. Their manager can not send them text instructions, because one-third of the workers are illiterate." On February 3, Prime Minister Miyazawa also "slipped out" in the reply of the Budget Committee, saying that the US workers were lack the work ethic of being diligent." The comment provoked strong national resentment in the United States.

For the United States, since the Cold War had ended, the original problem of military security had given way to economic security. Japan–United States relations were more uncertain in the early 1990s than at any time since World War II. Naturally, the economic friction with Japan came forward as the primary issue. "From the US point of view, with the end of the Cold War, the adverse factors in economy greatly exceeded the favorable political factors in its relations with Japan. The United States was now looking forward to re-arrange the pacific relations in order to meet its new demands."[25]

President Clinton proposed the policy of prioritizing economy in November, 1992 and highlighted the content related to economy in relations with Japan. At this point, two factions holding different opinions on its relations with Japan appeared in the United States, namely the so-called "Sakura faction" and "Beat faction." "Sakura faction" was mainly part of the US administration and bureaucratic machine, which only mildly blamed Japan for the conflicts, because they believed that Japan's political and economic system was strongly attached to US's global strategy. They also argued that Japan was closed, by virtue of numerous visible and invisible mechanisms, because Japan's political and business leaders liked it that way. And it would not open until the West forced it open—a task left chiefly to the Americans.

While the "Beat faction" was mainly strong in the US Congress, the business community and public, they thought the threat from Japan was far greater than the one from the Soviet Union, so they insisted applying tough policies towards Japan. In fact, no matter it was "Sakura faction" or "Beat faction", they both did not want to see Japan becoming stronger. Also some prominent commentators warned of a Japanese economic juggernaut, out of control of the Japanese government, which needed to be "contained" by the United States.

---

25 The Coming US-Japan War, co-authored by George Friedman & Merendith Lebard, translated by He Li, Xinhua Publishing House, 1992, p.416.

However, due to the long-term contradiction between the two countries which had hurt the nation's feelings and national mentality, the public opinion became one-sided. The slogan of "Japan threat", "beat the Japanese" and "contain Japan" continued to emerge in the US. According to the poll in March 1989, 68% of the US officials thought Japan would be the greatest threat to the United States, and 60 % of them confirmed that it was exactly right to drop the atomic bomb in Japan. The US had launched the "boycott" campaign since 1992, calling on the US officials to buy domestic products. Drastic emotion finally triggered drastic actions. The president of Chukyo University in Nagoya, Japan was shot by two whites in Boston on February 19, 1992. In just a few days later, a Japanese real estate broker in California was killed on February 24th.

About the tensions between the US and Japan in the first few years after the Cold War, there was a popular evaluation as "drifting alliance", which believed that the former US-Japan alliance which aimed to contain the Soviet Union was in a "drifting" state because of the loss of a common enemy.[26]

This was a major turning point in the history of the US-Japan alliance. Now, the US-Japan alliance was faced with two choices: One of them letting it to gradual fainting, while the other was to re-adjust itself in according to the new situation.

Redefinition of the "Treaty of Mutual Cooperation and Security" between the United States and Japan"

Facing the "drifting" state of the US-Japan alliance, political thinkers of both the US and Japan had become worrisome. They were not worried about the relations between the two countries, but the national interests, international status and common aspects regarding goals was imposing the maintenance of the relationship. Thus, the leaders of the two countries began to study the steps and measures to strengthen the alliance. They needed to figure out whether the US-Japan alliance should continue or to be improved and how should it improve since the changes in the international situation and the competitive environment after the Cold War.

Three of the US servicemen in Okinawa Island raped a Japanese girl in September 1995. The anti-US sentiment stirred by the event was unprecedented. The protest had two characteristics. One was that it directed at the problem of the US military bases in Japan, questioning the US-Japan military alliance. Okinawa county government and the people of Okinawa

---

26 The Drifting State of the US-Japan Alliance by Kuriyama Takakazu, Nikkei, 1997; Yoichi Funabashi, The Drifting Alliance, Iwanami Shoten Press, 1997.

initiated a campaign of requesting the withdrawal of the US troops from Okinawa. This marked that the US-Japan friction and conflict had turned its direction from economic areas to military security. Another feature was it changed from the form of civil protest in the past to the form of directly imposing pressure to the central government by the Okinawa local government. Okinawa Governor Masahide Ota publicly pledged to "achieve an Okinawa without the US bases," promising to build Okinawa an economic center and a tourist destination. In fact, such incidents had also occurred during the Cold War, but they never provoked such a huge wave of protest. The response to the Okinawa incident no doubt made those who worried about the US-Japan alliance more alarmed, so they accelerated the pace of repositioning the US-Japan alliance.

The US President Bill Clinton had a visit in Japan on April 16, 1996. He had talks on security issues with Prime Minister Ryutaro Hashimoto, and signed the US-Japan Joint Declaration on Security with the subtitle "Alliance for the 21st Century". This manifesto which redefined for the US-Japan military alliance marked the qualitative change in the system and nature of the US-Japan alliance, and also marked that the US-Japan relations gave priority to security instead of economy. The main contents of the declaration included:

Redefining the scope of the US-Japan security.

Back in February 1960, the Japanese government had defined the "Far East" in the security treaty, thinking its scope included the "north of the Philippines, South Korea and Taiwan." Today, the "Far East" was replaced by the Persian Gulf region or even any region in the world.

Redefining the precaution's object of the US-Japan security.

The declaration emphasized the close relationship between the US-Japan security and the Asia Pacific region and highlighted the "instability and un-certainty" in this region. The declaration paid special attention to the words saying "when the accidents occurred in the surrounding area of Japan have a significant impact on Japan's peace and security, the two countries will conduct consultation and cooperation". In public opinion, this was repla-cing the danger object of the Soviet Union by the "unstable and uncertain factors" in Asia-Pacific region and the surrounding area and the "peripheral events". It aimed directly at China.

Redefining the content and specifications of the US-Japan security cooperation.

The unilateral commitment by the US to defend Japan in the past has transformed into a bilateral military and defense cooperation. When the manifesto was published, the two countries signed the Agreements on the US-Japan Mutual Supply of Materials and Labor. The Agreement not only regulated providing arms and other military supplies by SDF to the US military but also the Japanese SDF could be in combat under the guise of providing "logistical support". This involved the term in the Constitution that Japan shall not exercise collective self-defense and participate in the war. On September 23rd, 1997, according to the spirit of the joint declaration, the United States and Japan issued the New Guidelines specialized the US-Japan Security Treaty in New York. Then, both houses of Japan passed the bill related to the new guidelines during April and May in 1999. Since then, the US-Japan military alliance got further strengthened. The Japan's efforts to break the post-War military constraints has also grown vigorously. (see Chapter II, Section 3).

It has been more than 60 years since the US-Japan alliance had come into force in 1952. Despite the "drifting" state during the early 1990s, it had "anchored its position" after being strengthened. Now we could not see the United States and Japan had the idea of changing their respective obligations in the security treaty, let alone the signs of abandoning the alliance. The reason for this was not so complicated. First, East Asia was the fundamental and strategic interests of the two countries. The US-Japan alliance had the function of protecting it. If the United States gave up the US-Japan alliance, it would not only lose Japan, a settled base in East Asia, but also likely to shake the whole alliance system in East Asia. As early as it concerned about the "drifting" of the alliance in February 1995, the US Department of Defense published the Report on East Asia and Pacific Security Strategy, which comprehensively expounded on the US Asia-Pacific policy, emphasized the importance of Asia-Pacific region for the US security and economy.[27]

It emphasized that it was of great significance to have an institutional security arrangement in Asia, to support the new system of international relations in the post-Cold War era, thinking that the US bilateral military alliance in this region should continue to maintain, especially the US-Japan alliance. "The US-Japan alliance is fundamental and is the cornerstone of

---

27   US Department of Defense 1995, United States Security Strategy for the East Asia and Pacific Region, http://www.defenselink. mil/pubs/easer95/.

the US security policy in the Asia-Pacific both for the United States' Pacific security policy and the US global strategic objectives." For Japan, the East Asian region was its base due to historical and cultural tradition. But in reality, Japan's economy, politics and security were all closely linked with East Asia. Japan could not pave the way to becoming a political power in East Asia on its own, so it must depend on the power of the United States. It could neither lose East Asia nor lose the United States. This was the reason why Japan's foreign policy was always swinging among "getting away from US to Asia" and "getting away from Asia to the United States" or "getting into the US and Asia". Therefore, in terms of geo-strategy the US-Japan alliance needed to be strengthened, so the US and Japan had no other choice. Secondly, the prevention and containment of potential threats became the main excuse of strengthening the US-Japan alliance. It was because they lost the main opponent namely, the Soviet Union that the US-Japan alliance began to "drift". To curb this "drift", they must create an alternative of the Soviet Union. Thus, they found that North Korea was a direct threat because of the nuclear issue; China with rapid economic development was the most uncertain factor; the Taiwan issue and the disputes about the sovereignty over the South China Sea were the most destabilizing factors. Therefore, in order to prevent and curb these potential threats, the US and Japan must continue to strengthen the US-Japan alliance and give it a new definition. In fact, these potential threats identified by the United States and Japan were all related to China. This meant that China had become the new opponent in the new definition of the US-Japan alliance. This was the reason of the prevalence of the "China threat theory" in the 1990s in the United States and Japan. Third, the highly consistent ideology and values also determined the need to strengthen the US-Japan alliance. Although Japan already had its own historical and cultural traditions, from the perspective of modern ideology and values, Japan was undoubtedly the country which shared the most similarities with the United States in East Asia.[28]

It should be noted that there was a long-standing view that the US-Japan alliance had played role of safeguarding the stability in East Asia and of preventing Japan becoming a new threat again to East Asia. Today, this is a question worth of studying and thinking. If we say the US-Japan alliance had a role in the containment of Japanese militarism in the early Post-War period and in balancing the expanding power of the Soviet Union during the Cold War, then we need to reassess the US-Japan alliance after the Cold War and the redefinition of the US-Japan alliance. There are two points should be noted. First, the redefinition of the US-Japan alliance meant that

---

28   Ibid.

the US-Japan alliance should be the only one who was responsible to the security and stability of the entire East Asian region. It not only regarded China as a new threat to prevent, which made people feel the threat of a new Cold War, but also made many East Asian countries the opponents of the US-Japan alliance, which implied its future interference in the internal affairs of other countries and created many new factors of insecurity in East Asia. Second, the redefinition offered Japan the more initiative. The original the US-Japan alliance mainly relied on the patronage of the US, but now it has become interdependent, and even sometimes the US demands more contribution from the Japan side, which not only provides a pretext for Japan's militarization, but also stimulated the Japanese ultra-nationalist right wing forces and promotes its ambition of becoming a great power which increases worries .and anxiety among East Asian countries.[29]

6.3 "9/11" Incident and International Cooperation against Terrorism

The terrorist attack of "9/11" was a deep imprint in the world history to some extent. It was a rare attack directly into the US, which had impact in both the US and the world. The event not only made the international system under transforming to re-regulate the principles of the relationship among great powers, but also put the Western alliance into a new round of test. It did not just stirred the accusation and anger of the people in the US and around the world towards the international terrorism, but also made people thinking about a lot of common issues that all human beings were faced with.

6.3.1 "9/11" Incident and the Afghanistan War

On September 11, 2001, at the US Eastern Time 8:46, a Boeing 767 air-liner which was the 11th flight of American Airlines took off from Boston was hijacked by terrorists, hit the north tower of the World Trade Center, New York, and caused the fire; at 9:03, another hijacked flight of the United Airlines Flight 174 crashed into the south tower of the World Trade Center; at 9:47, the third hijacked American Airlines' Flight 77 passenger plane crashed the US Defense Ministry of the Pentagon in Washington, causing a corner of the building collapsed; at 10:54, the fourth hijacked United Airlines' Flight 93 passenger plane crashed in Pittsburgh, Pennsylvania; within half an hour from 10:00 to 10:30, two hit skyscrapers of the World Trade Center both collapsed.

---

29 Eugene A. Matthews: "Japan's New Nationalism", in Foreign Affairs, November/December 2003.

The "9/11" terrorist attacks caused direct economic losses for the United States, which was estimated at between 10 billion to 15 billion US dollars initially. After a month, the direct property loss amounted to 40 billion US Dollars, according to the UN report excluding the loss of people. The loss amounted to 350 billion US Dollars would lower the world's economic growth by 1%. The number of people died in the "9/11" terrorist attacks reached 6700 according to the initial statistics. On October 8, 2002, according to the statistics from the New York office of medical examiners, the number of missing and the dead was 2797 in the "9/11" terrorist attacks, 59 were missing, only identities of the 1411 of the 2738 deaths could be confirmed.[30]

This unprecedented international terrorist attacks shocked the United States, and also shocked the whole world. The US President George W. Bush gave four public speeches within 24 hours after the incident. He believed that it was "an act of war" and vowed to crack the mastermind and their supporters behind the terrorist incidents, calling upon all countries to stand together with the United States and to punish the international terrorism. The US government began its investigation quickly, and locked the Islamic extremist terrorist leader Osama bin Laden hiding in Afghanistan as the prime suspect. On September 14 and 15, the US House and Senate both passed a resolution authorizing the president to use force against the terrorism. The United States issued an ultimatum on September 17 ordering the Taliban regime in Afghanistan to hand over Osama bin Laden within 72 hours. On September 20, President Bush made a speech in Congress, vowed to fight terrorism, and asked other countries to support the US anti-terrorist military operations. He delivered his memorable quote, "Either stand with us against terrorism or stand with terrorism against us." On October 7th, President Bush announced the launch of the military attack code named "lasting just action" to the Taliban regime in Afghanistan.

Osama bin Laden was born in the largest family which was one of the Muslim world's largest economic blocs in Saudi Arabia. Osama bin Laden graduated from the University of Aziz in 1979, majoring in engineering, and he had also majored in economic management. Influenced by the Iranian Revolution and the Soviet invasion of Afghanistan, he gave up the opportunity of taking over the family business, advocating himself to the "Islamic Jihad." Bin Laden had been in a fight with the Soviets in Afghanistan, and later became an extremist opposing the United States and Israel. He created the "Al-Qaeda" in 1988.[31]

---

30   Three years after the "9/11" affair in 2004, the number of death was reported 2749, 1570 of them had been identified. – Author's note.
31   Al-Qaeda has been a terrorist organization. The US government acclaimed that Al-Qaeda implemented the "9/11" terrorist attacks under the leadership of bin Laden. – Note by the Author.

Before and after the Gulf War, there was a fierce debate in Saudi Arabia on whether to support the US against Iraq and whether accepting the US troops were against the doctrine of Islam. Bin Laden insisted that working with the United States was a rebel against orthodoxy, was making friends with the devil. He was then deported due to his opposition to the royal family. The Taliban in Persian means Islam Students. Its official name is "Afghan Islamic Student Organization." The Taliban originated in Islamic fundamentalist movements in Afghanistan's Pashtun regions. After the Soviet invaded Afghanistan in 1978, the Afghan people became rebellious, and the Taliban was the backbone of their resistance. In order to defeat the Soviet Union, the United States established military training camps in the Afghanistan-Pakistan border, and recruited many unpopular Arabs and Muslims for the war against the Soviet Union.

Most of them became the backbone of the Taliban. The Taliban came to power with the support of the United States and Pakistan in 1994, and controlled 90% of the regions in Afghanistan. However, the Taliban regime in Afghanistan did not get on well with the United States. After the Soviet withdrawal, the United States abandoned the recruited fighters, which was known as the "Arab Afghans." The Taliban embraced Osama bin Laden as an anti-US leader in 1996, and bin Laden also married a daughter of the Taliban leader Mullah Omar.

On October 7th, 2001, the US war in Afghanistan took advantage of modern sophisticated weapons to attack the military strategic targets of the Taliban from the sea and in the air from the beginning. It took only three or four days to destroy 85% of the Taliban military targets. The US not only mastered the air, but also made the Taliban lost the communication of a unified command. The Taliban abandoned Kabul and retreated to their camp in Kandahar on November 13th. The US ground forces surrounded and attacked Kandahar with the cooperation of the armed Northern Alliance in Afghanistan at the end of the month. The Taliban surrendered on December 7th. The war lasted for 61 days. On December 22nd, each Afghan faction formed an interim government with the help of the United States. The military operation launched by the US in Afghanistan had been supported and understood by most of the world. Therefore, the military operation was the beginning of both the US anti-terrorist war and the international cooperation opposing terrorism. However, although the United States has defeated the Taliban and Al-Qaida at a minimum price, it could not achieve capturing of Osama bin Laden and his main aides and bring them to justice, so it had to launch a "protracted war on terror."

6.3.2 The International Response to "9/11" incident and the international cooperation against terrorism

Modern media tools and methods enabled all the people to feel the tragic scene almost at the same time when the "9/11" attacks broke out. After a short period of bewilderment, compassion and anger replaced the consternation and confusion of people. The people all around the world unanimously denounced the international terrorism when they were mourning for the innocent victims of the "9/11" attack.

Almost all countries' leaders and representatives of government expressed their sympathy and anger on behalf of their people in the shortest time through the US leaders and government to the US officials. After the "9/11", the leaders of Russia, China, Japan, Italy, Saudi Arabia, Egypt, Spain, Mexico and many other nations all delivered condolences to President Bush on the phone. The leaders of France, Indonesia, Britain, Jordan, Canada, Japan, Mexico and other countries met with President George W. Bush in the United States. Bush announced the partial lifting of the sanctions against India and Pakistan nuclear tests in 1998, and India and Pakistan both committed to assist in the fight against terrorists. Uzbekistan and Tajikistan agreed to open airspace and military bases for the United States' fighting against the Taliban. Even Russia also said it would allow the US aircraft performing humanitarian missions transiting. At last, 40 countries gave the US the permission of air transiting or landing rights, and 46 international organizations, including NATO, ASEAN, the EU, the OIC, the Organization of American States (OAS), issued a declaration to support United States' fight against terrorism. On September 28th, the United Nations passed a binding resolution, requiring all member states to track and arrest terrorists and their supporters and to cut off the financing source of terrorist activities. Six neighboring countries of Afghanistan, including China, committed to the fight against international terrorism at the UN General Assembly.

The US allies were even more eager to render support. After the "9/11" terrorist attacks, Japanese Prime Minister Junichiro Koizumi visited the United States. Japan adopted the Bill of Special Measures for Anti-terrorism, the Amendment of Self-Defense Forces Law and the Amendment of Coast Guard Law in accordance with the US war against terrorism. British prime minister Tony Blair visited the United States twice, and also had constant telephone contacts with President George W. Bush. The media commented that the two were ambitiously "contemplating on the war against terrorism and common global issues." Bush said, "In this world, the United States has no better friend than the UK." Britain was a staunch supporter of the

US global strategy and policies as ever been. It was the Anglo-American joint forces that fought against the Taliban in Afghanistan initiated by the US. After the "9/11" incident, the German government made a clear commitment that it would unreservedly support the United States in combating terrorism, and said it would send troops to the war against terrorism. The Federal German parliament approved the draft bill that proposed sending troops to Afghanistan by the Schroeder government. Schroeder announced that Germany would send 3900 troops and weapons to support the US military operations in Afghanistan on November 7.

Although only a few German soldiers were directly involved in the war, Afghanistan was the second war operation of the Germany after the NATO's air strikes targeting Yugoslavia in March 1999, and it was also the first time that German ground forces went into a fight after World War II. After the "9/11" event broke out, the most influential newspaper "Le Monde" in France, the nation which has always been considered as having frequent conflicts with the United States, published a comment entitled "Nous sommes tous Americains" "We are all Americans" on the front page in the name of its editor Jean-Marie Colombani, expressing a firm attitude of standing with the sufferings of American people.[32]

French President Jacques Chirac first went to the United States only after two days. He gave condolences to President Bush and the citizens in English on the ruins of the World Trade Center.

Also in the second day after the "9/11" attacks, NATO held an emergency meeting in Brussels, announcing the implementation of the fifth clause—"collective defense" in the North Atlantic Treaty. The provision stipulated that the attack on any NATO member state would be regarded as the attack on all member states, and the allies could take "collective defense" action including military actions. This provision was the most important commitment to member states given by NATO. NATO had never implemented it before since its establishment. It should be said that this was the most important international reflect on the "9/11" incident, and it was the most important support to the US.

The European Union had given great sympathy and support to the US after the "9/11" incident. Initially, the EU wanted to use the name of NATO to collectively participate in the United States' war against terrorism. The EU member in NATO insisted the implementation of the fifth clause—"collective defense". 15 countries of the EU convened a special emergency summit in Brussels on September 21st, adopting the "Anti-Terrorism Action

32   Jean-Marie Colombani, "Nous sommes tous Americains", Le Monde, 13, Septembre.

Plan", and advocated establishing a global coalition against terrorism within the UN framework. The EU had planned only to discuss the euro issue at the informal summit in Ghent. Later it expressed its support to the US military action in Afghanistan through a statement on October 19, and decided to implement the anti-terrorist plan as soon as possible, promising offering political and humanitarian aid after it had established a stable legal regime in Afghanistan.

If the change of regime was a sign, the US-launched war against terrorism in Afghanistan could be said to be over due to the collapse of the Taliban and the establishment of Afghan interim government. The small-scale war in Afghanistan did not last long. There still has been a wide variety of comments about it so far. Some say it was a "symbolic" war, because there was no opposing countries, no clear battlefield; some others say it was a war without winners nor losers, it could continue forever; some also say it was a "real war" and a "war of justice"; others say it was a very special war, because it was distinct from those conventional wars: There was no clear targets; it did not take some certain nation as an enemy; no one could win by conventional means. So, what kind of war was this in the end?

It should be said that this was a special war. Every argument above can prove its particularity. However, none of the comments has pointed out the most special feature of this war that: This was a war without obvious national opposition and was supported by almost all countries including all the major powers since the end of the Second World War.

The "9/11" terrorist attacks and the war on terror in Afghanistan made all countries which had problems with the United States in bilateral relations temporarily put their disputes and doubts aside. Russia seemed to forget the pressure of NATO's expansion and the hidden danger of the US military presence in Central Asia, and was willing to give convenient help for the US war on terror. China also left behind the pain caused by the bombing of the US embassy in Belgrade in 1999, and agreed to cooperate in the field of intelligence information. The US allies in Japan and Europe ceased to mention their different opinions with the United States on the US policy towards North Korea and on the establishment of a missile defense system, and they also stopped mentioning their quarrel in implementing the Kyoto Protocol and in the establishment of the International Criminal Tribunal. They would like to do everything possible, including sending troops to Afghanistan, to participate in the war on terror. For a time, the focus of international politics gathered in Afghanistan, and Osama bin Laden's fate became the headline news. It seemed that the whole world was gathering together under the banner of international anti-terrorism led by the US. Thus, some public opinion held that an international anti-terrorist coalition led by the US had already been formed. In fact, this saying was only a wish, or deliberately exaggerated and elevated the influence and status of the US in the specific international environment at that time. In fact, it was only a kind of international cooperation at best instead of a league of nations. One of the simplest features of coalition was that there should have been a statement of legal binding and an appropriate working mechanism among the units in the alliance. After the "9/11", although the United Nations adopted the proposals of international anti-terrorism, the international cooperation around the Afghan war against terrorism did not have this feature.

The war in Afghanistan was a war on terrorism without an apparent enemy and received support from all major powers. Though it cannot be regarded as a formal international alliance, it was still a large-scale international cooperation, rarely seen in world history. The reason behind such an alliance were the following: firstly, there were no rivaling—military and political—international alliances in the world. Although the NATO, the European Union, ASEAN and several other international unions still existed, but they did not have rivaling unions, consequently any state either within the above unions or outside them, could easily join this anti-terror alliance without feeling any pressure from its allies. Such a situation was rare during the Cold War era. Secondly, globalization had developed to a certain level; terrorism had become an international phenomenon, and one of the major threats to world peace and stability, so the anti-terrorism international cooperation was likely to become an important part of global cooperation. This was a rare large-scale international cooperation. Therefore, its practical significance was also important. It fully showed that despite the contradictions and conflicts and being on the verge of social collapse for many times, human society still had a common interest to be found since it was divided into different interest groups and states. Different countries and different interest groups were still likely to abandon their hatchet and past grievances at a certain moment in a certain event, and to stand together for the common interests of mankind. Of course, this was a possibility that had been confirmed. The problem was that whether such a possibility could generate more reality, and the key was how to understand the world and ourselves. This difference in understanding not only led to further difficulty in international cooperation of anti-terrorism among Afghanistan and other place in the world, but also led to a public quarrel within Western alliance due to the war in Iraq.

6.4 Iraq War and the Western Alliance

The EU External Relations Commissioner Chris Patten delivered his final address at the European Parliament on September 15, 2004. When talking about the relationship between Europe and America, he said he was worried that the transatlantic relations would deteriorate due to the US unilateralism, and believed that the war in Iraq split the Western alliance.[33]

Patten's words made sense to some extent. The world became more restless because of the US unilateralism. Not only new international cooperation was difficult to achieve, even decades of Western alliance got caught in an unprecedented crisis.

6.4.1 The US Unilateralism and the Bush doctrine

Before the "9/11" incident, there were a lot of criticism about the fresh President Bush administration's attempt to establish a uni-polar world in the circle of international politics. This criticism was not just from the countries which had been directly hurt by the United States and those which shared a common responsibility with the United States like Russia and China, but from the United States' Western allies. There was a common opinion in Europe held that the United States was increasingly keen to promote the unilaterally made policy in other parts of the world, and rarely took the interests and views of other countries into account. The US seemed often to confuse the global interest with the United States' national interests in international affairs. The US said that "the things benefits the United States are also good for the world." In the summer of 2001, the "Washington Quarterly" published the articles on analysis of the EU-US relations and the US unilateralism written by two European scholars. One was a professor of history at the German Friedrich-Alexander University, the chief correspondent of Die Welt, Michel Merle Styria. Another was the director of French Institute for International Strategic Pascal Boniface. The former directly asked in the article that "what kind of world does the US expect?" He believed that now "Europeans become more European, Americans become more American," "The US is not the US that Europe wants it to be, Europe is not the Europe that the US hopes it to be". As Washington was used to ignoring other people's desire, so the chance of other countries getting recognized by the United States was "as rare as looking for a monster in a bottle." As a historian, pointed out that the existence of the North Atlantic alliance proved that multilateralism was used to be the secret of the US success in the second half of the 20th century, and the "unilateralism is

---

33   http://europa.eu.int/comm../external relations/news/patten/sp04399.htm.

a natural expression of hegemony." Sturmer warned: "The US unilateralism and European localism must gain a common ground again."[34]

The French author's article was more forthright than the German's, and he wrote: "In the past people in Western Europe often worried that the US isolationism had been replaced by US unilateralism", the author also listed the "most remarkable unilateral policies by the US which offended the Europeans and the French people:

Failed to sign a treaty banning lethal landmines;

Refused to ratify the Comprehensive Nuclear-Test-Ban Treaty;

Repealed the relevant agreements of controlling global warming in the Kyoto Protocol;

(Together with the British) Bombed Iraq, continued sanctions against Iraq, and the main victim of the sanctions was not Saddam Hussein, but the ordinary people of Iraq;

Refused to recognize the problem related to the economy and the gap of development between the north and south;

Unwilling to help consolidate and legitimize multilateral organizations, especially the United Nations;

Supported Israel as a general policy, but due to public opinion in Europe, Israel seemed to be more like the aggressor, while the Palestine was more like a victim;

Pursued the "defense" or "protection" out of the national interest, rather than "preventive" measures of multilateral regulation.[35]

Later, he especially mentioned the controversial national missile defense program of the US.[36]

If people looked back at the newspapers and magazines at that time, in the opinion of international politics, it was easy to conclude that the US unilateralism had become the main target of criticizing of its allies.

After the "9/11" terrorist attacks there were some changes in public opinion. The "9/11" terrorist attacks as well as the following international cooperation of anti-terrorism caused a lot of speculation of people in academic

---

34 Michael Sturmer, "Balance from Beyond the Atlantic ", in Washington Quarterly, Summer 2001.

35 Pascal Boniface: "The Specter of Unilateralism", in: Washington Quarterly, Summer 2001.

36 In fact, the presentation of the US unilateralism also included its retreat from International Criminal Court against its promise. It forced a minority of countries which had asked it for help to sign the bilateral agreement endowing immunity to the US soldiers abroad, it rejected the Biological Weapons Convention, performed unequal trade competition by using the clause 301 and so on. – Author's note.

and political circles at home and abroad on the future of international relations. They believed that international relations had entered the transition period. As a result of the "9/11" incident, the US adjusted its foreign policy and international strategic priorities, which indicated that the US unilateralism and its hegemonic behavior would be constrained to a great extent, so that it would be conducive to the development of a multi-polar world.[37]

Later, however, the development of reality was completely the opposite. The United States did not constrain hegemony because of the "9/11" attack, but advocated the unilateralism under the slogan of fighting against terrorism. People wondered why the fact there had so such differences with their speculation. First, people's desire of pursuing democratization of international relations was too strong. They thought the United States would easily give up its unilateralism based on its culture, politics and economy through several communication and compromise. Second, because the entire international public opinion and social emotions were immersed in anger against terrorism and sympathy for the United States, people did not notice (or noticed but unwilling to say) even in the atmosphere of that time, the United States' unilateralism was manifested in a new form.

We need to start from the memorable words of President Bush—"Either stand with us against terrorism or stand with terrorism against us". President Bush's words were most agreed upon within the ten days after the "9/11" incident, but the international media did not have the time to figure out its hidden intention. When people calmed down, they soon felt the pressure of regarding the United States as the benchmark to determine a friend or a foe and to judge right and wrong from Bush's statement. Bush's words revealed the arrogance of the United States, revealed the true intention of the US unilateralism—"let those who comply with me thrive and those who resist me perish", and revealed the essence of the US foreign policy which was later known as the "Bush Doctrine". However, although dissatisfied, people could not change or shake the US established policy of unilateralism. Bush not only repeated the US ultimatum that "no country can remain neutral" in both the half-year anniversary and the one-year anniversary of the "9/11" incident, but also said Iraq, Iran and North Korea were the "axis of evil" in the State of the Union message delivering to the Congress in January 2002, expressing his determination of taking military action against the "axis of evil" with explicit words. The world was shocked by the term "axis of evil." The consternation of the US allies who knew nothing in advance turned into embarrassment, from embarrassment into wrath. Because they had not fully understood the "rogue states" in the age of Clinton, now, they were again

---

37   Immanuel Wallerstein & Brzezinski, The Great Change, Jiangxi People Press, 2002, p.9.

impacted by the term "axis of evil". It was like a blow especially for the South Korean government which was implementing the "sunshine policy" for the unification of North Korea. However, Bush continued in its own way. On March 6, 2002, the Japanese Asahi Shimbun newspaper published an interview with Harvard University professor Joseph Nye conducted by its reporter Miura Kasuga. Nye noted that the Bush administration had always been promoting the unilateralism, believing that the unilateralism would undermine the US national interests from a long-term point of view.

The United States announced the US National Security Strategy whose introduction was written by Bush on September 20, 2002. This report focused on the analysis of the security situation that the United States was faced with after the "9/11" incident and determined that terrorism was the main threat to the United States; the primary task of safeguarding the US security was fighting against terrorism and preventing the spread of weapons of mass destruction ; in order to protect the United States from planned terrorist attacks, the United States should remain strong armed forces to deter potential arms expansion of enemies and to stop their attempt to surpass or balance the status of the United States." The United States would, if necessary, implement "pre-emptive" attack, "recognize and destroy the threat before it enters the US border." The report emphasized that when the United States was implementing "pre-emptive" attack, "even though the United States will fight tirelessly for the support of the international community, it will not hesitate to act alone when it is necessary, and exert the power of self-defense through the pre-emptive strikes against terrorists in order to prevent our people and country from harm."[38]

The above Strategy document, has endorsed that the US's Cold War strategy targeting the Soviet Union (Russia) has ended and the "Bush Doctrine" began to appear in public, which attracted wide attention.

In April 1950, with the more and more dignified atmosphere during the Cold War, the US National Security Council issued a document of security strategy, known as document NSC-68.[39]

The document elaborated the current international situation, especially the balance of power and the prospects of the US and the Soviet Union, claiming that the confrontation between the Soviet Union and the US was inevitable. The Soviet Union and its group had posed the greatest threat on the United States and all the "free state", so the US determined the strategy of

---

38   The National Security Strategy of the United States of America 2002, www.whitehouse
.gov/nsc/nss.Gtml.
39   FRUS, Vol. 1, 1950, pp.235-292.

"deterrence" and "containment" that had been implemented in the decades during the Cold War. Although the US new government must submit the National Security Strategy to the Congress according to the Constitution, all reports were issued within the framework of the Cold War without changing the main objectives of prevention and major tasks in the document NSC-68. The US and other countries were all waiting for the United States to introduce a new strategy superseded the document NSC-68 after the end of the Cold War in the early 1990s. However, the new document did not appear in the 20th century, until the Bush administration released it a year after the "9/11" incident. Naturally, the public would consider the main points of the report a manifestation of the Bush Doctrine.

The essence of the Bush Doctrine was that: The US international position of being the most powerful country must not be violated. The United States had the right to take free pre-emptive attack against any action harmful to the US.

The Bush Doctrine adopted the pre-emptive policy which provided a dangerous example for the settlement of international disputes. Having such a policy as a criterion, the United States might implement pre-emptive military strike to any actual or potential competitors in the US mind by various means. No matter it was one-sided or not, this was unfair and unreasonable because the reason for pre-emptive strike was recognized by the United States only. If any big country or great power took this as an example, the whole world would completely lose its order, which was the same with returning to the jungle of human barbarism.

The Bush Doctrine refused to deal with international affairs with allies and friends or through international organizations on the basis of international law, refused to take advantage of these partnerships, organizations and legal provisions as an important means of protecting the interests of the United States, and refused to comply with the will of allies and international organizations. The Bush doctrine divided the world into the countries supported the United States and the ones did not support the United States. It established a temporary alliance of the same willingness to meet its purpose instead of using existed alliances, because it believed that friends, the allies, and international organizations might limit the United States to achieve the goals someday. It did not advocate conducting diplomacy and negotiations with rivals or enemies, but advocated the use of coercive means to promote the change of regime in the other, because it believed that it would be impossible for the terrorist who launched the attacks to obtain so much energy and efficiency if there was no support from "rogue states" or "axis of evil".

The Bush Doctrine ignored the UN Charter and the International Law, and clarified that military means was its preferred way of settling international disputes and conflicts, because the US needed to maintain full advantage of its military power. It did not allow any challenges to the US military dominance in the world. The United States would "do whatever it takes to thwart all possible military challenges in the future." The Bush Doctrine raised the role of military means in international relations to an unprecedented level, as it believed it was the military force of a country that decided the international political affairs rather than any other forces in this dangerous "jungle-like" world.

Bush Doctrine as defined in the US National Security Strategy of 2002 reflected US desire for its uni-polar hegemony in the post-Cold War era. It caused objections and doubts of all nations which had a sense of responsibility for the future of all mankind. In the relationship among the United States and its allies, the allies were sad to notice that their differences were increasing and became more and more profound, except for a very few countries (It should be noted that these very few countries did not stand with the United States on all issues). Using a metaphor in public, that was "the Atlantic becomes wider and wider."

6.4.2 The Quarrel Among Allies Related to the Iraq Issue

As early as during the Gulf War, Iraq, Iran and other countries had already been called as "rogue states" by the United States. After the Gulf War, the United States suspected that Iraq was manufacturing and had possessed weapons of mass destruction, thus, Iraq became the number one target of the United States. Driven by the United States, the United Nations adopted Resolution 687 in April 1991, demanding that Iraq must unconditionally destroy all chemical and biological weapons and other weapons of mass destruction under international supervision and promise there would be no innovation and development of nuclear weapons. To this end, the United Nations set up a special committee to oversee. Iraq thought that the special committee was a tool of the United States to make things difficult for Iraq and to perform espionage activities in Iraq. The US and Iraq started a round of confrontation lasting for a several years which was called "cat catching mouse" and "mouse playing cat" on the issue of weapon inspection. The United Nations Special Commission and the International Atomic Energy Agency completed the verification of a total of 188 terms in Iraq, confiscated Iraq's nuclear materials and destroyed a large number of chemical and biological weapons, proscribed missiles and their production facilities by the end of April in 1997. In January 1998, the United States' request of

verifying Iraq's presidential palace was refused. The United States developed a plan named "Desert Thunder," preparing to force Iraq to accept the
verification by force, which was given up after the mediation of the UN
Secretary-General Kofi Annan. Iraq decided to terminate the cooperation
with the United Nations Special Commission on October 31, and ordered
the UN inspectors to leave before deadline. The United States and Britain
angered by Iraq bypassed the UN and launched a military air strike codena-
med "Desert Fox" against Iraq from December 17 to 19. Since then, the verification in Iraq was interrupted. The United Nations passed a resolution to
set up a Commission of Monitor, Verification and Inspection in December
1999 to continue weapons inspections in Iraq. Due to the lack of cooperation in Iraq, the verification had not been restored in Iraq until November 8th,
2002, the United Nations adopted the Resolution 1441.

During the Gulf War, almost one hundred percent of the US allies gave
their support in different ways and participated in the US military attack in
Iraq. After the Gulf War, even France which used to maintaining a distance
from the United States also participated in the monitoring in the no-fly zone
of Iraq. However, the majority of the US European allies began to dislike
the US policy in Iraq soon. They believed that although Saddam's regime
was of no merit, it could not be an excuse for changing the regime of a
sovereign state by force. The US policy towards Iraq had become a part of
the US unilateralism strategy. The United States, together with Britain aim-
lessly bombed Iraq, implemented endless economic sanctions and rejected
the recommendations of other countries. Its actions of hegemony not only
could not solve the problem of Iraq, but made the Iraqi people suffer and
placed the Middle East in a new turmoil. Thus, when the war in Afghanistan
came to an end and the United States gradually moved its objectives of
opposing terrorism towards Iraq, the United States and Europe sparked a
quarrel over the Iraq issue.

On January 29, 2002, President George W. Bush's "axis of evil" theory,
triggered a strong reaction in his European allies. French Prime Minister
Jospin opposed to relate all problems to the fight against terrorism. He thought they could not only rely on military means to solve the problem of terrorism. British European Commissioner for External Relations Chris Patten
denounced Bush's assertion as "absolute and simplistic", saying that "it
is difficult to believe this is a deliberate proposal." The strongest reaction
occurred in Germany. Anyone would remember that just two months ago,
Germany was the most powerful supporter of the United States-launched
war in Afghanistan. German Chancellor Gerhard Schroeder had threatened
the German Bundestag with his resign, forcing it to adopt the resolution of

sending troops to Afghanistan. Now, facing Bush's "axis of evil" theory and implied invasion in Iraq, Schroeder said Germany would not participate in any "adventure" for "blind solidarity". He believed that people could not only connect the security and military power together, the expansion of armaments was one-sided, and the "guarantee of peace requires a comp-rehensive concept of security." German Foreign Minister Joschka Fischer was more eloquent. He criticized that Bush's "axis of evil" theory met with more failures than successes, and asked, "If we regard Iraq, Iran and North Korea as one, where will this thought take us?" He also noted that "the international coalition against terrorism is not used just to attack anyone, let alone to take unauthorized act." He also called for vigilance on the evo-lution of the US fight against terrorism into a global military action at the Cabinet meeting and warned that "Europeans must understand that this is not our policy."

In order to bridge the US-EU relations, President Bush began his tour in Germany, Russia, France, and Italy from May 2002. But the thing went against his wish. Voices of protest heated up wherever Bush went. It was estimated that the feeling of Bush in allied countries was not as comfortable as in Russia. On June 12, 2002, the German government passed the report on German cooperation with the United Nations. The report stressed that the United Nations was the only one international organization capable of safeguarding the security of the world; the measures of relevant parties in the fight against international terrorism were legitimized only after autho-rized by the United Nations. President George W. Bush said at the reporter conference on July 8 that: changing the regime of Iraq was a policy of the United States, the United States would achieve this goal by all means. French Foreign Minister Dominique de Villepin met with US Secretary of State Colin Powell on July 11, and hoped that the United States could con-sult with the allies and give full consideration to the legality of the action taken before military action against Iraq. For that fact that US President George W. Bush and British Prime Minister Tony Blair had declared that they had "sufficient evidence" to take military action against Iraq, and they were seeking international support and understanding, the governments or leaders of many countries had spoke out to oppose the US and Britain to act alone by taking military action against Iraq, and they called for using peace-ful diplomatic means to resolve the issue of Iraq. In early August and early September, German Chancellor Gerhard Schroeder stated his opposition to the military action against Iraq. He said the Bush administration's plan to attack Iraq was a serious mistake. It was possible to destroy the results of the war on terror to ignite the flames of war in the Middle East before the end of the war in Afghanistan. The European Commissioner for External Relations Chris Patten delivered a speech at the European Parliament on September 4, stressing again the importance of the UN Security Council and its resolutions in resolving the Iraq issue. Subsequently, France announced it would not participate in any military action without the permission of the UN Security Council. President Chirac criticized the United States attempt to launch "pre-emptive" military strikes against Iraq, thinking that such action would be "particularly dangerous." During this period, Italy, Spain and Portugal and other countries except for the United Kingdom had expressed support for US military action in Iraq in spite of strong domestic anti-war sentiment. Swabian Daily, a local newspaper in Germany, reported a news worsened the US-German relations On September 19, 2002: German Justice Minister, Herta Däubler-Gmelin, stated in a conversation with the cadres of the trade union the day before that the reason why Bush was rushing to launch a military strike against Iraq and to overthrow the regime of Saddam Hussein was that he wanted to divert the attention of the US officials on domestic issues and to relieve a variety of contradictions. She said: "This is a common practice. Hitler had also done so. The comparison between Bush and Hitler provoked protests in the United States.

People from government officials to public opinion all questioned the purpose of the Germans. Schroeder explained that there were some mistakes in the reports in his letter personally wrote to Bush, but also failed to obtain the understanding. Then the United States not only refused a meeting of the defense ministers of the two countries, but also did not send its congratulation to Schroeder by convention after he won the election in Germany. The US Senate and House authorized President Bush to use force against Iraq if necessary on October 11.

Even if Herta Däubler-Gmelin's comparison between Bush and Hitler was true, it was only his personal opinion, not necessarily realistic, nor praised by all the Europeans. However, it was no wonder that there were suspicions of all kinds in the mind of the Europeans, because they really could not understand why the US had to fight against Iraq; similarly, the European anti-war protesters' march confused the US, why the Europeans bothered to oppose the US war against Iraq?

In fact, the public reason of the US was simple, that Saddam Hussein's regime in Iraq had connections with the Al-Qaeda and possessed weapons of mass destruction. Now we see that these were only excuses for the United States to launch a war. Because the United States had repeatedly said that they neither find weapons of mass destruction in Iraq, nor conclusive evidence of keeping in touch with the Al-Qaeda. Since the public reason became groundless, then what was the real reason behind it? It was also very simple, that the United States would not tolerate the existence of a regime that opposed the United States. The US could ensure its security only by overthrowing the regime. And for many Europeans, the contrast between the tragic consequences of war and the peace after the war was crucial to the decision of whether to support launching war in Iraq. The Europeans still had fresh memories about wars. They knew that the war machine was difficult to control since it had been turned on, and no one would know the outcome. They did not believe that war can make the world safer. On the contrary, it will make the world more dangerous. Therefore, they were more inclined to take peaceful diplomatic means, and continued to delay the weapons inspection in order to find other solutions other than war.

It was totally reasonable that the Europeans were worried that violence would lead to greater violence. The wars in Bosnia and Kosovo were encouraged and participated by the Europeans. Although the wars had gone, the international peacekeeping force did not dare to leave; the war in Afghanistan supported by the Europeans could be considered to be over, but the fight did not stop, and the terrorist violence seemed to be endless; the Israeli-Palestinian conflict was more a typical painful example of using violence against violence. Would Iraq be a typical again? The Europeans did not think that Iraq constituted the major threat of the current world. If the US thought this way, then the US should ask why that was. After the "9/11", "Why do they hate us" became the number one question in the US which they could not or did not want to answer by themselves. In fact, this was a question to which everyone knew the answer except a part of the US. The editor of American magazine Newsweek Fareed Zakaria had analyzed that, "When someone asked why do you dislike the United States, people of many countries said it was because of Bush and his policies," "since Bush administration promoted the US power in a vulgar way and disregarded the international institutions and alliances, it has ruined decades of diplomatic efforts of the United States. So there is no wonder that people around the world are bearing resentment towards this kind of (uni-polar) imbalance and seeking ways to create obstacles for the US."[40]

It seemed unfair that Zakaria blamed Bush for all. Bush was just doing more obviously than his predecessors. This was what people said, "Rome was not built in a day." Someone had done the calculation that, after the end of World War II, the United States implemented about 110 times of unilateral economic sanctions in 26 countries whose population accounted

40 Fareed Zakaria, "Hating America", in Foreign Policy, September/October 2004.

for half of the world. The United States sent troops abroad about 13 times as the world's policeman. There were seven times were considered as illegal invasion. For example, the Korean war in 1950, the invasion of Vietnam in 1961, the invasion of Grenada in 1983, the invasion of Panama in 1989, the invasion of Haiti in 1993, the armed intervention in Yugoslavia in 1999, and the war in Iraq. The US always carried out economic sanctions and military intervention in other countries with its strength. Its behavior could be said as a violation of international law that undermined the accepted norms of international relations and international order; or could be said bringing the victims incalculable damage and unbearable suffering. What did the US get in the end? Of course, it stimulated the ambition of a small number of the US politicians to establish a "new empire of the United States," gained a large amount of wealth for a part of the US rich men, and also satisfied the US officials who believed in "the US first" and wanted a wealthy life.

However, the United States also gained something it did not expected before, that was distrust and suspicion of many countries and people, the protest and condemns of victims, and "asymmetric" terrorist violence stirred by a part of extremists who had nowhere to go. Only before the car explosion in the US embassy in Lebanon in September 1984 and the "9/11" incident in 2001, there were as many as over ten times of serious terrorist attacks in the United States and in its overseas institutions. For example, in the Lockerbie bombing on December 21, 1988, Pan Am Flight 747 exploded, killing 270 people; the explode at the parking lot of New York World Trade Center on February 26, 1993 injured more than 1,000 people and killed 6 people; a bomb exploded in the federal building of Oklahoma City on April 19, 1995, 168 people died; on June 25, 1996, a car bomb exploded in eastern Saudi Arabia, causing 19 US soldiers died; on August 7, 1998, the explosions happened in front of the US embassies in Kenya and Tanzania killed 224 people; October 12, 2000, the USS Cole was also attacked by the boat bombing while refueling in Yemen Aden harbor, 17 US soldiers were killed, etc. The United States became the main target of terrorist attacks, becoming a little confused, while Europe could see it clearly as a "bystander".

European countries do not want too many enemies. It did not want that the United States to expand the war on terror, let alone agreeing with implementing military strikes without authorization to a sovereign country in the absence of sufficient evidence. Its difference on the issue of Iraq with the United States was inevitable. Moreover, since the United States had operated in Europe for years, and established its position and influence, while many countries were dominated by the orientation of interests after the big change in Europe, therefore, the split also eroded the EU.

6.4.3 The "Split" in the Western Alliance

Using quotation marks in "Split" is because the Western alliance's "split" is not the same kind of organizational split that we usually think. In commonsense, "the split" means that the organization no longer existed, the alliance members went their separate ways, unrelated, or participated in or form a new coalition. However, the term "split" here referred to the increasingly deepened contradictions and conflicts within the existing alliance. Although, it had not yet led to the disintegration of the alliance, it led to a complex situation in the international stage during the transition period after the Cold War, because of its uncertain situation swinging between unity and split.

Iraq War led by US and Britain

After entering the 2003, the US war against Iraq was already imminent. Bush reiterated that if Saddam Hussein refused to disarm, the United States would enter into Iraq and disarm it for "peace and security". Although the president of the UNSCOM Blix and the IAEA's Director General Baradei led the UN weapons inspection team implementing the verification task in Iraq, and proposed a report of verification. But the United States clearly expressed its distrust towards this report. The US Secretary of State Colin Powell briefed to the UN Security Council providing some evidence that Iraq produced and hid weapons of mass destruction on February 5th, but the Council and other countries opposed to the use of UN approved force against Iraq as proposed by the Western powers. In the meantime, Iraqi government also felt the critical risky situation of US attack. In order to express its cooperative attitude towards the UN inspection, Iraq announced the formation of a larger-scale commission that would search for prohibited weapons, the weapons development program and related documents to help inspectors to settle the problems remaining since the weapons inspection of the 1998. Iraq also agreed to the use of the American U-2 spying aircrafts in the verification and declared it would destroy its "Al Samoud-2" missiles exceeding the allowed legal range under international supervision. In the eyes of the US, all these concessive acts by Iraq were just tricky attempts to stop her. The United States, Britain and Spain might veto the proposal by France and Russia to continue the verification and avoid the use force. [41]

41 On March 10, the Foreign Minister of Russia announced that Russia would veto the new resolution authorizing use of force in Iraq. In the evening of the same day, President Chirac accepted the joint interview of TF1 and TF2, saying that France would veto the new resolution authorizing implementing force in Iraq, and France would not participated in the war against Iraq without authorization. See Interview televise de Jaques Chirac sur l'Irac par Patrick Poivre d'arvor (TF1) et David Pujadas (TF2), Palais de l'Elysee–Lundi 10 mars 2003.

But given that the UN Secretary General Kofi Annan had warned that "the military action against Iraq without the Security Council's authorization lacks legal basis and would violate the UN Charter," there was a slight possibility that they could gain more than 9 votes in the Security Council. On March 17, the United States, Britain, Spain abandoned the request of the Council voting on the new draft resolution proposed by the three countries, and announced an ultimatum ordering Saddam and his sons to exile within 48 hours, or a war would be approaching. On March 20, at 5:35 of Iraq time (GMT 10:35), the United States and its allies air raided Baghdad. In half an hour after the raid began, President George W. Bush made a televised speech at the White House at 10:15 in the evening of 19th (GMT 11:15 on 20th), announced the beginning of the war to overthrow the Saddam Hussein regime of Iraq launched by the US and its allies.

The US war against Iraq was much simpler than people's anticipation. From the US military launched a ground offensive through Kuwait to Iraq on March 21, the US troops gradually encircled Baghdad on April 5, and captured Baghdad on April 10, to President Bush delivered a speech on the "Lincoln" aircraft carrier at 9:00 (GMT 9:00 on May 2) on the night of May 1 to announce the end of the major military operations in Iraq (without announcing the victory of the war and the end of the war), it only lasted for no more than 40 days.[42]

The US and its allies were neither resisted by large amount of Iraqi soldiers as they had estimated, nor had the danger and harm caused by weapons of mass destruction.

When it came to injuries, one of the biggest victims of this war was Iraqi people. According to the incomplete statistics, about 14,000 Iraqis were killed in the war. Besides, the violence in the post-war continued as expected, as well as the bloodshed. Another victim was the Western alliance. As a result of the different attitudes towards the war, the Union was torn apart. The war "split the Western alliance" as Patten said.

"Divisions" in the NATO

The world still remembered the same attitude of the NATO countries towards armed intervention in Yugoslavia, and also would not forget the NATO countries' support and cooperation with the United States during the war on terror in Afghanistan. In fact, this cooperation was still in progress. However, faced with the war in Iraq, NATO met the biggest crisis since the

---

42   During the war, Iraqi army was beaten and dissolved, and Saddam was nowhere to find. On December 13, 2003, the US army caught him in his home country in Tikrit. – Author's note.

resistance of Charles de Gaulle-led France against NATO's military integration in the 1960s.

The United Nations passed the resolution No. 1441 on the issue of weapon inspection in Iraq on January 8, 2002; on November 21, NATO issued a statement at the summit where it decided to invite seven new member states, that it would give full support the implementation of resolution 1441 of the UN Security Council. But when discussing whether to take "effective measures" to force Iraq to comply with United Nations' resolution, NATO failed to put forward plans for military action due to French opposition. Besides, German Chancellor Gerhard Schroeder expressed his determination of not involving in wars at the meeting. On January 15, 2003, the United States formally asked NATO to provide logistical support and to protect Turkey from Iraqi violations in the Iraq war. The support included the deployment of troops from the Balkans and other European countries to aid for the war and the arrangement of the Patriot missile defense system, warning aircraft and equipment against biological and chemical weapons attacks in Turkey. But there was no decisions made on this issue at the NATO Convention on January 22, 2003 because of the opposition of France, Germany, Belgium and other countries. After the discussions and negotiations in several meetings, the NATO Council did not reach an agreement. NATO Secretary General Robertson decided to start the "Default Programs", which meant if there was no objection until 10:00 on February 10, it would be regarded as default consent. Robertson's intention was clear. He hoped this move could avoid direct embarrassment, and could leave a secret space for compromising, so that the protocol could be adopted. France, Germany and Belgium expressed their opposition to NATO's adoption of related resolutions before the war at 8:00 on February 10. They thought that it would be equivalent to supporting the war. So the "Default Programs" failed, and Turkey immediately called for the launch of the Article IV in the Convention. According to this provision, when a NATO member was threatened in the territorial integrity, independence and security, NATO would conduct emergency consultations at the request of any member. This was the first time that this provision was activated since NATO was founded 53 years ago. There was no result of the emergency consultations of NATO Council began from the 11th February On February 16th, 2003, the NATO Defense Planning Committee replaced the NATO Council to pass a new program planned by the United States,. As France was no longer a member of the committee since it exited from the NATO military integration mechanism in 1966, an agreement on cooperative defense of Turkey was finally achieved without the intervention of France.

The high level of the US was very dissatisfied with the rejection of France and Germany in NATO, which was undoubtedly an act of perfidy in the eyes of the US. Burns, the US ambassador in NATO, said the decision of France, Germany and Belgium was "unfortunate" and would cause "a crisis of credibility" for NATO. President Bush also expressed disappointment, and he said the French were "short-sighted." However, whether it was short-sighted or not, and no matter whom was short-sighted, the objection of France, Germany and other countries in NATO made the United States unable to launch the war in Iraq in the name of the United Nations or in the name of NATO. The helpless United States had to form a new wartime alliance outside the existing alliance to carry on the war in Iraq. What caused a headache for the United States was not only the French-German alliance, but also their flirting with Russia, which was West's common enemy during the Cold War. It also showed that although NATO looked more populated and influential after two important expansions, in fact, the NATO was not at the US disposal like in the past. This "iron plate" already had cracks, and the cracks were getting bigger and bigger. The leader was still France which inherited the Gaullist approaches. However, the difference was that France was not as alone as it was in the 1960s, and it had strong sympathizers and supporters in the Western alliance.[43]

The "split" of the EU as old and new Europe fractions and the US

Among the countries opposing the Iraq war, France and Germany formed the anti-war alliance with the active support and participation of Russia. France and Germany not only became the world leader in anti-Iraq war, but also constituted the most steadfast and the most influential cooperation in the history of French-German relations during the course of anti-Iraq war.

The peace in Europe after the war was connected with the European alliance, and with the French-German reconciliation and cooperation. The whole process of post-war development of the European alliance was closely linked with the French-German relationship. The French-German relationship was the foundation of the European alliance. In the process of the EU's development when there were some difficulties and differences which needed to be discussed and solved at the summit, they only could reach an agreement at the plenary session after the leaders of Germany and France reached a consensus on coordination and compromise. Decades of historical experience of European integration after the war had proved that as long as France and Germany worked together, the European integration would

---

43 Immanuel Wallerstein, "France is Key", in: Fernand Braudel Center, Binghamton University, Commentary No.106-Feb. 1, 2003.

be able to deepen its development; otherwise, it might suffer a setback. This was the origin of the "French-German axis," "joint engine", "locomotive" and "barometer of European integration". But in a few years after the mid-1990s, people's view on the "French-German axis" was shaking, thinking that the "engine" of the EU was out of order.

Since the end of the Cold War, especially after the reunification of Germany, the differences between France and Germany seemed to multiply than ever. Although the meetings between the two leaders still continued, their disagreements over the development of the EU, the EU's future political structure and pattern, single currency, common agricultural policy reform and even nuclear policy frequently hit the newspapers. In 2000, Germany even unilaterally put forward the scenario of "United States of Europe" without the two countries consultation. Besides, the two countries often kept in touch with Britain in order to put pressure on the other side, no wonder someone would think that the "French-German axis" did not exist anymore, and the EU should be replaced by a new axis. Actually, the two leaders had already sensed the implied crisis in the French-German relationship. The German post-war generation of leaders in 1998 represented by Schroeder were not only unwilling to continue to bear the burden of war crimes, but also wanted to serve as the European "leader" role to "more confidently safeguard national interests" by virtue of the strength of unity. Of course, Germany could no longer give others an impression that "it could only achieve something by relying on the political strength of France". However, after years of governing, the Schroeder government felt that the problem was not so simple. Europe had more concerns about the unified Germany which was trying to "surpass Europe". Given the fact that German economic situation was not better than France in recent years and its position on the Middle East and Iraq issues was similar with France, Schroeder realized that Germany had not yet have the ability to dominate Europe. Only when working with France, could Germany continue to promote the European construction and play a role in the integration of Europe. Thus, the German leaders re-emphasized the relationship between Germany and France was "irreplaceable". The French-German relationship, "as the engine of European integration, is more important than ever." Compared with Germany, France undoubtedly needed to rely on the power of European integration. Although it could not completely be at ease about Germany, it still had to find ways to repair the relationship between France and Germany. After Chirac defeated the leader of the extreme right-wing Le Pen, and was re-elected as the president. Chirac finally got rid of the political situation whether the left or the right wing in May 2002, the leaders of

France had a free hand to make the revival of the French-German relationship as one of the key foreign policies. In Chirac's proposal, the two leaders decided to take the chance of the 40th anniversary of the French-German Cooperation Treaty and the Elysee Palace treaty on January 22, 2003, and launched a series of commemorative activities to show the world the friendship between France and Germany. In the comprehensive and grand commemoration, because it was held against the background of the imminent war in Iraq, so the public paid particular attention to the joint statement and content on foreign policy in the speech of leaders. And all statements and measures related to the strengthening of bilateral relations were all seen as support and commitment to foreign policy.

Both countries declared their attitude towards the issue of Iraq which was different from the United States and Britain, expressed support for the extension of the UN weapons investigation in Iraq, and opposed taking military action against Iraq without the UN Security Council's authorization. The statement emphasized that when the UN Security Council was voting on the Iraq crisis and other major issues, the two governments should carry out bilateral consultations, and then took their positions. When mentioning the issue of Iraq in his speech, Schroeder thought that the European countries should have a comprehensive negotiation at the United Nations, and take the same position. He also believed that this was a very important time for the current international situation. Chirac who was standing beside him interjected: "I totally agree with this!" (C'est d'accord!) While the leaders of France and Germany were opposing military action against Iraq, the NATO Council failed to pass the decision of giving logistical support to the war in Iraq and helping defending Turkey because of the opposition of France and Germany. The United States was angry about this. On the same day, Secretary of Defense Rumsfeld said publicly at the news conference of Washington's National Press Club that the stance of France and Germany on the Iraq issue could not represent the attitude of whole Europe. He said, "Germany is a tough issue, France is also a tough issue ...... but you should look at many of the other European countries, they do not agree with the views of France and Germany, they stand on the US side." He added, "You think Germany and France can represent Europe, but I do not think so. If so, it was only on behalf of the old Europe. If you look carefully at the European countries in NATO, you will find Europe's focus has moved eastward, where there are many new NATO members."[44]

---

44   "L'Allmagne et la France,c'est la vieille Europe", assure M. Ramsfeld, Le Monde, 23 Janvier 2003; La petite phrase de Ramsfeld secoue le monde politique, "l'Allmagne et la France de representants de la 'vieille Europe'", Le Figaro, 28 Janvier 2003.

It seemed that the US were really irritated, or, regardless of its intention, it would not say these provocative words to separate the EU to the two largest member states of the EU after the EU had just made a resolution on its enlargement at the end of last year.

Why the US had got very angry? First the United States could accept the attitude of France to which the US had been used to since the era of Charles de Gaulle. So it was not surprising. But the resistant attitude of Germany was stronger than France and this was unexpected and intolerable for the US because Germany was always considered to be bounded with the US. Although during the last election, Schroeder had expressed his disagreement on Iraq issue with the United States, it generally would be considered as a strategy that met the needs of the campaign, which would change sooner or later. The US did not expect that Schroeder would become aggravated and tougher after he came to power. Everyone knew that, after the signing of French-German Cooperation Treaty forty years ago, when the German Federal Parliament was approving it, there was an intervention to maintain the "transatlantic relations," – unilaterally adding a preface aimed at consolidating and developing the relationship between Europe and the US to distinguish it from de Gaulle's policy towards the United States, and to avoid the suspicion of working with France against the United States. This time, however, when the United States needed the support of its allies, Germany took the opportunity of the fortieth anniversary of the French-German Cooperation Treaty, not only announced its cooperation with France in public, but also launched an attack to the United States in the name of the "representative of Europe" under the banner of reviving the French-German axis. This was sprinkling a handful of salt on the wound of the US-European relations that had been torn apart several times in recent years. Second, the US had established the principle of "prioritizing the US interests" in international affairs, and tried to establish an international political and economic order on the basis of this principle. Thereby the United States could judge its friend and enemies. And with this principle the United States could launch pre-emptive attack by unilateralism without any restrictions of any treaty or organization. In fact, the United States had implemented the pre-emptive principle of the Bush Doctrine in Iraq, implemented "either stand together with us, or stand with the terrorists" in the attitude whether to agree on the Iraq war and the destruction of Saddam Hussein's regime. The joint resistance of France and Germany undoubtedly touched the US taboos. This move of France and Germany might not prevent the US military action, but its political effect and significance was enormous, because although allies might also have different views in such a major operation in the past, it did not lead to the cancel of action in the name of allies. This was a blow to NATO, and also a hit to the United States

Rumsfeld referred France and Germany as the representatives of the "old Europe". His statement was so striking phrase that awakened the Europeans from the dream of achieving a "big unified Europe". There was the "old Europe", naturally there would be a "New Europe". Who would be the representative of the "new Europe"?

During the development process of the post-war European integration, some European countries already had objections about the pivotal role of Germany and France. They had complaints about France and Germany using their power to influence and even manipulate the EU affairs, and were much annoyed by the assertion of France and Germany being spokesperson in Europe. It had long been expected that with the further enlargement of the EU, the contradiction would be more acute when countries competed for dominance in the European Union. This time, activated by the "old Europe" theory of the United States, a "New Europe", secretly operated by Tony Blair administration of the United Kingdom, taken care by Spanish People's Party government, and having a group of Eastern European countries which were eager to show themselves in order to "return to Europe" as the main character, finally emerged out of the water.

On January 30, 2003, the European Parliament passed the French-German-sponsored resolution requesting a peaceful solution to the Iraq crisis by all means and opposing unilateral military action against Iraq after a heated debate, thinking that "pre-emptive" military combat violated the international law. But the result of 287 votes to 209 votes made people feel that Europe had been divided into two at that time. Almost at the same time on that day, 12 European influential newspaper published the open letter co-signed by the leaders of five EU countries Britain, Italy, Spain, Portugal and Denmark, as well as three candidate countries Poland, Hungary and the Czech Republic, expressing their strong support for the US policy towards Iraq, and also called on European countries to disarm Iraq together with the United States. This statement not only showed the different position of France and Germany from other countries, the way it had been introduced was also rare in the EU's history calling for "speaking with one voice". Because it not only put aside those anti-war countries such as France and Germany, but also put aside Prodi, the President of the current Presidency of the EU Greek and the president of the EU Commission, and Solana, the chief of the EU common foreign policy. By February 6, 2003 another 10 Eastern European countries issued a statement to support the United States.

At the weekend on February 15th, 2003 large antiwar demonstrations of nearly ten million people broke out in about 600 cities all over the world, of which the demonstrations in Madrid, Rome, Italy, London and the anti-war Paris, Berlin, Germany became the vastest momentum. On February 17, in order to eliminate the public suspicion on the EU's "split", and also to cope with the rising European anti-war sentiment in general public, 15 EU countries held an emergency summit. By a joint statement on the Iraq crisis, they suggested that the EU hoped to seek a peaceful solution to the crisis and agreed to consider using force as the last resort. After the meeting, President Chirac said publicly that he was dissatisfied with the statement proposed by the 10 candidate countries to support the US, called it "reckless action", and believed it would be uneasy for them to join the EU if they stood in the United States side, because some EU countries had to go through a referendum to decide whether to accept new members. Losing the trust of these countries was obviously not conducive for accession. Chirac's words provoked the anger of candidate countries, which saw it as a threat. Then, Prime Minister Tony Blair sent letters to the Prime Minister of the candidate countries, claiming to be their closest ally in Europe, and praised them for keeping consistent with the United States. He said he was very impressed by the leadership exhibited on these issues. It should be noted that the European Union already had splits since the war in Iraq. The split was reflected in two aspects: the first was the split among the member states, they were divided into states supporting wars and antiwar states; the second was the split between the government and the general public in states supporting wars: the government advocated wars, the people declared against wars.

According to Rumsfeld's words, "New Europe" referred to those Eastern European countries which recently participated in and asked to participate in NATO. Why were these Eastern European countries so determined to be consistent with the US while actively requiring participating in the EU's plan of "return to Europe"?

First, the shadow of the Cold War was still haunting the Eastern European countries. Although they were free from the control of the former Soviet Union, they still had lingering fear towards the successor of the Soviet Union, Russia. How to maintain and consolidate the independence towards Russia was an important issue in the foreign policies of these countries. In their view, the EU had no unified foreign and defense policy, and could not shoulder the burden of European security by itself, so it would not choose to rely on itself in security. Only the United States and NATO under the leadership of the US had decades of experience fighting against the Soviet Union, and also strength to dominate Russia. Thus, when the United States judged its friends by approving the war in Iraq, the Eastern European countries had no alternative but the United States. Secondly these Eastern European countries were aware that their foundation of development still lay in the European Union, which was decided by the geopolitical economy, so they could not get rid of the European Union. But as new members with relatively weak political and economic strength, Eastern European countries felt annoyed about the harsh conditions for joining the EU. They worried and unwilling to be seen as "second-class citizens" in the European Union, so they took every possible opportunity to show and improve their strength and status. They choose to stand together with the United States and Britain to launch the war in Iraq. Besides, the countries with the Prime Minister who is member of the Communist Party Political Bureau, such as Poland, often behaved unexpectedly in order to represent a clean break with the past. It also showed that these countries which had just completed the transformation of the political system were not mature enough.

The appearance of the "New Europe" was more a challenge to the European Union than to the "French-German axis". Some people said "an ax of the United States hews out two Europe", some said, "because of an open letter to the 8 countries, Europe becomes fragmented", some others said "the primary victim of the war in Iraq is not Saddam, but Europe. The US shows by creating discord among Europeans that its main goal is not to eliminate terrorism, but to rule the world. In the eyes of the United States, the control over Europe is as important as the control over the Near East. If the war in Iraq leads the disintegrating elements into the politics of Europe, then the United States will get a double benefit."[45]

Europe had hoped Eastern Europe to "return to Europe", but the Eastern European countries choose the side of the United States in return. This even aroused the resentment of France and Germany, which had always been pursuing the independence of Europe, against the United States. It seemed that people did not only have to study the new topic of differentiation in European integration in world history, but also have to study the deep-seated problems underlay the relationship between the US and Europe.

6.5 The Analysis of US-Europe Alliance Relations

The war in Iraq launched by the United States and Britain had a profound and comprehensive impact on the future global trend of the international politics and economy from beginning to end. The impact on the traditional

---

45   La Chronique de Jacques Julliard, "Non a l'Europe americaine", Le Nouvel Observateur, No 1996-6/2/2003.

relationship between Europe and the US was even more compelling. What was the most profound change in the relationship between Europe and the US? Would the partners in the North Atlantic alliance become rivals?

6.5.1 The Historical and Realistic Aspects of Internal Conflicts in the Western Alliance

Since European countries transformed from wartime alliance to the North Atlantic Alliance within the Yalta system after the end of World War II, the differences and contradictions in EU-US relations had never stopped, of which especially the Suez event in 1956 and the conflict between France and the US in 1966 were the most prominent.

The Suez event in 1956 was a battle over sovereignty of the Suez Canal between the emerging independent countries represented by Egypt and old colonial powers represented by Britain and France. In this war, the US which wanted to replace the position of Britain and France in the Middle East not only refused to support the British and French to maintain their interests in the Middle East by force, but used oil and dollar to put pressure on Britain and France, and voted to force a cease-fire of Britain and France together with the Soviet Union.

In 1966, France exited the military integration mechanism of the North Atlantic Treaty, and expelled NATO headquarters and all of its military bases from France. This was the concentrated presentation of dissatisfaction of European countries represented by France with the US "patriarchal" behavior of hegemony after Charles de Gaulle returned to power in 1958 and their request to share decision-making power of the league. Any historian could not underestimate the impact of these two historical events to the Western alliance. They could not ignore their long-term influence over the international situation and relations among the big powers. Those events were the evidence utilized when politicians were dealing with the relationship between Europe and the US during a half century and the typical cases which need to be studied by scholars when looking at the relationship between Europe and the US. So, when there was intense confrontation in the US-European alliance because of the issue of Iraq, many people compared it with the events in 1956 and 1966, expecting to get some answers.

In fact, this crisis of the alliance between Europe and the US half a century later had big differences with the two crises in 1956 and 1966. On the surface, first, there was a big change in the major character of the events. The anti-war faction and the pro-war faction exchange their position between France and the United States; the United Kingdom, Germany, Russia (the Former Soviet Union) replaced their allies. Second, Europe with a tradition of pursuing to "speak with one voice" was divided into two factions after constant expansion. Third, there were changes in the international anti-war movement. The protests against the Anglo-French invasion of Egypt in 1956 mainly took place in Asia, Africa and criticized by the socialist countries, while this time, anti-war demonstrations by millions of people were held in Western countries (especially in those countries which launched the wars). Nevertheless,the real factors behind the crisis of the alliance cannot be explained by the above facts.

The main reason of the US-European alliance after World War II was their consensus of agreeing that the Soviet Union constituted a major military threat. After the upheaval of Eastern Europe, the dissolution of the Soviet Union and the Warsaw Pact, this major threat no longer existed, so the US-European alliance lost the original meaning of existence. In order to keep the alliance between the United States and Europe, many European and the US thinkers, statesmen and military strategists had been constantly exploring strategic theory and practicing the policy more than a decade, trying to find and identify a new basis for maintaining the alliance in the new situation. However, since the different opinions around the question of whether to stick to the US dominance in the alliance or to construct a new partnership of equality and many other issues, the new basis for the alliance between Europe and the US had always been difficult to be established. Without this basis, Europe and the US finally trigger the intense conflict on the issue of the war in Iraq after a decade of quarrels. Therefore, if the existence of the Soviet as a threat in the past confined the differences between Europe and the US to a certain extent, even the events in 1956 and 1966 failed to destroy the US-European alliance, then, at the absence of a solid limit for more than a decade until now, the conflict this time was possible to become a symbol of ending the traditional alliance between Europe and the US in the actual sense. This was where the real difference between the US- European conflict on the Iraq war in 2003 and events in 1956 and 1966 truly lay.

The influential events in history often reproduce themselves in a strikingly similar way. (Marx quoted from Hegel: "Hegel remarks somewhere that all great world-historic facts and personages appear, so to speak, twice. He forgot to add: the first time as tragedy, the second time as farce."[46]

This is why people have to constantly sum up the history, study the history, and learn from the history. However, the reproduction of history that

---

46   Karl Marx, "The 18th Brumaire of Louis Bonaparte", Selected Works of K. Marx and F. Engels. Vol.1, Beijing: People's Publishing House, 1972, p.603.

people are faced with, will not simply repeat itself without change. Thus, the crisis of the US-European alliance in 2003 did not simply repeat their crisis happened in 1956 and 1966, so people could not simply draw a conclusion with the old way of thinking.

6.5.2 The Reasons behind Conflicts between the US and Europe

Contradictions and conflicts between Europe and the US existed since the foundation of their alliance. This was the truth that both sides had admitted. For a long time, in people's general impression, the reason for the conflicts between Europe and the US was mainly because of the collision of national interests in a particular issue or a particular problem, thus they were reflected more in economic benefits, such as the debate on the expansion of trade and on handling the crisis of dollar around the 1960s, even if there was some controversy related to strategic issues, it was only an argument about strategic direction of their own interests, not involving strategic nature and the whole board. For example, European countries were more cautious in the Korean War, because they feared that the United States might be at a loss; the reason why the United States opposed British and French use of force in the Suez was that it wanted to further weaken the British and French forces in the Middle East and replace them; Charles de Gaulle stood against the United States was because he was unwilling to be controlled by the United States and wanted to restore the status France as a great power. But no matter how he fought, he was just moving inside the North Atlantic Alliance. Neither Europe nor the US had doubted their clash would lead to the collapse of the alliance. From the end of the Cold War to the war in Iraq, internal contradictions and disputes within the Western alliance became increasingly sharp and open. Due to the concerns about the outlook of the alliance, many in the West were analyzing and discussing the reasons for the conflict. Some said it was caused by the differences in social structural patterns between Europe and the US, some else said it was because of the large gap of strength between Europe and the US, some others also believed it was because of the similarities and differences of values between Europe and the US. Opinions varied.

The view of pattern differences held that although the United States was Europe's "daughter", it was not carved out from the same mold as Europe. There were big differences in their social structures. Of course, the economic pattern was the most fundamental. The German social market economy was the most typical one of the economic patterns enshrined in the Europe (see Chapter II of the book). It had created an economic miracle for Europe in Germany, and made the whole European economy comparative to the

United States and Japan. Its main feature was that, under the premise of respecting the laws of the market economy, it did not allow a laissez-faire market and capital, and maintained the balance of capital and labor through the nation to achieve social justice and equity. What the United States implemented was the free market economy, which paid more attention to the spontaneity of capital and market. This difference in the economic pattern was reflected in the parliamentary system in which the rulers were decided by party elections in the politics of Europe, while the United States decided the ruling party through presidential campaign. Europe and the US both considered their patterns of social development as the representative of the future development of the world. Over the past decade, the US economic model used its favorable position in the international politics to seize the limelight and sold or output the US pattern to the rest of the world, including Europe, with an overwhelming superiority. The combination of the US unilateralism developed on the basis of unlimited expansion of private capital and the US unmatched strength determined that the US not only acted as a world leader, but also followed their own pattern to output the strategic objectives of the US democracy. Anything caused damage to the US interests and violated its goal might be attacked by the US unfettered, pre-emptive, military means. But Europe did not think the US pattern was the "model of democracy" or "the best model of development of human society." Europe rejected the US-style ruling, refused to accept the democracy and freedom different from the European tradition that the United States exported to the world by all means. Europe preferred to strengthen collective consultation and cooperation on issues of common concern within the existing international framework, and to promote the development of capital in different societies. The dispute of two models led to conflicts and contradictions between Europe and the US on a range of issues.

The view of strength gap believed that the conflicts and contradictions between Europe and the US derived from the difference in strength between the two sides. The strength of the United States, especially the powerful military strength, and the strength of Europe, especially the weak military strength, led to the disagreement on some problems between the two sides. Europe advocated applying peaceful means to solving international problems—by negotiation, diplomacy and persuasion rather than military means. In the settlement of disputes, Europe tended to rely on international organizations, international conventions and public opinions. On the contrary, the United States resorted to military force. It lacked of patience in diplomatic actions, skeptical of international law, and more willing to take action without constraints of international law. Why would the United

States and Europe adopt different ways of doing things? The senior fellow of Carnegie Endowment for International Peace Foundation, a famous conservative commentator of the Washington Post, Robert Kagan published a series of articles, which caused a sensation in the United States and Europe.[47]

Kagan believed that the growing gap of strength since the 1990s was the root of the disharmony in strategies between the United States and Europe. He said, "Compared with those countries with weak military power, the countries with strong military strength is more likely to resort to force as an effective means of dealing with international relations." Kagan cited an example in history. He said in the beginning period of the founding of the United States, the European powers controlled the world, conquering colonies by force, while the United States was pursuing a policy of opposing wars and force. Now the situation had been reversed. Since the United States had become strong, it would act as a powerful state, while European countries had become weak, so they would see the world as weak countries. He hoped Europe could increase investment to and improve its military strength, while the United States could restrain some "arrogance" in order to narrow the gap and to make up the differences.

Kagan's argument irritated the Europeans, because in Kagan's opinion, Europe seemed to become like a person who "was saying grapes are sour when he was not able to eat them". They did not only argue that Kagan's interpretation of history was wrong, but also reflected the anti-US sentiment in Europe. They have argued that, it was more beneficial for the world stability and security to invest nearly 30 billion US. dollars a year for the development of 15 countries of the EU, than investing nearly 400 billion US. dollars a year in military like the United States.

Compared with other theories, the value differences did not put forward additional arguments. Its key was the conclusion drew from similar evidence that "Europe and the US have different values and cultural values", which was refreshing. Because both the West and the East always had a common view that "Europe and the US have the same roots and veins, and the same values, so they will not split." This view did not change much until the great upheaval in the Eastern Europe, the disintegration of the Soviet Union, and the end of the Cold War. Because at that time, the whole Europe and the US were rejoicing, cheering for the "end of history" based

---

47   Robert Kagan, "The US-Europe Divide", The Washington Post, May 26th, 2002; Robert Kagan, "Power and Weakness", in: Policy Review, June/July 2002, Number 113; Robert Kagan, Of Paradise and Power: America and Europe in the New World Order, Alfred A. Knoff, New York, 2003.

on the principles of democracy and freedom in Europe and the US (Francis Fukuyama, 1989). In their view, even if history had no "end", there would be "clash of civilizations", which was only the clash happened to the Western civilization represented by the United States and Europe and other civilizations (Samuel Huntington, 1993). Under the premise of consistent values between Europe and the US, the commercial disputes involving the US, such as Helms—Burton Act and the D'Amato Act, the banana deal, Boeing and Airbus orders, steel imports, sales of gene transferred agricultural products, and so on, showed that Europe and the US were only economic competitors. It was also at this time, due to the large-scale ease of political and military confrontation, academics paid more attention to civilization (culture), values (worldview) and other factors in studying international relations, but rarely in the study of the relationship between Europe and the US.

Since Europe and the US had more and more conflicts over the issue of the Balkans, the Middle East, Afghanistan, and North Korea, and had opposing attitudes towards the application of anti-personnel mines, the establishment of the International Criminal Court, Comprehensive Nuclear-Test-Ban Treaty, Biochemical Weapons Convention, Kyoto Protocol, and Anti-Missile Treaty, especially the contest between the US unilateralism and the Europe-advocated multilateralism after the" 9/11 "incident, made the traditional interpretation of the US-European conflict unconvincing. Thus, the role of the similarities and differences of cultural beliefs and values in international relations began to get involved in the research of the relationship between Europe and the US.

On February 26, 1998, the French magazine "Le Nouvel Observateur" criticized the US cultural hegemony and promoted cultural diversity with the title of "50 years of Cultural Battle between France and the United States", pointing out that the essence of French-US cultural confrontation was that the United States was intended to implement the cultural monopoly, while the Europeans required respect for cultural diversity. In the French view, the root of confrontation between European culture and the US culture was not the different cultural concepts. In terms of cultural values, the French people believed that they could defend their cultural tradition, because France did not want to compete with others in this regard. In contrast, what the United States pursued was to play a leading role in popular culture.[48]

---

48   Jean-Gabriel Freset, "France/Etats-Unis La guerre culturelle a cinquante ans", Le Nouvel Observateur, No.1738-26/2/1998.

On July 31, 1999, the British magazine Economist published an article on geopolitics of the 21st century. It pointed out that culture would dominate geopolitics in the 21st century, and the possibility of conflict within the same cultural area was greater than the possibility of conflict among different cultural regions. The article held that the United States and Europe might develop in different directions. In the spring of 2001, only a few months after George W. Bush took office, European and the US politicians, academics and the media started a heated discussion on the "values differences" between Europe and the US. Many people stressed the "strategic differences" between Europe and the US, and some even expressed their concerns about the prospect of such a disagreement. Robert Kagan who we have previously mentioned wrote in his sensational article "The US-Europe Divide" that "Europeans and the US no longer have a common view of the world." Because of this, "on the issues of major international strategy, the US are from Mars and Europeans are from Venus, so it may be hard to reach an agreement between them, and their mutual understanding will become less and less." Almost at the same time, he once again denied that Europe and the United States shared a common view of the world in another striking article "Power and Weakness". He said, "Some people say that Europeans and the US share a common view of the world, or even say that they occupy the same world. Now is the time to stop this thought." Following his lead, Francis Fukuyama who always regarded the victory of Western values and system as the end of history was also undetermined about the common values of Europe and the US. He said, "The history should take the victory of the values and institutions of the West, not just the United States, as its end, making the democracy and market economy the only feasible option. The allies with common values of freedom and democracy had fought side by side in the Cold War. But now the United States and Europe have a large gap in the evaluation of world affairs. The common values that have been existing for a long time are gradually declining."[49]

Of course, there were also different opinions on the judgment of this worldview difference theory. On June 12, 2001, when a debate on "values difference" was held in the United States, the national security adviser Rice published an article entitled "The United States and Europe, the Future Partnership" at the International Herald Tribune. Rice said, it was said that there were strategic differences between the United States and Europe, some people even thought that the US and Europe were destined to become rivals, but "the President and the government under his leadership firmly

---

49   Francis Fukuyama, "The West may be cracking", in International Herald Tribune, August 9, 2002.

oppose this hypothesis." She believed that Europe and the United States were partners for now and forever. They were the most intimate partners. "This is not only because of historical inertia, but also because we have common interests, in fact, common values."

By the end of 2002, directed against Kagan's article, the US bimonthly published magazine Foreign Policy published an article entitled "The Real Difference of Both Sides of the Atlantic" and co-written by Craig Kennedy, the director of Marshall Fund, and Marshall M. Bouton, the president of Chicago Diplomatic Society. Based on the US and European media and the public survey, the article found that conflict and confrontation between the United States and Europe did not reach the level of severity that Kagan claimed. It believed that the common economic interests and the same values of the US and Europe provided a solid foundation for maintaining strong transatlantic relations, and the US and Europe had the same stance in many areas.[50]

In early 2003, when Europe and the US were at an intense debate on the issue of Iraq, the US bimonthly published Foreign Affairs published an article entitled "Bridging the Atlantic Divide" by Philip H.Gordon, a senior fellow of Brookings Institution and the director of the US and French Research Center. Gordon said, "The fundamental values and interests of the United States and Europe do not deviate off. If we see from a broader perspective, we can find that the views and values of the US and Europe have more similarities than differences."[51]

During the ongoing war in Iraq, French Foreign Minister Dominique de Villepin gave a lecture entitled "Right, Force and Impartiality" at the annual meeting of the International Institute for Strategic Studies in London. He believed that people saw two views of the world through the Iraq crisis, but he also said, "They are destined to restore close and strong partnership, because the United States and France share common values."

The debate on differences of values between Europe and the US was a little like a discussion on "how to understand the world and how to change the world". Regardless of the difference between the debate on values and the values of Marxism, the essence of the problem was: it was related to whether the differences between Europe and the US were the fundamental differences, related to how to treat the current status and role of the Western

---

50   Craig Kennedy and Marshall M. Bouton, "The Real Trans-Atlantic Gap", in Foreign Policy, November/December 2002.
51   Philip H. Gordon, "Bridging the Atlantic Divide", in Foreign Affairs, January/February 2003.

alliance, or the United States and Europe no longer needed such an alliance because they could find a more suitable ally. As capitalism had been developed until today, its inherent contradictions has been effecting the values (worldview) of the capitalist society, i.e. the core of the superstructure of this society. How do they affect our world in theory and practice? It must not be taken lightly for the United States, Europe, and even the whole world.

6.5.3 The Future Prospects of Western Alliance

It may seem too early to make certain judgements for the future prospects of the Western alliance, because, after all, the conflict between Europe and the US was still in deep change. Sometimes, however, the analysis in discussion was more enlightening than conclusive statement. Take a look at various claims about the future of the Western alliance, a certain thought of them would probably be confirmed by history in the future.

The first question is whether the traditional Western alliance will further exist. We can say that it is impossible for the US and Europe to maintain the traditional alliance of the past. It can be seen from the previous analysis that there were mainly two reasons for US-European alliance after World War II: one was a common threat from the outside, and the other was the common values inside. Today, not only the common threat of the Soviet Union did not exist anymore, the shared values also had been fully questioned. The base of the alliance collapsed. As this book said previously, NATO as an organization for the alliance of Europe and the US would continue to exist in form. However, there were two important changes: one was that its military functions would gradually stop working with the changes in the international environment and the disagreement in alliance. However, for 50 years, multilateral and bilateral military alliance had always been the main part of the US strategy in its foreign affairs and national security; the other is that several major military operations launched by the United States intentionally or unintentionally –frequently– bypassed its traditional allies in the post-Cold-War era showing that the US was returning to the policy of forming temporary alliances as it has done before World War II, selecting more temporary allies of the same interests and formed a "coalition of the willing." It was for this consideration that Francis Fukuyama suspected "whether the notion of 'the West' still has any meaning in the first decade of the 21st century."[52]

---

52 Francis Fukuyama, The West May Be Cracking", International Herald Tribune, 09.08.2002.

Immanuel Wallerstein, one of the founders of the world system theory, has also questioned: "whether the Western world still exists." He has argued that the Western world is not an embodiment of culture and history, but a contemporary geopolitical issue. In the world politics from 1945 to 2001, no one had doubted whether there was "the West" or "Western world", but since the US embraced unilateralism across the whole globe, although the "West" did not completely disappear geopolitically, "it has indeed weakened."[53]

From above evaluations, it seems that people should be cautious when talking about the "US-European alliance" because although it is difficult to assert that "Europe is splitting," Europe is indeed divided into several factions, which is an open fact. Moreover, intentionally or unintentionally, the United States causes the disintegration of Europe. Europe in the context of "Europe and the US" in fact refers to Western Europe or the EU, and there arises a question if EU, means the Europe with or without Russia. There are some concepts put forward as "fringe Europe" referring to weaker nations of Europe, ore "core Europe", and also "old Europe" and "new Europe". What do the terms "Europe in general" or "Europe and the US" refer to in the final analysis?

Secondly, will the Western alliance eventually split and will partners become rivals? As mentioned earlier, the former US President's national security adviser Condoleezza Rice had firmly denied "the assumption that the United States and Europe will eventually become rivals," but there were a lot of people who not only did not hold hopes for the prospects of the Western alliance, but also believed that the alliance would be definitely broken, and the United States and Europe would eventually become rivals. The most outstanding one among them was Charles A. Kupchan.

Kupchan is a professor of international relations at Georgetown University in the US, the leader of European research team in the US Institute of Foreign Affairs, and an expert in studying the relationship between Europe and the US and European issues at the security conference of the Clinton administration. Kupchan said the next clash of civilizations would not happen between the West and the non-West, but between the United States and Europe, which has not realized among the most US officials. In Kupchan's opinion, the current dominance of the US was not as solid as it looked like, but had begun to wane. The challenger who forced the weakening of the US was not China, nor the Islamic world, but the European Union. He believed that as a new political entity, the EU was strengthening the collective

---

53   Immanuel Wallerstein, "Does the Western World Still Exist?" speech in Fernand Braudel Center, Binghamton University, Commentary No 112, 1 May, 2003.

consciousness and character, and was forming a more definite and different concept of interests and values from the United States. The gap of annual economic output between the EU and the United States was very small, and the euro also threatened the status of the dollar. As the EU further strengthened its institutions of integration and took in new members, the EU would become a strong power that could compete with the United States on the international stage. With the uprising of the EU's strength, its economic and political interests were likely to have continuous conflict with the US, which would aggravate mutual maliciousness. Kupchan asserted that the results of the expanding of differences between the US and Europe is just emerging. As a consequence, the competition among the Atlantic partners will inevitably grow.

Of course, Kupchan's argument has many assumptions as its premise, such as what extent could the European Union develop in economy, politics, and even military integration and whether it could play a role as expected; or whether the United States will adjust its policy, insist on its unilateral approach, or chose other policies to avoid being further isolated. Therefore, his conclusion was not necessarily the inevitable tendency. Moreover, Kupchan did not want the United States to become weaker from the bottom of his heart, since he believed that if the US weakens, the world might be more unstable and insecure. In fact, no alliance, no cooperation, including the transatlantic alliance can be understood in the conceptual framework of "friends or foes" for allies, this is an outdated conceptual framework.[54]

The third was how to repair and maintain the cracks in the Western alliance. Although, some theorists believe that the traditional Western alliance would not continue to exist as in the past, and even raised the possibility of the alliance being divided and even predicting rivalries but in the West, most people still favored the maintenance of the alliance and lobbied in this direction. By the end of 2003, the chief representative of the EU foreign policy and security affairs Javier Solana wrote that Europeans and the US were members with common values of a large family. He said, "Even the world's most powerful countries also need friends and allies ...... However, they must treat the allies as allies, not only allowing them to participate in the implementation of the policy, but also in the process of policy-making. In the long run, the idea that thinks one can pick or abandon the alliance composed by obedient followers is neither attractive nor permanent." He believed that if the partnership across the Atlantic was going to be persistent

---

54   Charles A. Kupchan, "The End of the West", article in The Atlantic Monthly, November 2002; Charles A. Kupchan, The End of the American Era: US Foreign Policy and the Geopolitics in the Twenty-first Century, Alfred A. Knopf, 2002.

and dynamic, "it must not be merely a pure alliance of pragmatism and expediency." He reminded the United States that it would be much easier to solve major international problems in the future if it worked with a strong and confident Europe.[55]

As the highest representative of the European Union for foreign affairs and security policy, Javier Solana's analysis of the current situation and prospects of the alliance, of course, had the tendency to urge the United States assume more responsibility, which was not surprising. While more people hoped that both the United States and Europe could take some action. Dominique Moisi, a senior fellow at the Institute of International Relations in France, pointed out that the West was divided into two Western areas represented by the United States and Europe, "but Europe and the United States today still need each other." He suggested the Europeans learn from "the US ambition" and accept the unique international position of the United States, while the United States should learn from "Europe's virtues of modesty and self-restraint."[56]

The senior adviser of RAND Corporation, the former US Ambassador to NATO Robert · E. Hunter suggested that the US and Europe establish a new relationship beyond the North Atlantic and Europe in geographic and functional aspects—a new type of strategic partnership complemented NATO. He believed that the Iraq war had proved that, compared with separate action, it was easier to achieve strategic objectives for the US to build alliance.[57]

The United States and Europe will certainly try to maintain the Western alliance and are bound to do so. But the Western alliance torn by the Iraq war, will find it hard to patch itself up. Some people have argued that the contradiction between Europe and the US is a structural issue. As a general view a "structural" contradiction can be alleviated or eliminated through adjustment and reforms. But, if the contradiction is not only "structural", but also includes historical and cultural factors and differences in social attitudes and values, then it will not be possible to bridge differences only through adjustment and reforms. Because national interests adjusted by compromises and concessions, but differences in social and cultural attitudes and values cannot be surpassed by compromises, let alone allow long-term alliances between partners, or allow one accept the other's leadership.

---

55   Javier Solana Madariaga, "The Transatlantic Rift", in Harvard International Review, Winter 2003.
56   Dominique Moisi, "Reinventing the West", in Foreign Affairs, November/December 2003.
57   Robert E. Hunter, "A Forward-Looking Partnership", in Foreign Affairs, September/October 2004.

Of course, when we are analyzing the future prospects of the Western alliance, the analysis should also be extended to the status of the Western alliance in the Eastern hemisphere. A famous Japanese scholar, the director of the Institute of Peace and Security in Japan Akio Watanabe has argued that the transatlantic alliance is obviously at stake, but in Asia-Pacific region a variety of alliances with United States being at the core are in good condition. "The countries of this region react more insipid to US's unilateralism." He said: Among the most significant global effects outside the US of the terrorist attacks are the realignment of today's major powers and a larger global international security role for Japan, including a transformed military posture."[58] However, this is only one of the positions among the think tanks. After half a century, since the Western alliance began, we can observe certain degree of turmoil and division during the first decade of the 21st century. Will it find the new bonds to reconnect and revitalize itself or face a crisis? History will answer this question.

---

58   Akio Watanabe, "A Continuum of Change", in Washington Quarterly, Autumn 2004, Volume 27, Number 4.

References

Documents in Chinese

Ed. Wang Chunliang: "World modern history literature and to discuss the election 1900-1988", Oriental Publishing House, 1990.

"Compilation of Germany Issue Documents", People's Publishing House, 1953 edition.

"Tehran, Yalta, Potsdam Conference Minutes", Shanghai People's Publishing House, 1974 edition.

"Tehran, Yalta, Potsdam Conference Documents Collection", Sanlian Bookstore 1978 edition.

International Treaties Collections (1934-1944), World Knowledge Publishing House, 1961 edition.

"Concise Japanese Encyclopedia" by CASS scholars, China Social Science Press, 1994 edition.

"Collection of De Gaulle's Lectures (May 1958–January 1964)" Compiled by Institute of International Relations, World Knowledge Publishing House 1964 edition.

"European Community Treaty Documents", Dai Bingran, Fudan University Press, 1993 edition.

"Palestine Issue Reference Materials" published in the International Relations Research Series, World Knowledge Publishing House, 1960 edition.

"European Integration Theory and Historical Literature and Documents" ed. by Li Wei, Wang Xueyu, Shandong People's Publishing House, 2001 edition.

Books in Chinese

"Marx and Engels, Selected Works", People's Publishing House, 1972 edition.

Pogue, Forrest C. "George C. Marshall, Statesman, 1945-1959", World Knowledge Publishing House 1991 edition.

Henry Kissinger, "Diplomacy", translated by Gu Shuxin, Lin Tiangui, Hainan Publishing House 1997 edition.

Henry Kissinger, "White House Years–Memoirs of Kissinger", translated by Chen Yaohua, World Knowledge Publishing House 1980 edition.

"The US Diplomatic History in the Post-War Era", by Zhong Zhongjun, World Knowledge Publishing House, 1994 edition.

Chen Lemin: "Post-War, British Diplomatic History", World Knowledge Publishing House, 1994 edition.

"Post-War International Relations of Western Europe" by Chen Lemin, China Social Science Press, 1987 edition.

"History of International Relations", by Wang Shengzu, World Knowledge Publishing House 1995 edition.

"Cold War History", by Liu Jin, World Knowledge Publishing House, 2003 edition.

"The US's Foreign Policy History", by Yang Shengmao, People's Publishing House 1991 edition.

"1945-1980 United States, the Soviet Union and the Cold War", by Walter LaFaber, the Commercial Press 1986 edition.

"The Coming US-Japan War", by George Friedman, Merendith Lebard, translated by He Li "The Next US-Japan war", Xinhua Publishing House 1992 edition

"The US Policy on Japan", by Yu Qun, Northeast Normal University Press, 1996 edition.

"US-Japan alliance: Past, Present and Future", by Michael J. Green, Patrick M. Cronin editor, translated by Hua Hongxun, Xinhua Publishing House 2000 edition.

"Memoirs of Konrad Adenauer", Volume I and III, Shanghai People's Publishing House, 1976 edition.

"Corporations and the Cold War", by D. Horowitz, Shanghai People's Publishing House, 1974 edition.

"German Economic History of the Twentieth Century", by Karl Hardach, Commercial Press 1984 edition.

"The Rise of the Fourth Empire", by Edwin Hartridge, World Knowledge Publishing House, 1982 edition.

"Friends and Foes" by Michael H. Armacost, translated by Yu Tiejun, Xinhua Publishing House 1998 edition.

Willi Brandt, "In Exile, Essays Reflections and Letters", translated by Yu Tiejun, Commercial Press, 1979 edition.

Pierre Gerber, "Construction of Europea, History and Reality of European Unity", translated by Ding Yifan, China Social Science Press, 1989 edition.

Chen Yugang: "State and Super National–European Integration Theory Comparative Study", Shanghai People's Publishing House 2001 edition.

Jean Monnet, "The Father of Europe–Monnet's Memoirs", the translated by Sun Hui Shuang, International Cultural Publishing Company, 1989 edition.

Alfred Grosser, "French Foreign Policy 1944-1984", translated by Lu Boyuan, Mu Wen, World Knowledge Publishing House 1989 edition.

"The Origin and Evolution of Britain's Integration Policy towards Western Europe (1945-1960)", Hong Yusheng, Nanjing University Press, 2001 edition.

"European Economic Community" by Wu Yikang, "European Economic Community", People's Publishing House 1983 edition.

"F. Mitterrand's Biography", by Zhang Xichang,World Knowledge Publishing House 1997 edition.

"Biography of Charles de Gaulle" by Zhou Rongyao, Oriental Publishing House 1994 edition.

"Post-Cold War Era in the East and West" by Zhou Rongyao, China Social Science Press, 1997 edition.

"Strategic Relationship among Major World Powers after the 9/11 Incident" by Zhou Rongyao, China Social Science Press, 2002 edition.

"Churchill: Memoirs of the Second World War", Commercial Press, 1975 edition.

"Path of Jewish National Revival", by Pan Guang, Shanghai Academy of Social Sciences Press, 1998 edition.

1999: Victory Without War: Richard Nixon, World Knowledge Publishing House 1997 edition.

"Grand Failure: The Birth and Death of Communism in the Twentieth Century" by Z. Brzezinski, Military Science Press, 1989 edition.

Foreign documents

Archives of the US Foreign Ministry
FO 371/29421, N 1307/87/30
FO 371/61054
Archives of British Cabinet
CAB 130/27, Gen.197/1
CAB 129/23, CP (48)6
Winston Churchill, The Complete Speeches of Churchill, Vol. 7, N.Y. Chelsea House Pub
FR. US (The Department of State, Foreign Relations of the United States)
Diplomatic Papers, the Conferences of Cairo and Teheran 1943, GPO.1961.
Diplomatic Papers, the Conferences of Malta and Yalta 1945, GPO. 1955.
Diplomatic Papers, the Conference of Berlin 1945, GPO. 1960
1943, Vol. 3, GPO. 1957
1946, Vol. 5, GPO. 1967
1948, Vol. 3, GPO. 1973
United States Department of State, Historical Office, The US Foreign Policy, 1950-1955, Basic Documents, GPO, Washington D.C., 1957.
State Department Records, PPS Records, Box 32, National Archives, Washington D.C.
PPS Records, Box 33
Treaty Establishing the European Economic Community and Connected Documents, Publishing Services of the European Communities, 1962
Bulletin of the EC
Bulletin of the EU
European Documents
The Washington Quarterly
News Week
Contemporary European History, Vol.9, Part 1, March 2000
The National Interest
Foreign Affairs
Foreign Policy
Le Nouvel Observateur

Foreign books

Arthur M. Schlesinger, The Dynamics of World Power: A Documentary History of United States Foreign Policy, 1945-1973, Vol. 1, Western Europe, Chelsea House Publishers, New York, 1973.

Don Cook, Forging the Alliance: NATO, 1945-1950, Arbor House/William Morrow, New York, 1989.

Olav Riste: "Norway's 'Atlantic Policy', The Genesis of North Atlantic Defense Cooperation", in Nicholas Sherwen ed.,NATO's Anxious Birth, The Prophetic Vision of the 1940s, St.Martin's Press,New York, 1985.

John Lamberton Harper, The US Visions of Europe: Franklin D. Roosevelt, George F. Kennan and G. Acheson, Cambridge University Press, 1994.

Charles E. Bohlen, Witness to History, 1929-1969, Norton, New York, 1973.

Walter Lippmann, U.S. Foreign Police: Shield of the Republic, Little Brown, Boston,1943.

Charles de Gaulle, Memoires de Guerre, L'unit 1942-1944, Librairie Plon, 1956.

Memoires de Guerre, Le Salut 1944-1946, Librairie Plon, 1959.

Memoires d'Espoir, Le Renouveau 1958-1962, Librairie Plon, 1970.

Memoires d'Espoir–Le Renouveau, Librairie Plon, 1971.

Discours et Méssages, V, Librairie Plon, 1970.

Robin Edmonds, The Big Three: Churchill, Roosevelt, Stalin in Peace and War, W.H. Norton & Co.,New York, 1991.

Wilson D. Miscamble, George F. Kennan and the Making of The US Foreign Policy, Princeton University Press, Princeton, New Jersey, 1992.

Irwin M. Woll, The United States and the Making if Post-War France, 1945-1954, Cambridge University Press, 1991.

Elisabeth Barker, The British between the Superpowers, 1945-1950, University of Toronto Press, Toronto and Buffalo, 1983.

Ronald E. Powaski, The Entangling Alliance: the United States and European Security, 1950-1993, Greenwood Press, Westport, 1994.

John W. Spanier, The Truman-MacArthur Controversy and the Korean War, The Norton Library, W.W. Norton &Company Inc. New York, 1965.

Richard H. Rovere & Arthur Schlesinger, General MacArthur and President Truman, the Struggle for Control of The US Foreign Policy, Transaction Publishers, New Brunswick, U.S.A. and London, 1992.

Philip M. Williams, The Diary of Hugh Gaitskell, 1945-1956, Jonathan Cape, London, 1983.

Alfred Grosser, La IVe Republique et sa Politique extérieure, Armond Colin, 1961.

The Western Alliance: European-American Relations Since 1945, The Macmillan Press, London, 1980.

André Fontaine, Un Seul lit pour deux réves – Histoire de la "détente" 1962-1981, Fayard, 1981.

Martin J. Dedman, The Origins and Development the European Union, 1945-95, Routledge, London, 1996.

F. Roy Willis, France, Germany, and the New Europe, 1945-1967, London: Oxford University Press, 1968.

R. Schuman, Foreign Policy towards Germany Since the War, London, 1953.

Louis Lister, Europe's Coal and Steel Community, New York: Twentieth Century Fund, 1960.

John W. Yang, Britain and European Unity, 1945-1999, Macmillan Press Ltd, 2000.

Desmond Dinan, Ever Closer Union: An Introduction to European Integration, The Macmillan Press Ltd, 1999.

Pierre Gerbet, La Construction de l'Europe, Nouvelle edition revisee at mise a jour, Imprimerie Nationale, 1994.

Cordell Hull, Memoirs of Cordell Hull, vol.2, Macmillan, New York, 1948.

Anthony Eden, the Memoirs – The Reckoning, Cassell Company Ltd, London, 1965.

Elliot Roosevelt, As He Saw It, Duell, Sloan and Pearce, New York, 1946.

Harold Wilson, The Labour Government, 1964-1970: A Personal Record, London, Weidenfeld and Nicolson, 1971.

Max Beloff, The United States and the Unity of Europe, London, Westport: Green Press, 1976.

John Killick, The Unites States and European Reconstruction, 1945-1960, Kneele University Press, 1997.

Michael Hogan, The Marshall Plan: America, Britain, and the Reconstruction of Western Europe, 1947-1952, Cambridge University Press, 1987.

Maurice Couve de Murville, Une politique étrangére, 1958-1969, Paris, Plon, 1971.

Francis Fuknyama, The End of History and the Last Man, New York: Free Press, 1992.

Bruce Russett, Grasping the Democratic Peace, Princeton University Press, 1993.

www.ingramcontent.com/pod-product-compliance
Lightning Source LLC
Chambersburg PA
CBHW020431130626
46549CB00001B/84